ACADEMIC READING

ACADEMIC READING

Reading and Writing
Across the Disciplines

Janet Giltrow

broadview press

Canadian Cataloguing and Publication Data

Academic reading: reading and writing across the disciplines
ISBN 1-55111-057-1

1. English language — Rhetoric. 2. College readers.
I. Giltrow, Janet Lesley

PE1417.A33 1995 808 .0427 C95-931111-4

Broadview Press
Post Office Box 1243, Peterborough, Ontario, Canada k9j 7h5

in the United States of America:
3576 California Road, Orchard Park, ny 14127

in the United Kingdom:
B.R.A.D. Book Representation & Distribution Ltd., 244A, London Road, Hadleigh, Essex ss7 2DE

Broadview Press gratefully acknowledges the support of the Canada Council, the Ontario Arts Council, the Ontario Publishing Centre, and the Ministry of National Heritage.

PRINTED IN CANADA

5 4 3 2 1 95 96 97

Contents

Introduction

Academic Reading selects fourteen publications from recent scholarly research — fourteen from many, many thousands. The selection process did not begin in a systematic search of the many thousands. Instead, on visits to the periodical reading room, I picked up and carried off what I came across — instances that seemed to me representative and portable. So *Academic Reading* is more like a collection of souvenirs than the product of a large-scale quantitative survey. No doubt, my choices could be interpreted as evidence of a personal itinerary, and biased in certain directions. Readers will soon find recurring themes among the articles in this book, even though the selections come from different disciplines. Gender, class, ethnicity and race show up again and again, sometimes announced as topics, sometimes unannounced, embedded in other topics. Yet, if I am in fact preoccupied with these themes, I am not alone. They are prominent concerns among scholars in many disciplines. If readers find themselves getting fed up with these topics, they can go ahead and quarrel with the arrangements which have produced the prevailing constellation of issues. They can say, "No, it can't be gender again. It's a worn-out idea." This is how intellectual paradigms get changed: thinkers find that some ideas are depleted or fatigued from over-use.

Before they even have a chance to get fed up, though, some readers, on their first approach to these articles, may find that scholarly preoccupations seem far away from the world's everyday business. But I hope these readers will come to see that researchers' concerns are not just the in-house fascinations of minor enclaves. Scholarly concerns are contiguous with worldly matters: they touch some ordinary materials, and refer to common experience. Dorothy Counts and David Counts, for example, talk about RV campsites; the research of Apter et al. has to do with food and weight loss; Penelope Eckert refers to high-school popularity; Min-Zhan Lu refers to schooling; Harriet Baber and Mary Lynn McDougall each discuss maternity leave. And the researchers represented in this volume also summon grander conceptualizations that involve us all: power and constraint, identity and difference, for example. Every article in this book can contribute to our understanding of the social order and the forces immanent in it, this understanding refining our interpretations of the world. For my part, I can say, for example, that Naila Kabeer's research among Bangladeshi garment workers in London and Rebecca Scott's historical analysis of labour relations after the abolition of slavery have led me to revised understandings of labour and power: I don't think of either piece-work employment or seasonal work in the same way anymore. I see that conventional interpretations of these forms of work — as signs of subjugation, say, or desperation — oversimplify the real case, which is more complicated.

Indeed, just about everything is *more complicated* — according to the research represented in this book. As worldly concerns are translated into research discourse, the simple and everyday turns complex and difficult. The translation of the everyday into an object of study leads to an unavoidable circumstance: these articles are not entirely easy reading. Easy stories of eating disorders or the workplace appear in newspapers or magazines, or on television. Slightly more difficult versions are in textbooks which set out to tell students all about psychopathologies or about nineteenth-century America or the labour economy. Newspapers and magazines address a "popular" audience (pretty much everybody, or a sector of everybody); textbooks address undergraduates. The writers of these articles address neither a popular nor an undergraduate audience but other scholars. So, rather than telling all about feminism, Cheshire Calhoun, for example, assumes in her readers some background knowledge of feminist theory. Presupposing familiarity with established concepts, she defines her readers as already knowing these things. These presuppositions may seem to exclude or disallow people who don't fit the definition. I believe, however, that these writers' practice of assuming some background knowledge does not constitute an insurmountable barrier between scholarship and non-specialist readers.

I base my optimism on a natural feature of communication, one linguists call *accommodation*. Say, for example, an air traveller — an inexperienced one, a first-time flyer, perhaps — approaches the threshold of the security area through which passengers move on their way to departure lounges. An official says to the traveller, "Could I see your boarding pass, please?" The traveller does not in fact know he has a "boarding pass." He doesn't know there is such a thing. Yet the official, with her question, has defined the traveller as someone who does know these things: "your boarding pass" *presupposes* both the existence of the document and the traveller's possession of it. (A non-presupposing, telling-all-about-departure version would be something like this: "There are documents called 'boarding passes' which are scrutinized by security officials and ground crews. You have one.") We could say that the traveller, in actuality, is *not* the audience defined by the official's utterance. What does he do? Does he give up and go home? Probably not. Instead, he will *accommodate* the utterance's presuppositions. He will *infer* the existence of things called "boarding passes" and infer that he has one — somewhere in the folder the clerk at the check-in counter returned to him. With some inferential effort on the part of the traveller, the communication is ultimately successful. I expect that readers of the articles in this book will be able to adjust similarly and accommodate presuppositions, and that they will be rewarded for the extra inferential effort required of them. We are all beginners at some point — first-time flyers. Only by hazarding that moment at the threshold, when we are not precisely the audience the speaker assumes, can we go beyond the discourse of the popularization and the textbook, into the realms where knowledge is being made, and where we can hear the authentic sounds of its production.

This collection counts on readers' ability to accustom themselves to a sense of not always being quite the reader defined by the text, and to the effort of accommodating statements that don't explain themselves fully, and take some things for granted. Even under these conditions, readers can conduct themselves thoughtfully and observantly in new domains where — to borrow Bruno Latour and Steve Woolgar's (1978) name for the researchers in a neuroendocrinological lab — members of various scholarly "tribes" are at work. Once transported to these regions, what will we see? What are these tribal people doing? What are they like?

From the evidence of the way they write, we might conjecture that, for one thing, these people are compulsive *readers*: they can scarcely begin to tell about their own ideas without mentioning books or articles they have read. We might also notice that they concentrate their readings in scholarly areas close to their own. At the same time as they quote and paraphrase one another, they also tend to find fault with others' work: something is missing, or not quite right, or not right at all. Yet, despite their fault-finding, they can also be very polite: while they can seem to magnify apparently small flaws in others' reasoning and research, they can also minimize their own claims. Even after lengthy evidence and discussion, they can modestly excuse themselves, saying, well, this is just our idea and it might be true.

These tribespeople also have a taste for going after settled ideas, rousing common notions from their comfortable state, getting them riled up so they can't settle down again. Taking a solid commonplace, they trouble it with fantastical attention to detail and particulars or to previously invisible inconsistencies. To get people nearby to share their interest, they call on big, sedate words rarely heard in other neighbourhoods. Like incantations, these words invoke recognized authority and traditions of reverence. To get along under these conditions, the observer-reader has to learn to be patient with the swarms of detail that disturb settled ideas, and to respect the wordy invocations of abstraction and revered theory.

The observer-reader will also find that, while the tribes have a lot in common, they also each cultivate their own routines and proprieties, their own sayings, and ideas of what counts. The philosophy tribe doesn't sound exactly like the history tribe, or the history tribe like the anthropology tribe, and none of these sounds like the psychology tribe. Defining themselves by their distinctive ways of making statements about the world, scholars can be somewhat jealous of tribal boundaries. So, observer-readers exposed to several speech varieties — as university undergraduates are — may pick up the sounds of one variety and then another, and, innocently mixing them, get a surprisingly intense response when their audience hears the competing sounds of another tribe. A newcomer to the tribal cultures might notice that intense feelings are liable to be aroused in the areas the tribes seemed to share — citations, notes and references, the display of detail and abstraction. While, to an outsider, these features unite the scholarly tribes, for local people they are sites of distinction among them.

I hope readers will come to feel comfortable amidst the writers and researchers brought together in this book. To this end, I have composed introductions to the selections — guides to reading. These guides are designed to help readers prepare for difficulty and for the effort of accommodation. Like maps of unfamiliar territory, they sketch terrain where readers new to the area might lose their way, or become discouraged; they indicate landmarks by which readers can orient themselves. And, like guide-books to tourist attractions, they point out distinctive features representative of local culture.

The introductions also pose questions about the articles' contents. In this, they tend towards a genre many will remember from the schoolroom: the short interrogations that followed stories or essays in the readers used in English class. I remember this genre as a nuisance. The questions were so insipid as to suggest that the questioner had no real interest in the reading itself. Or they took an unnatural interest in matters that would never occur to a normal reader. Or the questions showed such a fussy attention to specifics — things a sensible reader would not have memorized — as to suggest that the questioner's greatest interest was verifying that students had actually read the selection. I have tried to avoid being either insipid or unnatural or fussy. Questions are intended to be aids to understanding the articles and the implications of the research they report. At the same time, they gesture to ways readers might prepare to become writers themselves, and to participate in the kind of reasoning prized among members of these disciplinary cultures.

The introductory questions may instigate writing projects. Or, in their own travels through these articles, readers may spy avenues connecting them. Such connections can in themselves generate writing projects. And, for starters, all the articles in this book are summarizable. Summary is a highly valued procedure in the academic disciplines, and challenging, too. Even if users of this book wrote only summaries of its articles, they would be developing a style and voice recognized and respected in research communities. (**Counts and Counts** (RVing), **Tiratsoo and Tomlinson** (restrictive trade practices), **Dasenbrock** (multicultural literature), and **Calhoun** (feminist and lesbian theory) would be especially good candidates for summary.)

Academic Writing, the textbook that is companion to this anthology, offers advice on scholarly summary. It also suggests writing opportunities that could develop from readings in this volume. Partly repeating *Academic Writing*'s suggestions for writing, the suggestions which follow here point to areas of shared concern which show up when we put some of these articles next to each other. Like the questioning which introduces selections, the listings below can provide materials for developing a writing topic. But they are not assignments in themselves — only guides to shared ground, to sites where the intersection of research concerns makes fertile space for further reasoning and writing. Just as researchers themselves are not assigned topics ("Write a 4000-word ethnographic article discussing community among RVers: what role does 'reciprocity' play?"), neither do I assign students particular topics. Rather, students are encouraged to acquire the research techniques and habits of mind that look for interstices in established knowledge, places to take a stand, to investigate a position, to construct a research question.

Grounds for writing

- Education/literacy

Lu	(Basic Writing)
Englund	(Mary Englund remembers)

- Work

Kabeer	(London garment trade)
Scott	(after abolition of slavery)
Tiratsoo and Tomlinson	(restrictive trade practices)
McDougall	(maternity leave)
Baber	(feminist epistemology)

- Community

Counts and Counts	(RVing)
Kabeer	(London garment trade)
Chavez	(imagined community)

- Gender

Calhoun	(lesbian and feminist theory)
Baber	(feminist epistemology)
Kabeer	(London garment trade)
Eckert	(adolescent "girl talk")
Apter et al.	(attitudes towards eating)
McDougall	(maternity leave)

- Race and ethnicity

Kabeer	(London garment trade)
Verkuyten, de Jong and Masson	(anti-racist and racist discourse)
Dasenbrock	(multicultural literature)
Englund	(Mary Englund remembers)

Touching more tangentially on race and ethnicity ,

Chavez	(imagined community)

| Apter et al. | (attitudes towards eating) |
| Lu | (Basic Writing) |

Comparable in looking at race and ethnicity along the lines of

- *Immigration*

Chavez	(imagined community)
Verkuyten, de Jong	
and Masson	(anti-racist and racist discourse)

- Work

| Kabeer | (London garment trade) |
| Scott | (after abolition of slavery) |

Finally, the scholarly voices which this volume convenes can themselves provide a research site. Students could investigate and compare, for example, the ethnographic methods of **Counts and Counts, Eckert, Kabeer, Verkuyten, de Jong and Masson**, and **Chavez**, using **Apter et al.** as a contrastive methodological case. Or they could inspect different disciplines' techniques of representing and consulting the past, investigating and comparing **Scott, McDougall, Baber**, and **Tiratsoo and Tomlinson**. Finally, they might take **Mary Englund** as an example of oral narrative and compare this document to scholars' ways of telling about the past.

Introduction

Labour supply decision making, female labour supply behaviour, game-theoretic bargaining models — these are not terms that most people run across in their everyday lives. Yet the activities they describe are part of most people's everyday experience. Naila Kabeer's "The Structure of 'Revealed' Preference: Race, Community and Female Labour Supply in the London Clothing Industry" looks into how people make decisions about where to work, when to work, and whether to work, and how families come to agreements (or fail to come to agreements) about the work lives of their members.

Kabeer's article is about labour *supply* (so it differs from analyses of labour which focus on *demand* — the labour requirements of employers and how these requirements structure the workforce). It is also about "choice and constraint, culture and economy" (308) — big issues embodied in very high-level abstractions. These are the things her research is *about*. Her research site — the "place" she goes to find out about these things — is a group of Bangladeshi women "employed in the homeworking sector of the East London rag trade" (307). These women have chosen to work at home, sewing for garment-industry contractors who pay them by the piece. It is the experience of these particular women — 60 of them — which provides her with the data that contribute to our understanding of "labour supply decision making," "culture and economy."

We might ask two questions about the connection between these abstractions and the lives of Bangladeshi women in East London. First, we might ask how Kabeer turns their life experience into data, and, second, we might ask how she extracts from these data illuminating information about culture and economy.

Looking to answer the first questions, we see that Kabeer tells about conducting interviews with the women (and some husbands). Their life experience has been turned into words, translated and transcribed. Segments of these stories appear frequently in the body of the article (for example, [30]), and we come into a kind of contact with these people and their voices. But it is a restrained or controlled contact. For one thing, nobody gets to tell her whole story. The whole stories have been broken up, and the fragments sorted and organized to support certain themes (for example, "Attitudes to outside work" [32-34]) which provide headings for sections of the discussion. For another thing, we are never left alone with these speakers, to make what we like from their stories. Rather, we are always accompanied by the researcher (for example, "Summing up these various responses, it is clear that by and large, purdah was not the main factor which lay behind the homeworking decision" [34]). Moreover, Kabeer says that only to a certain point will these people speak for themselves: "The objective of the research was to *go beyond* the immediate reasons given for observed labour market outcomes and to explore the actual decision-making processes which generated these outcomes" (25, emphasis added). When the women say that they work at home because of lack of education or limited command of English, Kabeer discounts these answers as sufficient explanations for the homeworking decision. She also moderates or qualifies "childcare" and "housework" as adequate explanations. So we might go on to our second question: how does Kabeer get from the interview data more general information about culture and economy? How does she "go beyond" what the women actually say?

Although you are told early on that this article investigates the decision-making of a particular group of women, you may lose sight of that group as you proceed through the first three or four pages of the article. In these pages, Kabeer briefly summarizes four or five theoretical approaches to decision-making, from "mainstream economic explanations," through variations on these to emphatically sociological explanations. It is these theoretical models which guide her interpretations of interview data: these are the means of "[going] beyond" what appears on the surface. To get a good grasp of this article, you might estimate the connections between the interpretations of interview data and each of the theoretical models.

Kabeer's article is a good example of scholarly procedures which investigate human behaviour by asking people what they think about what they are doing. In effect, the interviewer appears to have asked, "why have you chosen to work at home?" But the researcher does not take the answers to the question at face value, although she respects their wording and sincerity. You can measure the productivity or effectiveness of this procedure by estimating the power of Kabeer's explanations of the decision:

- Are Kabeer's explanations more comprehensive and illuminating than simply saying "these women don't speak enough English to work outside the home," or "they have to stay home to look after the children?" What do these explanations miss that Kabeer's work uncovers?

- What do we learn about "culture and economy" from this research?

Piece-work employment has traditionally been stigmatized as exploitative. When women do piece work, they seem especially liable to be seen as subjugated.

- How does Kabeer's research refine our idea of women's decision to do piece work at home?

- How do racialist contexts influence the decision to work? What does "community" have to do with the decision to work at home? What is the connection between racialism and community?

The Structure of 'Revealed' Preference: Race, Community and Female Labour Supply in the London Clothing Industry

NAILA KABEER

ABSTRACT

This article takes as its starting point the overwhelming concentration of Bangladeshi women in the homeworking sector of the clothing industry in London. This pattern forms a
contrast to the large numbers of male Bangladeshi workers
also concentrated in the garment industry but who are to be
found mainly in the factories and sweatshops. The article uses
the accounts given by the Bangladeshi homeworkers themselves for their concentration in this form of work to explore
different theoretical explanations of female labour supply behaviour, focusing in particular on questions of choice and
constraint, culture and economy.

The study suggests that the 'preferences' revealed by the
labour market behaviour of Bangladeshi women cannot be
attributed solely to them, but must be seen in terms of bargaining and negotiation with other, more powerful members
of the family. Furthermore, the intra-household decision-
making process is itself embedded within a broader institutional environment which determines the access enjoyed by
different groups to socially-valued resources. For Bangladeshis, a key factor in this broader environment is the operation of racially-based forms of exclusion from the mainstream opportunities. Consequently, community solidarity
and networks represent important symbolic and material resources for members. However, these resources are distributed in highly gender-specific ways, with very clear implications for women's place within the community. The article
argues therefore that any attempt to explain Bangladeshi
women's concentration in homework has to move beyond a
focus on either individual circumstances or cultural norms to

This article is based on a project on Bangladeshi women in the London garment industry, funded by the Economic and Social Research Council in Britain.

an exploration of the interaction of racism, community identity and gender relations in shaping women's labour market options.

INTRODUCTION

This article analyses labour supply decision-making for a particular group of women workers in a particular segment of the London clothing industry. It takes as its starting point the concentration of Bangladeshi women in the homeworking sector of the East London rag trade (Mitter, 1986a). This pattern forms a contrast to female garment workers from other ethnic groups in London who, while also working predominantly as clothing machinists, are dispersed across factories and sweatshops as well as the homeworking sector (Mitter, 1986b; Phizacklea, 1990). It also contrasts with the large numbers of male Bangladeshi garment workers, again mainly machinists, who are to be found in the factories and sweatshops of the London garment industry (Carey and Shukur, 1985; Mitter, 1986a; Tower Hamlets Trade Union Council, 1986).

The article reports on the explanations given by the Bangladeshi homeworkers themselves for their concentration in this form of work. It uses these accounts to explore different theoretical explanations of female labour supply behaviour, focusing in particular on questions of choice and constraint, culture and economy. The accounts are taken from in-depth, semi-structured, interviews carried out in 1989 with 60 female homeworkers from the London garment industry. Supplementary information is drawn from interviews with 30 Bangladeshi men working in factories[1]. Because of the casual and intermittent nature of this work, many of the men and women interviewed were unemployed at the time of the interview; they qualified for inclusion in the sample if they had undertaken such work in the preceding year.

ECONOMIC FRAMEWORKS: CHOICES AND CONSTRAINTS

Rational choice decision-making has long been the hallmark of mainstream economic explanations of human behaviour: eco-

---

[1]   These interviews were carried out with the valuable assistance of Ms S. Joddar who spoke the Sylheti variant of Bangla which is mainly spoken by the community in East London.

nomic decisions are seen as attempts by individuals to maximize their utilities, subject to their budget constraints. However, since utility is a metaphysical concept, eluding measurement or observation (Robinson, 1962), it tends to be replaced in empirical analysis by the concept of 'revealed' preference: observed market behaviour is taken to *reveal* underlying preferences of economic agents by providing information on the actual choices they make. While households are recognized as collectivities rather than individuals, the same decision-making rules apply since households are considered to behave 'as if' they were seeking to maximize a unified preference function. The validity of attributing a unified preference function to the household depends on certain assumptions, namely that household members are altruistic to the extent that their individual utilities are interdependent; or that there is an authoritarian but benevolent household head who is able to impose choices which maximize the joint utility of members (Becker, 1981).

Within the choice-theoretic paradigm, the gender division of labour among household members, and hence women's labour market behaviour, is explained in terms of individual specializations on the basis of comparative advantage. In general, this suggests that, for equal endowments of human capital, women have a comparatively greater advantage than men in domestic labour because of its compatibility with their childbearing and nurturing responsibilities. In the context of this study, therefore, the choice-theoretic approach would draw attention to differentials in human capital endowments among household members as well as to women's domestic responsibilities in order to explain the latter's concentration in the homeworking sector. While culture is sometimes factored into neo-classical explanations as a potential constraint on optimizing behaviour, it is seldom explored in any systematic way; the focus is on prices, incomes and the intermediary variables through which they operate.

There are other paradigms within economics which challenge this assumption of unified decision-making within the household. Game-theoretic bargaining models put forward by McElroy and Horney (1981) and Manser and Brown (1980) allow for differential preferences among household members so that household decision-making takes the form of bargaining. Bargaining power is seen to depend on the relative 'fall-back' or 'threat' positions of the individuals concerned, generally measured by their income potential outside the household. Although these approaches begin out in the formal 'as if' tradition of neo-classical economics, they lend themselves more readily to the consideration of the broader structural context of decision-making (Folbre, 1986).

This broader focus is evident, for instance, in Sen's formulation of household decision-making as a form of 'co-operative conflict' (1990). He suggests that differentials in bargaining power between household members reflect both on their material resources and contributions as well as the cultural meanings ascribed to these contributions and resources. Gender is seen as a major dimension in this differential, based on men's greater ability — in most contexts — to mobilize material, symbolic and coercive capabilities. Their greater access to resources outside the household, the greater value attached to their contributions, the close convergence between their personal well-being and their longer term self-interests, and their greater ability to exercise coercion and threat to achieve their goals, all coalesce to produce an asymmetrical gender distribution of bargaining power within the household, favouring male preferences in household decision-making outcomes.

SOCIOLOGICAL FRAMEWORKS: RULES AND RESOURCES

If cultural factors are generally given short shrift in the formal choice-theoretic tradition, they occupy a privileged place in traditional sociological explanations of behaviour, where they are seen as powerful constraints on how people behave. In this tradition, gender differences in employment patterns would be explained in terms of powerful cultural norms defining gender roles in given contexts. Muslim women have attracted considerable attention within this culturalist paradigm because of the perceived power and pervasiveness of Islamic ideologies. Purdah in particular has been singled out to explain Muslim women's exclusion from public forms of employment (Jeffries, 1979; Mernissi, 1975). At the core of the institution of purdah is the idea that the honour of the family resides in the virtue of its women; constant surveillance is necessary to ensure that women do nothing to bring shame on their kin. The practice of female seclusion effectively cements the syndrome of family honour and female virtue by restricting women to the domestic domain and permitting them to intrude into 'male' space only in dire economic need. Purdah can be seen as a key institutional determinant of women's disempowerment in such cultures, explicitly linking male power with the maintenance of boundaries which contain women within a curtailed range of life choices and opportunities. As Mernissi puts it:

Institutionalised boundaries dividing parts of society express the recognition of power in one part at the expense of the other. Any transgression of the boundaries is a danger to the social order because it is an attack on the acknowledged allocation of power. The link between power and boundaries is particularly salient in a society's sexual patterns. (Mernissi, 1975: 81)

In the British context, where Bangladeshi migrant women are generally subsumed within the homogenizing category of 'Asian women' both within popular perceptions as well as in the early academic literature, they tend to be defined almost exclusively in terms of these apparently immutable cultural traditions. They are portrayed as passive, powerless, traditional and homebound. These stereotypes appear to be confirmed in the case of South Asian Muslim women by employment statistics which document their much lower levels of participation in the 'visible' waged economy: in the 1984 Labour Force Survey, only 17 per cent of women of Bangladeshi and Pakistani origin in the age group 25-44 were classified as economically active compared to 62 per cent of women of Indian origin, 66 per cent of indigenous white women and 77 per cent of Afro-Caribbean women (reported in the *Employment Gazette*, December 1985).

As Allen and Wolkowitz (1987) point out, there is a tendency in the British sociological literature to draw a contrast between white women whose work options are assumed to be affected by 'life-cycle' factors and women from ethnic minority groups who are assumed to be constrained by cultural norms peculiar to their community. The same point is made by Parmar (1982) who questions analytical explanations which hold cultural norms responsible for 'Asian' women's absence from the labour force. Such explanations are exemplified in studies such as that of Khan (1976) among the Pakistani community in Bradford which concluded that the majority of Pakistani women of rural origin do not go out to work because it is unacceptable for 'cultural religious reasons' (Parmar, 1982: 251). Parmar points out that, along with 'cultural religious reasons', attention should also be paid to the number of dependent children, the availability of child care facilities, the range of options available to women, and the structure of local labour markets. In other words, culturalist explanations would benefit from an exploration of the economic domain, of the material constraints and opportunities which characterize the lives of different cultural groups.

Recent work in sociology, associated in particular with Giddens (1979), Connell (1987) and others, has broken with the idea of culture as chronically constraining and sought to recognize its potential for generating resources as well as rules. Such ideas are reflected in some of the recent literature on ethnic minorities in Britain which stresses that, in a racially antagonistic environment, culture offers resources which minority communities are able to mobilize in their own interests: 'differences and complexities . . . are called up as resources socially and economically, in addition to offering a sense of self and identity to minority peoples' (Mars and Ward, 1984: 11). Studies of the 'ethnic economy', for instance, point to the importance of kinship and community networks in generating employment in the context of racially-segmented labour markets. Within this body of literature, there is some difference of emphasis in the way in which gender relations are incorporated. The work of some researchers draws attention to the extent to which women are used as unpaid family labour or underpaid workers to subsidize the ethnic economy, *precisely* because of these cultural ties and affinities (Mitter, 1986a; Phizacklea, 1990). The work of others points to the need to disaggregate the category 'Asian women' to take account of the gender implications of different cultural traditions and the kinds of cultural resources they may offer to their women (Westwood and Bhachu, 1988).

BANGLADESHIS AND THE LONDON CLOTHING INDUSTRY

These cross-cutting debates in economics and sociology throw up a number of interesting questions concerning labour market behaviour which will be explored further in this article. For instance, whose preferences are revealed by Bangladeshi women's labour market decisions in the London garment industry? Are these preferences best understood in terms of voluntaristic rational choice within households or do they reflect differential decision-making power among household members? What role does culture play in shaping these 'revealed' preferences — is it purdah which explains Bangladeshi Muslim women's concentration in homework? However, before attempting to explore these questions, it is necessary to provide a background on the Bangladeshi community and its involvement in the garment industry in London. The following account draws heavily on Carey and Shukur (1985).

Bangladeshis first arrived in Britain in the early 1950s when men from the Sylhet district who had worked in the British Merchant Navy jumped ship to take up low-paid jobs in the catering industry. However, the bulk of the migrants began to arrive in the early 1960s, again largely unaccompanied men, sponsored by the seafaring kinsmen who had preceded them. The first area of settlement was Tower Hamlets, a borough in the East End of London. Wives and children followed later when it became clear that the original plan of accumulating savings and returning to Bangladesh was not going to be realized.

In the early stages, Bangladeshi immigrants found jobs in a variety of industries, although catering and clothing received a major share. However, as the recession of the early 1970s hit large sections of British manufacturing, Bangladeshis began to drift into the East End of London from other cities, many of them going into clothing (Mitter, 1986a). During this period the clothing industry was undergoing its own restructuring process both in response to economic recession and in order to compete against cheaper imports. The search for lower-wage and more flexible labour led to the closing down of many of the larger factories and the expansion of the practice of subcontracting out the more labour-intensive machining and assembly stages of production to small 'outdoor' units (or sweatshops) operating largely in the informal economy. Many Bangladeshi men moved into the jobs created by this dense network of subcontracting chains. The labour force in this sector is highly casualized and the men are therefore subject to long periods of seasonal unemployment. The large numbers of Bangladeshi men working as machinists in the East End clothing industry explains why a survey carried out in the Tower Hamlets area noted a much higher proportion of *male* machinists in this area compared to predominantly *female* machinists in other areas of the London clothing industry (Tower Hamlets Trade Union Council, 1986).

The other major form of subcontracting was to the homeworking sector, where it was mainly women from minority communities who took up the new opportunities. Here too the work was extremely erratic and even more poorly paid. The Bangladeshi women interviewed reported earnings of around £20 to £50 a week compared to the wages reported by men of over £100. These differentials are not 'pure' discrimination: they partly reflect the vulnerability of homeworkers but they also reflect the irregularity of the hours worked and the levels of skill entailed in the machining tasks usually assigned to the Bangladeshi women (mainly belts and linings).

This brief background helps to spell out some of the demand factors in the clothing industry which led to these different forms of employment being made available in its East London sector:

however, it leaves unanswered the question of why Bangladeshi men, as well as women, entered what is generally considered a female labour-intensive segment of the labour market, and why their participation took such different forms. In other words, it leaves the supply side of the labour market behaviour untouched. It is this aspect that the rest of the article addresses.

We begin our analysis in the next section by examining the explanations which emerge from the women's accounts of their labour market behaviour. The actual reasons given for the choice of homework appear perfectly compatible with a conventional economic framework: low educational qualifications; little or no command of English; child care and domestic responsibilities; the cultural constraints of purdah. However, by themselves, they throw little light on whether the labour supply decision-making within the household is one of consensus or of bargaining. Poorer educational qualifications and linguistic ability may explain women's concentration in homeworking on the grounds of comparative advantage. Alternatively, they may simply reflect, along with women's assignment to a badly remunerated form of labour, their weaker bargaining position within the household. Similarly, cultural norms of purdah may be either shared or imposed within the household.

The objective of the research was to go beyond the immediate reasons given for observed labour market outcomes and to explore the actual decision-making processes which generated these outcomes. This fuller analysis helped to highlight the multidimensional nature of the labour decision. In this context the decision to enter the labour market was first and foremost — and not unexpectedly — a response to economic need, most frequently for basic necessities, less often to acquire the accoutrements of status within the community, and least often to earn 'pin money' for personal consumption. However, a number of other subsidiary decisions had to be made simultaneously with this preliminary decision to earn money. Thus the homeworking decision could be seen as expressing a positive preference for earning money through home-based work, a positive opposition to work outside or a failure to find work outside. It could be seen as expressing either a temporary preference for home-based work or a permanent one. Finally it could be seen as an expression of women's own preferences, an expression of the preferences of other decision-makers within the household, or as the outcome of a consensual decision-making process within the household.

The analysis which follows will explore these broader dimensions of the homeworking decision. We will consider in greater detail the reasons given by women for doing homework; ask whose preferences were dominant in the decision; and explore attitudes to outside work, in general, and to garment factory work, in particular. We will conclude by returning to the theoretical explanations for women's labour market behaviour outlined at the start and consider their usefulness in the light of this account.

Why homework?

As noted above, women cited a variety of reasons for taking up domestic outwork. These reasons were not mutually exclusive and many women gave more than one: each of them will be considered in turn. First of all, there was a group of women who stressed purdah considerations as the reason for undertaking homework. As one women put it 'The gaze of any man over the age of 12, be he Bengali, or Jamaican or English, violates a women's [sic] purdah'. To this group, all forms of labour market activity which exposed women to such a gaze would constitute a violation of purdah. However, this strict definition of purdah was not widely held; most of the women interviewed expressed the view that purdah was not broken by going out of the house as long as they dressed and behaved with modesty.

Low educational attainment was another reason put forward for choosing homework and it was indeed the case that, on average, the women interviewed had lower levels of education than the male respondents. There were, however, a number of reasons why this did not constitute an adequate explanation for their differing employment patterns. A comparison of simple group averages frequently disguises the degree of overlap between group members. In this case, it disguises the fact that while some of the women interviewed had completed secondary education or more, many of the men interviewed had not completed primary education. If education alone was the key, then clearly the more educated women interviewed would have found jobs in the clothing factories while less educated men would have been excluded. Moreover, some of the men explicitly blamed their own *lack* of educational qualifications for their confinement to garment factory jobs:

> When I got here, my landlord's son told me I would get work in garment factories because they do not ask for educational qualifications.
> We go for these garment jobs because we have little educa-

tion.

We came here without the education to get good jobs. We
needed to earn money quickly so we couldn't even study for
better jobs. We had to go into jobs which relied on physical
labour, like these factories.

A related and more common explanation for women's concentration in homework was their poor command of languages other
than Bengali. In fact, education was sometimes mentioned as a
way of explaining the lack of linguistic skills. Not only did this
prevent women from finding jobs outside the home, it often prevented them from even looking. Again, gender differences in language proficiency did exist within the community, but other factors came into view, once the focus was shifted from differentials
in language proficiency to the process by which English was acquired. Many of the men interviewed also reported having arrived
in the country without any knowledge of English. However, they
had managed to improve their proficiency informally through
conversations with English speakers:

When I came here, I learnt to speak English through trial and
error.
After my arrival, I started to attend 'English as a second language' classes, but I had to stop shortly after. I could not
work and study at the same time. Instead I learnt by listening
to other people and trying to reply when spoken to.

The men acquired English because most of them worked in, or
had worked in, racially-mixed environments or had interacted in
other contexts with English speakers. It was this more frequent exposure to conversations conducted in English which was missing
in the lives of many of the women interviewed. The reasons they
lacked this regular exposure were bound up with the same considerations which kept them in homework and will be examined in
the course of this article.

There is one further reason to believe that gender difference in
linguistic proficiency was not an adequate explanation for the
marked gender difference in employment patterns. Along with the
many women who were able to speak English, there were also a
number of men interviewed who spoke little or no English, despite their long residence in the country. This had not prevented
them from finding jobs in the outdoor units since many such units
were owned by Bangladeshis or other Asians and often staffed en-

tirely by men from the community. There was little need here for proficiency in English.

The fourth, and most widely cited, reason that women gave for doing homework was their domestic responsibilities. While child care and housework are separate forms of labour, they are treated together here because they were frequently linked in the women's descriptions of the responsibilities associated with Bengali wifehood. Given that social services (including crèches and schools) are much poorer in this borough than in many other parts of London, and given that private child minders are generally very expensive, child care responsibilities constituted a real and widespread constraint on the ability of mothers to work outside. The advantage of homeworking was that it permitted them to combine child care and income earning.

Responsibility for children was one constraint: women also placed a great deal of stress on other domestic responsibilities. Families expected cooked meals at home. Since many husbands were unemployed and at home during lunch hours, this generally entailed at least two cooked meals a day. Women also performed other services which added to the comforts of home life for men: 'I have to attend to my husband when he comes home from work, he has to wash and I have to find his towel or sandals and get him tea and something to eat . . . '

Furthermore, as with other South Asian communities, Bangladeshis have brought with them into the British context a strong culture of hospitality. For many Bangladeshi Muslim men, bars and pubs, with their connotations of alcohol and hostile white drunks, were not welcoming prospects. Local cafés, home videos and visiting and receiving friends and relatives made up a major part of social life for the community. While the 'intense sociability' of community life made demands on both men and women, women's labour was in fact central since theirs was the primary responsibility for preparing tea, snacks or meals for their guests and attending to them.

To summarize this section, therefore, it appeared that for the majority of the women interviewed, the chief advantage of homework was its compatibility with the different cultural dimensions of being a housewife within the Bengali community — primarily looking after children and keeping the house in order, but also servicing the needs of male breadwinners, usually husbands, and fulfilling the family's hospitality obligations. This finding echoes those of other studies of homeworkers, which have included women from a variety of majority and minority ethnic groups:

Any explanation of why it is mainly women who do home-work . . . cannot ignore the family roles of these women . . . All the women in our sample considered housework and child-care to be their responsibility and regarded help from their husbands as a generous concession. (Hope, Kennedy and de Winter, 1976: 98–9)

The explanatory emphasis put on the care of young children obscures what is a life-long experience of women, namely that of servicing others on an unwaged basis. (Allen and Wolkowitz, 1987: 79)

It seems clear that while women's primary responsibilities for child care and domestic labour are elaborated in culturally-specific forms and language[2], they are common to women of different ethnic groups. At the same time, the constraints of purdah and the problems of language mentioned by the Bangladeshi women, together with differences in their community's location in relation to the labour market and the broader society, suggest that the specificities of their circumstances have also to be considered in any explanation of their labour market behaviour.

The decision to do homework: whose preference?

In attempting to determine whose preferences underpinned women's homework decision, the problem of disentangling choice from constraint was often difficult because of constant slip-page between the two — 'I didn't want to do it, and anyway my husband wouldn't allow me to'. In such situations, it was hard to determine whether the situation being described was one of shared preferences, or *ex post* rationalization of male preferences. In general, however, the decision to earn money appeared most often to have been made by the women themselves, sometimes with the support of their guardians, but more often meeting with

---

2   Allen and Wolkowitz (1987:82) point to interesting differences in the way in which white and Pakistani homeworkers formulated what appeared to be a similar point. The former were more likely to say that their husbands 'preferred' them to work at home while the latter tended to say that their husbands would not 'allow' them to take outside employment. Whether this reflected minor differences in language use or major differences in perceptions of male authority, the authors note that the influence of husbands' wishes had the identical effect of constraining women's work options.

initial resistance so that adjustments had to be made to accommodate conflicting preferences. In these cases, therefore, homeworking was a negotiated outcome rather than one which emerged out of identical or altruistic preferences.

Those who saw their lack of educational and language qualifications as the reason for working at home could be said to have exercised their own preferences. From their own viewpoint, they felt that they had very little choice in the matter of labour supply decision-making:

> I have never looked for outside work. I don't want to because you would need to know English.
>
> Since coming here, I have never tried for a job outside because I can't speak English. Without that there is no prospect of outside work.
>
> I can say yes and no in English and I can understand if someone speaks to me, but I can't speak it. So I have never looked for outside work.
>
> I didn't try and work outside because I couldn't make people understand or travel around by myself.
>
> Without the education, how can we get the jobs?

Of those who had cited purdah constraints as their reason for doing homework, there were some differences as to whether this constraint was self-imposed or imposed by other family members. As noted above, a few women in this group expressed their adherence to the constraining view of purdah:

> The gaze of any man over the age of 12 violates my purdah.
>
> I would not take an outside job. Should I discard my purdah because I have come to this English country?

However, the majority did not hold to this narrow definition. While acknowledging the strictures of purdah, their accounts suggested a more problematic version of decision-making with frequent evidence of power being exercised by dominant members, husbands, parents and in-laws in determining the options available to women.

> Going out to work is not an option, my husband would not want it, we are Muslims and it would be a sin. My parents in law would criticise me too.
>
> My husband's family haven't actually forbidden me to go

out to work but in a way they have. They think purdah would be spoilt.

My husband doesn't let me go out very much, he thinks I will learn bad ways. I have never looked for work outside as a result.

The large numbers who cited their domestic responsibilities as the reason for working at home were similarly divided into those who clearly subscribed to the dominant definitions of women's domesticity within the community and those who did not. In that the former group were not seeking to challenge these community norms, the decision could be interpreted as a consensual one:

It is better for women to work at home. If I went to work outside, somebody would have to look after my children and cook for my husband. Cooking is our main duty. So it is not a question of breaking purdah — just a question of getting the housework done.

I can't do regular work. I have to cook for the children by 12. And I am often interrupted by our visitors. Then I have to make my husband's tea.

The advantage of homework is that I can stay at home, earn money, pray, fast, cook and feed my husband and son. They come home at lunch for only 45 minutes. When people come visiting, they just sit there and chat, but the hostess has to cook and give attention to guests who are just sitting there.

I have never looked for outside work, I have two children, who would look after them? I have to look after the children, look after the house and attend to my guests.

However, for the rest, the homeworking decision represented the outcome of a process of negotiation and compromise, where the terms of the compromise were generally laid down by husbands or (less frequently) by parents. In most cases, the idea of earning an income had come from the women. Some had started out wanting to work outside, and in the face of resistance from dominant family members, had confined themselves to homework. Others had faced resistance to the idea of homework itself because it was seen as interfering with their other responsibilities. The compromise reached here was adjustment of working hours so as to accommodate the routine demands on their time from domestic chores.

My husband doesn't want me to work outside, he is even reluctant to let me work at home. He thinks I should look after
the children, help them with their education and keep the
house clean.

I wanted to learn tailoring outside, I was bored and
wanted to meet people. But my husband said he would teach
me at home. I have to stop machining when he comes home,
otherwise he tells me off. He thinks the children are becoming bad-mannered. I may have to give up all together now
because he doesn't like it.

I needed to earn some money. My husband was worried I
would neglect the children and not feed them on time, but I
showed him I could manage. It is not difficult to look after
the children, clean the house, do the cooking and earn
money homeworking, is it? (laughs)

It was my idea, my husband wasn't very keen, but said I
could do it if I could manage all my other work.

My husband doesn't like my working like this; he says you
can't look after the children and the house and work at the
same time. He is getting used to it now, but still raises objections.

This conditional support was echoed in the comment of one of
the husbands who was present at the latter part of an interview:
'My wife's sewing does not interfere with the housework or the
cooking. My house is clean, as you can see.'

Attitudes to outside work

Further insights were obtained into the homeworking decision by
considering women's attitudes to the question of outside work.
For those few for whom purdah considerations were voluntarily
accepted as the reason for homework, any form of outside work
was obviously out of the question. Among those on whom cultural and religious restrictions had been imposed by others, attitudes to outside work were more equivocal and varied, although
none of them considered the act of working outside sufficient to
be a violation of purdah.

I don't know what jobs are available outside. I don't think
purdah gets spoilt by going out — I don't understand why
my husband's family forbid it. Purdah is only spoilt by what
you do. I could only go out to work if my husband let me. If

he let me, I would work anywhere, except perhaps in factories.

I wanted to do a course at our local college but my parents won't let me as there is no one to accompany me. I want to do a job that requires academic qualifications, people respect those kinds of jobs, but my parents refuse their permission.

People have many reasons for not working outside, but I will tell you my own experience. I wanted to work outside, but my husband won't let me. I once went and worked in a factory for 3 days without telling anybody.

Finally, of those for whom domestic responsibilities were the most important factor in their decision to do homework, the majority appeared to have no inherent objections to the idea of outside work. However, this apparent willingness was hedged with certain conditions. Some were prepared to consider outside work only if it was compatible with child care or once their children were at school, suggesting both that there was a life cycle dimension to their work patterns and that child care was perceived as a more inflexible demand on their labour time than other domestic responsibilities. Others stressed a preference for 'respectable' jobs, suitable for Bengali women. In practice this led to a converging and fairly restricted range of jobs for both groups: work within the community, in crèches, nurseries or in schools. In addition, a few with formal educational qualifications stated their preference for working in offices or in shops. Factories were generally not considered one of the preferred options.

I would work outside if I found an opportunity to work with the Bengali community. It wouldn't break purdah.

I am looking for work suitable for Bengali women. Perhaps a crèche worker in this area, because they often take Bengali women.

I would like a job in a crèche. Sewing gives me a headache. I would work outside, but among women, not with men.

I would do any work now, even in a factory, as long as it was from 10 to 3 and with women. I have tried for work in crèches, clinics or looking after small children. I would work now if I could get a job in a creche and take the children with me.

I would work in a shop which was suitable for women like me, or teaching our children Bengali or babysitting. The salary would have to be very good. I would have to earn at least

80-100 a week after deductions to make it worth my while to work outside.

I learnt English because I wanted to work in an office or shop. My mother won't let me work in a shop in this area because I would be harassed by local boys.

I am doing college to improve written English; I want to work in an office.

Summing up these various responses, it is clear that by and large, purdah was not the main factor which lay behind the home-working decision. Many accounts stressed that it was possible to maintain purdah outside work by dressing modestly: 'even if you go out without a *burkah*, you are not behaving like white people. You cover yourself with your sari, cardigan, coat, scarf, they serve the same purpose as a *burkah*'.

Attitudes to factory work

Cultural norms clearly played an important role in shaping the kinds of outside jobs that women were prepared to consider, with age and life-cycle acting as further influences on their attitudes. Such norms were in even greater evidence in shaping women's responses to the idea of working in the garment factories. The near-unanimity of their rejection of such work was based on their fear that routine contact with strange men would excite community censure. However, while unanimous that contact with male strangers would be a problem, the women varied in their categorization of which male strangers constituted the difficulty. For some women, it was the presence of *men per se* in the factories that constituted a problem. For others, it was the presence of *Bengali men*, while for a third group the stress was on the *class background* of Benagli men in the factories. Gender-related factors therefore appeared as a common dimension in these accounts; what distinguished them was the extent to which community and class considerations were also featured.

For some women, the problem with working in garment factories lay quite simply in the fact that it entailed routinized contact with male strangers. Here some of the accounts were specifically couched in terms of purdah and religion, while others also stressed the social problems that were likely to ensue if Bengali women worked alongside men.

I couldn't work with men, I could only work in a factory full of women. It is forbidden by our religion and also there are many people in this community who like to spread bad stories. Also there are many bad women and men. I have heard many incidents from people about this boy falling in love with that girl or saying some bad things to that girl . . . Even if you are a virtuous woman and are seen talking to a virtuous man, people will say bad things about you, they will blame you. I would feel ashamed if that happened to me.

If there were just women in the factories, and only one or two men, there is no problem about purdah. But how can men and women work together, we are Muslims and our religion is against it. I couldn't work in a factory. I would be embarrassed, it wouldn't be normal.

Our women don't work in factories, our women have a lot of shame. It is shameful to work with men. Even when we go in front of strangers or talk to them, we feel shame, so how could we work in factories? Decent women don't work in factories because they are full of men. Any other kind of work is better than that. Our people would laugh and say things.

My father wouldn't let me work in a factory. I wouldn't like it either, I would have to appear in front of so many men. I would get more money, but I wouldn't want to go.

For a second group, the problem lay not in the presence of men *per se* in the garment factories, but in the presence of large numbers of Bengali men. Much of the literature on the garment industry in British cities has emphasized the female-intensiveness of its labour force, as well as the disproportionate presence of women from ethnic minorities. What was striking about the East London segment of the industry was the extensive presence of male machinists from the Bangladeshi community working in its factories and sweatshops. Many of the sweatshops were entirely made up of Bangladeshi male machinists. This was the product of racial segmentation of the local labour market which closed off most mainstream employment opportunities to members of the Bangladeshi community. As one of the male workers interviewed bitterly pointed out, 'When I first came to this country, my brother told me straightaway that there are only two types of jobs permitted to us Bengalis — catering and tailoring factories'.

However, the closure of large segments of the labour market to the Bangladeshi community and the resulting concentration of its men in the garment factories in turn had the effect of closing off these jobs to women from the community. Their reluctance to enter the factories was based in this case, not on religious strictures against working alongside men, but on the responses they anticipated from Bangladeshi men in the workplace and from the community in general:

> I don't want to work in the factories . . . there are English and Bengali men working in them. I would feel ashamed, purdah is spoilt for Muslim women and it is a sin . . . The English men may ignore you, but however good you are, men from our community will spread scandal about you. They won't say it in front of you, but they will go somewhere else and say it. I don't know about this area so much, but you must know what it is like in Bangladesh as well, they just make things up.

> There would be a problem working in factories, there are too many Bengalis in them. It is hardest for me, they will say things about me, I cannot behave as I might have been able to. People will say, Look at her, she hasn't got a husband and she is working in a factory.

> Women feel embarrassed because they didn't go out in front of men in Bangladesh . . . they feel ashamed in front of Bengali men because they will say that the husband sent his wife out to work because he can't feed her himself, that is how they will think.

> Our women feel shame in front of Bengali men. Even though they are from our country, there is still shame. People are different, some are good, some bad. Many look at you in a bad way. If there is any other reason that our women don't work, I don't know what it is. I wouldn't go into the factories because I would feel ashamed.

> My husband wouldn't let me work in a factory and I wouldn't go. There are many different kinds of men, and so many Bengalis. I would feel embarrassed in front of them.

Finally there was a third group of women for whom objections to the presence of Bengali men in the factories had a strong class dimension. Although racist stereotyping has often led to all Bangladeshis in the East End of London being lumped together as a homogenous group, there are of course class and status differences within the community. The garment factories were perceived by some women as inhabited by men from lower status groups within the community who could not be relied on to conduct themselves with propriety in the presence of women:

I don't want to work in garment factories. Too many different kinds of Bengali men there. After all, we are not all the
same. There is too much mixing in the factories.

There are all kinds of men from our community there. If a
man is only used to driving rickshaws and has never held a
book in his hand, he will not know how to behave anywhere. That is that type of man who seems bad, it is not his
fault, he did not get any education.

Many of the Benagli boys here don't know how to behave
around us; they have not been to college and they have
grown up according to the culture of this country.

There are so many different types of Bengalis in the factories and I would feel embarrassed. Some of these men . . . if
they see a smart well-dressed woman from the community,
they will inspect her from head to foot.

There was thus a strong sense in which factory work was perceived by Bangladeshi women as a male domain, and in particular,
the domain of a specific group of men who subscribed to the same
notions about female propriety and shame as they did and operated
by the same codes of behaviour. The presence of men from their
community within the factories meant that rather than being an impersonal space, inhabited simply by fellow workers, the factory floor
was perceived as an extension of the moral community. The values
and mores of the community were not left behind at the factory gates
but were actively reconstituted within its space. In a culture where
norms of sexual propriety are closely bound up with the maintenance of spatial boundaries, encounters between women and men
outside accepted boundaries can never be sexually neutral. Women
who trespass lay themselves open to the defining — and dishonour-
ing — power of the male gaze. As far as the factories were concerned,
Bangladeshi women would literally be under the gaze of the community and since it was overwhelmingly a male gaze, the sense of being under constant community surveillance would be further compounded by sexual unease and shame.

Discomfort in the presence of men from their community was
not restricted to the factory context, but manifested itself in other
situations where women felt they were trespassing on 'male space'.
This was evident for instance in discussions about their behaviour
around shopping. Weekly provisions were generally bought by
male members of their households; this is customary in Bangladesh
as well. Many of the women hesitated about going into the local
Bangladeshi grocery shops because they were usually patronized

by men from their community. They had no problems about going into saree shops because these were seen as 'female' spaces and mainly patronized by women, but for groceries, they preferred shops like their local supermarket where they felt anonymous.

> I don't go into grocery shops in this area because they are all owned by men from our community. I feel embarrassed in those shops. If you go into them, the men look at you. If one of them says something, how can you protect your reputation. I prefer to go to Sainbury's, no one looks at you.
>
> I try not to go in Bengali shops very often because there are too many Bengali men in them and find it shaming to go in front of them.
>
> My husband does the shopping, not me. I don't go for groceries, those shops are full of Bengali men, and though we are from the same country, our norm is not to go in front of men. I still feel the shame. I don't feel embarrassed in front of English people, they don't look at you twice. But some people in our community spread gossip without reason. Even if you behave, they say bad things. I know because I hear them talking about other people; if they can do that, they can talk about me as well. I don't mind the saree shops, because there are more women there.

Male perspectives on women's work

Before assessing the implications of these accounts of labour market behaviour for the different theoretical explanations outlined earlier, it is worth touching briefly on how this behaviour was represented in the accounts of the male workers interviewed. Here there was some reference to perceived gender differences in abilities and aptitudes, but the presence of women from other ethnic communities within the garment factories put definite limits on how far this explanation could be taken. Religion had too limited a role, because Muslim women from the Turkish community were observed in many of the factories. By and large, the weight of men's explanations of Bangladeshi women's work patterns tended to focus on the need to maintain the boundaries of gender propriety inscribed in community norms and consequently echoed what the women had said:

> There are many reasons why Bengali women don't work in factories. Their husbands don't want it and even if they did,

our community would not allow it. Our people think it is shameful for women to work in factories — because they are full of men. People say bad things about women working in factories. Friends and relatives will dislike such women.

Our society and culture keeps our women away from work. It is best our women don't work in these factories because men and women work together, mix freely, talk and laugh. Our women do not like these things. The Turkish women are Muslims, but very different, very westernized. It is best for Bengali women to work at home; the money is a little less, but they will have privacy. Or they can work in playgroups with children; they can also become dinner ladies if they want to.

I have never seen a Bengali woman in factories. Lack of education, purdah and household duties prevent Bengali women from working in factories. But many women are getting community jobs. I don't think purdah is ruined if women go out to work, as long as they wear loose clothing and don't mix freely with men.

There are some African, Indian and Irish women working in my factory. Their culture is very different from ours, they don't think it is bad for women to go out to work. But our culture is very much against this. If my wife goes out to work, we lose our family prestige. It is not religion that stops our women. Purdah is not ruined as long as women keep their hair and bodies well-covered. Our religion is not against this, but our culture is.

I have only even once seen a Bengali woman in a factory and she was a widow trying to make ends meet. Our women do not like to work in factories because of our religion and culture. Our religion does not allow women to work with men; neither does our culture, particularly where there is a large group of men. People think badly of such women. Husbands and fathers will not allow this to happen. Anyway, our women have to look after the children and do all the housework, they have too much to do at home.

Purdah would be ruined if Bengali women came to work in the factories because it is difficult for them to work with men. Men would also find it difficult because there often has to be body contact. We have to push and shove in order to move around because these units tend to be small. Bengali women are very different from the English. Whatever the English do, our religion, our culture and our social views prevent our women from doing the same. Some of our women are going to work wearing English clothes, which don't cover their body properly. They are not maintaining purdah.

RACISM AND THE CONSTRUCTION OF COMMUNITY

Although the accounts given by the women of their labour market behaviour touched on a variety of considerations, the empirical frequency with which certain explanations cropped up in these accounts pointed to some of the structural regularities which featured in their lives. One such regularity was the overarching presence of 'the community' as a factor in shaping the lives and choices of Bangladeshi women *and* of their families. Even in the more voluntaristic accounts, decisions were rarely presented as entirely freely chosen. Community norms were implicit in the taken-for-granted assumption that women are primarily, often solely, responsible for child care and housework and hence the assignment of women to home-based forms of income-earning. The presence of community — its perceptions, rules and information networks — was more explicitly stated as a factor in closing off certain segments of the outside labour market to women and making others more attractive. Even when it appeared that more powerful household members (husbands or parents) were imposing constraints on women workers' choices, it was frequently in the context of observing community norms and mores, rather than as an expression of their own individual preferences. Similarly, when women presented the decision to take or avoid certain actions, it was frequently fear of community censure, rather than the prospect of violating religious precepts, that proved to be the motivating factor.

Why did the community loom so large in the lives and choices of the Bangladeshis in East London? After all, migration can be a time for cultural renegotiation as individuals leave behind the society in which strong sanctions and incentives exist to ensure conformity to traditional 'rules'. However, both the character and experience of the migration process for the Bangladeshi community has militated against this happening. In the first place, its members tended to be from particular villages in one particular district in Bangladesh. Early legislation had helped to perpetuate a very selective process of migration as kinsmen and fellow-villagers stood a better chance of being sponsored under the voucher system than those who had no kinship links to Britain. They had then become concentrated in certain boroughs of the East End of London. Even after the halting of new immigration, a steady flow of Bangladeshis into Tower Hamlets borough from other parts of Britain continued, as manufacturing industry began to lay off labour in the cities of the Midlands and the North. The geographical cohesiveness of the community, both in terms of its origins in the villages of Sylhet and its subsequent settlement patterns, meant it was constituted as a highly localized community, based on face to face interaction 'where the presence of known others was a major precondition for all social encounters' (Giddens, 1979). The anonymity usually associated with urban life was not a feature here.

While this cohesiveness helped to keep alive the cultural rules of the community, it would be wrong to portray this culture as purely constraining. The continued concentration of the Bangladeshis in the East End of London should also be understood as a response to the hostile racial environment in which they found themselves. Most of them chose to live in council housing in 'safe' neighbourhoods rather than owner-occupied housing elsewhere, because of fear of racial harassment in white owner-occupied areas. Many white areas were effectively no-go areas for Bangladeshis. Commenting on the seriousness of the problem of racial attacks on white housing estates, Carey and Shukur (1985) note that on one white estate, seven out of nine Bangladeshi families had to be evacuated to safe accommodation in 1984 after a year of constant and severe harassment by local youths. During this period, the National Front polled only 2-4 per cent of votes in the three wards of Tower Hamlets in which the Bangladeshis were concentrated: it polled between 9 and 19 per cent in the other eleven wards. The community was thus hemmed into a small area within the borough: to move east or north of the areas of most Bengali concentration was to venture into NF territory.

Aside from the hard-core racism of the far right organizations, there was also the more hidden, but more persistent and pervasive racism entrenched in the segmented structures of the labour market and public provision of social services, particularly housing and education. Indeed, the highly discriminatory character of local housing policy by a Liberal-led local council has proved to be one of the most racially explosive issues in the area, and in 1993 helped to catapult a member of the fascist far right British National Party onto the local council for the first time in the area's history. The intersection of these acute forms of racially-based exclusion has produced a community that has been forced to draw heavily on its own resources in order to survive. This is the Bangladeshi version of the ethnic economy referred to at the beginning of this article. Through a dense network of exchanges, encounters and transactions, important resources are distributed within the community and serve simultaneously to reconstitute its boundaries.

The importance of these social networks surfaced continuously in the accounts of both the women and men interviewed. It was through relatives and acquaintances already resident in London that later immigrants were able to obtain the information and sponsorship which made their journey possible. They relied on these networks to find them lodgings when they first arrived, to help them make contact with local social services and to direct them towards employment possibilities. Furthermore, these mutual support networks continued after the initial critical period of settling in. The women, being more circumscribed in their movements, were clearly dependent on their husbands or on family friends to participate in community information circuits, to alert them to homeworking opportunities and to act as middle-men for their products. But the men were also dependent on their contacts within the community. The majority of them worked in units owned by a Bangladeshi subcontractor or had heard of factory jobs through Bangladeshi informants in the factories or through the community grapevine. In the words of one of the male workers:

> It is only possible to move from one job to another with the help of a friend or a relative. It is only through them that you learn about new openings. You can't get a job just by asking the owner of the factory to give you one. You must go with a reference. That is how many Bengalis find jobs in Turkish or Greek factories.

Community cohesion offered symbolic as well as material resources. Faced by a closed and hostile ethnic majority, the Bengali community has mobilized its own religion, norms and customs to assert a separate — and preferred — cultural identity. Cultural functions have been on the increase, with dancers and musicians brought over from Bangladesh by local entrepreneurs (Carey and Shukur, 1985). Community organizations put on musical shows and dramas regularly. The local mosque also plays an important role in the community's political and cultural life. Where lesser antagonism from ethnic majority groups might have led to greater mutual exploration of cultural difference, what has occurred instead is a sharper definition of difference, of discourses based on 'them' and 'us'. As Carey and Shukur (1985:416) point out, 'even young Bangladeshi children, whose command of English is indistinguishable from that of their white peers, and whose leisure patterns have absorbed elements from the local white (and black) working-class youth cultures, have found that skin colour and negative stereotypes about "Asians" have erected formidable barriers to interaction'.

The bitter realities of 'skin colour and negative stereotypes' surfaced particularly frequently in the accounts of the Bangladeshi men interviewed, who appeared to be more exposed to the risk of direct attacks or had witnessed or knew of attacks on other male acquaintances:

They don't like us because we are foreigners. They think we are taking everything away from them, especially their jobs. But they don't realise they allowed us in when there were plenty of jobs available. Now they don't need so much labour they treat us badly in order to scare us into going home. I know of so much racial harassment of Bengalis.

The white skinheads beat us up really badly. It is different now. We are more alert and stand up for ourselves. Many white people in the area are OK, but some are really bad and there are still a lot of attacks.

The English, especially the ones living in London, are always abusing and attacking our people. Outside the London area it may not be so bad.

I travel alone a lot. All men have to do this because it is not possible to have someone with you all the time. So you have to get used to it. On two occasions I was threatened with attack — once at Stepney and once at Shadwell Garden. On both these days I was alone and returning home late in the evening. A group of teenage boys swore at me and followed me for a while. Thank God I was not attacked. They don't like us because we are foreigners.

I always return home by 9 o'clock in the evening. I have never been attacked because I never stay out late at night. Most attacks happen late at night. Last year, my friend was badly beaten up at midnight. He was in hospital for many days. He has recovered from his wounds, but mentally he will never recover from the experience. He is now unbalanced by his fear. It is frightening what is happening to our people.

Sometimes I have to work till late in the evening. I have

often heard of Bengalis being attacked. One night I was returning home and on the underground. Three white men got on the train and beat me up quite badly. I don't like white people because they hate us.

In the face of persistent racial antagonism which regularly spills over into physical harassment and violence, the community remains a source of strength, safety and solidarity for its members. It can only continue to play this role if it is constantly and actively reaffirmed and reconstituted. Hospitality, gossip, conformity to community customs and norms, cultural occasions — all these are aspects of this reconstituting practice. But also critical to it is the reproduction of social hierarchies of the community and here gender takes on a particular significance. Women are assigned a place within the community which seeks to reproduce the one that they are seen to occupy in the 'home' culture, that is, as dependent mothers, wives and daughters. Despite their ambivalence towards many aspects of community culture, therefore, women paradoxically are the main bearers of the culture of the homeland.

GENDER, RULES AND RESOURCES IN THE COMMUNITY

All this has a bearing on the theoretical questions we raised at the start of this paper concerning the role of culture in economic decisions. The analysis presented here bears out the dual nature of culture as a source of both rules and resources. In situations where minority communities are excluded from mainstream labour markets, their social networks offer alternative ways of mobilizing material and symbolic resources: support, identity, employment and safety. At the same time, these practices also help to shape and constrain daily behaviour and interactions, introducing areas of "inertness" in house-hold decision-making, in that responses to opportunities are shaped by a concern with cultural propriety rather than by any immediate economic payoff.

The major point that emerges from the accounts given by women and men is that these rules and resources are not neutral between members of the community, but markedly gendered in their content and consequences. The same set of rules have very differing symbolic and material implications for women and men. Thus women may benefit from the presence of the community in that they are able to move about more safely in the locality than might have otherwise been the case. On the other hand, the same presence ensures that their mobility is a highly selective one, so that a form of gender-segregation is evident in community life, where women are confined to family-based or women-dominant spheres and avoid public areas where groups of men from the community are likely to congregate.

Gender asymmetry in community rules and resources is also apparent in the gender division of labour sanctioned by cultural norms. Rules which uphold men as primary breadwinners and women as dependent housewives not only shape the conduct permissible to women and men, but have important material implications. On the one hand, they assure men of prior claims to the labour market opportunities available to the community. On the other, women's near full-time responsibility for domestic chores assures men of what is probably a fairly cost-effective way of achieving comforts which conform as closely as possible to life back home: home-cooked lunches and dinner, clean house, clean clothes, hospitality for friends and all the small services which, if they could be purchased on the market, would entail a considerable strain on the family budget. As we have seen, a common objection to women's income-earning activities, even within the home, was that it would interfere with their performance of household chores and might even require men to help out, if they were unemployed.

The idea that woman's first obligation is to her children and husband has an important symbolic value. It upholds a specific version of masculinity in a context where such masculinity is being constantly threatened and undermined by racist violence on the streets, segmentation in the labour market and discrimination in public services. The gender division of labour within the garment industry itself, with men occupying the more visible factory roles while women engage in the hidden labour of homework, allows households to reproduce themselves without threatening the gender hierarchies of the community[3].

---

3   This point echoes the observations made by Ben Birnbaum in his historical review of the clothing industry in East London (nd). Focusing on the pre-war period when the industry relied mainly on workers from the Jewish community in East London, Birnbaum notes that tasks carried out by male machinists were graded as skilled, while those carried out by women were graded as semi-skilled, classifications which bore little relationship to complexity of the actual work performed. He attributes this apparent anomaly to the struggle of men workers from the local immigrant communities to retain their social status within the family, despite being excluded from mainstream employment opportunities: 'the Russian, Polish, Jewish community was isolated with little hope, or desire, of finding alternative employment outside the community. Consequently, male employ-

The unequal position from which Bangladeshi women and men entered the British context — and their subsequent experiences within a highly racialized society — have allowed the cultural renegotiations necessitated by immigration to take on a highly constraining form for the women. Most of the women interviewed were part of a first-generation of immigrants. Coming from a conservative rural area of Bangladesh, many of the disadvantages of a patrilineal and patrilocal kinship system have been compounded for them by the move to urban Britain. They have married outside their own lineage groups, left behind their natal family networks and moved to a strange country with alien, and inhospitable, culture. In these circumstances, the community represents a context that is both familiar and supportive while the risks associated with survival outside community networks are likely to be higher for women than for men. Although the women interviewed frequently expressed their antagonism to constraining cultural practices, and although they have sought to renegotiate them with dominant members of their households, by and large they have not succeeded in re-writing the cultural rules: power relations, as Giddens (1979) has pointed out, help to determine whose accounts will count. This is likely to change, of course, as a younger generation of women, who have grown up in England, begin to challenge the rules from a stronger bargaining position (for the different form that cultural renegotiation around gender relations has taken for women workers in the garment industry in Bangladesh, see Kabeer, 1989).

CONCLUSION: THE STRUCTURE OF REVEALED PREFERENCE

Let me conclude by returning to the title of this paper. The possibility that individual preferences are structured by institutional contexts rather than shaped by purely individual circumstances is not generally one that receives much space in the neo-classical economic tradition out of which the concept emerged. Altruistic models of the household assume that women's labour supply behaviour reveals their own preferences, or at least their voluntary deference to a uni-

---

ment was restricted to a few occupations, and to retain his social status, his job had to be designated as skilled. Initially the family unit was the production unit and it would have been socially difficult for large differentials in skills and earnings to exist in one family' (Birnbaum, nd: 7 cited in Phillips and Taylor, 1980: 84).

fied household preference function. Bargaining models assume that it is the more powerful member of the household whose preferences are revealed in decision-making outcomes.

My reading of the accounts given by the women workers — and supported by those of the men — leads me to conclude that the question must be answered at a number of different levels. It would clearly go against the grain of the accounts presented here to suggest that Bangladeshi women's concentration in the home-working sector of the London garment industry revealed their own freely chosen preferences. It was more often the result of a bargaining process in which the preferences of other key members — husbands but also mothers and fathers — play an important role in determining actual decision-making outcomes. However, while these decisions may be seen to benefit dominant, usually male, decision-makers in the household, the preferences themselves appear to reflect structural as well as individual factors. Thus while men may have a disproportionate influence in shaping women's labour supply behaviour, male preferences are here shaped by the defensive social relations of a community responding to the racism of British culture and practice. Had Bangladeshi immigrants found themselves in a more hospitable society, the negotiation process within the household would probably have taken on a very different complexion and a different set of preferences are likely to have emerged.

Nor is the consideration of this larger context relevant only for minority ethnic communities. Just as the preferences of the individuals interviewed for this research cannot be understood without reference to the broader context of a racially divided society, so too the labour market behaviour of women and men from the dominant cultural groups who benefit from this segmentation would need to be located in this broader context rather than studied as purely individual choices. All labour market behaviour in the real world is shaped by structurally generated and cross-cutting inequalities in the distribution of rules and resources. The extent to which choices are exercised or constrained, the forms that these choices take and their practical outcomes, are all likely to vary according to whether the actors being studied belong to the privileged groups or to the marginalized ones.

REFERENCES

Allen, S. and C. Wolkowitz (1987) *Homeworking. Myths and Realities.* London:

Macmillan.

Becker, G. S. (1981) *Treatise on the Family*. Cambridge, MA: Harvard University Press.

Birnbaum, B. (nd) 'Women, skill and automation: a study of women's employment in the clothing industry 1946-1972', unpublished.

Carey, S. and A. Shukur (1985) 'A profile of the Bangladeshi community in East London', *New Community* XII (3): 405-17.

Connell, R. W. (1987) *Gender and Power*. Cambridge: Polity Press.

Folbre, N. (1986) 'Cleaning house: New Perspectives on Households and Economic Development', *Journal of Development Economics* 22: 5-40.

Giddens, A. (1979) *Central Problems in Social Theory. Action, Structure and Contradiction in Social Analysis*. London: Macmillan.

Hope, E., M. Kennedy and A. de Winter (1976) 'Homeworkers in North London', in D. L. Barker and S. Allen (eds) *Dependence and Exploitation in Work and Marriage*, pp. 88-108. London: Longman Press.

Jeffries, P. (1979) *Frogs in a Well: Indian Women in Purdah*. London: Zed Books.

Kabeer, N. (1989) '"Rational Fools" or "Cultural Dopes?" Women and labour supply in the Bangladesh garment industry', *European Journal of Development Research* 3(1): 134-60.

Khan, V. S. (1976) 'Purdah in the British situation', in D. L. Barker and S. Allen (eds) *Dependence and Exploitation in Work and Marriage*, pp. 224-5. London: Longman Press.

Mars, G. and R. Ward (1984) 'Ethnic Business Development in Britain: opportunities and resources', in R. Ward and R. Jenkins (eds) *Ethnic Communities in Business. Strategies for Economic Survival*, pp. 1-19. Cambridge: Cambridge University Press.

Manser, M. and M. Brown (1980) 'Marriage and household decision- making: A bargaining analysis', *International Economic Review* 21(1): 31-44.

McElroy, M. and M. J. Horney (1981) 'Nash bargained household decision: Toward a generalization of the theory of demand', *International Economics Review* 22(2): 333-50.

Mernissi, F. (1975) *Beyond the Veil. Male-Female Dynamics in Modern Muslim Society*. New York: John Wiley and Sons.

Mitter, S. (1986a) 'Industrial restructuring and manufacturing homework: immigrant women in the clothing industry', *Capital and Class* 27: 37-80 (Winter).

Mitter, S. (1986b) *Common Fate, Common Bond*. London: Pluto Press.

Parmar, P. (1982) 'Gender, race and class: Asian women in resistance', in Centre for Contemporary Cultural Studies *The Empire Strikes Back. Race and Racism in 70s Britain*, pp. 236- 75. London: Hutchinson and Co.

Phillips, A. and B. Taylor (1980) 'Sex and Skills: Notes towards a Feminist Economics', *Feminist Review* 6: 79-88.

Phizacklea, A. (1990) *Unpacking the Fashion Industry. Gender, Racism, and Class in Production*. London: Routledge.

Robinson, J. (1962) *Economic Philosophy*. London: C.A. Watts and Co.

Sen, A.K. 'Gender and Co-operative Conflicts', in Irene Tinker (ed.) *Persistent Inequalities*, pp. 123-49. Oxford: Oxford University Press.

Tower Hamlets Trade Union Council (1986) *Silk, Satin, Muslin, Rags*. London: Tower Hamlets Trade Union Council.

Westwood, S. and P. Bhachu (1988) 'Introduction', in S. Westwood and P. Bhachu (eds) *Enterprising Women: Ethnicity, Economy and Gender Relations*, pp. 1-19. London: Routledge.

2

Introduction

Most North Americans know something about the phenomenon Dorothy Ayers Counts and David R. Counts write about in "'They're My Family Now': The Creation of Community Among RVers." Most North Americans have seen motor homes cruising the continental highways. Many have some personal contact with the phenomenon: family members or friends disappear for months at a time — they're on the road. In fact, we may have become so familiar with this circumstance that we have come to take for granted something that, from another cultural perspective, might seem quite remarkable: a generation of elders roaming the interstates. Whereas one might predict that such migrations would be undertaken in youth, we find instead that the young (or younger) are relatively sedentary, compared to their travelling elders. So, even though this phenomenon is familiar to us — Counts and Counts do not surprise us with news of elders' remote venturing — it is worth investigating.

In the process of investigation, RVers become less familiar to us, and more exotic: their ways are compared to those of other "nomads," "the Gabra of Kenya" (78, 82). This defamiliarization involves abstractions (e.g., "reciprocity") which interpret RVers' customs and culture, and definitions of concepts which theorize the authors' findings (e.g., "community" [53], "key principle" [65], "lifestyle enclave" [71], "margins" [73], "home" [77]). Like most researchers represented in this volume, Counts and Counts refer to theory to develop interpretations of their data. But unlike some others, they introduce theory throughout the discussion. This seems to be an effective alternative, in this discipline at least, to massing theory at the beginning of an article: Counts and Counts present concepts as are called for, to explain the unfolding story of RV culture.

Counts and Counts' study is *ethnographic*: an account of a people's ways developed from firsthand observation. In their "Method" section they explain their positions as *participant observers* — that is, as researchers to some degree involved in the situation they are studying — and explain how they collected their data: they conducted numerous structured but flexible interviews. Although they often present substantial portions of these interviews, they, like other ethnographic researchers in this book, do not exactly allow their informants to speak for themselves. Anthropological wordings like "ritual greetings" and "ritual food sharing" supersede RVers' own words, and when RVers' own words are significant, we are explicitly instructed in how to read them: "Particularly note the use of the words *family, trust, home, friend, help* — terms that describe the essential relationships of community (Nisbet 1966:48)" (63). Finally, what RVers say leads to a conclusion they would (probably) never say themselves: " ... when RV nomads set up at a new site, their repetition of spatial patterns reinvents and reinforces their cognitive structure of home, society, and community" (82).

This process of defamiliarization — transforming the everyday into an object of study — is characteristic of much ethnographic research. But at least one aspect of Counts and Counts' article is unusual in that it arrests the process, stops it for examination, as research method itself becomes an object of interest. In their "Method" section, the authors report that they gave up administering questionnaires (57). Later in the article (69-70), they relate this research-method decision to their larger findings about RV culture.

- What is the connection between the fate of the planned questionnaires and the "key" feature of RV culture?

- Compare Counts and Counts' report of informants' response to the study to the presence or absence of such reports in, for example, Kabeer and Verkuyten, de Jong, and Masson.

And, to confirm your understanding of the overall findings of this article, consider this question:

- The researchers describe at some length full-time RVers' experience of divesting themselves of their possessions: how is this relevant to larger claims (such as those regarding "reciprocity")?

Finally, try to take a step beyond the terrain specifically surveyed by Counts and Counts:

- What does their research suggest about ageing in North America?

"They're Family Now": The Creation of Community Among RVers

DOROTHY AYERS COUNTS
University of Waterloo

DAVID R. COUNTS
McMaster University

Abstract: This paper examines living in a recreational vehicle as an alternative lifestyle for retired people in North America. Based on fieldwork in trailer parks and on "boondocking" sites on government land, the paper argues that RVers experience a greater sense of community and fewer of the emotional problems common in old age than those who have chosen other forms of retirement living. It is further argued that the reciprocity which anthropologists have often noted as a key factor in creating social bonds is more easily achieved among RVers than in other settings in North America.

Résumé: Cet article examine la vie dans un véhicule de rentrée (RV) comme mode de vie alternatif pour les retraités en Amérique du Nord. Cette étude est basée sur des enquêtes effectuées dans les parcs pour roulottes et dans des sites de "boondocking" sur des terrains gouvernementaux. L'auteur constate que les adeptes des véhicules de rentrée ont un plus grand sens de la communauté et moins de problèmes émotionnels liés à l'âge, que les retraités qui ont opté pour un autre mode de vie. L'auteur note aussi que les adeptes des RV réussissent plus facilement à développer la réciprocité que les anthropologues considèrent comme un facteur indispensable à la création de liens sociaux.

Living either full- or part-time in a recreational vehicle has been an alternative lifestyle in North America since the 1920s, when the first tent trailers were manufactured. By the 1930s, during the depth of the depression, Wally Byam's Airstream company could not keep up with the demand for his self-contained "house trailers." By 1936 there were about 200 000 "trailer nomads" (see Hartwigsen and Hull 1989 for a brief history on the house trailer phenomenon). In the past 50 years there has been an enormous proliferation of RVers of all ages and interests, and these have formed a multitude of clubs and associations. Today there are at least 40 RV clubs with over a million members that meet a variety of needs or reflect particular interests. There are, for instance, clubs for people who own a particular type (motorhome) or brand (Airstream, Avion, Holiday Rambler) of RV. Clubs may be organized according to gender, age, marital status or social group (women, people over 50, singles, singles who drive motorhomes, blacks); clubs may appeal to people with a special interest, hobby or former occupation (the deaf, birdwatchers, Christians, submarine veterans); or clubs may be organized by people committed to a particular style of RVing (boondocking, full-timing, flea-marketing, even singles who return to boondock in a particular spot year after year). The largest organization of RVers is the Good Sam Club, which currently has 800 000 members (Estes 1992:7). Good Samers identify their rigs with a bright orange decal showing a smiling good samaritan. This organization is founded on the principle that RVers *can trust each other.*

This paper, which is a preliminary report based on a two-and-a-half month pilot study, examines RVing as a modern retirement alternative for North Americans. After a brief discussion of our research methods and the variety of RVing styles, we compare RVers who follow two markedly distinct RV lifestyles: private resort or membership park residents and boondockers. We then turn to the question of how elderly RVers establish the ties that enable them to cope with the problems that more sedentary elders solve by turning to friends and relatives. In other words, how do RV nomads form community?

Sociological and socio-ecological definitions of community traditionally focussed on shared interest and common territory and on social organization and activities based on this shared territory (Bender 1978:5; Osgood 1982:23). However, as North American society has become more mobile, social interaction based on shared territory has become less important. How, as Bender observes, "A preoccupation with territory . . . ultimately confuses our understanding of community" (1978:6). Besides territory, feelings of community are created by shared social organization and "we-feeling" (Osgood 1982:23). Or, as Bender says:

> A community involves a limited number of people in a somewhat restricted social space or network held together by shared understandings and a sense of obligation. Relationships are close, often intimate, and usually face to face.

Individuals are bound together by affective or emotional ties rather than by a perception of individual self-interest. There is a "we-ness" in a community. One is a member. (1978:7)

There is a concern that social change has resulted in the destruction of community in contemporary North America (Bender 1978:4). For instance, Bellah et al., argue that although Americans value mobility and privacy, these values "rob us" of "opportunities to get to know each other at a reasonably intimate level in casual, unforced circumstances" (1985:135). North Americans' high regard for these values have, in other words, robbed them of a sense of belonging — of a sense of community. If this is true, we would expect RVers, who choose their lifestyle at least partially *for* its mobility, to be isolated, lonely people who have difficulty in establishing a network or a community to help them cope with crises. Such is not the case.

Although retired RVers do not share a common territory or a common history, they have developed strategies that allow them to establish instant community. These strategies include the use of space to define a sense of "we-ness" and insistence on reciprocity. RVers expect to provide help and support to others in their RV community in time of crisis, to share food when there is surplus and to engage with each other in ways that assure security of person and property. Reciprocity demonstrates the equality of those who share and expresses the principle, "We're all the same here."

RVING AS A RETIREMENT ALTERNATIVE

Since the end of World War II, retired North Americans have increasingly turned to RV living as an alternative lifestyle (see Hoyt 1954 for an early discussion of trailer living by retirees). Estimates of the size of this population vary from 350 000 (see Hartwigsen and Null 1989:319; Howells 1990:64) to eight million (Born 1976:257).

The popular press has been sensitive to the interest of the elderly in RVing as an alternative lifestyle, as a casual glance through the pages of *Trailer Life* and *Motorhome* will attest. Most of the models in the advertisements in those magazines belong to the "active elderly" category. Publications outlining retirement alternatives also focus on the RV lifestyle as one of those alternatives. For example, *On the Road in an RV* is published by the American Association of Retired Persons; the August 1990 issue of *Aide* magazine, a publicaion of the USAA, an organization for retired U.S.

military, FBI and Secret Service agents, has an article on RVing as its lead article; the how-to-do-it book *Full Time RVing*, published by *Trailer Life*, acknowledges that "Most full-timers are retirees" (Moeller and Moeller 1986:6) and contains several sections on retirement; Howells' book *Retirement Choices* includes information on RV retirement (1987:271-81); and the volume *Retirement Guide for Canadians* has a section on RV living (Hunnisett 1981).

Anthropologists and gerontologists have not been as sensitive to RVing as a retirement alternative. Although there is a considerable gerontological literature on seasonal migration, we found only two scholarly articles focussed on full-time RVing. One (Born 1976) was a typology of desert RVers based on brief interviews. The research procedure on which the other publication was based was limited to questionnaires distributed to members of a nationally based camping organization with a resort format (Hartwigsen and Hull 1989).

There are difficulties with a research method that depends on questionnaires distributed in private resort and membership parks. First, this approach misses entirely those RVers who avoid resort parks, preferring to "boondock" — to park with few amenities at little or no cost on public lands. As we argue below, boondockers have different assumptions about what makes a good quality of life than do people who spend most of their time in private parks. Second, in our experience many RVers — especially boondockers — are hostile to questionnaires and either refuse to answer them or lie on them. For reasons we discuss below, this attitude toward questionnaires is consistent with the values that underlie the ability of RVers to quickly form communities. Researchers who depend on questionnaires distributed in private parks would, therefore, have at best a distorted picture of a distinctive group of RVers.

RESEARCH METHOD

Our field research on RVers was conducted between October 1 and December 15, 1990. Our goals were to interview as many different kinds of retired RVers as possible and to focus on Canadians travelling in the United States. We attempted to live and be like the people we wished to study. Our age and appearance facilitated this (we did not alienate potential informants by our youth, a problem encountered by some researchers attempting to work in retirement communities; see Streib, Folts and La Greca 1984). We rented a 12-year-old, 25-foot Prowler trailer and pulled it from British Columbia to the U.S. southwest with an aging van. We stayed in private and public RV parks in British Columbia, Nevada, Arizona and California. We boondocked on U.S. Bureau of Land Management (BLM) land in the southwestern desert and (with hundred of others) we tresspassed on an abandoned World War II Army training base — popularly known as The Slabs or Slab City — near Niland, California. We slept overnight in private parks, in public campgrounds, in roadside rest areas and in parking lots of truck stops. In short, for two-and-one-half months we became RVers.

We conducted 50 interviews with retired RVers, some who were singles and others who were couples. Of our interviews, 34 were with full-timers and 16 were with part-timers; 25 were with Americans, 24 were with Canadians and 1 was with a British couple. Of the 24 Canadians, 16 were full-timers, while 18 of the 25 Americans were full-timers. We were able to ascertain the ages of 81 of our informants: 2 of these (both women married to older men) were in their 40s, 13 were in the 50s, 45 in their 60s, 19 in their 70s, and 2 in their 80s. Our youngest informant was 46, the oldest 86.

We followed an interview guide and asked everyone the same questions, although not necessarily in the same order (also see Kaufman 1986:22-23). We did not tape our conversations, which were informal and intended to encourage people to talk in a relaxed context about what was important to them. Some of our informants were curious about us and our project and asked us as many questions as we asked them; others seemed delighted to find an audience interested in RVing and talking with enthusiasm about their RVing experiences. Some of the interviews were brief, lasting only an hour or so. Others last for hours over several days. People were interested in our research and most were extremely co-operative and helpful. Many spoke of a need for the general population to know more about RVing and some hoped the wider exposure would dispel a lingering stereotype of RVers as "trailer trash." Other labelled themselves as trailer trash or "trailerites" with irony and fierce pride, as if daring the world to despise them. A number of people said they had thought about writing a book on RVing themselves. Some brought us magazine articles relevant to our research; other introduced us to people whose stories they thought we should hear; and some sought us out to discuss the advantages of RV retirement. One couple even led us to a park 45 miles from where we and they were camped to show us where we could find Canadian boondockers.

We initially intended to supplement interviews with a questionnaire asking questions about age, former occupation, estimated income before and after retirement, length of time retired, type of RV selected, etc. Many people were suspicious of the questionnaire and resisted it. Some flatly refused to fill it out. Others declined to answer particular questions — especially the ones about income; "I forget," we were told. One couple, themselves members of a membership park, suggested we join a membership park organization such as Thousand Trails or Coast-to-Coast (at a cost of several thousand dollars). Then we could introduce ourselves and our research at Saturday morning coffee get-togethers in park club houses. Under these circumstances, they thought, people would willingly complete a questionnaire. Another couple commented that they did not mind answering questions in conversation because this made us all equals and they could ask *us* questions too. They would, however, respond to a questionnaire either by throwing it away or by lying. And one man, when asked to fill out a questionnaire, inquired "Are you going to ask me if I eat dog food?" In his experience, he said, this was the sort of question asked by people who pass out questionnaires. We abandoned the questionnaire after two weeks.

THEY SPEAK WITH MANY VOICES: ALTERNATIVE VERSIONS OF THE RV LIFESTYLE

At the beginning we assumed that retired RVers were a more-or-less homogeneous group, an assumption reinforced by reading the mass-market periodicals that target RVers. We further assumed that they would spend most of their time in private resort parks. We were wrong on both counts. Retired RVers are not homogeneous; there are a variety of alternative RV lifestyles.

Some people sell their homes when they retire, buy an RV and live in it; as one informant said, "Home is where I turn off the key." They call themselves full-timers, although the term is not necessarily limited to them (Moeller and Moeller 1986:16). Others retain a home base (their family home or a summer cottage) where they return for part of the year. Some regard their home base as their true residence and say they are on vacation when they are in their RV, even though they travel for more than six months a year. Others stay in permanent homes only a few weeks (or even days) a year, but keep them against the time when they will be too ill or infirm to RV.

Some RVers move from a summer site to a winter one, only travelling when moving from one settled spot to another. These people tend to return to the same place year after year, and many park on the same site — they refer to it as "our site" — each time. Others move in an annual cycle, travelling from one favourite spot to another, staying two weeks (the maximum allowed at most public campgrounds) at each place before moving on. Still others treasure life "on the road" with no planned or detailed itinerary that cannot be quickly and easily changed. "We can," said one informant, "go where we want, stay where we want, stop when we want, leave when we want or stay a little longer."

Some RVers work to supplement their retirement income and keep in touch with each other and with job opportunities through the *Workamper News*. Flea marketers, who sell everything from solar panels to knitted fly-swatter covers, are the most numerous type of working camper (Leonard 1987).

Some RVers willingly pay fees for overnight campsites while travelling and would not consider sleeping in a rest area or parking lot where they could stay free. Others make it a point of honour to pay as little as possible (preferably nothing) for an overnight stop. These folks exchange information on where safe, free camping is available in "Day's End," a regular column in the *Newsletter of Escapees*, an organization for full-timers. Others publish *A Guide to Free Campgrounds*, listing spots where RVers can camp for $8.00 or less.

Finally, some RVers prefer to camp in private resort parks or in membership parks. RV resorts provide amenities such as swimming pools, game rooms and organized recreational activities as well as full hookups — electricity, water, sewage or even phones and cable TV. They often cater to people who stay for months at a time or who rent sites by the year and leave an RV or "park model"[2] trailer set up on a permanent basis. Some resort parks actively discourage overnighters.

A membership park is one which requires residents to purchase membership in the organization with which the member's "home park" is affiliated. Coast-to-Coast, Thousand Trails and NACO are the three membership organizations we heard mentioned most often. Members may stay at their home park for 30 days free or for a nominal fee (usually $1.00 a night), and may stay for one or two weeks at a time at other parks affiliated with the organization. Ordinarily, reservations must be made well in advance, and after spending the allowed time in the affiliated park the member must leave for a set time (usually two weeks to a month) before being permitted to return for another week. Members are often prohibited from staying in another affiliated park within a prescribed distance (from 30 to

100 miles) of their home park. Consequently, full-time RVers who spend most of their time in membership parks are constantly on the move.

Other retired RVers prefer to "boondock," to live in self-contained units and park on public land (often in desert wilderness) where they pay little ($25 to park for six months) or nothing at all and where they are provided no hook-ups. We encountered boondockers at The Slabs near Niland, California, at BLM Long Term Visitor Area (LTVA) campgrounds in California and Arizona near the Mexican border and in Quartzsite, Arizona where as many as 1.4 million people were expected to gather in January and February of 1991 to attend the annual Gemboree rock show and swap meet. Most of these people boondock on BLM land in the desert surrounding Quartzsite.

EQUALITY, COMMUNITY AND THE GOOD LIFE

A tension exists between the values of equality that most RVers espouse and the widely held notion that people selected their type of RVing because of their educational/occupational background or social class. Many of the private park residents we met believed that social class and income distinguished them from boondockers. In fact, former occupation and income level is significant only at the ends of a continuum. At one end are expensive membership parks and exclusive resorts that refuse entry to rigs[3] more than five or ten years old (the standards vary). These places are well known among RVers. Boondockers interpreted such policies as being supported by well-heeled snobs who were insulating themselves from association with the common folk. Certainly such parks do limit residence and membership to the affluent. At the other end of the continuum were a few boondockers at the Slabs who were living — apparently permanently — in broken down RVs (unlikely ever again to go on the road) and subsisting on welfare. Other boondockers said of these folks that you dared not smile in their presence if you had a gold tooth.

In general, however, there was no perceptible difference between boondockers and their rigs and the people and rigs to be found in private parks. Motorhomes retailing at more than $100 000 and trailers even older than ours were parked side-by-side at both kinds of campgrounds. Retired white-collar professionals — chartered accountants, school teachers, civil servants, a communications specialist for the U.S. Apollo program — were boondocking, while residents at private parks included retired blue-collar workers — factory workers, auto mechanics, plumbers and career-enlisted military personnel. Both kinds of RVers emphasized economy as a principle, although they disagreed whether RVing is an expensive or an inexpensive way of life. In both areas some people told us that they were living in their RVs because they could not afford to live any other way. Informants in private parks stressed that living in an RV and paying rent for a site is less expensive even than paying property taxes on a home. Membership park residents stressed the economy of the RV lifestyle and insisted that these parks quickly become a bargain for the full-time RVer who pays only $1.00 a night to stay in affiliated parks. Otherwise, they said, park fees plus high gasoline prices and the costs of maintaining a rig made RVing extremely expensive.

One difference between private park campers and boondockers is their attitude toward what makes a good quality of life. When we asked RVers "What kind of campground do you like and why?" those who preferred private resort parks stressed the comfort and convenience of full-hookups. Some talked about being on an "endless vacation." Others warned that the "endless vacation" mentality often results in overeating or alcoholism. They also emphasized their concern for security — both from "the crazies out there" and from possible theft or violence from their RV neighbours. They wanted the security of living in a park that was separated from the outside world by a fence or wall and patrolled by a security guard. One resident of a membership park that had gone bankrupt and was admitting anyone who could afford $14 a night, commented that before the park opened its gates to the public he could leave his doors unlocked and his belongings out on his picnic table while he was gone. Now he worried about "the type of people we get in here. Anybody can come in now." He referred particularly to the fact that in the park there were "trailers with flat tires and people live in them anyway."

In contrasting answers to the same question, boondockers talked about the space they enjoyed, space lacking in private parks. One woman explained her preference for boondocking by telling of her visit to a friend in a resort park. Her friend's RV was so close to her neighbours' that when the women sat outside to talk the neighbour sat in a chair by her window and listened. She continued, "When I first read about Quartzsite 10 years ago or so [in the *National Geographic*] I thought, 'How can they sit out there in the desert like that?' Now, we have some friends who are coming down but they're going to stay in an RV park. I can't imagine staying in an RV park."

Boondockers also like their freedom from rules, pointing out that nobody told them where to park, where they could walk their dog or limited the amount of time they could be visited by their grandchildren. One man expressed it eloquently:

> I don't have to be here at a certain time or there at a certain time. If I want to stay up until 2 o'clock in the morning I can, if I want to sleep until noon I can. If I don't like it here I can go somewhere else. I have no worries, I save $700 a month over the expenses I used to have. It's money in the bank and I'm enjoying life. If I have food to eat and gas to travel, then I'm happy. If I spend a little too much one month, I spend a little less the next. If more people were doing it, there'd be fewer of them laying up in nursing homes.

Boondockers also stressed equality: they asserted that all those who boondock are equals, no matter what their income, previous occupation or the cost of their RV. One man said he liked boondocking specifically because "the fellow next door to us has an $80 000 rig but we're all the same here."

There are also important qualities shared by boondockers and those who stay in private resort parks. First, RVers share values. Boondockers and private park campers alike speak of the freedom RVing gives them, of a sense of adventure, of equality and of their appreciation of nature and the out-of-doors. RVers told us that they were living the "old values" of friendship, sharing and co-operation on which North American society was built and which has, for the most part, been lost. These values create a set of attitudes and a quality of life for retired RVers of all types that contrast markedly with those reported for other elderly people, both those living at home and those living in retirement communities. Jacobs comments, for instance, that residents in settled retirement communities pursue a passive way of life and are characterized by a pervasive "sense of social and physical isolation, apathy, and loneliness" (Jacobs 1974:101).

Another researcher reports that when she asked her elderly informants, "What do you look forward to now?" she found that the answer was always some variation of "There is nothing to look forward to now. I just live from day to day" (Kaufman 1986:111). She concludes: "The vast majority, even those in their early 70s, do not think in terms of the future, do not make long-range plans, and assume their own future to be short. The future is not perceived as a source of meaning" (ibid.)

These feelings of isolation, apathy, loneliness and the absence of a future were not true of the retired RVers we met during our research. Although our informants admitted that boredom and excessive alcohol use was a problem for some people, only one man, alienated from his wife and children and living on Social Security, complained of being lonely and isolated. This man talked about weeping over his estrangement from his family and added, "I've got no place to go and nothing to do when I get there."

Instead it was typical to hear the life of the RVer assessed as in the following description offered by a full-timer: "A full-timer is an adventurous soul, a saddle trap who wants to go and see what is over that hill." When asked why he chose to retire to an RV, another full-timer responded, "I didn't want to sit around and watch the boob tube 24 hours a day!"

Most people compared RV life favourably to retirement in a house or apartment. In response to the question, "What do you do all day?" one full-timer said, "I have my sewing machine, my crafts, my computer. What else do I need?" Then she added, "What do you do all day if you're retired and in your house?" In the same vein, a full-time boondocker answered, "People ask me what I do all winter — Hell, I'm so busy doing nothing that I haven't got time to worry about it."

Others described sight-seeing trips they had taken or planned to take or spoke of the pleasure they found in shopping or selling in the flea-markets that are ubiquitous in many boondocking areas. Still others spent hours each week gleaning harvested fields, collecting pop and beer cans to sell or taking adult-interest courses offered in local schools. Some commented that volunteer work was available for all with time on their hands. In brief, unlike some other seniors, most retired RVers seem to have social vitality: they are vigorous, look forward to the future and feel in control of their lives.

A second characteristic shared by RVers, one of special interest to us here, is a sense of community. Indeed, comments about friendship and community made by RVers contrast markedly with those cited by Kaufman, whose informants are saddened by the loss of "close" friends whom they have known for 20 years or more. She says:

All of those who discuss friendship state that one does not make close friends when one is old. They feel that friendships depend upon building a life together, looking forward to the future and sharing expectations. When one is old, there is no future, few expectations, and thus no basis for the creation of friendship. (Kaufman 1986:110)

She quotes an 81-year-old woman:

> The friends I've made recently I consider very much on the surface. When you're older you don't go deep into friendship. You aren't relying on them in the sense that you did at 35 or 40. . . . You have no place to grow together. When you're younger you do. . . . When you're older, you've heard it all before . . . and anyway, what more is there to say? (1986:110)

As the following quotation from Kay, one of our informants, illustrates, RVers are aware of the transitory quality of their friendships. "Full-timers," she said, "strike up immediate bonding. Within an hour you'll know everything you wanted to know about each other. Your lives touch, bounce, and then they go off. Some people we tend to stay with. Others we may never see again." RVers do not seem to feel that these friendships are superficial, futile or useless. Rather, they speak with pride about their many friends, about the places where they may stay for a night or two in the driveway of someone they met in an RV park the year before, about the many RVers on their Christmas card list with whom they exchange greetings but whom they may never see again. They share the attitude of Kay who added that she and others like her are "going back to the old time values." Although they highly value mobility and freedom to "turn on the key" and leave incompatible neighbourhoods or an uncomfortable situation, RVers like Kay insist that they quickly make friends with whom they share community. Indeed, as on RV park managers suggests in a statement quoted below, some people apparently adopt the RV lifestyle *because* it provides them with a sense of community lacking in the suburbs where they lived for decades. A selection of quotations from our informants and from the RVing literature illustrates this feeling of community. Particularly note the use of the words *family, trust, home, friend, help* — terms that describe the essential relationships of community (Nisbet 1966:48).

In an article on the RV lifestyle and under the subheading entitled "Campgrounds are Communities!" Paula and Peter Porter write:

> It didn't take us long to realize that the RV parks along our favourite north-south and east west routes were the friendliest places we had ever stayed on vacation. Everywhere we

travelled, people were open and helpful, sometimes insisting on setting up our awning for us, or helping Pete level the trailer. On a couple of occasions, when we forgot the technique for setting something up, we knew that there was always a neighbour ready to lend a hand. It was like joining a club . . . every RV couple we met wanted to drop by and say "welcome to the campground." (1991:13)

In another article, the welcome RVers receive when they arrive at the home park of Escapees is described as follows:

Your first act at Rainbow's End is to pull the rope on the big ol' bell. As the tones ring over the grounds, people with smiles as big as Texas appear, and they're there for one reason: to welcome you. Hugs all around. Handshakes and introductions. Invitations to happy hour, dinner, a trip into town. Offers to help find a spot, hookup, settle in. Oh, boy, your tired bodies say gratefully, this feels like home! And that's exactly the intent. (Courtney 1991:76)

In *Highways*, the official publication of the Good Sam Club, a senior who is a long-time RVer writes: "RVing . . . is about a way of life that has revolutionized recreation for a vast number of people . . . it has taken senior citizens out of their rocking chairs and created a travelling community with a camaraderie that can't be matched" (Edwards 1991a:55). During a discussion about why people become full-time RVers, Dwayne — a full-time RVer and a part-time manager of a resort park — explained that it is possible to live in a subdivision in southern California for 20 years and not know the name of the people next door. "Here, and in RV parks generally," he observed, "you get a real sense of community and people becoming friends and helping each other. It is as if people see others living like themselves and feel they can trust them."

Another RV resort owner-manager, in response to our observation that people in the park were friendly and all seemed to know each other, explained, "That's what they come here for. They have it here and they don't have it back home. They get back home and they miss it. That's why they keep coming back. Almost all of our people come back here every year. When they come back here they're coming home."

When we asked Vanessa, a full-timer, why she and her husband returned to the Slabs every year she explained, "It's like coming home. They're your family." It was also important to her that

We can trust the people in our area because they're like we are. They try to make the area look homey. They want it to look like home and smell like home. Everybody watches out for everybody else. Everybody's so eager to help. When you get situated in one group it's like a family, but we don't have a name yet.

On what is this sense of community based? As we noted above, in modern, mobile North American society people who have a sense of community are likely to base it on something other than shared territory and history. Indeed, as Bender observes, "Community, then, can be defined better as an experience than a place. As simply as possible, community is where community happens" (1978:6). What makes it happen for RVers?

COMMUNITY AND RECIPROCITY

One basis for the creation and expression of community among RVers is the principle of balanced reciprocity among equals (Sahlins 1972). This notion is strong, pervasive and so important to the establishment of community among RVers that it is for them a key principle. Ortner says that something — be it a symbol, a principle, a value, an idea, a practice — is "key" to the culture or way of life of a people if more than one of the five indicators of keyness is present (Ortner 1973:1339). The principle of reciprocity between equals has at least three of Ortner's indicators: our informants say it is important; they become aroused about it, particularly if it is violated in a way that suggests that they are inferior; and it arises in many different contexts: for example, in giving and receiving food, goods and help, in the exchange of information and in the response to questionnaires.

Many RVers, and most full-timers, are retired. They share with other elderly folks the problems of trying to live on a fixed income in an inflationary economy, declining health, concern about violence and isolation from family and friends. In addition they have the problems unique to a nomadic lifestyle: difficulty getting access to funds; illness far from one's own physician; mechanical breakdown; the fact that they spend much of their time among strangers. It is critical, therefore, that RVers develop a strategy for coping with crisis and they have, indeed, done so: the strategy of and mutual assistance. RVers expect to be able to give and receive help from each other in an emergency; reciprocity is essential to the success of this strategy.

The principle that RVers can expect reciprocity and mutual assistance from each other was the basis for the establishment of the
Good Sam Club, the largest and most influential of the RV clubs
in North America. In a reprint of the original letter to the June
1966 issue of *Trail-R-News*, Joens describes the founding of the organization on the assumption that if you are an RVer and are in
trouble you can safely call on other RVers for help (Joens 1991:4).
Good Sam was begun in 1966 by people who agreed to carry a
sticker on their car or RV. The sticker indentifies the bearers as
club members who were willing to stop and help, and to accept
the help of, others also carrying the decal (Joens 1991:4). Today
most of the RVs on the road carry the emblem, which portrays a
smiling face with a halo. Joens states that he has often given and
received help from other "trailerists," and has "yet to find an un-
friendly trailering family." By giving and receiving help he says he
has "made many life-long friends." Extension of trust and expectation of reciprocity are essential to the success of the enterprise. In
spite of a pervasive fear of violence from strangers, from "the
crazies out there," Good Sam members extend trust to, and expect
help rather than violence from, other RVers. We were repeatedly
advised to seek out other RVers in rest areas and truck stops for
mutual security. In isolated areas, we were warned, we should
park beside other RVers so that we could look out for each other.
This trust and the expectation of reciprocity are created in a number of ways.

EXCHANGE OF PERSONAL HISTORY

First, as the earlier quotation from Courtney suggests, the introduction of an RVer into a community begins as soon as the newcomer arrives, particularly where people may be expected to stay
for several weeks or months. Rituals of greeting and of parting occur both in private parks where people rent sites by the month or
season and in boondocking areas. During the greeting ritual,
neighbours surround the new RV to provide assistance in parking
and setting up, to offer the loan of needed equipment and to swap
biographies. There is an immediate exchange of personal histories
and information. People are careful to let newcomers know the
rules: where you may not walk your dog in a resort park, the location of the nearest "glory hole,"[4] and instructions on how to use
it, at the Slabs. As our informant Kay observed above, this exchange results in "immediate bonding," a fact that provides security for boondockers. One Canadian man in an LTVA area told us: "I

always go right over to get to know people when they first pull in. If they don't know me they might rip me off, but once we know each other they'll even look after our things while we're gone." RVers also have rituals of parting. Because we were not present when people dispersed during the spring, we observed only part of the full parting ritual, carried out when we left sites after a stay of several days. During the ritual, neighbours gathered around to help with unhooking and hitching up, make photographs, exchange addresses and invitations to visit, make suggestions about desirable routes and places to stay overnight that are both safe and free, and offer gifts of food. Parting rituals at the end of a season of shared community are said to be lengthy and elaborate and involve planning future reunions and exchanging gifts as well as food and addresses.

RITUAL SHARING OF FOOD

The food-giving that occurs when RVers part brings into focus another aspect of reciprocity that reinforces the feeling of community: the ritual sharing of food. RVers recognize the importance of food-sharing in establishing community (Sahlins 1972:218) and the necessity of trusting those with whom one shares meals. This latter point as well as one about instant community was articulated by Karl. Discussing his pleasure in the potluck dinners organized by the campground hosts at an Arizona state park, he said, "I'm not big on eating stuff made by people I don't know, but it doesn't take long to get to know these people and then it's OK."

RVers exchange and share food both formally — as part of ritual, for example, Thanksgiving or Christmas dinners — and informally. Newcomers are often given food within the first 24 hours of their arrival but not, in our experience, as part of the greeting ritual. Among boondockers especially, food-sharing has great social importance, for it permits the redistribution of an essential resource without challenging the ideal that "we're all the same here." Contrast the following accounts of the chariable distribution of free food at Slab City with the resident-run system of food-sharing at another boondocking area. The attitudes of the residents illustrates the importance of self-reliance and equality to RVers and the role of reciprocity in maintaining these attributes.

Slab City is a place with no formal organization or system of control. No park rangers or hosts patrol the area, there are no amenities and no one is required to check in or out of the area when arriving or leaving. Indeed, everyone parked there is technically trespassing, though the State of California and the U.S. government generally ignore them and no one is sure how many people are actually there at any one time. As the sign welcoming newcomers says: "SLABS Population Unknown Most Residents Live Somewhere Else." The only institution linking Slab residents with the outside world and external organizations (such as state government agencies and charitable groups) is the Christian Center. The Center is staffed by a resident missionary and by Slab residents who volunteer their time. It is located in a trailer positioned near the entrance to the Slabs. People who want information are referred there, and on entering the Center's trailer newcomers are asked to register, identify the named area where they are parked and give the names and addresses of their next-of-kin in case of emergency. State officials go first to the Christian Center to locate Slab residents being sought by members of their family and to get information about rumoured illegal activities. Slab residents registered with the Center can pick up their mail there and get help for others who are ill. The Center also serves as a distribution point for food provided by the Salvation Army and other charities. People wishing to receive the food must sign forms declaring their income and stand in line to get it. Few do so.

Center volunteers expressed frustration over the lack of participation in the food distribution program by needy Slab City residents. In the opinion of the volunteers, may people who should have been taking food are "too lazy" or "think they are too good" to stand in line for it. Consequently, proffered food is often unclaimed and vegetables are left on the ground in front of the Center to rot.

The self-administered system for distributing free food in an LTVA area less than 50 miles from Slab City contrasts sharply to the charitable one at the Slabs. In the LTVA, the system was organized by the residents and was informal, involved reciprocal exchange and was viewed with pride. To them it exemplified their self-sufficiency, their frugality, their enterprise and their ingenuity in taking advantage of opportunity.

Imperial Valley farmers permit LTVA residents to glean their fields after harvest and farm workers — some of whom lived at the LTVA — often carried home large boxes of sub-standard fruits and vegetables. When gleaners and farm workers arrived at the LTVA with their crates of free produce they distributed the surplus first among those people with whom they shared a residence circle and then among friends who lived outside the circle (we discuss the significance of the residence circle below). Remaining food was left in boxes at the foot of the bulletin board at the entrance to the LTVA where anyone could help themselves. Recipients of the food were expected to make a return eventually, although the return did not have to be in kind but could be in the form of aluminum cans to be sold for cash, books or magazines, help with projects, loan of tools and the like. Some LTVA residents specifically gave this food distribution system as a reason for returning to the spot year after year. "If you're a vegetarian," one said, "you can live here for almost nothing." Then he added, "None of us are on charity here."

Among RVers the most common food-sharing ritual is the potluck dinner. Weekly potluck dinners are a regular event at resort parks, at many Arizona state parks during the winter season and at RV parks of all sorts at Thanksgiving and Christmas. RVers who are away from their families during the holiday season may pool their funds to buy a turkey and share a holiday meal. Some RVers travel every year to the same park where they meet friends to share Christmas or Thanksgiving dinner. Finally, any important celebration — such as a wedding — includes a potluck dinner. Newcomers join the community by participating in ritual food-sharing.

Our experience of incorporation into community through food-sharing is an example of how the system works. We pulled into an LTVA boondocking area only two hours before a wedding was to be held. Before we had unhooked our trailer we were invited to take part in the festivities. People acknowledged that we had just arrived and were not expected to provide anything elaborate, but we were advised to "bring something if you can." We prepared a small salad and took photographs of the ceremony, copies of which we gave the bride and groom. Other RVers noted our participation with approval. Subsequently we were invited to join campfire songfests and received shares of gleaned fruits and vegetables. We were also invited to join in other activities including community cleaning of the local hot spring (where residents bathed) and a weekend trip to Las Vegas planned by members of the group.

The values that retired RVers assign to the principles of equality and reciprocity are so basic, so "key" to their way of life, that any research method that fails to recognize their importance is bound to produce a skewed view of RV culture. Earlier in this essay we argued that the questionnaire is a flawed research tool. Kaufman is correct in her assertion that the use of a questionnaire forced people to structure their discussions and answers "according to the researcher's priorities rather than their own" (1986:22). In addition, questionnaires are predicated on a one-sided and unequal relationship. Informants have no part in the construction of the instrument; their needs, priorities and interests may not be addressed; there is no mechanism that allows them to ask the researcher questions. There is, in short, no provision for the give-and-take between equals that is of basic importance to RVers. The absence of this reciprocal balance is, we think, the reason why our attempts to do questionnaire-based research failed. People who willingly engaged in a reciprocal exchange of information rejected a relationship which they saw as one-way and, therefore, demeaning to them. It does not matter whether, in fact, any researcher's questionnaire ever asked about the consumption of dog food. Our informant's protest was not really about dog food; it was about his perception that he would be the inferior party in an unequal, non-reciprocal relationship.

COMMUNITY, SPACE AND PLACE

In one sense shared territory does not create community for RVers who treasure their mobility and their ability to turn on the key and be gone if they don't like their neighbours. In another sense it does. As Davis observes, "People cluster together for protection, contact, organization, group integration, and for the purpose of exploitation of a particular region and the community is the smallest territorial group that can embrace all aspects of social life" (Davis 1949:312). As we have said, RVers choose different sorts of places to cluster and they define themselves and are defined by others by where they park. These definitions reinforce the sense of community among RVers who cluster together, but also emphasize differences that alienate RVers from each other. We look first at the way in which their choice of place separates RVers and then turn to a discussion of how space unites them through common values, interests and experience.

When RVers select a place to park their rigs they are also making a choice about lifestyle and about identity. Some choose private resort parks where their personal space is limited but where they feel safe and comfortable. They seek the protection of walls and guards; they enjoy the luxury of water and sewer hookups, electricity and cable TV; their space is organized into streets and blocks where each RV has its own "pad";[5] and leisure activities are organized by professionals who encourage and promote contact among park residents. Many private resort parks have strictly enforced rules about how a rig may be parked, where dogs may be walked, the conditions under which residents may have guests, and for how long and under what circumstances children and grandchildren may visit. Many of the people who choose this lifestyle see themselves holding standards of affluence, respectability and orderliness and they particularly appreciate the fact that the other park residents are similar to themselves in age, social standing, consumption level and interests. In thinking about private resort parks one is reminded of the distinction made by Bellah et al. between "lifestyle enclaves" and communities. Lifestyle, they point out, "brings together those who are socially, economically, or culturally similar, and one of its chief aims is the enjoyment of being with those who 'share one's lifestyle'" (Bellah et al 1985:72). In their terms, groups such are retirement "communities," organized around a common lifestyle, are "lifestyle enclaves," not communities. A community is inclusive and focusses on the interdependence of private and public life while recognizing and tolerating the differences of those within it. In contrast, "lifestyle is fundamentally segmental and celebrates the narcissism of similarity. It usually explicitly involves a contrast with others who 'do not share one's lifestyle'" (Bellah et al. 1985:72). Resort park residents make a sharp distinction between their standard of living and lifestyle and that of boondockers. Our non-boondocking informants advised us that, as part of our research, we should go to one of the boondocking areas. "You should spend one night there, just to see it, but you won't want to stay longer," one couple said about Slab City. Another marvelled that boondockers "sit out there on the desert, happy as clams," adding, "but I couldn't do it."

Boondockers agree that they are unlike the folks who live in resort parks and many of them treasure the difference. They are not a homogenous lot, for people from all social classes, levels of education and degrees of affluence can be found boondocking. They opt for economy and simplicity, the absence of rules and organization and unlimited external space. They particularly want to avoid the crowding — what one person calls sites "like cemetery plots" and another referred to as being "crammed in like sardines" — that they see as characteristic of private parks. Boondockers often used the term "freedom" to describe their way of life and many of them said that resort park residents had simply exchanged the restrictions and crowding of urban life for an RV version of the same thing.

Boondockers are regarded by others (and sometimes they regard each other) with considerably ambivalence. On the one hand, the lives of boondockers epitomize the values on which America was founded: they are independent of rules and regulations, they live simply with a minimum of luxury and expense, they embody the qualities of individualism and ingenuity and they co-operate on their own terms for mutual security and to share re-sources. On the other hand, they are marginal to North American society. Many of them have no fixed address — not even a mail box in an RV park. Many, particularly those who are flea market-ers, participate in an underground economy that avoids regula-tions and taxes — a fact that is not lost on officials of nearby towns. Most instructive and, we think, representative of the attitude of civic officials toward boondocking flea marketers, is a letter cited by Errington that expresses the resentment of a small-town busi-nessman toward transient vendors (1990:642). He bitterly resents the fact that they pay no taxes and little rent and face none of the risks and costs endured by town retailers. "Let's tax 'em," he says, "Let's set up a licensing procedure that will discourage the money hounds" (Errington 1990:642).

Boondockers are also marginal because of the kind of place they park and the kind of life they lead: they camp on the desert — often in the shade of a creosote bush or small thorn tree — with-out amenities, recreation facilities, or external protection from ruffians who might harass or rob them. In the Slabs at least many of them dump their sewage in to glory holes, a practice that pri-vate-park residents consider to be filthy. They are in charge of their own lives. No one else organizes their neighbourhoods, tells them where or how they may park their rigs or guarantees them a pad. And no one else is responsible for their comfort or their en-tertainment.

For some boondockers the absence of amenities is a source of wry humour. In the Slabs, for instance, several people parked side-by-side had gone to elaborate trouble to fit out their rigs with fake hook-ups. Electric cords led from their RVS to metered posts, hoses led from water taps to water tank inlets and sewage pipes drained into concrete pipes that appeared to lead into septic tanks. The realistic-looking setup was a joke designed to fool the unwary newcomer. When we asked our neighbours how hook-ups were possible our ignorance was met with guffaws of laughter. Al-though they say that "We're all the same here," boondockers do make distinction among themselves and are ambivalent about those whom they perceive to be different. In the Slabs, for exam-ple, people warned us about others in the "wrong" areas who had turned the space surrounding their RVs into junk yards. They were not "like us" and, therefore, not to be trusted. As one woman cautioned, "Be careful where you park. The people on "vendors row" are the children of God just like I am, but I wouldn't want to camp with them." Another person distinguished between "permanent" Slab residents and RVers who lived there only during the winter. "Most full-time Slabbers are OK," he said, "but with some of them you don't want to smile if you have a gold tooth." He then identified those Slabbers who were "OK," and pointed out the sections where those who were not to be trusted congregated. We should, he advised us, avoid going into those areas.

The belief (unfounded as we discovered) of our resort park informants that boondockers are likely to be poor, dirty and lawless is widespread. In an article on campground etiquette, Gordon Symons notes that it is often assumed that one can tell which campers are "the filthy ones by looking at their rigs," and that "people with older model trailers and motorhomes — the less affluenct, in other words — were most likely to be the worst offenders. He observes: "I haven't found that to be true" (Symons 1991:11).

The categorization of boondockers as embodying despised characteristics, and the ambivalence felt toward them by other RVers, is reportedly characteristic of the attitude of members of mainstream society toward those on the margins. In his discussion of places on the margin, Shields observes: "The social definition of marginal places and spaces is intimately linked with the categorisation of objects, practices, ideas and modes of social interaction as belonging to the 'Low culture,' the culture of the marginal places and spaces, the culture of the marginalised" (1991:4-5). He maintains that the marginal is categorized as being "at the 'edge of civilisation'" and that the "high" or dominant culture is ambivalent toward it: "The social 'Other' of the marginal and of low cultures is despised and reviled in the official discourse of dominant culture and central power while at the same time being constitutive of the imaginary and emotional repertoires of that dominant culture" (Shields 1991:5). The ambivalence cuts both ways. Some boondockers take exception to resort park rules that they think are designed to keep them out. Valerie — a state campground host and active member of Singles International (SI) who spends her nonworking months either at SI rallies, in public parks or boondocking — candidly admitted that she would love to spend her time in a park with a swimming pool and a spa. She was prevented from doing this, she said, by the age of her motor home and by the high fees that would strain her limited retirement income. Valerie also avoids resort parks because the people there are "cliquish." They are, she said, "all better fixed than I am, and I wouldn't be welcome. So I don't do it."

Boondockers bitterly resent RVing acquaintances who live in

resort parks and who make remarks such as "How can you live out here like this?" They ridicule these people as being ignorant, fearful, wasteful of money and resources and prejudiced. They also maintain that people who "badmouth" the boondocking way of life usually have not tried it, arguing that those who do give it a chance often find, to their surprise, that they like it.

Some boondockers are of the opinion that boondocking is for the youthful in spirit while resort parks are for the old. This was the attitude of Mabel, a woman in her mid-70s who had boondocked for a decade but who, for health reasons, was now headed for her second year in a private park. She wryly observed that resort parks cater to "the blue rinse bunch" and complained (with an ironic chuckle) that the problem with resorts is that they are "full of old people." Another boondocker commented that people who spend six months at a time in RV resorts are "just waiting to die." He went on: "When I get so old that I can't [boondock], then I'll go into one. They have schedules up on the wall to tell you what you can do and when you can do it. Not me!" A friend, listening to the conversation, chimed in: "Me neither."

The most scathing, and articulate, critique of resort park residents was made by Randy and Rachel, working RVers. This couple had dropped out of society when they were in their 40s to boondock and work as flea marketers. Now in their late 50s, they are still "hustling" to survive. One of the ways they make a living is by providing entertainment in resort parks in exchange for parking space and hookups. Although they were dependent on them for a livelihood, they were contemptuous of their resort park neighbours whom they scornfully categorized as "snowbirds" who "would like to live in Sun City but can't afford it." They described the residents as "people who have no imagination and no sense of adventure and who continue living the constricted lives they've always lived, taking orders." They added that although they live in RVs, resort residents typically try to re-create living in a house and pretend they own their territory. They do this by placing lawn ornaments in their "front yards," putting down artificial turf for grass and bounding their "yards" with portable fences. Randy characterized snowbirds as conformists who "always do their laundry on Monday" because "they have followed orders all their lives and are still doing it."

Part of the tension existing between resort park residents and boondockers derives from the image of "trailer trash" that is left over from the stereotypical association of trailer parks with poverty. Thus, although RVers espouse a philosophy of equality ("we are all the same here!"), they distance themselves from those who are categorized as "trash." An excellent example of the rejection by RVers of any suggestion that they are "lower class slobs" is found in a collection of letters to the November 1988 issues of *Trailer Life* magazine. The letters were in response to an advertisement published in the May 22, 1988, issue of *Advertisement Age* for *US Magazine*. It consisted of a two-page spread showing an RV campground peopled with aging, slovenly men and women sitting in disarray around shabby RVs. The caption noted the high median income, the active social life and the generally upscale lifestyle of *US readers*. Though nothing was said in the caption about the RVers in the photo, the constrast was clear from the ad's title "Definitely Not *US*!" The advertisement was reprinted in *Trailer Life* because the magazine editors considered it to be "insulting to all RVers." Readers were asked to send letters to the publisher of *US Magazine* with copies to *Trailer Life*. Some of the letters characterized the advertisement as intolerable, "condescending snobbishness" (*Trailer Life* 1988:7) and focussed on the value of an alternative lifestyle based on simplicity and love of nature. "RVers are adventurous, fun people, a class unto themselves," said one correspondent (Montelpasse 1988:7). Another responded:

> You will often see my husband and me relaxing in camp, but usually after a day of hiking nature trails, bird watching, breathing fresh air and just plain enjoying nature. My idea of relaxation is definitely not going to an expensive resort crawling with snobs showing off their expensive clothes. (Noon 1988:169)

And another: "We are college-educated, affluent, active, healthy, outdoor-loving, trim, family-loving, book-and-Bible-reading, retired happy people" (Green 1988:165). Others emphasized their affluence and their credentials both as typical RVers and as members of the upper-middle class. For example: "As a typical RV person, I am 60, own a $75 000 home on a half acre, have a $22 000 truck and a $30 000 fifth-wheel trailer. My retirement income, completely disposable, is well over $31 000 a year" (Lewis 1988:165). And:

> The average RVer today is . . . educated and affluent. He actually buys second cars or thirds, coats, and clothes. He "goes out like crazy" in a variety of locales. He isn't necessarily retired, but may very likely be a professional and even single.

His RV probably has an air-conditioner and a furnace, TV (and a satellite dish on top), a microwave oven, stereo, full bath, etc. (Robinson 1988:165,169)[6]

Although RVers reject the "slob" image, they are not agreed on whether they place more value on equality (and eschew snobs) or on a hierarchy of respectability evidenced by affluence and lifestyle and expressed by conspicuous consumption. There is tension here in the notion of place that both creates and destroys community: there is a contradiction between the notion that all RVers are equal and the recognition that they are not. We have already referred to the desire of people in resort parks to avoid sharing space with people who, because of their consumption level (older trailers) or their lifestyle (those who live in trailers with flat tires) are likely to be untrustworthy. This directly contradicts the egalitarian ideal, the notion that, as one RVer put it: "The biggest adjustment that RVers have to make is getting used to the idea that everybody is equal."

RVERS AND THE PROBLEMS OF LIMITED SPACE

Although the choices that RVers make about where they will camp and how they use their space may divide them, their common experiences in adjusting to the spatial problem inherent in RVing draws them together.

One problem that every RVer must face is that space inside a trailer, fifth-wheel or motor home is severely limited. People who take up the RV lifestyle, especially full-timers for whom the rig is truly home, must adjust to the fact that the limited space affects (1) the relationships between people sharing the space and (2) the number of possessions they can carry with them. RVers are well aware of the tensions that develop between people who share restricted space. When we asked what was required for full-time RVing, a frequent reply was "a happy marriage" or "a congenial husband/wife." Some people said they were able to begin RVing only after divorce or the death of a spouse; others commented that while RVing was possible with their current mate, it would have been impossible with an earlier one. The level of stress that can develop between incompatible RV partners was brought home to us as we were ending our research when we had a brief encounter with another RVing couple who were also heading north rather than south. When we remarked that we were all going the wrong direction, the man responded by warning us never to sell our home and buy an RV. They had done this and had also purchased expensive memberships in two park organizations during the past summer. Now, only six months later, he was headed home to get divorced, having been financially ruined by the investment and "by that piece of shit back there," pointing toward the RV. The trailer was a new and expensive one, so we asked, "What's wrong with it?" "I'm not talking about the rig," he snarled, "I'm talking about the woman in it."

The interpersonal problems of living in the confined space of an RV are sometimes addressed in the popular RV press. For example, in an article in *Trailer Life* one author suggests ways to organize life in order to live compatibly in the restricted space of an RV. In what he calls "the ten commandments of the psychology of living in small spaces," Jim Luce focusses on considerate behaviour, the wise and creative use of space and proper care of one's body and spirit. The practice of these commandments, according to Luce, results in Tender Loving Concern or TLC (Luce 1991). TLC "can make even the most trying times in an RV bearable," while its absence "can let the air out of a trip like a nail does in a radial tire." It is, he says, "what puts the 'home' in motorhome" (Luce 1991:80).

In addition to the practice of TLC, an RV is also a home because, as Mary Douglas suggests, it has "structure in time" (1991:290). A home's complexity of orientation and boundary "depends on the ideas that persons are carrying inside their heads about their lives in space and time. For the home is the realization of ideas" (ibid.). Douglas argues that a distinctive characteristic of the idea of home is revealed if we "focus on the home as an organization of space over time" (1991:294). Home, she says, is "always a localizable idea," one that is located in space, but not necessarily in a fixed space. "Home starts by bringing some space under control. . . . For a home neither the space nor its appurtenances have to be fixed, but there has to be something regular about the appearance and reappearance of its furnishing" (Douglas 1991:289).

"Home" involves a response to events that happened in the past — to memory — and a prediction of events that will happen in the future. For example, people remember cold winters and respond by installing storm windows or buying extra blankets. As Douglas notes, an essential aspect of home is storage: space dedicated to memory and to planning for the future. A home contains things that will be wanted through the years and organizes them so that they can be found when they are required. The severe limitation of storage space in rigs creates for RVers the problem of anticipating their future needs in order to reduce their possessions to essentials. "No matter how large a motorhome you may own, the storage problem is soon upon you," warns Norman Lusk in a letter to *Trailer Life* (Lusk 1991:19). The ability to fit essential possessions and the artifacts of memory into a limited space is a must for full-time RVing. One full-timer, explaining the need to cull belongings, told us, "You do not put anything in here that you do not use or wear." He added that he had only three pairs of trousers: one in the dirty clothes, one he was wearing and a clean pair. His wife commented that she had reduced her formal wardrobe to one "little blue dress" for funerals and weddings. Similarly, Courtney quotes Kay Peterson, one of the founders of Escapees, who urged those on the brink of full-timing, but hesitant to give up their "things," to order their priorities. "Do you own things or do they own you?" she asks (Courtney 1991:78).

Limited storage means that RVers must restrict the artifacts containing their memories and histories to basics. With little room for nostalgia, the past must be condensed to its essence. This constraint is common to nomads. Prussin, who worked with the Gabra of Kenya, observes that for nomads the past persists in limited boundaries. "Constancy and continuity are . . . concentrated within, and bounded by, the moving container," she says (1989:155).

In a sense, full-time RVers must relinquish the past. As one said, "It's not giving up the things that's hard, it's giving up what has been." Many RVers reduce their memories to the pages of a photograph album which they share with others within hours of their first meeting. The pictures are usually of their family members and of their RV history and RVing friends. They place the subjects in a recognizable context and permit other RVers with whom they do not share a common history to recreate their past, identify with their experiences and to share photographs, adventures and family histories of their own.

Giving up home and possessions is a rite of passage, especially for full-time RVers. Those who have done it share a unique experience that sets them apart, even from other RVers, and creates among them a sense of community. As onlookers we witnessed, but could not participate in, the comradeship shared by full-timers as they swapped stories about how they decided to give up their homes, how they established priorities in determining which of their possessions to keep and the difficulties of actually carrying through with their decision. Most full-timers said they spent a long time deciding to do it and many took several years and more than one start before they completed the process. As Randy expressed it:

People who want to go full-time have a set of problems. The first is letting go of their house. You can't have a nest. You must strip your belongings down to the bare essentials and get rid of the rest. You can't take a lot of things with you. Too many people try to hang onto their house and rent it out. Renters tear the place up and they lose their shirts. I tell them, "Give it up and sell."

The full-timers with whom we talked had tried a number of approaches to "letting go." A few people said they had no difficulty divesting themselves of their excess property once they made the decision to do it, but — as the previous quotation suggests — many more sought some kind of compromise that permitted them to keep the treasures they could neither part with nor fit into their RV. Some people gave their homes and family heirlooms to a child with the understanding that they could return there to live if poor health forced them off the road; others called in their children to claim what they wanted of the family treasures before the rest was sold at auction; others moved things they could not part with to a summer cottage or into storage where they sat for years before finally being discarded.

After they make the decision to sell their home and strip themselves of unnecessary possessions, RVers must develop strategies for making the best use of the limited space in their rigs. Ideas on how to accomplish this are a favourite topic of conversation and whenever they get together RVers share information on how to organize their interiors most efficiently. They spend hours exchanging views on which kinds and models of RVs have the most space available, ways in which things can be made to do double duty and ideas on how to modify one's rig to make it "livable" nomadic space. Veteran full-timers invited us inside to demonstrate how they had solved the problems of limited storage. One full-timer couple pointed with pride to the retaining bars along the upper walls of the rig that held their entire collection of music transcribed onto cassette tapes, while another described an innovative RVer who had installed his model train track along the walls of his trailer. Luce's suggestions for the creative use of wall space is a published example of this kind of information exchange (Luce 1991). Another is the article "Playing Solitaire" in *Highways* in which Edwards suggests modifications that make the space in rigs more useful to single RVers (Edwards 1991b).

Because interior space is so limited, RVers spend a lot of time outdoors and include the area where the rig is parked as part of their home or dwelling space. Interior space is private; most socializing occurs in the external space adjacent to the RV: in lawn chairs under an awning, at a picnic table or on the astroturf "lawn" in front of the rig. The notion that one's home or dwelling includes the out-of-doors is well known cross-culturally. In his definitive study of dwellings in many societies, Oliver observes that they do not require permanent structures. He says:

> To dwell is to . . . live in, or at, or on, or about a place. For some this implies a permanent structure, for others a temporary accommodation, for still others it is where they live, even if there is little evidence of building. . . . It is this double significance of dwelling — dwelling as the activity of living or residing, and dwelling as the place or structure which is the focus of residence — which encompasses the manifold cultural and material aspects of domestic habitation. (Oliver 1987:7)

As we observed above, one distinction between boondockers and resort park residents is that boondockers refuse to accept limits that restrict them to only a few feet of external space or rules defining how they are expected to use it. Typically, the area that boondockers claim for their dwelling is more extensive than the area allowed residents of private parks and greater even than the sites in many park or forest service campgrounds. Those who return to the same site year after year may stake out a considerable area for themselves. In the Slabs, for instance, we saw a "No Trespassing" sign blocking off a dirt track leading down into a shallow ravine where a trailer was parked. When we asked our neighbours whether individuals did, in fact, own land in the Slabs they confirmed that the sign had no legitimacy. As one said, "We're all trespassers here."

According to Randy, to be a full-timer it is necessary to give up notions of territoriality. "People have a lot of trouble with the fact that they don't own the land where they are parked," he said. "You can't put a fence around the place where you park." This is true and it is the source of a fascinating paradox, for although they cannot own the space outside their RV, they attempt to make it their own; as one of our informants said, to "make it like home."

Even if they plan to be in a place only a few days, many people attempt to personalize their outside space. They brush it clean and hang bird feeders and baskets of plants; they fly over it flags that proclaim their nationality (U.S., Canadian), affiliation (RV club) or ideology (Christian cross, the Jolly Roger, the Confederate Stars and Bars); they bound it with stones, bits of broken glass, small white picket fencing or strings of coloured lanterns; they plant flowers, cactus or vegetables; they put down an astroturf "lawn"; they decorate it with pink flamingos, fountains, coloured rocks, hunting trophies, cow skulls and Christmas trees; and they build patios, campfire circles and barbecue pits. In short, anything that might be found outside a suburban home to identify it as personal space may also be found in the space outside an RV. Furthermore, people who stay in one spot for months, or who return to the same site year after year — whether it is a pad in a resort park rented by the month or year or a spot in the Slabs — attempt to establish "ownership" of their space. They put up signs naming their area ("Rattlesnake Flats") and listing the names of the people who live there (recall the comment of Vanessa, "When you get situated in one group it's like a family, but we don't have a name yet"). In boondocking areas, a site that appears to be empty may in fact be "owned" by former residents who have improved it and intend to return. Newcomers who try to park in one of these sites are warned that they should move because it "belongs" to someone who will be returning to claim it. If the rights of the absent "owner" are not respected, fights may occur.

Social space for community activity is an important part of any RV setting. This is the shared idea where people socialize and in which everyone involved has rights. In private parks where the requirement of water mains, sewage lines and electrical connections dictate that RVs must park in rows, social space may be formally organized. In these parks, too, the desire for privacy and the recapitulation of suburban neighbourhoods are manifested by aligning the rigs so that the entrance of each one faces its private pad and the back of its neighbouring RV. Such parks often advertise their social space such as recreation halls or swimming pools. In public parks, individual sites are usually larger and are also organized in rows along roads. Public space in these parks includes campfire circles where officials deliver talks, recreation areas such as playgrounds or swimming beaches and picnic areas where potluck dinners organized by the host are held.

In desert boondocking areas there is no imposed external organization. People may park wherever they wish, and an individual RVer's personal territory can take up as much area as she wishes or can lay claim to by establishing boundaries. Neighbourhood design is not limited by the constraints of hookups and, although they do sometimes park along access roads, people are free to form communities of whatever shape they wish. They most often arrange themselves in circles with their doorways facing inward. The circle formation seems to be spontaneous and, although no one has the authority to tell anyone else where to park, a newcomer who unwittingly disrupts a circle will be directed to "a good place to park" on the periphery. The inside of the circle is community space where circle residents may construct a fireplace or barbecue pit or decorate a tree in December. Other community spaces — used by all residents of a boondocking area — include canals, river banks or springs where people go to wash and talk or the area in an LTVA near the host's rig. Social events may be organized (a potluck dinner) or spontaneous (singing around an evening campfire) and contribute to a strong sense of belonging among the participants.

CONCLUSION

In her discussion of the Gabra of Kenya, Prussin observes that the repetition of fixed spatial pattern reinforces the cognitive structure of interior space for nomads (1989). We would take this further and argue that when RV nomads set up at a new site, their repetition of spatial patterns reinvents and reinforces their cognitive structure of home, society and community. Although RVers carry with them the form of their social structure, the form is empty. Because they share no history with their RV neighbours, there is no one to fill the status of "neighbour," "friend" or "family," but the ideal content of these forms is shared knowledge. Therefore, when a newcomer pulls in, the strangers who are instant neighbours immediately begin to perform the roles of friend and family by sharing substance and labour. They help the newcomer set up, bring food, give advice and exchange information about personal history. This sharing and exchange allows RVers, who have no common past, to recreate the structure of history from one park to another and to embed themselves in a familiar social structure given substance. Like the Gabra, their reconstruction of history and society enables them to insulate themselves from a hostile environment — the "Crazies" out there — and to transform the stranger who might "rip you off" into the friend who will look after you in your time of need.

NOTES

1. Our research was supported by an Arts Research Board grant from McMaster University, using funds supplied by the Social Sciences and Humanities Research Council of Canada (SSHRCC). All names used in the manuscript have been changed to protect the privacy of our informants.

2. A "park model" trailer is not quite a recreational vehicle, nor is it quite a "mobile home." Such fine distinctions are important in the world of RVers. A *real* RV must be capable of being towed by the owner's private vehicle at will. A mobile home is essentially a moveable house — often 10 or 12 feet in width — and can only be moved by a proper tractor. A "park model" is no more than eight feet wide and may, therefore, be parked in an "RV" park, but it is furnished with regular furniture (rather than built-ins) and may even have sliding patio doors as one of its accessories. It is *not* meant to be moved without considerable professional planning.

3. Among RVers, a "rig" refers to the recreational vehicle *including* the tow vehicle, e.g., the truck that pulls a fifth-wheel or conventional trailer. When the RV is parked for residence, it is termed the "unit," even if it is an inseparable marriage of living quarters and motive power, as with a motor home. Living quarters that are detachable from their motive power, such as trailers, fifth wheels or truck campers are referred to as "units" when distinguishing them from the truck, van or other tow vehicle.

4. A "glory hole" is a hole in the desert, often dug by an earlier user of the site, into which one drains either sewage (black water) or wash water (grey water) or both. These holes may be as much as six feet deep and are considered by those who use them to be ecologically sound, sanitary, odourless and sensible. State health officials and RVers who prefer sani-dumps may disagree.

5. A pad is the private space that includes the place where the RV is parked and an area round it that is usually only a few feet wide.

6. "Going out like crazy" appears in this letter because in the advertisement for *US* magazine, its readership was characterized as doing just that — they "go out like crazy!"

    The point of the ad was that the slobbish RVers in the accompanying photograph were definitely NOT *US* readers — RVers and other non-*US* readers sat around in their undershirts and drank beer in the woods near their rigs.

REFERENCES CITED

American P. C. Campground Directory
1989   A Guide to Free Campgrounds. Dallas, Texas.
Bellah, Robert N., et al.
1985   Habits of the Heart: Individualism and Commitment in American Life. New York: Harper & Row.

Bender, Thomas
1978   Community and Social Change in America. Baltimore: Johns
              Hopkins University Press.
Born, T.L.
1976   Elderly RV Campers Along the Lower Colorado River: A Pre-
              liminary Typology. Journal of Leisure Research 8:256-262.
Courtney, Myrna
1991   Great Escape Artists. Trailer Life 51(6):76,78-79.
Davis, Kingsley
1949   Human Society. New York: Macmillan.
Douglas, Mary
1991   The Idea of Home: A Kind of Space. Social Research 58(1):287-
              307.
Edwards, Beverly
1991a   It was a Very Good Year. Highways 25(4):14,52-55.
1991b   Playing Solitaire. Highways 25(6):38-39.
Errington, Frederick
1990   The Rock Creek Rodeo: Excess and Constraint in Men's Lives.
              American Ethnologist 17(4):628-645.
Estes, Bill
1992   Driver's Seat. Trailer Life 52(6):7.
Green, Mr. and Mrs. L. Dexter
1988   Letter to The View from the Driver's Seat. Trailer Life
              48(11):7,165,169.
Hartwigsen, Gail, and Roberta Null
1989   Full-timing: A Housing Alternative for Older People. Interna-
              tional Journal of Aging and Human Development 29:317-328.
Howells, Bob
1987   Retirement Choices for the Time of Your Life. San Francisco:
              Gateway Books.
1990   RV Clubs. Trailer Life 50(11):62-70,78-79.
Hoyt, G.C.
1954   The Life of the Retired in a Trailer Park. American Journal of So-
              ciology 19:361-370
Hunnisett, Henry S.
1981   Retirement Guide for Canadians. Vancouver: International Self-
              Counsel Press.
Jacobs, Jerry
1974   Fun City: An Ethnographic Study of a Retirement Community.
              New York: Holt, Rinehart and Winston.
Joens, Ray D.
1991   Good Samartian Decal. Highways 25(4):4.
Kaufman, Sharon R.
1986   The Ageless Self: Sources of Meaning in Late Life. Madison: Uni-
              versity of Wisconsin Press.
Leonard, Barbara
1987   Flea for All. Trailer Life 47(5):62-64.
Lewis, Graydon
1988   Letter to The View from the Driver's Seat. Trailer Life 48(11):7,
              165, 169.
Luce, Jim
1991   Out of Space. Trailer Life 51(6):80,82-84.

Lusk, Norman M.
1991   Mail Box. Trailer Life 51(6):10,15-16,19,140,142.
Moeller, Bill, and Jan Moeller
1986   Full Time RVing: Complete Guide to Life on the Open Road.
            Agoura, California: Trailer Life Books.
Montelpasse, Lisa
1988   Letter to The View from the Driver's Seat. Trailer Life 48(11):7,
            165, 169.
Nisbet, Robert
1966   The Sociological Tradition. New York: Basic Books.
Noon, Marilyn
1988   Letter to The View from the Driver's Seat. Trailer Life
            48(11):7,165,169.
Oliver, Paul
1987   Dwellings: The House Across the World. Oxford: Phaidon Press.
Ortner, Sherry B.
1973   On Key Symbols. American Anthropologist 75:1338-1346.
Osgood, Nancy J.
1982   Senior Settlers: Social Integration in Retirement Communities.
            New York: Praeger.
Porter, Paula, and Peter Porter
1991   We Said Yes to the RV Lifestyle . . . RV Buyers Guide 19(7):8-
            10,13,16.
Prussin, Labell
1989   The Architecture of Nomadism: Gabra Placemaking and Culture.
            In Housing, Culture and Design, edited by Setha M. Low and
            Erve Chambers, pp. 141-164. Philadelphia: University of Penn-
            sylvania Press.
Robinson, Barbara Hicks
1988   Letter to The View from the Driver's Seat. Trailer Life 48(11):7,
            165, 169.
Sahlins, Marshall
1972   Stone Age Economics. Chicago: Aldine.
Shields, Rob, ed.
1991   Places on the Margin: Alternative Geographies of Modernity.
            London and New York: Routledge.
Streib, G. F., W.E. Folts and A.J. LaGreca.
1984   Entry into Retirement Communties: Process and Related Prob-
            lems. Research on Aging 6:257-270.
Symons, Gordon
1991   Roadwise: Campground Etiquette. Camping Canada 20(1):7,11.
Trailer Life
1988   The View from the Driver's Seat. Trailer Life 48(11):7,165, 169.

3

Introduction

In a very general sense, we could see Cheshire Calhoun's "Separating Lesbian Theory from Feminist Theory" as belonging to a debate in current public culture: how well does "feminism" represent actual women's actual experience? How capable is it of recognizing and accommodating differences among women, and of promoting their diverse interests? But you will find (from the title alone) that Calhoun's work investigates a particular sector of this debate, one less likely to receive public attention than, say, the issues of feminism's representation of the interests of the stay-at-home mother, or the woman seeking to benefit from advances in reproductive technologies. She addresses a deep but, she says, often obscured distinction between the interests of heterosexual feminists and those of lesbians. She argues that to fail to recognize this distinction is to "[miss] a good deal of what it means to live life as a lesbian as well as much of the political significance of lesbian practices ... " (95). Accordingly, "separating sexuality politics from gender politics is exactly what must happen if there is to be a specifically *lesbian* feminist theory rather than simply feminist theory applied to lesbians" (94, emphasis in original).

In identifying a knowledge deficit (the "missing" material) and claiming obligation as a result ("must"), Calhoun takes a stand typical of scholarly writers. Other features of her argument are similarly typical in situating her as a scholarly speaker. For example, you will find many messages about the argument itself. Forecasts occur at both global levels (where she provides an overview of the whole argument) —

> In what follows, I will be arguing.... I hope to establish two
> main points. First.... Second....

★ ★ ★

> In making this argument, I will take the category "woman"
> and the institution of heterosexuality in turn. My aim in
> both cases is to illustrate ... I begin with the category
> "woman." (94-95)

— and at more local levels, where the forecast is reinstated to
manage a smaller section of argument:

> I have been arguing so far that reading heterosexuality and
> lesbianism solely in relation to patriarchal gender politics
> fails to yield an adequate picture of lesbians' political posi-
> tion. I turn now to an exploration of the thesis that hetero-
> sexuality is itself a political system that shapes our social
> structure as systematically as do patriarchal, racial, imperialist
> and class systems. (113)

You can see, too, from this example, that forecast is accompanied
by summary of preceding argument: in the interests of managing
their readers' attention to complex argument, scholarly writers
often add backward-pointing signals (this is the gist of what I've
just said) to forward-pointing signals (this is what I'm going to
say). Backward-pointing gestures repeat points that have been established, and they come well flagged: "this is what you should
have understood from what has been said." But other forms of
repetition are not so well flagged. In fact, until you become somewhat familiar with this article, you may not realize how repetitive
it is. For example, a claim in the second paragraph —

> [early radical lesbians] argued either that the lesbian is *the*
> paradigm case of patriarchal resister or that she fits on a con-
> tinuum of types of patriarchal resisters (90)

— finds echoes five pages and then twenty-two pages later:

> [according to Monique Wittig] Lesbians ... refuse to partici-
> pate in heterosexual social relations. Like runaway slaves

who refuse to have their labour appropriated by white masters, lesbians are runaways who refuse to allow men to control their productive and reproductive labor within a nuclear family. (95)-(96)

... like Rich's notion of a lesbian continuum that includes both lesbians and heterosexual women, Raymond's "use of the term *Gyn/affection* expresses a *continuum* of female friendship" that includes some (but not all) lesbian women. In her view, it is gyn/affection that women seize power from men and engage in a woman-identified act. (112, emphasis in original)

Such repetition should be a comfort for readers facing an argument as demanding as Calhoun's. While first mention of the idea of the "continuum" and the "paradigm case of patriarchal resister" may be barely graspable, Calhoun provides several subsequent occasions for readers to meet these ideas, and handle them. So the central, commanding idea of "heterosexuality as a political structure separable from patriarchy" (91) appears over and over again. Different sections of the argument each approach this idea, confirming and reconfirming it until readers can approach it themselves, confidently.

It is not an easy idea, for reasons Calhoun most emphatically expresses at the end of the essay, where she talks about how the "socially foundational status of the male-female couple" naturalizes heterosexuality, and prevents people from seeing it as only a social practice rather than something prior to culture, something *natural*. And our access to this idea lies through some very abstract routes. So you may find the occasional clumps of examples (97-98, 114, 115) a boost to your understanding.

You may also have a feeling that you are eavesdropping on an ongoing conversation, the history of which is not available to you. For example, Calhoun refers to the "feminist critique of butch and femme lesbianism" (102). Perhaps you don't know the drift of this critique, or even that it exists. But you will find that the paragraphs which follow tell you what you need to know about feminist analysis of certain types of lesbian behaviour. And, more generally, if you feel unfamiliar with elements of feminist reasoning, you will find many occasions where they are set out for the purposes of this argument. So, while the article does not set out to tell you all about feminism, and its style assumes many things as familiar, you can nevertheless listen in, and pick up what you need to know.

Unlike many of the articles in this volume, this one introduces and summarizes the writing of others *throughout* — rather than only in introductory sections. It carefully and respectfully attends to each summarized position, even when that position will be partly discredited. So, along with its frequent messages about the argument, its repetitiveness, its few-and-far-between examples, and its way of assuming knowledge of certain areas of debate, we could say that this article is distinguished by its detailed summaries of many other arguments. In this, it belongs to the kind of scholarly writing that reasons about definitions, assumptions, and categories. It is theoretical rather than empirical. Calhoun didn't go out and investigate relationships and workplaces, homes and schools, or conduct a broad quantitative survey. Rather, she made new knowledge by turning over and examining existing knowledge, itself abstract.

There are many ways to approach the complexities of this argument and consolidate your understanding of it, and you may easily find your own way in. But here are some guiding questions which, although they appear to concentrate on one phase of the argument, can actually bring into focus its overall, main claims.

- What is the feminist critique of butch and femme lesbianism?

- What are some responses to this critique? In what way does Calhoun see these responses as inadequate?

- How do critique and response illustrate her central concern, that is, that patriarchy is separable from heterosexuality?

Separating Lesbian Theory from Feminist Theory

CHESHIRE CALHOUN

HEIDI HARTMANN ONCE SAID of the marriage of Marxism and feminism that it "has been the like the marriage of husband and wife depicted in English common law: marxism and feminism are one, and that one is marxism."[1] Lesbian theory and feminism, I want to suggest, are at risk of falling into a similar unhappy marriage in which "the one" is feminism.

Although lesbian feminist theorizing has significantly contributed to feminist thought, it has also generally treated lesbianism as a kind of applied issue. Feminist theories developed outside of the context of lesbianism are brought to bear on lesbianism in order to illuminate the nature of lesbian oppression and women's relation to women within lesbianism. So, for example, early radical lesbians played off the feminist claim that all male-female relationships are dominance relationships. They argued either that the lesbian is *the* paradigm case of patriarchal resister because she refused to be heterosexual or that she fits on a continuum of types of patriarchal resisters.[2] In taking this line, lesbian theorists made a space for lesbianism by focusing on what they took to be the inherently feminist and antipatriarchal nature of lesbian existence. Contemporary lesbian theorists are less inclined to read lesbianism as feminist resistance to male dominance.[3] Instead, following the trend that

---

1   Heidi Hartmann, "The Unhappy Marriage of Marxism and Feminism," in *Feminist Frameworks*, ed. Alison M. Jaggar and Paula S. Rothenberg, 2d ed. (New York: McGraw-Hill, 1984), p. 172.

2   On the former, see, e.g., Charlotte Bunch, "Lesbians in Revolt," in her *Passionate Politics, Essays 1968-1986* (New York: St. Martin's, 1987); and Monique Wittig, *The Straight Mind and Other Essays* (Boston: Beacon, 1992). Regarding the latter, see Adrienne Rich, "Compulsory Heterosexuality and the Lesbian Continuum," in *The Signs Reader: Women, Gender, and Scholarship*, ed. Elizabeth Abel and Emily K. Abel (Chicago: University of Chicago Press, 1983).

3   For instance, Jeffner Allen states in her introduction to the anthology *Lesbian Philosophies and Cultures*, ed. Jeffner Allen (Albany, N.Y.: SUNY Press, 1990), "The primary

feminist theory has itself taken, the focus has largely shifted to women's relation to women: the presence of ageism, racism, and anti-Semitism among lesbians, the problem of avoiding a totalizing discourse that speaks for all lesbians without being sensitive to differences, the difficulty of creating community in the face of political differences (e.g., on the issue of sadomasochism [s/m]), and the need to construct new conceptions of female agency and female friendship.[4] All of these are issues that have their birthplace in feminist theory. They become lesbian issues only because the general concern with women's relation to women is narrowed to lesbians' relation to fellow lesbians. Once again, lesbian thought becomes applied to feminist thought.

Now there is nothing wrong with using feminist tools to analyze lesbianism. Indeed, something would be wrong with feminist theory if it could not be usefully applied to lesbianism in a way that both illuminates lesbianism and extends feminist theory itself. And there would surely be something lacking in lesbian thought if it did not make use of feminist insights. My worry is that if this is all that lesbian feminism amounts to then there is no lesbian *theory*. Lesbian theory and feminist theory are one, and that one is feminist theory. What more could one want?

When Hartmann complained that Marxism had swallowed feminism, her point was that because traditional Marxism lacks a notion of sex-class, and thus of patriarchy as a political system distinct from capitalism, it must treat women's oppression as a special case of class oppression. Marxism is of necessity blind to the irreducibly gendered nature of women's lives. A parallel complaint might be raised about feminist theory. To the extent that feminist theory lacks a concepts of heterosexuals and nonheterosexuals as members of different sexuality classes and thus of heterosexuality as a political structure separable from patriarchy, feminist theory must treat lesbian oppression as a special case of patriarchal oppression and remain blind to the irreducibly lesbian nature of lesbian lives.

emphasis of this book is *lesbian* philosophies and cultures, rather than lesbianism considered in relation to or in contrast to, patriarchy, or heterosexuality" (p. 1).

4   See e.g., the recent anthology, Allen, ed., *Lesbian Philosophies and Cultures*; as well as Sarah Lucia Hoagland's *Lesbian Ethics: Toward New Value* (Palo Alto, Calif.: Institute of Lesbian Studies, 1990); and Janice G. Raymond's *A Passion for Friends* (Boston: Beacon, 1986).

Lesbian feminism is for several reasons at high risk of doing just that. First, the most extensive analyses of heterosexuality available to feminists are those developed in the late 1970s and early 1980s by Charlotte Bunch, Gayle Rubin, Adrienne Rich, Monique Wittig, and Kate Millet.[5] Heterosexuality, on this account, is both product and essential support of patriarchy. Women's heterosexual orientation perpetuates their social, economic, emotional, and sexual dependence on and accessibility by men. Heterosexuality is thus a system of male ownership of women, participation in which is compulsory for men and especially for women. The lesbian's and heterosexual woman's relation to heterosexuality on this account is fundamentally the same. Both experience it as the demand that women be dependent on and accessible by men. Both are vulnerable to penalties if they resist that demand. Thus heterosexuality is equally compulsory for heterosexual women and lesbians; and compulsory heterosexuality means the same thing for both. There is no specifically lesbian relation to heterosexuality.

Second, lesbian feminists have had to assert their differences from gay men and thus their distance from both the political aims and the self-understanding of the gay movement. The gay rights movement has suffered from at least two defects. On the one hand, in focusing on lesbians' and gays' shared status as sexual deviants, the gay rights movement was unable to address the connection between lesbian oppression and women's oppression. On the other hand, it tended to equate gay with gay male and failed to address the patriarchal attitudes embedded in the gay movement itself.[6] Making clear the difference between lesbians and gay men meant that lesbian feminists' focus had to be on the experience of lesbians in a patriarchal culture, not on their experience as deviants in a heterosexist culture.

5   Charlotte Bunch, "Lesbians in Revolt," "Learning from Lesbian Separatism," and "Lesbian-Feminist Theory," all in her *Passionate Politics*; Gayle Rubin, "The Traffic in Women," in *Toward an Anthropology of Women*, ed. Rayna Reiter (New York: Monthly Review, 1975); Kate Millet, *Sexual Politics* (New York: Doubleday, 1969); Rich; Wittig, *The Straight Mind*.

6   See, e.g., Marilyn Frye's critical assessment of the gay rights movement in "Lesbian Feminism and the Gay Rights Movement: Another View of Male Supremacy, Another Separatism," in her *The Politics of Reality* (Freedom, Calif.: Crossing, 1983); as well as John Stoltenberg's "Sadomasochism: Eroticized Violence, Eroticized Powerlessness," in *Against Sadomasochism*, ed. Robin Ruth Linden et al. (San Francisco: Frog in the Well, 1982).

Third, the fact that to be lesbian is to live out of intimate relation with men and in intimate relation with women encourages the reduction of 'lesbian' to 'feminist'.[7] Early radical feminists were quite explicit about this, claiming that lesbians are the truly woman-identified women. Contemporary lesbian feminists, recognizing that lesbians may share patriarchal attitudes toward women, resist such grand claims. But even if lesbian feminism is no longer at risk of equating being lesbian with being a "true" feminist, the danger remains that it may equate 'lesbian issue' with 'feminist issue'. If what count as lesbian issues are only those visible through a feminist lens, then lesbian issues will simply be a special class of feminist ones.

Finally, the historical circumstances that gave birth to lesbian feminism had a decided impact on the direction that lesbian feminism took. The first major lesbian feminist statement, "The Woman Identified Woman," was a direct response to Betty Friedan's charge that lesbians posed a "lavender menace" to the women's movement.[8] In Friedan's and many National Organization for Women (NOW) members' view, the association of feminism with lesbianism, and thus with deviancy, undermined the credibility of women's rights claims. Threatened with ostracism from the women's movement, the Radicalesbians argued in "The Woman Identified Woman" that lesbians, because they love women and refuse to live with or devote their energies to the oppressor, are the paradigm feminists.[9] The political climate of the 1970s women's movement thus required lesbian feminists to assert their allegiance to feminist aims and values rather than calling attention to lesbians' differences from their heterosexual sisters. It was neither the time nor the place for lesbians to entertain the possibility that heterosexuality might itself be a political system and

---

7   Charlotte Bunch, e.g., observes that "lesbianism and feminism are both about women loving and supporting women and women revolting against the so-called supremacy of men and the patriarchal institutions that control us" ("Lesbian-Feminist Theory," p. 196).

8   For brief historical discussions of this event, see Shane Phelan's "The Woman-identified Woman," in her *Identity Politics: Lesbian Feminism and the Limits of Community* (Philadelphia: Temple University Press, 1989); and Terralee Bensinger's "Lesbian Pornography: The Re/Making of (a) Community," *Discourse* 15 (1992): 69-93.

9   Radicalesbians, "The Woman Identified Woman," in *Radical Feminism*, ed. Anne Koedt et al. (New York: Quandrangle, 1973).

that heterosexual women and men, as a consolidated and powerful class, might have strong interests in maintaining a system of heterosexual privileges. In affirming their commitment to opposing patriarchy, lesbian feminists instead committed themselves to a specifically feminist account of the interests motivating the maintenance of a heterosexual system: men have patriarchal interests in securing sexual/emotional access to women, and heterosexual women have complicitous interests in securing access to a system of male privileges. This move effectively barred lesbian feminists from asking whether heterosexual women and men have, as heterosexuals, a class interest in constructing heterosexual sex as the only real, nonimitative sex, in eliminating historical, literary, and media representations of lesbians and gay men, in reserving jobs, public accommodations, and private housing for heterosexuals only, in barring lesbians and gay men from access to children in the educational system, children's service organizations, and adoption and artificial insemination agencies, in reducing lesbianism and homosexuality to biologically or psychodevelopmentally rooted urges while propagating the myth of a magical heterosexual romantic love, and in securing for the married heterosexual couple exclusive pride of place in the social world. Nor could or did lesbian feminists ask whether these privileges taken as a set could provide a sufficient motivating interest for maintaining a heterosexual system even in the absence of patriarchy.

For all four reasons, treating sexual orientation on a par with gender, race, and economic class — that is, as a distinct and irreducible dimension of one's political identity — may not come naturally to lesbian feminist thinking. But separating sexuality politics from gender politics is exactly what must happen if there is to be a specifically *lesbian* feminist theory rather than simply feminist theory applied to lesbians. A lesbian feminist theory would need, among other things, to focus on what is distinctive about the lesbian's relation to heterosexuality, to the category 'woman,' and to other women. That is, it would need to put into clear view the difference between being a lesbian who resists heterosexuality, being a woman, and loving men rather than women and being a feminist who resists the same things.

In what follows, I will be arguing that, like patriarchy and capitalism, or white imperialism, patriarchy and heterosexual dominance are two, in principle, separable systems. Even where they work together, it is possible conceptually to pull the patriarchal aspect of male-female relationships apart from their heterosexual dimensions. In arguing for the conceptual separability of the political structure of heterosexuality from patriarchy, I hope to establish two main points. First, lesbianism ought not to be read solely as resistance to patriarchal male-female relationships. One misses a good deal of what it means to live life as a lesbian as well as much of the political significance of lesbian practices by doing so. Second, even if empirically and historically heterosexual dominance and patriarchy are completely intertwined, it does not follow from this fact that the collapse of patriarchy will bring about the collapse of heterosexual dominance.[10] Heterosexual society may simply adapt to new social conditions. Thus it is a mistake for feminists to assume that work to end gender subordination will have as much payoff for lesbians as it would for heterosexual women. Only a political strategy that keeps clearly in mind the duality of the heterosexual-patriarchal structure, as well as the potential for conflict between feminist and lesbian strategies, could have such a payoff.

In making this argument, I will take the category 'woman' and the institution of heterosexuality in turn. My aim in both cases is to illustrate the difference between being a lesbian and being a feminist, between lesbian politics and feminist politics, and to sketch the directions that I think lesbian theory would need to go in order to make a space for fully lesbian theorizing within feminist thought. I begin with the category 'woman.'

THE LESBIAN NOT-WOMAN

Monique Wittig ends "The Straight Mind" with this sentence: "Lesbians are not women."[11] Wittig denies that 'man' and 'woman' are natural categories, arguing instead that the two sex-classes — men, women — are the product of heterosexual social relations in which "men appropriate for themselves the reproduction and production of women and also their physical persons by means of a contract called the marriage contract."[12] Thus, "it is oppression that creates sex and not the contrary."[13] Lesbians, however, refuse to partici-

---

10   I thank Ann Ferguson for pointing out that capitalism and patriarchy are empirically and historically intertwined, even if conceptually separate, and for suggesting that the same might be true of the heterosexual and patriarchal aspects of male/female relationships.

11   Monique Wittig, "The Straight Mind," in *The Straight Mind and Other Essays*, p. 32.

12   Monique Wittig, "The Category of Sex," in *The Straight Mind and Other Essays*, p. 6.

13   Ibid., p. 2.

pate in heterosexual social relations. Like runaway slaves who refuse to have their labor appropriated by white masters, lesbians are runaways who refuse to allow men to control their reproductive labor within a nuclear family. Thus Wittig observes, "Lesbianism is the only concept I know of which is beyond the categories of sex (woman and man), because the designated subject (lesbian) is not a woman, either economically, or politically, or ideologically. For what makes a woman is a specific social relation to a man, a relation that we have previously called servitude, a relation which implies personal and physical obligation as well as economic obligation ('forced residence,' domestic corvèe, conjugal duties, unlimited production of children, etc.), a relation which lesbians escape by refusing to become or to stay heterosexual."[14] What I want to highlight in Wittig's explanation of what bars lesbians from the category 'woman' is that it claims both too much and too little for lesbians as well as reads lesbianism from a peculiarly heterosexual viewpoint. To say that only lesbians exist beyond sex categories (in Wittig's particular sense of what this means) claims too much for lesbians. If to be a woman just means living in a relation of servitude to men, there will be other ways short of lesbianism of evading the category 'woman'. The heterosexual celibate, virgin, single-parent head of household, marriage resister, or the married woman who insists on an egalitarian marriage contract all apparently qualify as escapees from the category 'woman'.[15]

Although Wittig does remark that runaway wives are also escaping their sex class, she clearly thought that lesbians are in some special sense *not women*. But her own analysis does not capture lesbians' special deviancy from the category 'woman'. There is indeed no conceptual space in Wittig's framework for pursuing the question of how a heterosexual woman's refusal to be a woman differs from a lesbian's refusal to be a woman. It is in that failure that she claims too little for lesbians. Because lesbians and heterosexual resisters must have, on her account, the same relation to the category 'woman', there can be no interesting differences between the two. This, I think, is a mistake, and I will argue in a moment

14   Monique Wittig, "One is Not Born a Woman," in *The Straight Mind and Other Essays*, p. 20.

15   This point has been made by a number of authors, including Marilyn Frye ("Some Reflections on Separatism and Power," in *The Politics of Reality*) and Kathryn Pyne Addelson ("Words and Lives," *Signs* 7 [1981]:187–99).

that lesbians are in a quite special sense not-women.

Finally, to equate lesbians' escape from heterosexuality and the category 'woman' with escape from male control is to adopt a peculiarly heterosexual viewpoint on lesbianism. The fact that heterosexuality enables men to control women's domestic labor is something that would be salient only to a *heterosexual* woman. Only heterosexual women do housework for men, raise children for men, have their domiciles determined by men, and so on. Thus, from a heterosexual standpoint lesbianism may indeed appear to offer a liberating escape from male control. But from the standpoint of a woman unaccustomed to living with men, that is, from a lesbian standpoint, lesbianism is not about a refusal to labor for men. Nor is heterosexuality experienced primarily as a form of male dominance over women, but instead as heterosexual dominance over lesbians and gay men. Nor is the daily experience of lesbianism on of liberation, but instead, one of acute oppression.

Because Wittig looks at lesbianism from a (heterosexual) feminist perspective, asking how lesbians escape the kinds of male control to which paradigmatically heterosexual women are subject, she misses the penalties attached to lesbians' exit from heterosexuality. Indeed, contrary to Wittig's claim, the lesbian may as a rule have *less* control over her productive and reproductive labor than her married heterosexual sister. Although the lesbian escapes whatever control *individual* men may exercise over their wives within marriage, she does not thereby escape control of her productive and reproductive labor either in her personal life with another woman or in her public life. To refuse to be heterosexual is simply to leap out of the frying pan of individual patriarchal control into the fire of institutionalized heterosexual control. Wittig's claim that "lesbianism provides for the moment the only social form in which we can live freely" vastly underestimates the coercive forces brought to bear on the lesbian for her lesbianism.[16] She may be unable to adopt children or be denied custody of and visiting privileges to her children. In order to retain her job, she will most likely have to hide her lesbianism and pretend to be a heterosexual. She will likely be punished for public displays of affection. She may be denied the housing of her choice or be forced to move from her home as a result of harassment by neighbors. If she is "out," she will find herself alternatively abused and subjected to

16   Wittig, "One is Not Born a Woman," p. 20.

lascivious interest by heterosexual men. Even if she is no longer at risk of being burned at the stake or subjected to clitoridectomy or electroshock, she may still be subjected to "therapies" that insist that she cannot be both lesbian and a healthy, mature adult. She will be labelled a dyke and scrutinized for symptoms of mannishness in her anatomy, dress, behavior, and interests. She will not see her lesbian sexuality or romantic love for another woman reflected in the public media. And both because there are no publicly accessible models of lesbian relationships and because such coercive pressure is brought to bear against lesbian relationships, sustaining a stable personal life will be very difficult. The lesbian may be free from an individual man in her personal life, but she is not free.

What these criticisms suggest is, first, that the political structure that oppresses heterosexual women is patriarchy; but the political structure that most acutely oppresses lesbians is more plausibly taken to be heterosexuality. Second, these criticisms suggest that heterosexual women's (especially heterosexual feminists') and lesbians' relation to the category 'woman' are not the same.

From a feminist point of view, the problem with the category 'woman' is not so much that there is one. The problem lies in its specific construction within patriarchal society. 'Woman' has been constructed as the Other and the deficient in relation to 'man'. To 'woman' have been assigned all those traits that would both rationalize and perpetuate women's lack of power in relation to men. Women are weak, passive, dependent, emotional, irrational, nurturant, closer to nature, maternal and so on. This is to say that, from a feminist point of view, the problem with the category 'woman' is that 'woman' has been equated with subordination to men. The feminist task, then, is to rupture the equation. With the exception of early liberal feminists' recommendation of androgyny and possibly contemporary French feminists' deconstruction of 'woman', the feminist project has not been the elimination of the category 'woman'. Instead, the project has been one of reconstructing that category. That reconstructive project has had two phases within feminism. The first phase tried to reconstruct the category 'woman' so that it could no longer be used to rationalize male dominance. So, for example, some feminine traits were rejected, others, such as nurturance, were revalued and/or redefined, and some masculine traits (e.g., strength) were appropriated with or without redefinition.[17]

17   Joyce Trebilcott neatly summarizes these reconstructive strategies in "Conceiving

The more recent phase has been devoted to reconstructing the category 'woman' employed within feminism itself so that it cannot be used to rationalized white, middle-class, college-educated, heterosexual, Christian women's dominance within feminism.[18] This latter reconstruction has required the postulate of multiple categories of 'woman' to capture the intersection of gender with other political identities.[19]

The feminist experience of her relation to the category 'woman', thus, has been the experience of *being* a woman in a male dominant, as well as racist and classist, society, which imposes on her a conception of what it means to be a woman that she rejects. Her refusal to be a woman has extended only to refusal to be the kind of woman that a patriarchal, racist, and classist society demands that she be. And that refusal has gone hand in hand with claiming the category 'woman' (or categories of 'women') for herself and insisting on a woman-identified construction of that category.

This is not the lesbian relation to the category 'woman'. Although partly mistaken, I think, in her reasons, Wittig was correct to say that to be lesbian is to exit the category 'woman' altogether. It is to be ungendered, unsexed, neither woman nor man. This is because (here following Wittig) sex/gender is the result of institutionalized heterosexuality.[20] Heterosexual systems are ones that organize reproduction via hetero*sexual* practice. That practice requires the production of two sex/genders so that sexual desire can be heterosexualized. It also requires that sex/gender map onto reproductive differences. Thus, within heterosexual systems, "'intelligible' genders are those which in some sense institute and maintain relations of coherence and continuity among sex, gender, sex-

Women: Notes on the Logic of Feminism," *Sinister Wisdom*, vol 11 (1979), reprinted in *Women and Values: Readings in Recent Feminist Philosophy*, ed. Marilyn Pearsall (Belmont, Calif.: Wadsworth, 1986).

18   See, e.g., Marilyn Frye's "A Response to *Lesbian Ethics*: Why Ethics?" In *Feminist Ethics*, ed. Claudia Card (Lawrence: University Press of Kansas, 1991); and Elizabeth V. Spelman's *Inessential Woman: Problems of Exclusion in Feminist Thought* (Boston: Beacon, 1988).

19   Spelman argues elegantly for the necessity of multiple categories in *Inessential Woman*.

20   I used 'sex/gender' rather than 'gender' throughout the argument that lesbians are not-women in order to avoid implying that what makes lesbians not-women is simply their gender deviance (e.g., their butchness or refusal to be subordinate to men). I want to stress instead that lesbians are not clearly female. It is sex deviance combined with gender deviance that I think results in lesbians' exit from the category 'woman'.

ual practice, and desire."[21] Individuals who violate the unity of reproductive anatomy, heterosexual desire, and gender behavior fall out of the domain of intelligible gender identity. At best, lesbians are not-women. That is, for them the closest available category of sex/gender identity is one that does not fit. Neither anatomy nor desire nor gender can link her securely to the category 'woman'. Within heterosexist ideology her anatomy itself is suspect. Much was made, for example, in the sexologists' literature of physical masculinity in the lesbian, including reports of an enlarged clitoris. The postulate of a biological basis of homosexuality and lesbianism continues to guide research today. And many lesbians' insistence on having been born lesbian reinforces such suspicions about anatomical differences from heterosexual women. In addition, her anatomy cannot link her to 'woman' because what lesbianism reveals is the fundamental lie that differences in male and female anatomy destine a difference in males' and females' sexual and social relation to females, that is, destine on to be functionally a man or a woman. The lesbian's female body in no way bars her from functioning as a man in relation to women. She shares with members of the category 'man' a sexual desire for and love of women. Also, the very traits that Wittig took to be definitive of 'man' — the enactment of masculine dominance over women, physically, psychologically, socially, and economically — are an option for her in a way that they are not an option for heterosexual women. The lesbian thus exists the category of 'woman', though without thereby entering the category 'man'.

Gender-deviant heterosexual women (i.e., women who resist patriarchal understandings of what it means to be a woman) do not similarly exit the category 'woman'. Gender deviance would result in not-woman status only if the content of the category 'woman' were fully exhausted by a description, such as Wittig's, of what it means to be a woman. I have been suggesting, on the contrary, that heterosexuality is a critical component of the category 'woman'. Heterosexuality secures one's status as a "natural" woman, which is to say, as having a body whose sex as female is above suspicion. Heterosexuality also guarantees a significant nonidentity between one's own and men's relation to women. The heterosexual woman will not have a sexual, romantic, marital co-

21   Judith Butler, *Gender Trouble: Feminism and the Subversion of Identity* (New York: Routledge, 1990), p. 17.

parenting relation to other women; she will have instead a *woman's* relation to women. Thus even in her gender deviance, the heterosexual resister of patriarchally defined gender remains unambiguously a woman.

Because the lesbian stands outside the category 'woman', her experience of womanliness and its oppressive nature is not identical to that of the heterosexual feminist, who stands within the category 'woman', even if resistantly. Womanliness is not something the lesbian has the option of refusing or reconstructing for a better fit. It is a fundamental impossibility for her. To be a not-woman is to be incapable of *being* a woman within heterosexual society. The lesbian can thus be womanly only in the modes of being in drag and of passing. And if she experiences womanliness — the demand that she look like a woman, act like a woman — as oppressive, it is not because womanliness requires subordination to men (although this may also be her experience). It is instead because the demand that she be womanly is the demand that she pretend that the sex/gender 'woman' is a natural possibility for her and that she pass as a woman. It is thus also a demand that she not reveal the nonexhaustiveness and, potentially, the nonnaturalness of the binary categories 'woman' and 'man'.

The lesbian experience of her relation to the category 'woman', thus, is the experience of being a not-woman in a heterosexual society that compels everyone to be either a woman or a man and requires that she be a woman.[22] It is also the experience of being oppressed by a womanliness that denies her desire for women, and of being deviantly outside of sex/gender categories. That deviancy is harshly punished. In an attempt to compel her back into the category 'woman', her lesbian desire and unwomanly relation to women are punished or treated. At the same time, she is denied the heterosexual privileges to which "real" women have access.

From a lesbian perspective, the category 'woman' is oppressive, because, within heterosexual societies, that category is compulsory for all anatomically female individuals. Feminist reconstructions of 'woman' do not typically challenge compulsory sex/gender. They implicitly assume that 'woman' and 'man' exhaust the field of possible sorts of persons to be (even if it takes multiple categories of each to exhaust the taxonomy). Furthermore, insofar as lesbians are auto-

22 Frye quite vividly describes the phenomenon of compulsory sex/gender in "Sexism," in *The Politics of Reality*.

matically and uncritically subsumed under the feminist category 'woman', feminist theorizing presumes that membership in that category is determined by anatomy and ignores the extent to which the femaleness of the lesbian body is suspect. The lesbian objection to being a woman is not met by admissions that the category 'woman' as well as what it means to be anatomically female are open to social construction and reconstruction. Nor is it met by the suggestion that there is no single category 'woman' but instead multiple categories of women. From a lesbian perspective, what has to be challenged is heterosexual society's demand that females be women. For that demand denies the lesbian option. The lesbian option is to be a not-woman, where being a not-woman is played out by insisting on being neither identifiable woman nor man, or by enacting femininity as a drag, or by insisting on switching gender categories and thus being a man, which within patriarchy means being dominant in relation to women and potentially also misogynistic.

Failure to see the difference between feminist and lesbian relations to the category 'woman' may well result in mislocating lesbian politics and failing to see the potential friction between feminist and lesbian politics. I take the feminist critique of butch and femme lesbianism as a case in point. On that critique, both the lesbian appropriation of femininity by femmes (and more recently by lipstick lesbians) and the lesbian appropriation of masculinity through butch sexual-social dominance repeat between women the power politics and misogyny that typifies male-female relations in a patriarchal society. Julia Penelope, for instance, argues that "those aspects of behavior and appearance labelled 'femininity' in HP [heteropatriarchy] are dangerous for us. We still live *in* a heteropatriarchy and Lesbians who incorporate male ideas of appropriate female behaviors into their lives signal their acceptance of the HP version of reality."[23] In particular, the feminine lesbian confirms heteropatriarhy's acceptance of the feminine woman and rejection of any trace of mannishness in women.

From a feminist point of view there is no way of rendering politically harmless the appropriation of a role that requires sexual-social passivity and subordination, even if the appropriation is by a not-woman and even if she is not passive or subordinate primarily

23 Julia Penelope, "Heteropatriarchal Semantics and Lesbian Identity: The Ways a Lesbian Can Be," in her *Call Me Lesbian: Lesbian Lives, Lesbian Theory* (Freedom, Calif.: Crossing, 1992).

in relation to men. Here the argument against femininity in lesbians directly parallels the argument against the masochist role in lesbian s/m. The femme's and masochist's appeal to the voluntariness of their choices, the privacy of their practices, and the pleasure they derive from femininity and masochism, respectively, do not go all the way toward making what they do purely personal. Both femininity and female masochism acquire their meaning from what Penelope calls "heteropatriarchal semantics" as well as from the historical and material conditions of women's oppression. Those meanings cannot be dissolved at will.[24] To adopt either femininity or female masochism for oneself is to make use of a set of meanings produced through and sustained by men's oppression of women. It is thus to reveal one's personal failure to come to critical grips with the politics of women's position within patriarchy. Even if the femme's or masochist's personal choices are not political in the sense that they also publicly endorse femininity or masochism in women, they are still political in the sense that they make use of public meanings which are tied to gender politics.

Nor, the feminist critic might add, can the appropriation of masculine dominance, aggression, and misogyny be rendered politically harmless. What the butch (as well as the sadist in lesbian s/m) confirms is the patriarchal equation of power with sexual dominance and superiority with masculinity. Janice Raymond's caustic remarks about lesbian s/m might equally express the feminist critique of butch-femme roles: "It is difficult to see what is so advanced and progressive about a position that locates 'desire,' and that imprisons female sexual dynamism, vitality, and vigor, in old forms of sexual objectification, subordination and violence, this time initiated by women and done with women's consent. The libertarians offer a supposed sexuality stripped naked of feminine taboo, but only able to dress itself in masculine garb. It is a male-constructed sexuality in drag."[25]

I have no intention of disagreeing with the claim that butch-femme role-playing runs contrary to feminist politics. What I do intend to take issue with is the assumption that feminist politics are necessarily lesbian politics. Judith Butler gives a quite different

---

24   For critical discussions of the meanings employed within a/m, see esp. Susan Leigh Star, "Swastikas: The Street and the University," in Linden et al., eds.; and Stoltenberg.

25   Janice G. Raymond, "Putting the Politics Back into Lesbianism," *Women's Studies International Forum* 12 (1989): 149-56.

reading of the multiple appropriations of femininity and masculinity within the lesbian/gay community by butches, femmes, queens, dykes, and gay male girls. It is a reading that I take to be closer to a lesbian perspective, even if farther from a feminist one.

What the feminist critique omits is the fact that "Within lesbian contexts, the 'identification' with masculinity that appears as butch identity is not a simple assimilation of lesbianism back into the terms of heterosexuality. As one lesbian femme explained, she likes her boys to be girls . . . As a result, that masculinity, if that it can be called, is always brought into relief against a culturally intelligible 'female body'. It is precisely this dissonant juxtaposition and the sexual tension that its transgression generates that constitute the object of desire."[26] It is also precisely this dissonant juxtaposition of masculinity and female body that enables the butch to enact a comedic parody of masculinity that denaturalizes the category 'man'. Heterosexual society assumes that masculinity is naturally united to the male body and desire for women. Similarly, it assumes that femininity is naturally united to the female body and desire for men. Butler argues, however, that gender identity is not natural but the result of continuous gender performances. One can be a man, for example, only by continuously performing masculinity and desire for women through a male body. Heterosexual society sustains the illusion of natural gender identities — 'heterosexual man', 'heterosexual woman' — by outlawing alternative performances. The butch lesbian gives an outlawed performance. She performs masculinity and desire for women through a female body. The butch gay man similarly gives an outlawed performance by performing masculinity in tandem with desire for men through a male body. Such multiple locations of masculinity — on the heterosexual male body, the lesbian body, the gay man's body — help create a condition in which "after a while, everyone starts to look like a drag queen."[27] The categories 'woman' and 'man' cease to appear natural. Without such clearly natural or origi-

26 Butler, *Gender Trouble*, p. 123. For additional discussion of the creation of an apparently natural gender identity through repetitive gender performances, see Judith Butler, "Imitation and Gender Insubordination," in *Inside/Out: Lesbian Theories, Gay Theories*, ed. Diana Fuss (New York: Routledge, 1991).

27 Quote of the week from Allan Berube in *City on a Hill* 26, no. 30 (1992): 10. In "Sexism," Frye similarly comments that "heterosexual critics of queers' 'role-playing' ought to look at themselves in the mirror on their way out for a night on the town to see who's in drag. The answer is, everybody is." (p. 29).

nal gender identities, lesbians' subordinate status cannot be rationalized on the grounds that lesbians are unnatural, imitative beings. And, one might add, the exclusively heterosexual organization of sexuality, romantic love, marriage, and the family begin to appear arbitrary.

Because challenging heterosexual dominance and compulsory compliance with heterosexual sex/gender categories depends on deviant performances that reconfigure the elements of 'man' and 'woman', Butler rejects feminist attempts to "outlaw" butch and femme lesbian identities.

> Lesbianism that defines itself in radical exclusion from heterosexuality deprives itself of the capacity to resignify the very heterosexual constructs by which it is partially and inevitably constituted. As a result, that lesbian strategy would consolidate compulsory heterosexuality in its oppressive forms.
>
> The more insidious and effective strategy it seems is a thoroughgoing appropriation and redeployment of the categories of identity themselves.[28]

Terralee Bensinger gives a similar reading of butch-femme representations within lesbian pornography. Like Butler, she stresses the political significance of displacing "traditional heterosexual postures" of masculinity and femininity from their supposedly natural home on the heterosexual couple's bodies to lesbian couple's bodies.[29] "The important thing here is that the reworking of these codes, within a lesbian context, de-naturalizes the illusion of a 'natural' heterosexuality (where such codes are 'appropriately' attached to female and male bodies in a sex/gender suture)."[30] In her view, however, the effectiveness of butch-femme representations depends not only upon the displacement of masculinity and femininity onto nonheterosexual bodies but also upon their shifting and ambivalent inscription on lesbian bodies. When elements of masculinity and femininity appear on the same body or shift back and forth between the bodies of the lesbian couple, gen-

---

28   Butler, *Gender Trouble*, p. 128.

29   Bensinger, p. 84.

30   Ibid.

der is most fully destabilized and denaturalized.

But have Butler and Bensinger really responded to the *feminist* critique of butch-femme role-playing? I think not. A feminist might well raise the following objection: butch and femme lesbianism may indeed undermine heterosexual society. It does not follow, however, that butch-femme lesbianism undermines patriarchy. The original objection still stands: butch lesbianism leaves in place the patriarchal equation of masculinity with power and dominance, while femme lesbianism may indeed undermine heterosexual society. It does not follow, however, that butch-femme lesbianism undermines patriarchy. The original objection still stands: butch lesbianism leaves in place the patriarchal equation of masculinity with power and dominance, while femme lesbianism leaves in place the patriarchal equation of femininity with weakness and subordination. Butler's, and perhaps also Bensinger's, political program would at best simply replace heterosexuality-based patriarchy (male power), with masculinity-based patriarchy (masculine power). Under masculinity-based patriarchy, anatomical females and males would have an equal opportunity to appropriate masculine power of feminine individuals, who themselves could be either anatomically male or female.

What the disagreement between Butler and many feminists reveals is the fact that challenging heterosexual society and challenging patriarchy are not the same thing. The feminist political opposition to patriarchal power relations disables feminists from effectively challenging patriarchal society. But neither Butler nor feminists who critique butch and femme lesbians see this. Both assume the *identity* of feminist politics and lesbian politics. This is simply a mistake. Heterosexuality and patriarchy are analytically distinct social systems, just as capitalism and patriarchy are distinct. Patriarchy can survive just as easily in a nonheterosexual society. Heterosexual societies simply require that masculinity be united with a male body and desire for women and that femininity be united with a female body and desire for men. Heterosexual systems do *not* depend on femininity and masculinity being defined and valued the way they are in patriarchal societies. Matriarchies are heterosexual systems.[31]

Given this, one should expect that feminist politics and lesbian politics, though typically overlapping, may sometimes part com-

31   Wittig makes this point in "One is Not Born a Woman," p. 10.

pany. Moreover, when those politics do conflict, there is no reason to expect that feminist lesbians will or should give priority to feminist politics. Being a woman (or better, being mistaken for a woman) and being oppressed as a woman are often not the most important facts in a lesbian's life. Being a lesbian and being oppressed as a lesbian often matter more.

WHICH HETEROSEXUALITY?

I said at the beginning that one main reason why 'lesbian issue' tends to collapse into 'feminist issue' is that the most well-developed model of heterosexuality available to lesbian feminist theorizing is one that takes heterosexuality to be both product and essential support of patriarchy. The Radicalesbians, Monique Wittig, Charlotte Bunch, Adrienne Rich, and more recently Marilyn Frye all take this view.[32] On this feminist reading of heterosexuality, what defines heterosexuality is the requirement that women be in a dependent and subordinate relation to men. I have already argued that looking at heterosexuality this way results in claiming too much for lesbians. Lesbianism is mistakenly read as the quintessential form of feminist revolt. I intend to begin this section by expanding on the argument against reducing the institution of heterosexuality to (a part of) the institution of male dominance. I will then turn to Janice Raymond's and Sarah Hoagland's feminist attempts to avoid claiming too much for lesbians. Their strategy involves locating the political problem in a particular *style* of heterosexualist interaction rather than in heterosexuality itself. This strategy, I will argue, results in claiming too little for lesbians by denying that there is anything intrinsically political in lesbians' revolt against the rule of heterosexuality. I will conclude with quite a different reading of heterosexuality, one that I take to be closer to a lesbian view, if farther from a feminist one.

Heterosexuality as Male Dominance

Heterosexuality, in Wittig's view, is a political and economic system of male dominance. The heterosexual contract (to which only men have consented) stipulates than women belong to men. In

32   Marilyn Frye, "Willful Virgin or Do You Have to Be a Lesbian to Be a Feminist?" in *Willful Virgin: Essays in Feminism* (Freedom, Calif.: Crossing, 1992).

particular, women's reproductive labor, including both child rearing and domestic chores, belongs to men by "natural" right much as a slave's labor belongs to its master's by natural right. It is thus heterosexuality that enables men to appropriate women's labor and that supports a system of male dominance. In Wittig's view, lesbian refusal to be heterosexual challenges this system of male dominance because being lesbian fundamentally means refusing to accept the "economic, ideological and political power of men."[33] Wittig's equation of lesbian resistance with feminist resistance is both obvious and explicit. She claims that to be a feminist is to fight for the disappearance of the sex-class 'woman' by refusing to participate in the heterosexual relations that created the sex-class 'woman' in the first place.[34] To be a feminist just *is* to be a lesbian.

In "Lesbians in Revolt," Charlotte Bunch similarly equates heterosexuality with male control over women's labor; and like Wittig, she regards lesbianism as a political revolt against a system in which neither a woman nor her labor belong to herself. "The lesbian . . . refuses to be a man's property, to submit to the unpaid labor system of housework and childcare. She rejects the nuclear family as the basic unit of production and consumption in capitalist society."[35] In Bunch's view, commitment to heterosexuality is necessarily a commitment to supporting a male world, and thus a barrier to struggle against women's oppression. "Being a lesbian means ending identification with, allegiance to, dependence on, and support of heterosexuality. It means ending your personal stake in the male world so that you join women individually and collectively in the struggle to end oppression."[36]

At least two different objections might be raised to Wittig's and Bunch's implicit claim that one must be a lesbian and be a feminist. First, lesbianism only challenges male control in the family. But women's labor power is also extensively controlled in the public sphere through male bosses, absence of maternity leave, sexual harassment, the job requirement of an "approximately" feminine appearance, insufficient availability of day care, sex segregation of women into lower paid jobs, and so on. As Ann Fer-

33   Wittig, "One is Not Born a Woman," p. 13.

34   Ibid., p. 14.

35   Bunch, "Lesbians in Revolt," p. 65.

36   Ibid., p. 166.

guson observes, enforced heterosexuality "may be one of the mechanisms [of male dominance], but it surely is not the single or sufficient one. Others, such as the control of female biological reproduction, male control of state and political power, and economic systems involving discrimination based on class and race, seem analytically distinct from coercive heterosexuality, yet are causes which support and perpetuate male dominance."[37] Moreover, given both the decline of male power within the nuclear family and of the nuclear family itself, one might well claim that the public control of women's productive and reproductive labor is far more critical to the maintenance of patriarchy than the private control of women's labor within the nuclear family.

While the first objection focuses on the way that lesbianism may not be the only or even most fundamental means of resisting patriarchy, a second objection focuses on the fact that the kind of resistance being claimed for lesbians in fact belongs generally to feminists. As an empirical generalization about heterosexual relations, it is true that men continue to exercise control over women's private and public work lives. As Wittig might put it, it "goes without saying" in the heterosexual social contract that women will assume primary responsibility for child rearing and domestic labor, that they will adjust their public work lives to the exigencies of their male partner's, and that they will be at least partially economically dependent on their partner's income. But there are any number of ways of evading the terms of this contract without ceasing to be heterosexual. Thus the claim that heterosexual relations are male dominant ones in insufficient to support the claim that only lesbians are genuine resisters. Indeed, the heterosexual feminist who insists on a more equal partnership may resist patriarchy more effectively than many lesbians. As both Janice Raymond and Sarah Hoagland have argued, the importation of hetero-relations into lesbian relationships enables patriarchal ways of thinking to be sustained within lesbian relationship themselves.[38]

37   Ann Ferguson, "Patriarchy, Sexual Identity, and the Sexual Revolution," in Anne Ferguson, Jacquelyn N. Zita, and Kathryn Pyne Addelson, "Viewpoint: On 'Compulsory Heterosexuality and Lesbian Existence': Defining the Issues," Signs 7 (1981): 147-88, p. 159.

38   Hoagland.

Both Raymond and Hoagland avoid equating 'lesbian' with 'feminist' by distinguishing heterosexuality from 'hetero-relations' (Raymond) and 'heterosexualism' (Hoagland). Within their writing, 'heterosexuality' retains its customary referent to sexual object choice. 'Hetero-relations' and 'heterosexualism' refer to the patriarchal nature of male-female relations in both the private and public spheres. According to Raymond, in a hetero-relational society, "most of women's personal, social, political, professional, and economic relations are defined by the ideology that woman is for man."[39] Hoagland similarly claims that heterosexualism "is a particular economic, political, and emotional relationship between men and women: men must dominate women and women must subordinate themselves to men in any number of ways. As a result, men presume access to women while women remain riveted on men and are unable to sustain a community of women."[40] It is, in their view, hetero-relationalism, not heterosexuality, per se, that subordinates women to men.

By distinguishing hetero-relations and heterosexualism from heterosexuality Raymond and Hoagland avoid exaggerating the feminist element in lesbianism. Both recognize the potential failure of lesbians to disengage from heterosexualism. Lesbians themselves may be misogynistic and may engage in the same dominance-subordination relations that typify heterosexualism. Thus lesbian resistance to heterosexuality is not automatically a resistance to patriarchy. Because Raymond and Hoagland are sensitive to this fact, they are able to subject lesbian relations to feminist critique in a productive way. In addition, by recognizing that heterosexual women can redefine their relations to men in such a way that they both leave space for gyn-affectionate relations with women and refuse to participate in hetero-relations with men, Raymond avoids pitting lesbians against heterosexual women within the feminist community in a battle over who counts as a "true" feminist.

Their attempt, however, to avoid claiming too much for lesbianism comes at the cost of ultimately claiming too little for it. By

39   Raymond, *A Passion for Friends*, p. 11.

40   Hoagland, p. 29.

putting the concept of hetero-relations or heterosexualism at the centre of their lesbian feminism, both effectively eliminate space for a *lesbian* theory. Within their work, lesbian resistance to heterosexuality does not, in itself, have either political or conceptual significance. Whatever political significance lesbian personal lives may have is due entirely to the presence of or resistance to hetero-relations within those lives. The reduction of lesbian politics to feminist politics is quite obvious in Raymond's "Putting the Politics Back into Lesbianism."[41] There, Raymond sharply criticizes lesbian lifestylers and sexual libertarians for failure to see that in advocating an anything-goes sexuality (including lesbian pornography and s/m) as the path to liberation, they are simply repeating the patriarchal image of woman as essentially sexual being. Moreover, as I mentioned earlier, insofar as lesbian lifestylers advocate aggressive and violent forms of sexuality, they are simply putting a "male-constructed sexuality in drag."[42] What I want to underscore in Raymond's critique is that putting politics into lesbianism means putting *feminist* politics into lesbianism. She does not demand that lesbians put resistance to heterosexuality and to lesbian oppression at the centre of their lives. Thus she does not ask whether or not lesbian s/m promotes *lesbian* politics.

One important consequence of equating lesbian with feminist politics in this way is that lesbians who have suffered the worst oppression, for example, the 1950s butches and femmes who risked repeated arrest and police harassment, often turn out to be the least politically interesting from a feminist point of view. Shane Phelan's criticism of Adrienne Rich for marginalized "real" lesbians who resisted heterosexuality and for giving nonlesbians who resisted dependency on men pride of place on her lesbian continuum applies generally to those who equate lesbian politics with feminist politics: "It becomes clear that the existence of these women [lesbians], those who have been the targets of abuse for decades, is less interesting to lesbian feminists than the existence of women who never called themselves lesbians, never thought of themselves as such, and never faced the consequences of that. The sort of lesbian who laid the groundwork, built the urban subcultures, that allowed lesbians to find one another before feminism, is

---

41   Raymond, "Putting the Politics Back into Lesbianism." See also her criticisms of lesbian s/m in the chapter "Obstacles to Female Friendship," in *A Passion for Friends*.

42   Raymond, "Putting the Politics Back into Lesbianism," p. 150.

remembered primarily in the works of male historians. The relevant community is lesbian feminist, with the emphasis, curiously, on the feminist rather than the lesbian."[43]

From a feminist point of view whose political yardstick measures only distance from patriarchal practices and institutions, butches and femmes, lesbian sex radicals who promote pornography and s/m, lesbian mothers, and married lesbians all fail to measure up. All are vulnerable to the charge of appropriating for women and between women the very practices and institutions that have served so well to oppress women. Yet it is precisely these women, who insist on the reality and value of romance, sexuality, parenting, and marriage between women, who resist most strongly heterosexual society's reservation of the private sphere for male-female couples only. From a lesbian point of view whose political yardstick measures resistance to heterosexuality and heterosexual privilege, they are neither politically uninteresting nor assimilationist.

Not only does this focus on heterosexualism rather than heterosexuality leave no space for understanding the inherently political nature of lesbianism, it also leaves no space for understanding the significance of specifically lesbian love. For instance, like Rich's notion of a lesbian continuum that includes both lesbian and heterosexual women, Raymond's "use of the term *Gyn/affection* expresses a *continuum* of female friendship" that includes some (but not all) lesbian love as well as friendships between heterosexual women.[44] In her view, it is in gyn/affection that women seize power from men and engage in a woman-identified act. Thus it is gyn/affection that is politically significant. Specifically lesbian sexual and romantic attraction to women is left without any politically or conceptually interesting place to be. Raymond is by no means the first or only lesbian feminist to marginalize lesbian love in favor of a form of love between women that is more directly tied to feminist solidarity. Bunch, for example, claims that "the lesbian, woman-identified-woman commits herself to women not only as an alternative to oppressed male-female relationship but primarily because she *loves* women."[45] That

43 Phelan, p. 69.

44 Raymond, *A Passion for Friends*, p. 15.

45 Bunch, "Lesbians in Revolt," p. 162.

this is not a particularized conception of love but rather feminist "love" of women as a class becomes clear in the way she connects lesbian love with class solidarity: "When women do give primary energies to other women, then it is possible to concentrate fully on building a movement for our liberation."[46] In a more recent piece, Nett Hart similarly equates lesbian love with love of women as a class: "We love women as a class and we love specific women. We embrace the concept that women can be loved, that women are inherently worthy of love."[47] In both Bunch and Hart, there is a conceptual slide from 'love' in the sense of a sexual-romantic love of a particular woman to 'love' in the sense of valuing and respecting members of the category 'woman'. Although Raymond differs in being much more careful to keep the two sorts of love conceptually separated, all three prioritize love of women as a class. From a feminist point of view it is indeed the capacity to value members of the category 'woman' and to form strong primary bonds of friendship with many women that matters politically. But this is not lesbian love. Lesbians fall in love with, want to make love to, decide to set up a household with a particular other woman, not a class of women. It is for this particularized, sexualized love that lesbians are penalized in heterosexual society. Because of this, lesbian theory needs to move specifically lesbian love to the centre of its political stage.

None of these remarks are intended either to undercut the value for feminists of work being done by lesbians or the need to subject lesbian practice to feminist critique. They are meant to suggest that a full-blown lesbian feminism cannot afford to reduce the political institution of heterosexuality to an institution of male dominance.

Heterosexuality as a Political System

I have been arguing so far that reading heterosexuality and lesbianism solely in relation to patriarchal gender politics fails to yield an adequate picture of lesbians' political position. I turn now to an exploration of the thesis that heterosexuality is itself a political system that shapes our social structure as systematically as do patriarchal, racial imperialist, and class systems.

---

46   Ibid.

47   Nett Hart, "Lesbian Desire as Social Action," in Allen, ed., p. 297.

I do not mean to deny that in patriarchal societies heterosexuality enables what Gayle Rubin called the "traffic in women." I *do* mean to deny that heterosexual systems' only function is to support a system of male privilege. I suggest instead that heterosexual systems, whether patriarchal or not, function to insure reproduction by making the male-female unit fundamental to social structure, particularly, though not exclusively, to the structure of what might broadly be called the private sphere. That is, heterosexual systems assign the heterosexual couple-based family a privileged social status as the only legitimate site of sexuality, child bearing, child rearing, the care of individuals' physical and emotional needs, the maintenance of a household, and the creation of kinship bonds. It is because the purpose of heterosexual systems is to sustain reproduction that threats to that system — inevitably evoke in Anglo-American history some version of the race suicide argument.

Heterosexuality then is not just a matter of the orientation of individual sexual desire. It is a method of socially organizing a broad spectrum of reproductive activities. Accordingly, the taboo on homosexuality does not simply outlaw same-sex desire. More basically, it outlaws the female-female or male-male couple as the site of any reproductive activities.[48] Thus, if one wants a complete set of the regulations that constitute the taboo on lesbianism and homosexuality, one needs to look at all of the practices that directly or indirectly insure that the family will be built around a male-female pair. The social and legal prohibition of same-sex sex is only the tip of the iceberg of the systematic heterosexualization of social life.

This socially foundational status of the male-female couple gets ideologically expressed and reinforced through the language of naturalness: the individuals who make up society are taken to be naturally gendered as men or women, naturally heterosexual, and naturally inclined to establish a family based around the male-female reproductive unit. The alleged natural inevitability of gender differences, heterosexual desire, and heterosexually reproductive families enables heterosexual societies to take it for granted that

---

48 This helps to explain why it is relatively easy to garner toleration of lesbianism and homosexuality as private bedroom practices, while attempts to sanction lesbian and gay parenting and marriages meet with intense resistance. I thank Mary Going for bringing me to see the critical importance of challenging the heterosexual couple-based family.

"of course" the social, economic and legal structure of any society will, and ought to, reflect these basic facts.

Social practices, norms, and institutions are designed to meet heterosexual systems' needs to produce sex/gender dimorphism — masculine males and feminine females — so that desire can then be heterosexualized. Gendered behavioral norms, gendered rites of passage, a sexual division of labor, and the like produce differently gendered persons out of differently sexed persons. Prohibitions against gender crossing (e.g., against cross-dressing, effeminacy in men, mannishness in women) also help sustain the dimorphism necessary to heterosexual desire.

Children and especially adolescents are carefully prepared for heterosexual interaction. They are given heterosexual sex education, advice for attracting the opposite sex, norms for heterosexual behavior, and appropriate social occasions (such as dancing or dating rituals) for enacting desire. Adult heterosexuality is further sustained through erotica and pornography, heterosexualized humor, heterosexualized dress, romance novels, and so on.

Heterosexual societies take it for granted that men and women will bond in an intimate relationship, ultimately founding a family. As a result, social conventions, economic arrangements, and the legal structure treat the heterosexual couple as a single, and singularly important, social unit. The couple is represented linguistically (boyfriend-girlfriend, husband-wife) and is treated socially as a single unit (e.g., in joint invitations or in receiving joint gifts). It is legally licensed and legally supported through such entitlements as communal property, joint custody or adoption of children, the power to give proxy consent within the couple. The couple is also recognized in the occupational structure via such provisions as spousal health care benefits and restrictions on nepotism. Multiple practices and institutions help heterosexual individuals to couple and create families and support the continuation of those couples and couple-based families. These include dating services, matchmakers, introductions to eligible partners, premarital counseling, marriage counseling, marriage and divorce law, adoption services, reproductive technologies, family rates, family health care benefits, tax deductions for married couples, and so on.

The sum total of all the social, economic, and legal arrangements that support the sexual and relational coupling of men with women constitutes heterosexual privilege. And it is privilege of a particular sort. Heterosexuals do not simply claim *greater* socio-politico-legal standing than nonheterosexuals. They claim as natural and normal and arrangement where *only* heterosexuals have socio-politico-legal standing. Lesbians and gay men are not recognized as social beings because they cannot enter into the most basic unit, the male-female couple. Within heterosexual systems the only social arrangements that apply to nonheterosexuals are eliminative in nature. The coercive force of the criminal law, institutionalized discrimination, "therapeutic" treatment, and individual prejudice and violence is marshaled against the existence of gay and lesbian men. At best, lesbians and gay men have negative social reality. Lesbians are not-women engaged in nonsex within nonrelationships that may constitute a nonfamily.

It would be a mistake to think that legal prohibition of discrimination on the basis of sexual orientation or legal recognition of domestic partnerships would give lesbians and gay men any genuine socio-politico-legal standing. The legal reduction of lesbianism to mere sexuality which is implicit in "sexual orientation" legislation only reconfirms the heterosexual assumption that lesbianism cannot itself provide the site for the broad spectrum of reproductive activities. Only heterosexuality, which "everyone knows" is more than mere sexual desire, can provide this site in the form of the heterosexual couple. Because lesbianism is supposedly mere sex and not a mode of sociality, no fundamental alteration needs to be made in the social practices and institutions that constitute the private sphere. Domestic partnership laws fall in the same boat. They set up what amount to separate but allegedly equal spheres for heterosexuals and nonheterosexuals. Heterosexuals retain coverage by marriage laws. All other possible private arrangements are covered under domestic partnerships. The point of excluding lesbian and gay marriages from marriage law itself is, of course, to reaffirm heterosexual society's most basic belief that only the male-female couple constitutes a natural, basic social unit.

In short, unlike the heterosexual woman, including the heterosexual feminist, the lesbian experience of the institution of heterosexuality is of a system that makes her sexual, affectional, domestic, and reproductive life unreal. Within heterosexual society, the experience between women of sexual fulfilment, of falling in love, of marrying, of creating a home, of starting a family have no social reality. Unlike the heterosexual feminist, the lesbian has no socially supported private sphere, not even an oppressive one.

Failure to see the difference between the heterosexual feminist's and the lesbian's relation to the institution of heterosexuality may well result in mislocating lesbian politics. From a feminist point of view, sexual interaction, romantic love, marriage, and the family are all danger zones because all have been distorted to serve male interests. It thus does not behoove feminist politics to begin championing the importance of sexual interaction, romantic love, marriage, and the (couple-based) family. But it does behoove lesbian politics to start in precisely these places. Her recognition as a social being, and thus as an individual with socio-politico-legal standing, depends upon the female-female couple being recognized as a primary social unit. That in turn cannot be done without directly challenging the reservation of the primary structures of the private sphere for heterosexuals. Just as the heart of male privilege lies in the "right" of access to women, so the heart of heterosexual privilege lies in the "right" of access to sexual-romantic-marital-familial relationships.

4

Introduction

In late twentieth-century scholarship in many disciplines there is a propensity to seize highly regarded values — such as national "unity," for example, or "literacy" — and *problematize* them: to take, that is, a commonly recognized good, and discover in it questionable elements, elements which work to some people's advantage and other people's disadvantage. In "Conflict and Struggle: the Enemies or Preconditions of Basic Writing?" Min-Zhan Lu takes, broadly speaking, "education" and (slightly less broadly speaking) the education of minorities, and dismantles these notions. Like most arguments of this type, Lu's is complex, routed through many stages. She summarizes writers who exemplify certain positions, and interprets each of these positions, mapping an intricate landscape of related attitudes, interests, and strategies. Complexity is perhaps a necessary characteristic of such "problematizing" arguments, for simplified versions cannot resist the tendency of the concept to drift back into its accustomed place — as something OK, and self-evident. This is where we are used to seeing it, and our minds tend to restore it to its habitual setting.

Lu puts her argument in historical context, referring to the "open admissions" period of U.S. educational history in the 1970s, when new types of students were entering university in what people took to be great numbers. She further focusses her argument by concentrating on the teaching of writing. Although this focus may seem merely coincidental with her own professional interests (she is a teacher of writing herself), it is in fact an opportune one:

traditionally and currently, the health of "higher learning" has been gauged by measuring the quality of incoming students' writing. For a hundred years and more, people have expressed concern about students' writing. Such concern is liable to intensify during periods of relatively rapid social change.

As her title indicates, the writing Lu is interested in is "Basic Writing." What is this? One way of answering this question would be to say that Basic Writing is writing with quite a few departures from what is known as Standard English, or that Basic Writing is the kind of instruction inspired by such writing. People who produce this kind of writing are "Basic Writers." But this definition is scarcely adequate to fully identify Basic Writers, for the Basic Writing classroom often assembles people whose life experience is not equivalent to that of white, middle-class people. So Basic Writing is not just a name for a kind of writing, and the instruction it inspires, but also a sociopolitical definition. And the kind of learning that goes on in a Basic Writing classroom is not just about grammatical forms, even if this is often its overt concern.

Lu asks that we entertain ideas about language which would predict this. These ideas insist that a way of writing is a way of "consciousness" (122). So teaching people a new way of writing is much more than just correcting errors; it is confronting them with assumptions about the world which are embodied in these styles. (Hence, the resistance reported: students may not buy this new consciousness, or they may detect those assumptions, and find them in conflict with their own knowledge of the world.)

Is this acquisition of new consciousness a good thing? Lu's critique of the "acculturation" and "accommodation" models of education help us think about something we might easily accept as beneficial (of course it's good to learn new things). To get a grasp of her argument, you might keep these questions in mind:

- How does the acculturation model deny or disadvantage the experience of the "minority" student? How does it work to the advantage of those groups which already enjoy power?

- What part does the idea of "learning-for-itself" play in the acculturation model?

Perhaps more difficult to answer are these questions about the "accommodation" model, for accommodation can seem like a respectful and compassionate policy, a pleasant way to go about things:

- What is wrong with a teacher announcing that he will let students make their own "choices"? What is the difference between the "mere tolerance" of students' choices mentioned on page 135 and the better or more desirable "'tolerance for' ... contradictions and ambiguity" (Anzaldua 79) cited in the same paragraph?

The writings of Gloria Anzaldua accompany Lu through much of her argument, sustaining a vision of other possibilities for Basic Writing instruction (although we may come to the point where we don't want to use the term "Basic Writing" at all, once we recognize the way it defines enduring configurations of power and advantage). Anzaldua's wordings and thought have been, in the 1990s, often summoned to capture the spirit of analyses of the margins, the places where social categories and typifications collide, or contest one another. Eloquent as the quotations from Anzaldua are, you may find yourself uncertain as to the substance of her conceptualization of the "mestiza" consciousness. You may get a better grasp of her views by explaining to yourself the idea that "residents of the borderlands *act on rather than react to* the 'borders' cutting across society and their psyches, 'borders' which become visible as they encounter conflicting ideas and actions" (135). Consider what it means to "react to" a "border": to respect it, or submit to it, as a valid and incontestable definition of the end of one thing and the beginning of another; a manifestation of an agreed-upon division or distinction. So, for example, the 49th parallel says one is either in Canada or in the United States. It makes no provisions for being in both places at the same time, and its validity is confirmed by our "reactions" to it, our behaviour around this dividing line.

Conflict and Struggle: The Enemies or Preconditions of Basic Writing?

MIN-ZHAN LU

> Harlem taught me that light skin Black people was better look, the best to suceed, the best off fanicially etc this whole that I trying to say, that I was brainwashed and people aliked.
>   I couldn't understand why people (Black and white) couldn't get alone. So as time went along I began learned more about myself and the establishment
>
>   Sample student paper, *Errors and Expectations* 278.

> . . . Szasz was throwing her. She couldn't get through the twelve-and-a-half pages of introduction . . . .
>   One powerful reason Lucia had decided to major in psychology was that she wanted to help people like her brother, who had a psychotic break in his teens and had been in and out of hospitals since. She had lived with mental illness, had seen that look in her brother's eyes. . . . The assertion that there was no such thing as mental illness, that it was a myth, seemed incomprehensible to her. She had trouble even entertaining it as a hypothesis. . . . Szasz's bold claim was a bone sticking in her assumptive craw.
>
>   Mike Rose, *Lives on the Boundary* 183-84.

> In perceiving conflicting information and points of view, she is subjected to a swamping of her psychological borders.
>
>   Gloria Anzaldua, *Borderlands/La Frontera:*
>   *The New Mestiza* 79.

IN THE PREFACE TO *Borderlands*, Gloria Anzaldua uses her own struggle "living on borders and margins" to discuss the trials and triumphs in the lives of "border residents." The image of "border residents" captures the conflict and struggle of students like those appearing in the epigraphs. In perceiving conflicting information and points of view, a writer like Anzaldua is "subjected to a swamping of her psychological borders" (79). But attempts to cope with conflicts also bring "compensation," "joys," and "exhilaration" (Anzaldua, Preface). The border resident develops a tolerance for contradiction and ambivalence, learning to sustain contradiction and turn ambivalence into a new consciousness — "a *third* element which is *greater* than the sum of its *severed parts*": "a mestiza consciousness" (79-80; emphasis mine). Experience taught Anzaldua that this developing consciousness draws energy from the "continual creative motion that keeps breaking down the unitary aspects of each new paradigm" (80). It enables a border resident to act on rather than merely react to the conditions of her or his life, turning awareness of the situation into "inner changes" which in turn bring about "changes in society" (87).

EDUCATION AS REPOSITIONING

Anzaldua's account gathers some of the issues on which a whole range of recent composition research focuses, research on how readers and writers necessarily struggle with conflicting information and points of view as they reposition themselves in the process of reading and writing. This research recognizes that reading and writing take place at sites of political as well as linguistic conflict. It acknowledges that such a process of conflict and struggle is a source of pain but constructive as well: a new consciousness emerges from the creative motion of breaking down the rigid boundaries of social and linguistic paradigms.

Compositionists are becoming increasingly aware of the need to tell and listen to stories of life in the borderlands. The ccccBest Book Award given to Mike Rose's *Lives on the Boundary* and the Braddock Award given to Glynda Hull and Mike Rose for their research on students like Lucia attest to this increasing awareness. *College Composition and Communication* recently devoted a whole issue (February 1992) to essays which use images of "boundary," "margin," or "voice" to re-view the experience of reading and writing and teaching reading and writing within the academy (see also Lu, "From Silence to Words"; Bartholomae, "Writing on the Margins"; and Mellix). These publications and their reception indicate that the field is taking seriously two notions of writing underlying these narratives: a sense that the writer writes at a site of conflict rather than "comfortably inside or powerlessly outside the academy" (Lu, "Writing as Repositioning" 20) and a definition of "innovative writing" as cutting across rather than confining itself within boundaries of race, class, gender, and disciplinary differences.

In articulating the issues explored by these narratives from the borderlands, compositionists have found two assumptions underlying various feminist, marxist and poststructuralist theories of language useful: first, that learning a new discourse has an effect on re-forming of individual consciousness; and second, that individual consciousness is necessarily heterogeneous, contradictory, and in process (Bizzell; Flynn; Harris; Lunsford, Moglen, and Slevin; Trimbur). The need to reposition oneself and the positive use of conflict and struggle are also explored in a range of research devoted to the learning difficulties of Basic Writers (Bartholomae, "Inventing"; Fox; Horner; Hull and Rose; Lu, "Redefining"; Ritchie; Spellmeyer; Stanley). Nevertheless, such research has had limited influence on Basic Writing instruction, which continues to emphasize skills (Gould and Heyda) and to view conflict as the enemy (Schilb, Brown). I believe that this view of conflict can be traced in the work of three pioneers in Basic Writing: Kenneth Bruffee, Thomas Farrell, and Mina Shaughnessy. In what follows, I examine why this view of conflict had rhetorical power in the historical context in which these pioneers worked and in relation to two popular views of education: education as acculturation and education as accommodation. I also explore how and why this view persists among Basic Writing teachers in the 1990s.

Although Bruffee, Farrell, and Shaughnessy hold different views on the goal of education, they all treat the students' fear of acculturation and the accompanying sense of contradiction and ambiguity as a *deficit*. Even though stories of the borderlands like Anzaldua's suggest that teachers can and should draw upon students' perception of conflict as a constructive resource, these three pioneers of Basic Writing view evidence of conflict and struggle as something to be dissolved and so propose "cures" aimed at *releasing* students from their fear of acculturation. Bruffee and Farrell present students' acculturation as inevitable and beneficial. Shaughnessy promises them that learning academic discourse will not result in acculturation. Teachers influenced by the work of these pioneers tend to view all signs of conflict and struggle as the *enemy* of Basic Writing instruction. In perpetuating this view, these teachers also tend to adopt two assumptions about language: 1) an "essentialist" view of language holding that the essence of meaning precedes and is independent of language (see Lu, "Redefining" 26); 2) a view of "discourse communities" as "discursive utopias," in each of which a single, unified, and stable voice directly and completely determines the writings of all community members (Harris 12).

In the 1970s, the era of open admissions at CUNY, heated debate over the "educability" of Basic Writers gave these views of language and of conflict exceptional rhetorical power. The new field of Basic Writing was struggling to establish the legitimacy of its knowledge and expertise, and it was doing so in the context of arguments made by a group of writers — including Lionel Trilling, Irving Howe, and W. E. B. DuBois — who could be viewed as exemplary because of their ethnic or racial backgrounds, their academic success, and the popular view that all Basic Writers entering CUNY through the open admissions movement were "minority" students. The writings of Bruffee, Farrell, and Trilling concur that the goal of education is to acculturate students to the kind of academic "community" they posit. Shaughnessy, on the other hand, attempts to eliminate students' conflicting feelings towards academic discourse by reassuring them that her teaching will only "accommodate" but not weaken their existing relationship with their home cultures. Shaughnessy's approach is aligned with the argument of Irving Howe and W. E. B. DuBois, who urge teachers to honor students' resistance to deracination. Acculturation and accommodation were the dominant models of open admissions education for teachers who recognized teaching academic discourse as a way of empowering students, and in both models conflict and struggle were seen as the enemies of Basic Writing instruction.

This belief persists in several recent works by a new generation of compositionists and "minority" writers. I will read these writings from the point of view of the border resident and through a view of education as a process of repositioning. In doing so, I will also map out some directions for further demystifying conflict and struggle in Basic Writing instruction and for seeing them as the preconditions of all discursive acts.

EDUCATION AS ACCULTURATION

In *Errors and Expectations*, Mina Shaughnessy offers us one way of imagining the social and historical contexts of her work: she calls herself a trailblazer trying to survive in a "pedagogical West" (4). This metaphor captures the peripheral position of Basic Writing in English. To other members of the profession, Shaughnessy notes, Basic Writing is not one of their "'real' subjects"; nor are books on Basic Writing "important enough" either to be reviewed or to argue about ("English Professor's Malady" 92). Kenneth Bruffee also testifies to feeling peripheral. Recalling the "collaborative learning" which took place among the directors of CUNY writing programs — a group which included Bruffee himself, Donald McQuade, Mina Shaughnessy, and Harvey Wiener — he points out that the group was brought together not only by their "difficult new task" but also by their sense of having more in common with one another than with many of their "colleagues on [their] own campuses" ("On Not Listening" 4-5).

These frontier images speak powerfully of a sense of being *in* but not *of* the English profession. The questionable academic status of not only their students (seen as "ill-prepared") but also themselves (Basic Writing was mostly assigned to beginning teachers, graduate students, women, minorities, and the unemployed but tenured members of other departments) would pressure teachers like Shaughnessy and Bruffee to find legitimacy for their subject. At the same time, they had to do so by persuading both college administrators who felt "hesitation and discomfort" towards open admissions policies and "senior and tenured professorial staff" who either resisted or did not share their commitment (Lyons 175). Directly or indirectly, these pioneers had to respond to, argue with, and persuade the "gatekeepers" and "converters" Shaughnessy describes in "Diving In." It is in the context of such challenges that we must understand the key terms the pioneers use and the questions they consider — and overlook — in establishing the problematics of Basic Writing.

One of the most vehement gatekeepers at CUNY during the initial period of open admissions was Geoffrey Wagner (Professor of English at City College). In *The End of Education*, Wagner posits a kind of "university" in which everyone supposedly pursues learning for its own sake, free of all "worldly" — social , economic, and political — interests. To Wagner, open admissions students are the inhabitants of the "world" outside the sort of scholarly "community" which he claims existed at Oxford and City College. They are dunces (43), misfits (129), hostile mental children (247), and the most sluggish of animals (163). He describes a group of Panamanian "girls" taking a Basic Writing course as "abusive, stupid, and hostile" (128). Another student is described as sitting "in a half-lotus pose in back of class with a transistor strapped to his Afro, and nodding off every two minutes" (134). Wagner calls the Basic Writing program at City a form of political psychotherapy (145), a welfare agency, and an entertainment center (173). And he calls Shaughnessy "The Circe of CCNY's remedial English program" (129). To Wagner, Basic Writers would cause "the end of education" because they have intellects comparable to those of beasts, the retarded, the psychotic, or children, and because they are consumed by non-"academic" — i.e. racial, economic, and political — interests and are indifferent to "learning."

Unlike the "gatekeepers," Louis Heller (Classics Professor, City College) represents educators who seemed willing to shoulder the burden of converting the heathens but disapproved of the ways in which CUNY was handling the conversion. Nonetheless, in *The Death of the American University* Heller approaches the "problems" of open admissions students in ways similar to Wagner's. He contrasts the attitudes of open admissions students and of old Jewish City College students like himself:

> In those days ["decades ago"] there was a genuine hunger, and deprivation, and discrimination too, but when a child received failing marks no militant parent group assailed the teacher. Instead parent and child agonized over the subject, placing the responsibility squarely on the child who was given to know that *he* had to measure up to par, not that he was the victim of society, a wicked school system, teachers who didn't understand him, or any of the other pseudosociological nonsense now handed out. (138)

According to Heller, the parents of open admissions students are too "militant." As a result, the students' minds are stuffed with "pseudosociological nonsense" about their victimization by the educational system. The "problem" of open admissions students, Heller suggests, is their militant attitude, which keeps them from trying to "agonize over the subject" and "measure up to par."

Wagner predicts the "end of education" because of the "*arrival in urban academe of large*, indeed *overwhelming, numbers of hostile mental children*" (247; emphasis mine). As the titles of Heller's chapters suggest, Heller too believes that a "Death of the American University" would inevitably result from the "Administrative Failure of Nerve" or "Capitulation Under Force" to "Violence on Campus" which he claims to have taken place at City College. The images of education's end or death suggest that both Wagner and Heller assume that the goal of education is the acculturation of students into an "educated community." They question the "educability" of open admissions students because they *fear* that these students would not only be hostile to the education they promote but also take it over — that is, change it. The apocalyptic tone of their book titles suggests their fear that the students' "hostile" or "militant" feelings towards the existing educational system would weaken the ability of the "American University" to realize its primary goal — to acculturate. Their writings show that their view of the "problems" of open admissions students and their view of the goal of education sustain one another.

This view of education as a process of acculturation is shared by Lionel Trilling, another authority often cited as an exemplary minority student (see, for example, Howe, "Living" 108). In a paper titled "The Uncertain Future of the Humanistic Educational Ideal" delivered in 1974, Trilling claims that the view of higher education "as the process of initiation into membership" in a "new, larger, and more complex community" is "surely" not a "mistaken conception" (*The Last Decade* 170). The word "initiation," Trilling points out, designates the "ritually prescribed stages by which a person is brought into a community" (170-71). "Initiation" requires "submission," demanding that one "shape" and "limit" oneself to "*a* self, *a* life" and "preclude any other kind of selfhood remaining available" to one (171, 175; emphasis mine). Trilling doubts that contemporary American culture will find "congenial" the kind of "initiation" required by the "humanistic educational ideal" (171). For contemporary "American culture" too often encourages one to resist any doctrine that does not sustain "a multiplicity of options" (175). And Trilling admits to feeling "saddened" by the unlikelihood that "an ideal of education closely and positively related to the humanistic educational traditions of the past" will be called into being in contemporary America (161).

The trials of "initiation" are the subject of Trilling's short story "Notes on a Departure." The main character, a young college professor about to leave a university town, is portrayed as being forced to wrestle with an apparition which he sometimes refers to as the "angel of Jewish solitude" and, by the end of the story, as "a red-haired comedian" whose "face remained blank and idiot" (*Of This Time* 53, 55). The apparition hounds the professor, often reminding of the question "'What for?' Jews did not do such things" (54). Towards the end of the story, the professor succeeds in freeing himself from the apparition. Arriving at a state of "readiness," he realizes that he would soon have to "find his *own* weapon, his *own* adversary, his *own* things to do" — findings in which "the red-haired figure . . . would have *no* part" (55; emphasis mine).

This story suggests — particularly in view of Trilling's concern for the "uncertain future" of the "humanistic educational ideal" in the 1970s — that contemporary Americans, especially those from minority cultural groups, face a dilemma: the need to combat voices which remind them of the "multiplicity of options." The professor needs to "wrestle with" two options of "selfhood." First, he must free himself from the authority of the "angel"/"comedian." Then, as the title "Notes on a Departure" emphasizes, he must free himself from the "town." Trilling's representation of the professor's need to "depart" from the voice of his "race" and of the "town" indirectly converges with the belief held by Wagner and Heller that the attitudes "parents" and "society" transmit to open admissions students would pull them away from the "university" and hinder their full initiation — acculturation — into the "educated" community.

Read in the 1990s, these intersecting approaches to the "problems" of "minority" students might seem less imposing, since except perhaps for Trilling, the academic prestige of these writers has largely receded. Yet we should not underestimate the authority these writers had within the academy. As both the publisher and the author of *The End of Education* (1976) remind us within the first few pages of the book, Wagner is not only a graduate of Oxford but a full professor at City College and author of a total of twenty-nine books of poetry, fiction, literary criticism, and sociology. Heller's *The Death of the American University* (1973) indicates that he has ten years' work at the doctoral or postdoctoral level in three fields, a long list of publications, and years of experience as both a full professor of classics and an administrator at City College (12). Furthermore, their fear of militancy accorded with prevalent reactions to the often violent conflict in American cities and college campuses during the 1960s and 70s. It was in the context of such powerful discourse that composition teachers argued for not only the "educability" of open admissions students but also the ability of the "pioneer" educators to "educate" them. Bruffee's and Farrell's eventual success in establishing the legitimacy of their knowledge and expertise as Basic Writing teachers, I believe, come in part from a conjuncture in the arguments of the two Basic Writing pioneers and those of Wagner, Heller, and Trilling.

For example, Thomas Farrell presents the primary goal of Basic Writing instruction as acculturation — a move from "orality" to "literacy." He treats open admissions students as existing in a "residual orality": "literate patterns of thought have not been interiorized, have not displaced oral patterns, in them" ("Open Admissions" 248). Referring to Piaget, Ong, and Bernstein, he offers environmental rather than biological reasons for Basic Writers' "orality" — their membership in "communities" where "orality" is the dominant mode of communication. To Farrell, the emigration from "orality" to "literacy" is unequivocally beneficial for everyone, since it mirrors the progression of history. At the same time, Farrell recognizes that such a move will inevitably be accompanied by "anxiety": "The *psychic strain* entailed in moving from a highly oral frame of mind to a more literate frame of mind is *too great* to allow rapid movement" (252; emphasis mine). Accordingly, he promotes teaching strategies aimed at "reducing anxiety" and establishing "a supportive environment." For example, he urges teachers to use the kind of "collaborative learning" Bruffee proposes so that they can use "oral discourse to improve written discourse" ("Open Admissions" 252-53; "Literacy" 456-57). He reminds teachers that "highly oral students" won't engage in the "literate" modes of reasoning "unless they are shown how and reminded to do so often," and even then will do so only "gradually" ("Literacy" 456).

Kenneth Bruffee also defines the goals of Basic Writing in terms of the students' acculturation into a new "community." According to Bruffee, Basic Writers have already been acculturated within "local communities" which have prepared them for only "the narrowest and most limited" political and economic relations ("On Not Listening" 7). The purpose of education is to "reacculturate" the students — to help them "gain membership in another such community" by learning its "language, mores, and values" (8). However, Bruffee believes that the "trials of changing allegiance from one cultural community to another" demand that teachers use "collaborative learning" in small peer groups. This method will "create a *temporary transition* or 'support' group that [one] can join *on the way*" (8; emphasis mine). This "transition group," he maintains, will offer Basic Writers an arena for sharing their "trials," such as the "uncertain, nebulous, and protean thinking that occurs in the process of change" and the "painful process" of gaining new awareness ("On Not Listening" 11; "Collaborative Learning" 640).

Two points bind Bruffee's argument to Farrell's and enhance the rhetorical power of their arguments for the Wagners, Hellers, and Trillings. First, both arguments assume that the goal of education is acculturation into a "literate" community. The image of students who are "changing allegiance from one cultural community to another" (Bruffee), like the image of students "moving" from "orality" to "literacy" (Farrell), posits that "discourse communities" are discrete and autonomous entities rather than interactive cultural forces. When discussing the differences between "orality" and "literacy," Farrell tends to treat these "discourses" as creating coherent but distinct modes of thinking: "speaking" vs.

"reading," "clichés" vs. "explained and supported generalizations," "additive" vs. "inductive or deductive" reasoning. Bruffee likewise sets *"coherent* but *entirely* local communities" against a community which is "broader, highly diverse, *integrated"* ("On Not Listening" 7; emphasis mine). Both Farrell and Bruffee use existing analyses of "discourse communities" to set up a seemingly non-political hierarchy between academic and non-academic "communities." They then use the hierarchy to justify implicitly the students' need to be acculturated by the more advanced or broader "community." Thus, they can be construed as promising "effective" ways of appeasing the kind of "hostility" or "militancy" feared in open admissions students. The appeal of this line of thinking is that it protects the autonomy of the "literate community" while also professing a solution to the "threat" of open admissions students seem to pose to the university. Farrell and Bruffee provide methods aimed at keeping students like Anzaldua, Lucia, and the writer of Shaughnessy's sample paper from moving the points of view and discursive forms they have developed in their home "communities" into the "literate community" and also at persuading such students to willingly "move" into that "literate community."

Second, both Bruffee and Farrell explicitly look for teaching methods aimed at reducing the feelings of "anxiety" or "psychic strain" accompanying the process of acculturation. They thus present these feelings as signs of the students' still being "on the way" from one community to another, i.e., as signs of their failure to complete their acculturation or education. They suggest that the students are experiencing these trials only because they are still in "transition," bearing ties to both the old and new communities but not fully "departed" from one nor comfortably "inside" the other. They also suggest that these experiences, like the transition or support groups, are "temporary" (Bruffee, "On Not Listening" 8). In short, they sustain the impression that these experiences ought to and will disappear once the students get comfortably settled in the new community and sever or diminish their ties with the old. Any sign of heterogeneity, uncertainty, or instability is viewed as problematic; hence conflict and struggle are the enemies of Basic Writing instruction.

This linkage between students' painful conflicts and the teacher's effort to assuage them had rhetorical power in America during the 1970s because it could be perceived as accepting rather than challenging the gatekeepers' and converters' arguments that the pull of non-"academic" forces — "society" (Wagner), "militant parents"

(Heller), and minority "race" or "American culture" at large (Trilling) — would render the open admissions students less "educable" and so create a "problem" in their education. It feeds the fear that the pulls of conflicting "options," "selfhoods," or "lives" promoted by antagonistic "communities" would threaten the university's ability to acculturate the Basic Writers. At the same time, this linkage also offers a "support system" aimed at releasing the gatekeepers and converters from their fear. For example, the teaching strategies Farrell promotes, which explicitly aim to support students through their "psychic strain," are also aimed at gradually easing them into "interiorizing" modes of thinking privileged by the "literate community," such as "inductive or deductive" reasoning or "detached, analytic forms of thinking" ("Literacy" 455, 456). Such strategies thus provide a support system for not only the students but also the kind of discursive utopia posited by Trilling's description of the "humanistic educational ideal," Heller's "American University," and Wagner's "education." Directly and indirectly, the pedagogies aimed at "moving" students from one culture to another support and are supported by gatekeepers' and converters' positions towards open admissions students.

The pedagogies of Bruffee and Farrell recognize the "psychic strain" or the "trials" experienced by those reading and writing at sites of contradiction, experiences which are depicted by writers like Trilling ("Notes on a Departure"), Anzaldua, and Rose and witnessed by teachers in their encounters with students like Lucia and the writer of Shaughnessy's sample paper. Yet, for two reasons, the approaches of Bruffee and Farrell are unlikely to help such students cope with the conflict "swamping" their "psychological borders." First, these approaches suggest that the students' primary task is to change allegiance, to "learn" and "master" the "language, mores, and values" of the academic community presented in the classroom by passively internalizing them and actively rejecting all points of view or information which run counter to them (Bruffee, "On Not Listening" 8). For the author of Shaughnessy's sample student paper, this could mean learning to identify completely with the point of view of authorities like the Heller of *The Death of the American University* and thus rejecting "militant" thoughts about the "establishment" in order to "agonize over the subject." For Lucia, this could mean learning to identify with the Trilling of "Notes on a Departure," viewing her ability to forget the look in her brother's eyes as a precondition of becoming a psychologist like Szasz. Yet students like Lucia might resist what the classroom seems to indicate they must do in order to achieve academic "success." As Rose reminds us, one of the reasons Lucia decided to major in psychology was to help people like her brother. Students like these are likely to get very little help or guidance from teachers like Bruffee or Farrell.

Secondly, though Bruffee and Farrell suggest that the need to cope with conflicts is a temporary experience for students unfamiliar with and lacking mastery of dominant academic values and forms, Rose's account of his own education indicates that similar experiences of "confusion, anger, and fear" are not at all temporary (Rose 235-36). During Rose's high school years, his teacher Jack MacFarland had successfully helped him cope with his "sense of linguistic exclusion" complicated by "various cultural differences" by engaging him in a sustained examination of "points of conflict and points of possible convergence" between home and academic canons (193). Nevertheless, during Rose's first year at Loyola and then during his graduate school days, he continued to experience similar feelings when encountering texts and settings which reminded him of the conflict between home and school. If students like Rose, Lucia, or the writer of Shaughnessy's sample paper learn to view experiences of conflict — exclusion, confusion, uncertainty, psychic pain or strain — as "temporary," they are also likely to view the recurrence of those experiences as a reason to discontinue their education. Rather than viewing their developing ability to sustain contradictions as heralding the sort of "new mestiza consciousness" Anzaldua calls for (80), they may take it as signalling their failure to "enter" the academy, since they have been led to view the academy as a place free of contradictions.

EDUCATION AS ACCOMMODATION

Whereas the gatekeepers and converters want students to be either barred from or acculturated into academic culture, Irving Howe (Distinguished Professor of English, Graduate Center of CUNY and Hunter College), another City graduate often cited by the public media as an authority on the education of open admissions students (see Fiske), takes a somewhat different approach. He believes that "the host culture, resting as it does on the English language and the literary traditions associated with it, has . . . every reason to be *sympathetic* to the *problems* of those who, from choice or necessity, may *live with* the *tension of biculturalism*" ("Living" 110; emphasis mine).

The best way to understand what Howe might mean by this statement and why he promotes such a position is to put it in the context of two types of education stories Howe writes. The first type appears in his *World of Our Fathers*, in which he recounts the "cultural bleaching" required of Jewish immigrants attending classes at the Educational Alliance in New York City around the turn of this century. As Eugene Lyons, one immigrant whom Howe quotes, puts it, "We were 'Americanized' about as gently as horses are broken in." Students who went through this "crude" process, Lyons admits, often came to view their home traditions as "alien" and to "unconsciously resent and despise those traditions" (234). Howe points out that education in this type of "Americanization" exacted a price, leaving the students with a "nagging problem in self-perception, a crisis of identity" (642). Read in the context of Howe's statement on the open admissions students cited above, this type of story points to the kind of "problems" facing students who have to live with the tension between the "minority subcultures" in which they grow up and a "dominant" "Western" "host culture" with which they are trying to establish deep contact through education ("Living" 110). It also points to the limitations of an educational system which is not sympathetic to their problems.

The "Americanization" required of students like Eugene Lyons, Howe points out, often led Jewish students to seek either "a full return to religious faith or a complete abandonment of Jewish identification" (642). But Howe rejects both such choices. He offers instead an alternative story — the struggle of writers like himself to live with rather than escape from "the tension of biculturalism." In *A Margin of Hope*, he recounts his long journey in search of a way to "achieve some equilibrium with that earlier self which had started with childhood Yiddish, my language of naming, and then turned away in adolescent shame" (269). In "Strangers," Howe praises Jewish writers like Saul Bellow and the contributors to *Partisan Review* for their attitudes towards their "partial deracination" (*Selected Writings* 335). He argues that these writers demonstrated that being a "loose-fish" (with "roots loosened in Jewish soil but still not torn out, roots lowered into American soil but still not fixed") is "a badge" to be carried "with pride" (335). Doing so can open up a whole "range of possibilities" (335), such as the "forced yoking of opposites: gutter vividness and university refinement, street energy and high-culture rhetoric" Howe sees these writers achieving (338). This suggests what Howe might mean by "*living with* the tension of biculturalism." The story he tells of the struggle of these Jewish writers also proves that several claims made in the academy of the earlier 1970s, as Howe points out, are "true and urgent": 1) students who grow up in "subcultures" can feel "pain and dislocation" when trying to "connect with the larger, cosmopolitan culture"; 2) for these students, "there must always be some sense of 'difference,' even alienation"; 3) this sense of difference can "yield moral correction and emotional enrichment" ("Living" 110). The story of these writers also suggests that when dealing with students from "subcultures," the dominant culture and its educational system need, as Howe argues, to be more "sympathetic to" the pain and alienation indicated by the first two claims, and at the same time should value more highly the "infusion of vitality and diversity from subcultures" that the third claim suggests these students can bring (110).

Howe believes that the need for reform became especially urgent in the context of the open admissions movement, when a large number of "later immigrants, newer Americans" from racial as well as ethnic "subcultures" arrived at CUNY ("A Foot"). He also believes that, although the dominant culture needs to be more "responsive" and "sympathetic" towards this body of students, it would be "a dreadful form of intellectual condescension — and social cheating" for members of the "host culture" to dissuade students from establishing a "deep connection" with it. The only possible and defensible "educational ideal" is one which brings together commitments to "the widespread diffusion of learning" and to the "preservation of the highest standards of learning" ("Living" 109).

However, as Howe himself seems aware throughout his essay, he is more convinced of the need to live up to this ideal than certain about how to implement it in the day-to-day life of teaching, especially with "the presence of large numbers of ill-prepared students in our classroom" ("Living" 110, 112). For example, the values of "traditionalism" mean that teachers like Howe should try to "preserve" the "English language and the literary traditions" associated with "the dominant culture we call Western" (109, 110). Yet, when Howe tries to teach *Clarissa* to his students, he finds out that he has to help students to "transpose" and "translate" Clarrisa's belief in the sanctity of her virginity into their "terms." And he recognizes that the process of transposing would "necessarily distort and weaken" the original belief (112). This makes him realize that there is "reason to take seriously the claim" that "a qualitative transformation of Western culture threatens the survival of literature as we have known it" (112).

Although Howe promotes the images of "loose-fish" and "partial deracination" when discussing the work of Jewish writers, in his discussion of the education of "ill-prepared" students, he considers the possibility of change from only one end of the "tension of bi-culturalism" — that of "Western culture." His essay overlooks the possibility that the process of establishing a deep connection with "Western culture," such as teaching students to "transpose" their "subcultural" beliefs into the terms of "Western culture," might also "distort and weaken" — *transform* — the positions students take towards these beliefs, especially if these beliefs conflict with those privileged in "Western culture." In fact, teachers interested in actively honoring the students' decisions and needs to "live with the tension of bi-culturalism" must take this possibility seriously (see Lu, "Redefining" 33).

In helping students to establish deep connections with "Western culture," teachers who overlook the possibility of students' changing their identification with "subcultural" views are likely to turn education into an accommodation — or mere tolerance — of the students' choice or need to live with conflicts. This accommodation could hardly help students explore, formulate, reflect on, and enact strategies for coping actively with conflicts as the residents of borderlands do: developing a "tolerance for" and an ability to "sustain" contradictions and ambiguity (Anzaldua 79). Even if teachers explicitly promote the image of "partial deracination," they are likely to be more successful in helping students unconsciously "lower" and "fix" their roots into "Western culture" than in also helping them keep their roots from being completely "torn out" of "subcultures."

Two recurring words in Howe's essay, "preserve" and "survival," suggest a further problematic, for they represent the students as "preservers" of conflicting but unitary paradigms — a canonical "literary tradition" and "subcultures" with "attractive elements that merit study and preservation" ("Living" 110). This view of their role might encourage students to envision themselves as living at a focal point where "severed or separated pieces merely come together" (Anzaldua 79). Such perceptions might also lead students to focus their energy on "accommodating" their thoughts and actions to rigid boundaries rather than on actively engaging themselves in what to Anzaldua is the resource of life in the borderlands: a "continual creative motion" which breaks entrenched habits and patterns of behavior (Anzaldua 79). The residents of the borderlands act on rather than react to the "borders" cutting across society and their psyches, "borders" which become visible as they encounter conflicting ideas and actions. In perceiving these "borders" to identify the unitary aspects of "official" paradigms which "set" and "separate" cultures and which they can then work to break down. That is, for the mestizas, "borders" serve to delineate aspects of their psyches and the world requiring change. Words such as "preserve" and "survival," in focusing the students' attention on accommodation rather than change, could not help students become active residents of the borderlands.

The problematics surfacing from Howe's writings — the kind of "claims" about students from "subcultures" that he considers "true and urgent," the kind of "problems" he associates with students living with the tension of conflicting cultural forces, and the questions he raises as well as those he overlooks when discussing his "educational ideal" — map the general conceptual framework of a group of educators to whose writings I now turn. The writings of Leonard Kriegel, another member of the CUNY English faculty, seem to address precisely the question of how a teacher might implement in the day-to-day teaching of "remedial" students at City College the educational ideal posited by Howe.

In *Working Through: A Teacher's Journey in the Urban University*, Kriegel bases his authority on his personal experience as first a City undergraduate and then a City professor before and during the open admissions movement. Kriegel describes himself as a "working-class Jewish youth" — part of a generation not only eager to "get past [its] backgrounds, to deodorize all smells out of existence, especially the smells of immigrant kitchens and beer-sloppy tables," but also anxious to emulate the "aggressive intellectualism" of City students (32, 123). Kriegel maintains that in his days as a student, there existed a mutual trust between teachers and students: "My teachers could assume a certain intelligence on my part; I, in turn, could assume a certain good will on theirs" (29).

When he was assigned to teach in the SEEK program, Kriegel's first impression was that such a mutual trust was no longer possible. For example, when he asked students to describe Canova's *Perseus Holding the Head of Medusa*, a student opened his paper, "When I see this statue it is of the white man and he is holding the head of a Negro" (176). Such papers led Kriegel to conclude that these students had not only "elementary" problems with writing but also a "racial consciousness [which] seemed to obscure everything else" (176). Yet working among the SEEK students gradually convinced Kriegel that the kind of mutual trust he had previously enjoyed with his teachers and students was not only possible but necessary. He discovered that his black and Puerto Rican students "weren't very different from their white peers": they did not lack opinions and they did want in to the American establishment (175, 178). They can and do trust the "good will" of the teacher who can honestly admit that he is a product of academic culture and believes in it, who rids himself of the "inevitable white guilt" and the fear of being accused of "cultural colonialism," and who permits the students to define their needs in relation to the culture rather than rejecting it for them (180). Kriegel thus urges teachers to "leave students alone" to make their own choices (182).

Kriegel's approach to his journey falls within the framework Howe establishes. The university ought to be *"responsive* to the needs and points of view of students who are of *two minds* about what Western culture offers them" ("Playing It Black" 11; emphasis mine). Yet, when summarizing the lessons he learned through SEEK, Kriegel implies that being "responsive" does not require anything of the teacher other than *"permit[ting]* the student *freedom of choice*, to let him take what he felt he needed and let go of what was not important to him" (*Working Through* 207; emphasis mine). Kriegel ultimately finds himself "mak[ing] decisions based on old values" and "placing greater and greater reliance on the traditional cultural orientation to which [he] had been exposed as an undergraduate" (201-2). The question he does not consider throughout his book is the extent to which his reliance on "old values" and "traditional cultural orientation" might affect his promise to accommodate the students' freedom of choice, especially if they are of "two minds" about what Western culture offers them. That is, he never considers whether his teaching practice might implicitly disable his students' ability to exercise the "freedom" he explicitly "permits" them.

Kriegel's story suggests that business in the classroom could go on as usual so long as teachers openly promise students their "freedom of choice." His story implies that the kind of teaching traditionally used to disseminate the conventions of the "English language or literary tradition" is politically and culturally neutral. It takes a two-pronged approach to educational reform: 1) explicitly stating the teacher's willingness to accommodate — i.e., understand, sympathize with, accept, and respect — the students' choice or need to resist total acculturation; 2) implicitly dismissing the ways in which particular teaching practices "choose" for students — i.e., set pressures on the ways in which students formulate, modify, or even dismiss — their position towards conflicting cultures (for comparable positions by other City faculty, see Volpe and Quinn). This approach has rhetorical currency because it both aspires to and promises to deliver the kind of education envisioned by another group of minority writers with established authority in 1970s America, a group which included black intellectuals W. E. B. DuBois and James Baldwin. Using personal and communal accounts, these writers also argue for educational systems which acknowledge students' resistance to cultural deracination. Yet, because their arguments for such an educational reform are seldom directly linked to discussion of specific pedagogical issues, teachers who share Kriegel's position could read DuBois and Baldwin as authorizing accommodation.

For example, in *The Education of Black People*, Dubois critiques the underlying principle of earlier educational models for black students, such as the "Hampton Idea" or the Fisk program, which do not help students deal with what he elsewhere calls their double-consciousness (12, 51). Instead, such models pressure students to "escape their cultural heritage and the body of experience which they themselves have built-up." As a result, these students may "meet *peculiar frustration* and in the end be unable to achieve success in the new environment or fit into the old" (144; emphasis mine).

DuBois's portrayal of the "peculiar frustration" of black students, like Howe's account of the "problems" of Jewish students, speaks powerfully of the need to consider seriously Howe's list of the "claims" made during the open admission movement ("Living" 110). It also supports Howe's argument that the dominant culture needs to be more "sympathetic" to the "problems" of students from black and other ethnic cultures. DuBois's writings offer teachers a set of powerful narratives to counter the belief that students' interests in racial politics will impede their learning. In fact, DuBois's life suggests that being knowledgeable of and concerned with racial politics is a precondition to one's eventual ability to "force" oneself "in" and to "share" the world with "the owners" (*Education* 77).

At the same time, DuBois's autobiography can also be read as supporting the idea that once the teacher accepts the students' need to be interested in racial politics and becomes "sympathetic to" — acknowledges — their "peculiar frustration," business in the writing classroom can go on as usual. For example, when recalling his arrival at Harvard "in the midst of a violent controversy about poor English among students," DuBois describes his experiences in a compulsory Freshman English class as follows:

> I was at the point in my intellectual development when the content rather than the form of my writing was to me of prime importance. Words and ideas surged in my mind and spilled out with disregard of exact accuracy in grammar, taste in word or restraint in style. I knew the Negro problem and this was more important to me than literary form. I knew grammar fairly well, and I had a pretty wide vocabu-

lary; but I was bitter, angry and intemperate in my first thesis. . . . Senator Morgan of Alabama had just published a
scathing attack on "niggers" in a leading magazine, when my
first Harvard thesis was due. I let go at him with no holds
barred. My long and blazing effort came back marked "E"
— not passed. (*Autobiography* 144)

Consequently, DuBois "went to work at" his English and raised
the grade to a "C." Then, he "*elected* the best course on the campus for English composition," one which was taught by Barrett
Wendell, "then the great pundit of Harvard English" (144-45;
emphasis mine).

DuBois depicts his teacher as "fair" in judging his writing
"technically" but as having neither any idea of nor any interest in
the ways in which racism "scratch[ed] [DuBois] on the raw flesh"
(144). DuBois presents his own interest in the "Negro problem" as
a positive force, enabling him to produce "solid content" and
"worthy" thoughts. At the same time, he also presents his ra-
cial/political interest as making him "bitter, angry and intemperate." The politics of style would suggest that his "disregard of ex-
act accuracy in grammar, taste in word or restraint in style" would
have constrained his effort to "let go at [Senator Morgan] with no
holds barred" (emphasis mine). But statements such as "style is *subordinate* to content" but "*carries* a message further" suggest that
Dubois accepts wholeheartedly the view that the production of
"something to say" takes place before and independent of the
effort to "say it well" (144; emphasis mine). Nor does DuBois fault
his teachers for failing to help him recognize and then practice
ways of dealing with the politics of a "style" which privileges "restraint." Rather, his account suggests only that writing teachers
need to become more understanding of the students' racial/politi-
cal interests and their tendency to view "the Negro problem" as
more important than "literary form." Thus, his account allows
teachers to read it as endorsing the idea that once the teachers
learn to show more interest in what the students "have to say"
about racism, they can continue to teach "literary form" in the
way DuBois's composition teachers did.

Neither do the writings of James Baldwin, whom Shaughnessy
cites as the kind of "mature and gifted writer" her Basic Writers
could aspire to become (*Errors* 197), provide much direct opposition to this two-pronged approach to reform. In "A Talk to
Teachers" (originally published in the *Saturday Review*, 21 December 1963), Baldwin argues that "any Negro who is born in this

country and undergoes the American educational system runs the risk of becoming schizophrenic" (*Price* 326; see also *Conversations* 183), thus providing powerful support for Howe's call for sympathy from the dominant culture. Baldwin does offer some very sharp and explicit critiques of the view of literary style as politically innocent. In "If Black English Isn't a Language, Then Tell Me, What Is?" Baldwin points out that "the rules of the language are dictated by what the language must convey" (*Price* 651). He later explains that standard English "was not designed to carry those spirits and patterns" he has observed in his relatives and among the people from the streets and churches of Harlem, so he "had to find a way to bend it [English]" when writing about them in his first book (*Conversations* 162). These descriptions suggest that Baldwin is aware of the ways in which the style of one particular discourse mediates one's effort to generate content or a point of view alien to that discourse. Yet, since he is referring to his writing experience *after* he had become what Shaughnessy calls a "mature and gifted writer" rather than to experience as a student in a writing classroom, he does not directly challenge the problematics surfacing in discussions of educational reform aimed at accommodation without change.

The seeming resemblances between minority educators and Basic Writers — their "subculture" backgrounds, or the "psychic woe" they experience as a result of the dissonance within or among cultures, their "ambivalence" towards cultural bleaching, and their interest in racial/class politics — make these educators powerful allies for composition teachers like Shaughnessy who are not only committed to the educational rights and capacity of Basic Writers but also determined to grant students the freedom of choosing their alignments among conflicting cultures. We should not underestimate the support these narratives could provide for the field of Basic Writing as it struggled in the 1970s to establish legitimacy for its knowledge and expertise. I call attention to this support because of the intersection I see between Shaughnessy's approach to the function of conflict and struggle in Basic Writing instruction and the problematics I have sketched out in discussing the writings of Howe, Kriegel, DuBois and Baldwin.

Like Howe and DuBois, Shaughnessy tends to approach the problem of Basic Writers in terms of their ambivalence toward academic culture:

> College both beckons and threatens them, offering to teach
> them useful ways of thinking and talking about the world,

promising even to improve the quality of their lives, but threatening at the same time to take from their distinctive ways of interpreting the world, to assimilate them into the culture of academia without acknowledging their experience as outsiders. (*Errors* 292)

Again and again, Shaughnessy reminds us of her students' fear that mastery of a new discourse could wipe out, cancel, or take from them the points of view resulting from "their experience as outsiders." This fear, she argues, causes her students to mistrust and psychologically resist learning to write. And she reasons that "if students understand why they are being asked to learn something and if the reasons given *do not conflict* with deeper needs for self-respect and loyalty to their group (whether that be an economic, racial, or ethnic group), they *are disposed* to learn it" (*Errors* 125; emphasis mine).

Shaughnessy proposes some teaching methods towards that end. For example, when discussing her students' difficulty developing an "academic vocabulary," she suggests that students might resist associating a new meaning with a familiar word because accepting that association might seem like consenting to a "linguistic betrayal that threatens to wipe out not just a word but the reality that the word refers to" (*Errors* 212). She then goes on to suggest that "if we consider the formal (rather than the contextual) ways in which words can be made to shift meaning we are closer to the kind of practical information about words BW students need" (212). Shaughnessy's rationale seems to be that the "formal" approach (in this case teaching students to pay attention to prefixes and suffixes) is more "practical" because it will help students master the academic meaning of the word *without* reminding them that doing so might "wipe out" the familiar "reality" — the world, people, and meanings — previously associated with that word.

However, as I have argued elsewhere, the "formal" approach can be taken as "practical" only if teachers view the students' awareness of the conflict between the home meaning and the school meaning of a word as something to be "dissolved" at all costs because it will make them less "disposed to learn" academic discourse, as Shaughnessy seems to believe (Lu, "Redefining" 35). However, the experiences of Anzaldua and Rose suggest that the best way to help students cope with the "pain," "strain," "guilt," "fear," or "confusions" resulting from this type of conflict is not to find ways of "releasing" the students from these experiences or to avoid situations which might activate them. Rather, the "contextual" approach would have been more "practical," since it could help students deal self-consciously with the threat of "betrayal," especially if they fear and want to resist it. The "formal approach" recommended by Shaughnessy, however, is likely to be only a more "practical" way of preserving "academic vocabulary" and of speeding the students' internalization of it. As Rose's experiences working with students like Lucia indicate, it is exactly because teachers like him took the "contextual" approach — "encouraging her to talk through opinions of her own that ran counter to these discussions" (Rose 184-85) — that Lucia was able to get beyond the first twelve pages of Szasz's test and learn the "academic" meaning of "mental illness" posited by Szasz, a meaning which literally threatens to wipe out the "reality" of her brother's illness and her feelings about it.

Shaughnessy's tendency to overlook the political dimensions of the linguistic choices students make when reading and writing also points to the ways in which her "essentialist" view of language and her view of conflict and struggle as the enemies of Basic Writing instruction feed on one another (Lu, "Redefining" 26, 28-29). The supposed separation between language, thinking, and living reduces language into discrete and autonomous linguistic varieties or sets of conventions, rules, standards, and codes rather than treating language as a site of cultural conflict and struggle. From the former perspective, it is possible to believe, as Shaughnessy seems to suggest when opting for the "formal" approach to teaching vocabulary, that learning the rules of a new "language variety" — "the language of public transactions" — will give the student the "ultimate freedom of deciding how and when and where he will use which language" (*Errors* 11, 125). And it makes it possible for teachers like Shaughnessy to separate a "freedom" of choice in "linguistic variety" from one's social being — one's need to deliberate over and decide how to reposition oneself in relationship to conflicting cultures and powers. Thus, it might lead teachers to overlook the ways in which one's "freedom" of cultural alignment might impinge on one's freedom in choosing "linguistic variety."

Shaughnessy's approach to Basic Writing instruction has rhetorical power because of its seeming alignment with positions taken by "minority" writers. Her portrayal of "ambivalent feelings" of Basic Writers matches the experiences of "wrestling" (Trilling) and "partial deracination" (Howe), "the distinctive frustration" (DuBois), and "schizophrenia" (Baldwin) portrayed in the writings of the more established members of the academy. All thus lend validity to each other's understanding of the "problems" of students from minority cultures and to their critiques of educational systems which mandate total acculturation. Shaughnessy's methods of teaching demonstrate acceptance of and compassion towards students' experience of the kind of "dislocation," "alienation," or "difference" which minority writers like Howe, DuBois, and Baldwin argue will always accompany those trying by choice or need to "live with" the tensions of conflicting cultures. Her methods of teaching also demonstrate an effort to accommodate these feelings and points of view. That is, because of her essentialist assumption that words can express but will not change the essence of one's thoughts, her pedagogy promises to help students master academic discourse without forcing them to reposition themselves — i.e., to re-form their relation — towards conflicting cultural beliefs. In that sense, her teaching promises to accommodate the students' need to establish deep contact with a "wider," more "public" culture by "releasing" them from their fear that learning academic discourse will cancel out points of view meaningful to their non-"academic" activities. At the same time, it also promises to accommodate their existing ambivalence towards and differences from academic culture by assuming that "expressing" this ambivalence and these differences in academic "forms" will not change the "essence" of these points of view. The lessons she learns from her journey in the "pedagogical West" thus converge with those of Kriegel, who dedicates his book to "Mina Shaughnessy, who knows that nothing is learned simply." That is, when discussing her teaching methods, she too tends to overlook the ways in which her methods of teaching "linguistic codes" might weaken her concern to permit the students freedom of choice in their points of view. Ultimately, as I have argued, the teaching of both Shaughnessy and Kriegel might prove to be more successful in preserving the traditions of "English language and literature" than in helping students reach a self-conscious choice on their position towards conflicting cultural values and forces.

CONTESTING THE RESIDUAL POWER OF VIEWING CONFLICT AND
STRUGGLE AS THE ENEMIES OF BASIC WRITING INSTRUCTION:
PRESENT AND FUTURE

The view that all signs of conflict and struggle are the enemies of Basic Writing instruction emerged partly from a set of specific historical conditions surrounding the open admissions movement. Open admissions at CUNY was itself an attempt to deal with immediate, intense, sometimes violent social, political, and racial confrontations. Such a context seemed to provide a logic for shifting students' attention *away* from conflict and struggle and *towards* calm. However, the academic status which pioneers like Bruffee, Farrell, and Shaughnessy have achieved and the practical, effective *cures* their pedagogies seem to offer have combined to perpetuate the rhetorical power of such a view for Basic Writing instruction through the 1970s to the present. The consensus among the gatekeepers, converters, and accommodationists furnishes some Basic Writing teachers with a complacent sense that they already know all about the "problems" Basic Writers have with conflict and struggle. This complacency makes teachers hesitant to consider the possible uses of conflict and struggle, even when these possibilities are indicated by later developments in language theories and substantiated both by accounts of alternative educational experiences by writers like Anzaldua and Rose and by research on the constructive use of conflict and struggle, such as the research discussed in the first section of this essay.

Such complacency is evident in the works of compositionists like Mary Epes and Ann Murphy. Epes's work suggests that she is aware of recent arguments against the essentialist view of language underlying some composition theories and practices. For example, she admits that error analysis is complex because there is "a crucial area of overlap" between "*encoding*" (defined by Epes as "controlling the visual symbols which represent meaning on the page") and "*composing* (controlling meaning in writing)" (6). She also observes that students are most likely to experience the "conflict between composing and decoding" when the "norms of the written code" and "in conflict" with "the language of one's nurture" (31). Given Epes's recognition of the conflict between encoding and composing, she should have little disagreement with compositionists who argue that learning to use the "codes" of academic discourse would constrain certain types of meanings, such as the formulation of feelings and thoughts towards cultures drastically dissonant from academic culture. Yet, when Epes moves from her theory to pedagogy, she argues that teachers of Basic Writers can and ought to treat "encoding" and "composition" as two separate areas of instruction (31). Her rationale is simple: separating the two could avoid "exacerbating" the students' experience of the "conflict" between these activities (31). The key terms here (for me, at any rate) are "exacerbating" and "conflict." They illustrate Epes's concern to eliminate conflict, disagreement, tension, and complexity from the Basic Writing classroom (cf. Horner).

Ann Murphy's essay "Transference and Resistance" likewise

demonstrates the residual power of the earlier view of conflict and struggle as the enemies of Basic Writing instruction. Her essay draws on her knowledge of the Lacanian notion of the decentered and destabilized subject. Yet Murphy argues against the applicability of such a theory to the teaching of Basic Writing on the ground that Basic Writers are not like other students. Basic Writers, Murphy argues, "may need centering rather than decentering, and cognitive skills rather than (or as compellingly as) self-exploration" (180). She depicts Basic Writers as "shattered and destabilized by the social and political system" (180). She claims that "being taken seriously as *adults* with something of value to say can, for many Basic Writing students, be a *traumatic* and *disorienting* experience" (180; emphasis mine). Murphy's argument demonstrates her desire to eliminate any sense of uncertainty or instability in Basic Writing classrooms. Even though Murphy is willing to consider the implications of the Lacanian notion of individual subjectivity for the teaching of other types of students (180), her readiness to separate Basic Writing classrooms from other classrooms demonstrates the residual power of earlier views of conflict and struggle.

Such a residual view is all the more difficult to contest because it is supported by a new generation of minority educators. For example, in "Teacher Background and Student Needs" (1991), Peter Rondinone uses his personal experiences as an open admissions student taking Basic Writing at CCNY during the early 70s and his Russian immigrant family background in the Bronx to argue for the need to help Basic Writers understand that "in deciding to become educated there will be times when [basic writers] will be forced to . . . reject or *betray* their family and friends in order to succeed" ("Teacher" 42). Rondinone's view of how students might best deal with the conflict between home and school does not seem to have changed much since his 1977 essay describing his experience as a senior at City College (see Rondinone, "Open Admissions"). In his 1991 essay, this time writing from the point of view of an experienced teacher, Rondinone follows Bruffee in maintaining that "learning involves shifting social allegiances" ("Teacher" 49). My quarrel with Rondinone is not so much over his having opted for complete deracination (for I honor his right to choose his allegiance even though I disagree with his choice). I am, however, alarmed by his unequivocal belief that his choice is the *a priori* condition of his academic success, which reveals his conviction that conflict can only impede one's learning.

Shelby Steele's recent and popular *The Content of our Character* suggests similar assumptions about experiences of cultural conflict.

Using personal experiences, Steele portrays the dilemma of an African-American college student and professor in terms of being caught in the familiar "trap": bound by "two equally powerful elements" which are "at odds with each other" (95). Steele's solution to the problem of "opposing thrusts" is simple: find a way to "unburden" the student from one of the thrusts (160). Thus, Steele promotes a new, "peacetime" black identity which could "release" black Americans from a racial identity which regards their "middle-class" values, aspirations, and success as suspect (109).

To someone like Steele, the pedagogies of Bruffee, Farrell, and Rondinone would make sense. In such a classroom, the black student who told Steele that "he was not sure he should master standard English because then he 'wouldn't be black no more'" (70) would have the comfort of knowing that he is not alone in wanting to pursue things "all individuals" want or in wishing to be drawn "into the American mainstream" (71). Furthermore, he would find support systems to ease him through the momentary pain, dislocation, and anxiety accompanying his effort to "unburden" himself of one of the "opposing thrusts." The popular success of Steele's book attests to the power of this type of thinking on the contemporary scene. Sections of his book originally appeared in such journals as *Harper's, Commentary*, the *New York Times Magazine*, and *The American Scholar*. Since publication of the book, Steele has been touted as an expert on problems facing African-American students in higher education, and his views have been aired on PBS specials, *Nightline*, and the *MacNeil/Lebrer News Hour*, and in *Time* magazine. The popularity of his book should call our attention to the direct and indirect ways in which the distrust of conflict and struggle continues to be recycled and disseminated both within and outside the academy. At the same time, the weight of authority of the Wagners and Hellers should caution us to take more seriously the pressures the Rondinones and Steeles can exert on Basic Writing teachers, a majority of us still occupying peripheral positions in a culture repeatedly swept by waves of new conservatism.

But investigating the particular directions taken by Basic Writing pioneers when establishing authority for their expertise and the historical contexts of those directions should also enable us to perceive alternative ways of conversing with the Rondinones and Steeles in the 1990s. Because of the contributions of pioneers like Bruffee, Farrell, and Shaughnessy, we can now mobilize the authority they have gained for the field, for our knowledge as well as our expertise as Basic Writing teachers. While we can continue to benefit from the insights into students' experiences of conflict and struggle offered in the writings of all those I have discussed, we need not let their view of the cause and function of such experiences restrict how we view and use the stories and pedagogies they provide. Rather, we need to read them against the grain, filling in the silences left in these accounts by re-reading their experiences from the perspective of alternative accounts from the borderlands and from the perspective of new language and pedagogical theories. For many of these authors are themselves products of classrooms which promoted uncritical faith in either an essentialist view of language or various forms of discursive utopia that these writers aspired to preserve. Therefore, we should use our knowledge and expertise as compositionists to do what they did not or could not do: re-read their accounts in the context of current debates on the nature of language, individual consciousness, and the politics of basic skills. At the same time, we also need to gather more oppositional and alternative accounts from a new generation of students, those who can speak about the successes and challenges of classrooms which recognize the positive use of conflict and struggle and which teach the process of repositioning.

The writings of the pioneers and their more established contemporaries indicate that the residual distrust of conflict and struggle in the field of Basic Writing is sustained by a fascination with cures for psychic woes, by two views of education — as acculturation and as accommodation — and by two views of language — essentialist and utopian. We need more research which critiques portrayals of Basic Writers as belonging to an abnormal — traumatized or underdeveloped — mental state and which simultaneously provides accounts of the "creative motion" and "compensation," "joy," or "exhilaration" resulting from Basic Writers' efforts to grapple with the conflict within and among diverse discourses. We need more research analyzing and contesting the assumptions about language underlying teaching methods which offer to "cure" all signs of conflict and struggle, research which explores ways to help students recover the latent conflict and struggle in their lives which the dominant conservative ideology of the 1990s seeks to contain. Most of all, we need to find ways of foregrounding conflict and struggle not only in the generation of meaning and authority, but also in the teaching of conventions of "correctness" in syntax, spelling, and punctuation, traditionally considered the primary focus of Basic Writing instruction.

Author's Note: Material for sections of this essay comes from my dissertation, directed by David Bartholomae at the University of Pittsburgh. This essay is part of a joint project conducted with Bruce Horner which has been supported by the Drake University Provost Research Fund, the Drake University Center for the Humanities, and the University of Iowa Center for Advanced Studies. I gratefully acknowledge Bruce Horner's contributions to the conception and revisions of this essay.

WORKS CITED

Anzaldua, Gloria. *Borderlands/La Frontera: The New Mestiza.* San Francisco: spinsters/aunt lute, 1987.

Baldwin, James. *Conversations with James Baldwin.* Ed. Fred L. Standley and Louis H. Pratt. Jackson: UP of Mississippi, 1989.

——. *The Price of the Ticket.* New York: St. Martin's, 1985.

Bartholomae, David. "Inventing the University." *When a Writer Can't Write: Studies in Writer's Block and Other Composing Process Problems.* Ed. Mike Rose. New York: Guildford, 1985. 134-165.

——. "Writing on the Margins: The Concept of Literacy in Higher Educations." *A Sourcebook for Basic Writing Teachers.* Ed. Theresa Enos. New York: Random, 1987. 66-83.

Bizzell, Patricia. "Beyond Anti-Foundationalism to Rhetorical Authority: Problems Defining 'Cultural Literacy.'" *College English* 52 (Oct. 1990): 661-75.

Brown, Rexford G. "Schooling and Thoughtfulness." *Journal of Basic Writing* 10.1 (Spring 1991): 3-15.

Bruffee, Kenneth A. "On Not Listening in Order to Hear: Collaborative Learning and the Rewards of Classroom Research." *Journal of Basic Writing* 7.1 (Spring 1988): 3-12.

——. "Collaborative Learning: Some Practical Models." *College English* 34 (Feb. 1973): 634-43.

DuBois, W. E. B. *The Autobiography of W. E. B. DuBois: A Soliloquy on Viewing My Life from the Last Decade of Its First Century.* New York: International, 1968.

——. *The Education of Black People: Ten Critiques 1906-1960.* Ed. Herbert Aptheker. Amherst: U of Massachusetts P, 1973.

Epes, Mary. "Tracing Errors to Their Sources: A Study of the Encoding Processes of Adult Basic Writers." *Journal of Basic Writing* 4.1 (Spring 1985): 4-33.

Farrell, Thomas J. "Developing Literacy: Walter J. Ong and Basic Writing." *Journal of Basic Writing* 2.1 (Fall/Winter 1978): 30-51.

——. "Literacy, the Basics, and All That Jazz." *College English* 38 (Jan. 1977): 443-59.

——. "Open Admissions, Orality, and Literacy." *Journal of Youth and Adolescence* 3 (1974): 247-60.

Fiske, Edward B. "City College Quality Still Debated after Eight Years of Open Admission." *New York Times* 19 June 1978: A1.

Flynn, Elizabeth. "Composing as a Woman." *College Composition and Communication* 39 (Dec. 1988): 423-35.

Fox, Tom. "Basic Writing as Cultural Conflict." *Journal of Education* 172.1 (1990): 65-83.

Gould, Christopher, and John Heyda. "Literacy Education and the Basic Writer: A Survey of College Composition Courses." *Journal of Basic Writing*

5.2 (Fall 1986): 8-27.

Harris, Joseph. "The Idea of Community in the Study of Writing." *College Composition and Communication* 40 (Feb. 1989): 11-22.

Heller, Louis G. *The Death of the American University: With Special Reference to the Collapse of City College of New York.* New Rochelle, NY: Arlington House, 1973.

Horner, Bruce. "Re-Thinking the 'Sociality' of Error: Teaching Editing as Negotiation." Forthcoming, *Rhetoric Review.*

Howe, Irving. "A Foot in the Door." *New York Times* 27 June 1975: 35.

——. "Living with Kampf and Schlaff: Literary Tradition and Mass Education." *The American Scholar* 43 (1973-74): 107-12.

——. *A Margin of Hope: An Intellectual Autobiography.* New York: Harcourt, 1982.

——. *Selected Writings 1950-1990.* New York: Harcourt, 1990.

——. *World of Our Fathers.* New York: Harcourt, 1976.

Hull, Glynda, and Mike Rose. "'This Wooden Shack Place': The Logic of an Unconventional Reading." *College Composition and Communication* 41 (Oct. 1990): 287-98.

Kriegel, Leonard. "Playing it Black." *Change* Mar./Apr. 1969: 7-11.

——. *Working Through: A Teacher's Journey in the Urban University.* New York: Saturday Review, 1972.

Lu, Min-Zhan. "From Silence to Words: Writing as Struggle." *College English* 49 (Apr. 1987): 433-48.

——. "Redefining the Legacy of Mina Shaughnessy: A Critique of the Politics of Linguistic Innocence." *Journal of Basic Writing* 10.1 (Spring 1991): 26-40.

——. "Writing as Repositioning." *Journal of Education* 172.1 (1990): 18-21.

Lunsford, Andrea A., Helene Moglen, and James Slevin, eds. *The Right to Literacy.* New York: MLA, 1990

Lyons, Robert. "Mina Shaughnessy." *Traditions of Inquiry.* Ed. John Brereton. New York: Oxford UP, 1985. 171-89.

Mellix, Barbara. "From Outside, In." *Georgia Review* 41 (1987): 258-67.

Murphy, Ann. "Transference and Resistance in the Basic Writing Classroom: Problematics and Praxis." *College Composition and Communication* 40 (May 1989): 175-87.

Quinn, Edward. "We're Holding Our Own." *Change* June 1973: 30-35.

Ritchie, Joy S. "Beginning Writers: Diverse Voices and Individual Identity." *College Composition and Communication* 40 (May 1989): 152-74.

Rondinone, Peter. "Teacher Background and Student Needs." *Journal of Basic Writing* 10.1 (Spring 1991): 41-53.

——. "Open Admissions and the Inward 'I'." *Change* May 1977: 43-47.

Rose, Mike. *Lives on the Boundary.* New York: Penguin, 1989.

Schilb, John. "Composition and Poststructuralism: A Tale of Two Conferences." *College Composition and Communication* 40 (Dec. 1989): 422-43.

Shaughnessy, Mina. "Diving In: An Introduction to Basic Writing." *College Composition and Communication* 27 (Oct. 1976): 234-39.

——. "The English Professor's Malady." *Journal of Basic Writing* 3.1 (Fall/Winter 1980): 91-97.

——. *Errors and Expectations: A Guide for the Teacher of Basic Writing.* New York: Oxford UP, 1977.

Spellmeyer, Kurt. "Foucault and the Freshman Writer: Considering the Self in Discourse." *College English* 51 (Nov. 1989): 715-29.

Stanley, Linda C. "'Misreading' Students' Journals for Their Views of Self and

Society." *Journal of Basic Writing* 8.1 (Spring 1989): 21-31.

Steele, Shelby. *The Content of Our Character: A New Vision of Race in America.* New York: St. Martin's, 1990.

Trilling, Lionel. *The Last Decade: Essays and Reviews, 1965-75.* Ed. Diana Trilling. New York: Harcourt, 1979.

——. *Of This Time, Of That Place, and Other Stories.* Selected by Diana Trilling. New York: Harcourt, 1979.

Trimbut, John. "Beyond Cognition: The Voices in Inner Speech." *Rhetoric Review* 5 (1987): 211-21.

Volpe, Edmond L. "The Confession of a Fallen Man: Ascent to the DA." *College English* 33 (1972): 765-79.

Wagner, Geoffrey. *The End of Education.* New York: Barnes, 1976.

Introduction

In "Defining the Boundaries of Freedom in the World of Cane: Cuba, Brazil, and Louisiana after Emancipation," Rebecca J. Scott compares three entities: three systems of producing cane sugar in periods following the abolition of slavery in the three economies which supported these systems. So Scott, as a scholar interested in "discerning patterns in [the] complex struggle" (158) for control in post-emancipation labour markets, does something students are often asked to do: she writes a comparison.

Scott follows a classic form in developing the comparison. Early stages (156-59) of the discussion introduce the general issues at stake — "the boundaries of freedom," control, "the organization of work and the evolution of labor relations" — and tells that differences are to be found: "the patterns of labor that emerged in these three societies varied." (The differences themselves await disclosure.) We learn too that similarities are also to be found: "In each of the cases examined here, planters' class power was reconstructed — but the work relations on which it rested were shaped by the assertions and challenges of former slaves and other rural workers." (The nature of these "work relations" also await disclosure.) So readers approach a long and detailed account of three historical labour markets prepared to observe differences in "patterns of labor" and, amongst these differences, a resemblance in the part that workers themselves played in determining these patterns.

In other disciplines, especially those which specify findings in introductions, readers might approach the body of the comparison with a little more guidance — firmer, more pronounced claims about the outcome of the comparative process. But you will find that Scott's evidence is very complex, and perhaps not so open to being represented in a handful of introductory statements. Partly owing to the nature of its data and perhaps partly owing to suspicion of over-simplification, history appears to resist the commanding generalities which would reduce rather than respect complexity.

In this instance of comparison, readers are to a certain degree left to maintain their own hold on those opening claims: as you read about what happened during and after the Civil War in Lou-isiana, during the late colonial period in Cuba, and after abolition in Brazil, remind yourself of what you have been led to expect — evidence of the power of the dominant class reconstructing itself, and, at the same time, more subtle evidence of the way the choices and resistances of workers modified that power.

Although you will benefit from keeping these ideas handy, you will still not be left entirely alone in your encounter with the ma-terials of the comparison. At each transition point — as discussions of Louisiana, Cuba, and Brazil each conclude — summary para-graphs tell you what you should have in mind as you proceed to the next section. And the conclusion is also thorough and detailed in generalizing findings about changes in ways of "eliciting labor" and changes in "class relations" (192). Moreover, after the case of Louisiana has been established, explicit comparisons help you un-derstand the relevance of statements about Cuba to statements about Louisiana, or statements about Brazil to statements about Cuba and Louisiana. For example, in Cuba, "the concentration of seasonal Spanish workers meant that the field work force was not *the highly segregated one that prevailed in Louisiana*" (179, emphasis added); "[t]he *usinas* more closely *resembled the central mills of Louisi-ana and Cuba*, and they became the dominant form in much of the Brazilian northeast by the end of the century" (185, emphasis added); "[a]s in Cuba, cane farmers [in Brazil] bought their partial independence at the cost of absorbing the impact of low sugar prices" (187). These explicit points of comparison are likely to be part of the overall outcome of the comparison.

While textbook history may represent the past in compact and portable generalities, scholarly history is more likely to present readers with the kind of detail and complexity Scott offers — de-tail that can leave readers on their own for noticeable stretches. In those stretches of particulars, Scott presents the materials from which a plausible version of the past can be constructed. So, in dealing with the question of "continuity" (how much did emancipation really change things?), she reaches the conclusion "Continuity, yes: but it was a continuity of complex negotiations and renegotiations, carried out with few resources and great tenacity" (192) only after contacting some very specific, local materials: the wording of a 1922 government report; information on labour arrangements in the Brazilian states of Bahia and Pernambuco.

"Defining the Boundaries of Freedom" is characteristic of history scholarship in its repeated pattern of incursions into detail — telling the story of what happened, for example, in 1862-1864 in Louisiana (160-62) — followed by briefer interpretive statements — "[the effort to impose year-long contracts] fit with the long-standing desire of planters to control their workers' mobility and be assured of labor at harvest time" (162) — followed by return to detail. The degree to which such contact with detail is valued is further illustrated by Scott's first paragraph. Unlike other scholarly writers represented in this volume, she begins not with commanding abstractions and generalities but with a specific case: the words of a man named William Dougherty, composed in January 1866, regarding two parishes of southern Louisiana.

And on another, related dimension, Scott's article differs from those from other disciplines. You can see this difference at a glance, for it has a graphic profile: big clumps of footnotes at the bottom of each page. Looking a little closer, and inspecting the text itself, you will see that, unlike writers working in other disciplines, and with only a few exceptions in this long article, Scott does not *report* historical statements about Louisiana, Cuba, and Brazil 100 years ago and more. So whereas other writers repeatedly cite other writers — for example,

> In rejecting the tenets of 'universalist' criticism, Achebe calls his vision 'necessarily local and particular' (69) (Dasenbrock (11).

> Anorexia nervosa most often occurs in upper and middle-class adolescents and young women in affluent western countries (Prince, 1985; Szmulker, 1985) (Apter et al. 85)

— Scott appears at first to be not similarly constrained. She can simply say, "In the antebellum United States, the cultivation of sugar cane was concentrated in the rich delta and riverfront parishes of southeastern Louisiana" (159). But a still closer look reveals that the general picture of the Louisiana sugar economy is eventually secured by a very long footnote listing seven sources —

seven other histories of the time and place she describes. So, while the surface of the discussion does not overtly entertain other voices, the footnotes establish statements about the past as the co-operative work of a community of scholars. So, is this what scholarly history amounts to — a compilation of histories? Not exactly, for if you look closer still, you will see two kinds of footnote. One kind is like footnote 3, the seven-source one just mentioned; some of these are "discursive" — that is, they carry on some discussion themselves. The other kind of note is like footnote 32, which accompanies a quotation from a letter written by a planter's wife. You will find quite a few of these quotation-footnote pairs, where the words not of historians but of people of the time are reported (diarists, letter- and report-writers, even a Cuban cane-hauler who owned a cart), and the footnote leads not to published sources but to archives. So we could say that scholarly history is a fusion of the collated voices of other scholars and the voices of those who speak directly from the past — a fusion of what are known as "secondary" and "primary" documents. This fusion then materializes as a delicately negotiated sequence of steps from stories — what happened in 1873 — to generalizing interpretations and then back to more stories. The shape of scholarly history is embedded in these fused, footnoted voices and these rhythmic moves — a shape less overt than that of, say, psychology or ethnography, but deeply formed nevertheless.

In this characteristically historical fashion, Scott approaches issues reached through other routes by other articles in this volume. In a certain sense, her research brings into focus what Kabeer talks about: "labour supply decision-making." Cane workers in Louisiana, Cuba, and Brazil made choices, resisted or submitted to authority, negotiated — if only, as Scott says, "with few resources" — the terms of their working life. While, from a distance, or from a certain perspective, Bangladeshi women's piece-work employment can seem coerced, Kabeer's account reveals it as a much more complicated reconciliation of risks and advantages, conducted in a racialist society. Similarly, having read Scott's article, you might consider, or reconsider "seasonal work" as a "labour supply decision." Perhaps we too automatically associate seasonal employment with desperation or destitution, or with marginalization, and thereby oversimplify its meaning.

- What is the meaning of "seasonal work" in the contexts Scott describes? What part does it play in the struggle for "control" and "freedom" in the labour economy?

- What is a "reliable" labour supply (keeping in mind that one person's idea of "unreliability" [87] may be another person's idea of freedom)?

- What is the significance of racial segregation or racial mix in the work force?

Defining the Boundaries of Freedom on the World of Cane: Cuba, Brazil, and Louisiana after Emancipation

REBECCA J. SCOTT

IN JANUARY 1866, William Dougherty, an agent of the Bureau of Refugees, Freedmen, and Abandoned Lands, filed his inspection report on the state of plantations in two parishes of southern Louisiana. In it, he bemoaned the influence of black soldiers returning from service in the Union Army: "Possessing as they do erroneous and incongruous notions of liberty they decline to make an agreement by which they are to be in any manner restrained for a period of a year, and as most of them have considerable money when they are discharged it is optional with them whether or not they go to work, along with their example, their advice to other colored people is not of the best kind."[1]

I would like to thank Judith Allen, Ira Berlin, Fernando Coronil, Frederick Cooper, Astrid Cubano, Paul Eiss, David Eltis, Ada Ferrer, Josep Fradera, Jeffery Gould, Albert Hirschman, Thomas Holt, Earl Lewis, Sidney Mintz, Brian Pollitt, Peter Railton, Joseph Reidy, Leslie Rowland, Steven Topik, Harold Woodman, and several anonymous reviewers for the *AHR* for their very useful comments on previous versions of this material. I also owe a great debt to the late Peter Eisenberg for his generous assistance and advice. Earlier versions of this essay were presented to the Conference on Cultivation and Culture, University of Maryland, 1989; as the 1990 Elsa Goveia Lecture at the University of West Indies, Cave Hill, Barbados; to the John Hopkins Seminar in Atlantic History and Culture; and to the Comparative Studies in Social Transformation faculty seminar, University of Michigan.

1   See Wm. Dougherty to Capt. A.F. Hayden, in Inspection report of Plantations, freedmen, &c. in the parishes of Jefferson and Orleans, Right Bank, January, 1866, in Inspection Reports of Plantations from Subordinate Officers, January 1866 — November 1868, series 1312. Louisiana Assistant Commissioner, Bureau of Refugees, Freedmen, and Abandoned Lands. Record Group 105, U.S. National Archives (hereafter, BRFAL, RG 105, USNA), available as Microfilm Publication M1027, Roll 28.

As Dougherty's exasperation suggests, struggles over labor arrangements in the postemancipation world were also struggles over values.[2] Moreover, the different parties to those struggles had "incongruous notions" of how and where to define the boundaries of freedom.

Slavery, however complex its internal variation within the Americas, had been at its core a system of labor discipline. Africans had been forcibly transported to the New World in order to labor under compulsion. Once they and their descendants had escaped from that system of coercion, the question of what would — or could — come in its wake took on great urgency.

For those who commanded resources in society, the question had a particular meaning: if stable production was to be maintained, some scheme to secure reliable access to labor had to be put in place. But the range of possibilities was relatively broad: there were precedents in most agrarian societies for wage labor and tenantry, labor rents and share rents, sharecropping and small-holding. Land could be allocated to or withheld from the former slaves: labor could be compensated in money or goods: wages could be paid by the day, the task, the week, or the year. Contracts could be for varying lengths of time and could be written, oral, or customary. As employers sought strategies that would ensure their continued control, policy makers debated the implications of juridical freedom in the sphere of production and pondered the precise meaning of the concept of "free labor."[3]

For those who had been slaves and who did not command sub-

2   I am indebted to Julie Saville for making this point succinctly in her presentation to the Conference on Slavery and Freedom in Historical Perspective, University of California, San Diego, October 4-6, 1991. She traces it to the arguments of E.P. Thompson in *The Poverty of Theory and Other Essays* (New York, 1978). See also Julie Saville. "A Measure of Freedom: From Slave to Wage Labor in South Carolina, 1860-1868" (Ph.D. dissertation, Yale University, 1986).

3   For discussion of this contest, see Barbara J. Fields and Leslie S. Rowland. "Free Labor Ideology and Its Exponents in the South during the Civil War and Reconstruction" (forthcoming, *Labour History*). See also Steven Hahn. "Class and the State in Postemancipation Societies: Southern Planters in Comparative Perspective," *AHR, 95* (February 1990): 75-98.

stantial material resources, the question of the nature of free labor had a special significance and urgency. Not only material well-being but social and cultural life and the possibility of political voice were at stake. Recent research had made it clear that former slaves throughout the Americas sought access to productive resources and deployed whatever power they could to try to shape both the character of their labor and the social relations in which their work was embedded.[4]

One way of discerning patterns within this complex struggle is to examine its unfolding in areas that shared a concentration on the same crop — in this case, the cane regions of Louisiana, Cuba, and Brazil. The perishability of cane put a premium on reliable access to a disciplined seasonal work force, and sugar production increasingly required large-scale units for profitable processing. All sugar producers faced similar uncertainties in markets and instabilities in prices. But the patterns of labor that emerged in these three societies varied. The specific features of cane as a crop and sugar as a commodity seem to have constrained, but not determined, the organization of work and the evolution of labor relations.

These variations represent something more than different strategies adopted by planters under different circumstances. Sugar plantation societies had long been a locus not only of coerced production and exceptionally high mortality but also of communities of enslaved workers capable of rebellion and day-to-day negotiation. Moreover, the process of emancipation had in nearly every instance witnessed important initiatives taken by those who were enslaved. In each of the cases examined here, planters' class power was reconstructed — but the work relations on which it rested were shaped by the assertions and challenges of former slaves and other rural workers.

Exploring this contest in comparative perspective reveals the importance of a shared reliance on a crop with specific characteristics

4   Studies in postemancipation societies have multiplied in the last decade, and regional case studies are now too numerous to list individually. A major recent monograph is Thomas C. Holt, *The Problem of Freedom: Race, Labor and Politics in Jamaica and Britain, 1832-1938* (Baltimore, Md., 1991). For a recent collection, see Frank McGlynn and Seymour Drescher, eds., *The Meaning of Freedom: Economics, Politics, and Culture after Slavery* (Pittsburgh, Pa., 1992). For a comprehensive bibliography, see Leslie Rowland, Rebecca Scott, Thomas Holt, and Frederick Cooper, eds., *Societies after Slavery: A Select Annotated Bibliography of Printed Sources on the United States, Africa, Brazil, and the Caribbean* (forthcoming, University of Michigan Press).

but also affords evidence against the "crop determinism" that sugar sometimes inspires. Such comparison illuminates the ways in which work relations in sugar conditioned the character of collective action in each region. The process was a reciprocal one: individual and collective challenges by former slaves helped to determine the disposition of resources and the patterns of work that emerged, and the composition of the labor forces and the organization of work in turn shaped the possibilities for further collective action. Thus the dramatic strikes in the 1870s and the 1880s in Louisiana, and the cross-racial and anti-colonial insurgency that shook Cuba from 1895 to 1898, reflected the specific ways in which many of their participants earned a livelihood in the world of cane.

IN THE ANTEBELLUM UNITED STATES, THE cultivation OF sugar cane was concentrated in the rich delta and riverfront parishes of southeastern Louisiana. By the middle of the nineteenth century, most of the land suitable for cane had been occupied, and the slave population of the sugar regions had reached 125,000. About 1,300 plantations grew and ground cane for sale to markets elsewhere in the country, and the great majority of sugar houses used steam mills. Some seventy planters had also installed efficient vacuum pans for boiling the cane juice. The industry was characterized by a high level of capital investment, and it operated profitably behind tariff barriers that provided a variable degree of protection from foreign sugars, essential for a region with a shorter growing season and smaller mills than its major Caribbean competitor, Cuba. Average annual output between 1857 and 1861 was approximately 161,000 metric tons, culminating in a bumper crop in 1861 worth 25 million dollars.[5]

5   On the history of the industry, see J. Carlyle Sitterson, *Sugar Country: The Cane Sugar Industry in the South, 1753-1950* (Lexington, Ky., 1953); Sam B. Hilliard, "Site Characteristics and Spatial Stability of the Louisiana Sugarcane Industry," and Mark Schmitz, "The Transformation of the Southern Sugar Cane Sector," both in *Agricultural History*, 53 (January 1979): 254-69, 270-85; and Roderick A. MacDonald, "Independent Economic Production by Slaves on Antebellum Louisiana Sugar Plantations," in Ira Berlin and Philip D. Morgan, eds., *Cultivation and Culture: Labor and the Shaping of Slave Life in the Americas* (Charlottesville, Va., 1993), 275-99. Between 1847 and 1862, the average duty was approximately 1.11 cents per pound, at a rate of 24 percent ad valorem. For production figures, see Noel Deerr, *The History of Sugar*, 2 vols. (London, 1949), 1:250. On the bumper crop of 1861, see Walter Prichard, "The Effects of the Civil War on the Louisiana Sugar Industry." *Journal of Southern History*, 5 (August 1939): 315-32.

The outbreak of the Civil War placed this prosperity at great risk. New Orleans fell to the Union Army in the spring of 1862, and shortly thereafter Union troops occupied the major sugar regions of the state. Planters found themselves in a delicate situation. Many had been Whigs and Unionists, opponents of Confederate secession. But they were entirely reliant on slavery for their prosperity, and Union occupation threatened to undermine their authority over their slaves. While Union officers generally focused on maintaining security, tranquility, and production, they were divided on the necessity of transforming the character of labor in areas under their control. Some officers were content to allow planters to continue in more or less the old ways, while other officers and enlisted men saw in Louisiana an opportunity to demonstrate antislavery commitments and the virtues of free labor. Slaves themselves took the logic of occupation a step further and pushed for full freedom, with many fleeing to Union lines and presenting the army with a *fait accompli*.[6]

Military exigency combined with slave restiveness, and the institution of chattel slavery broke down rapidly under the pressure of occupation, black enlistment, and intermittent Union support for fugitive slaves. Planters could no longer, on their own, effectively assert authority over those they still considered their slaves. Thus, well before final emancipation, Union officers faced the problem of defining the character of work obligations.

General Benjamin F. Butler, commander of the Department of the Gulf, required fugitive slaves who had reached the Union lines to work, usually in menial and service jobs under direct military supervision. During the harvest of 1862, Union officers forced fugitives to work on the sugar estates, provided military enforcement of labor discipline on the plantations of "loyal" slaveholders who promised to pay wages to their slaves, and organized the production of sugar on confiscated estates. The experience left a bitter taste: many laborers were never paid, and some were subjected to corporal punishment.[7]

6   For a vivid picture of these conflicts, and of the shifting positions of the participants in them, see Ira Berlin, Barbara J. Fields, Thavolia Glymph, Joseph P. Reidy, Leslie S. Rowland, and Julie Saville, eds., *Freedom: A Documentary History of Emancipation, 1861-1867*, Series 1, Vol. 1, *The Destruction of Slavery* (Cambridge, 1985), chap. 4.

7   See the succinct and insightful account of the interplay of Union policy and Louisiana workers in Ira Berlin, Thavolia Glymph, Steven F. Miller, Joseph P. Reidy, Leslie S.

The results of congressional elections held in the occupied parishes in late 1862 met with federal approval, thus exempting slaves in the Louisiana sugar parishes from the Emancipation Proclamation in 1863, which was aimed only at areas still deemed to be in rebellion. So, during 1863, Union officers again improvised. General Nathaniel Banks, Butler's successor, attempted to institute contracts between planters and the government in which slaves would be bound for a year to labor for a nominal wage or a fractional share of the crop. Both planters and slaves balked at these arrangements, planters seeking greater direct control, slaves seeking greater mobility and liberty as well as more appropriate remuneration. The struggle became an open one, and slaves refused to work, seized equipment, and, in some cases, tried to work independently on abandoned plantations.

In early 1864, under increasing criticism of the Union-supervised labor system, Banks drafted new regulations, slightly more generous than the previous year's but still based on the assumption of wage labor and annual contracts. The new regulations did mandate the allocation of an acre of land to each first-class hand with a family and recommended larger allocations as part of the "encouragement of independent industry." Treasury Department rules issued the following month barred the raising of cotton or cane on such land, thus signaling that the allotments were an extension of the old provision grounds rather than a first step toward subdivision of land for staple production.[8]

Intense military recruitment of black soldiers further disrupted work on the estates, but, by the summer of 1864, Thomas Conway, head of the "Bureau of Free Labor," reported that some 50,000 freed people in southern Louisiana were employed as wage laborers on plantations, 35,000 of them with formal contracts.[9]

Rowland, and Julie Saville, eds., *Freedom: A Documentary History of Emancipation, 1861-1867*, Series 1, Vol. 3., *The Wartime Genesis of Free Labor: The Lower South* (Cambridge, 1990), 347-77. My own narrative draws on that chapter, and I am very grateful to the members of the Freedmen and Southern Society Project for sharing the typescript of it with me prior to its publication. See also C. Peter Ripley, *Slaves and Freedmen in Civil War Louisiana* (Baton Rouge, La., 1976); Joe Gray Taylor, *Louisiana Reconstructed: 1863-1877* (Baton Rouge 1974); and William F. Messner, *Freedmen and the Ideology of Free Labor, 1862-1865* (Lafayette, La., 1978).

8   On work regulations, see Berlin, *et al., Wartime Genesis*, chap. 2, documents 81, 109, and 113.

9   The figures from Conway are cited in Berlin, *et al., Wartime Genesis*, 371.

The effort to impose year-long contracts, with significant constraints on freedom of movement, had multiple origins. It arose in part from the specific needs of the occupying Union forces and the lessees to whom they had granted permission to operate abandoned or confiscated estates. But it also fit with the longstanding desire of planters to control their workers' mobility and be assured of labor at harvest time. It contrasts, interestingly, with the pattern that emerged later in Cuba and Brazil, where wage employment of former slaves, or of others, was more likely to be by the day or by the job.

Radical activists in New Orleans, particularly artisans and professionals among the *gens de couleur* and their white Unionist allies, denounced the efforts of planters to reassert full control over those who had been slaves. However great the social gaps between the *gens de couleur* and field slaves in the pre-war period, the necessity of an alliance had now become evident, as Louisiana became a focus for the national struggle over civil rights and the meaning of free labour.[10] "We have no rights which we can reckon safe while the same are denied to the fieldhands on the sugar plantations," observed one free man of color to the journalist Whitelaw Reid in 1865.[11] Not all of the *gens de couleur* agreed, but the vocal contributors to the New Orleans *Tribune* kept up the pressure.[12]

Parallel to the explicit effort by organized activists in New Orleans was a prior and decentralized effort by hundreds of former slaves in the sugar parishes. Working independently on old estates, sometimes organized into formal "labor companies," men and women on plantations like Potts, Johnson, and Woodlawn tried to assert a degree of proprietorship to the land and the right to choose their own crops and their own leaders. They planted corn, cotton, and occasionally cane on abandoned estates, in some cases fending off the claims of the lessees. During 1863, 1864, and early 1865, it looked as though this vision might occasionally prevail

10   See Eric Foner, *Reconstruction: America's Unfinished Revolution, 1863-1877* (New York, 1988), 62-65.

11   Whitelaw Reid, *After the War: A Southern Tour, May 1, 1865 to May 1, 1866* (London, 1866), 244. Also quoted in Eric Arnesen. *Waterfront Workers of New Orleans: Race, Class and Politics, 1863-1923* (New York, 1991) 16.

12   For a careful discussion of the *Tribune*, see the introduction to Jean-Charles Houzeau, *My Passage at the New Orleans "Tribune": A Memoir of the Civil War Era*, David C. Rankin, ed., Gerard F. Denault, trans. (Baton Rouge, La., 1984)

and substitute various forms of family labor in the production of subsistence and market crops for gang labor in the production of sugar. But these partial forms of proprietorship had survived only in the interstices of a wartime economy operating under clumsy and divided federal supervision, at a time of mixed signals from Union authorities; they were crushed in the restoration of peace.[13]

Although it would have been technically feasible to allocate cane lands to the freed people, as cotton lands were divided under sharecropping arrangements in northern Louisiana, and as cane lands had long been divided in Brazil, most planters in the Louisiana "Sugar Bowl" appear to have been convinced that former slaves would not be suitable partners in the enterprise of cane growing. The assistant inspector of freedmen for the Parish of Lafourche reported in 1866 that the planters "are generally averse to leasing land to the freedmen, though a very few in the Parish have done so."[14]

The planters preferred long-term contracts that ensured gang labor and limited the freed people's access to productive resources. A few of the terms of a contract from William J. Minor's plantation capture the spirit: "the laborers agreed to be respectful, obey orders, comply with all the rules and regulations (so long as sustained by the superintendent of freedmen of the district), work 10 hours each day except Sunday, keep no animals, cultivate no cotton, cane, or corn, take regular watches during the grinding season, and report every morning at the hospital when too unwell to work."[15]

A number of African-American delegates to the Louisiana constitutional convention of 1868 proposed breaking up the large estates by limiting the size of tracts that could be bought at distress sales and by increasing the tax on uncultivated land. But their challenge was

---

13 Evidence of these independent efforts can be found in a variety of wartime documents. See Berlin, et al., Wartime Genesis, chap. 2, Documents 91, 97, 106A, 114, and 133, for examples. A suggestive preliminary analysis of the labor companies is Paul Eiss, "Sharing the Land? The Production of Politics on Government Plantations, Terrebonne and Lafourche Parishes, Louisiana, 1863-1865," paper presented to the Third Michigan/Chicago Conference on Slavery, Emancipation, and Postemancipation Societies, April 1993.

14 Monthly report of Capt. C.E. Wilcox, Asst. Inspr. Freedmen, Parish of Lafourche, La., January 31, 1866, in Louisiana Assistant Commissioner. BRFAL, RG 105, USNA (M1027, Roll 28).

15 As described in J. Carlyle Sitterson, "The Transition from Slave to Free Economy on the William J. Minor Plantations," Agricultural History, 17, (1943): 216-24.

turned back. Sugar plantations changed hands but continued to operate as large-scale units. The number of working mills returned almost to its pre-war number, with 1,224 mills operating in 1873.[16] An increasing number were owned by partnerships and corporations, often with a significant component of Northern capital.

Even though cane land was rarely divided, some allocation of provision grounds continued. At the same time, planters had to relent on the number of days and hours of work that they could expect from laborers. The 1867 diary of the DeClouet family reflects both the concessions and the bad grace with which they were made: "Holy Friday. No work this morning the negroes being too pious to violate such holiness *by work*, but not too much so to go & harpoon fish in the high water. They however took up work at 2 o'clock as usual." And a week later: "Gave the negroes their land this evening."[17]

Although some planters found it difficult to raise capital for improvements working capital was available, and sugar prices in the late 1860s and early 1870s were relatively good.[18] Continued tariffs on foreign sugar partially insulated Louisiana from the competitive threat of Cuba. Planters did not have to resort to the subdivision of land as a measure of cash-poor desperation, but neither did they have the processing capacity that might encourage them to seek ways to arrange for an expansion of the total area under cane. Paying wages and permitting slaves to live in the old "quarters" may have seemed the optimum way to obtain labor while perpetuating dependent social relations. Moreover, the cultivation of food crops as well as cane tended to spread work demands relatively evenly across the year, making annual contracts an attractive proposition.

Within these constraints, the freed people sought to influence

16   In addition to the more recent sources cited above, see Roger Wallace Shugg, "Survival of the Plantation System in Louisiana," *Journal of Southern History*, 3 (August 1937): 311-25; and Prichard, "Effects of the Civil War."

17   See entries of April 19 and April 27, 1867, in Vol. 2, Diary, Box 2, Alexandre E. De-Clouet and Family Papers, Louisiana and Lower Mississippi Valley Collections, LSU Libraries, Louisiana State University (hereafter, LLMVC). Later references in the diary suggest that potatoes were an important crop on the land allocated to the freed people.

18   Sitterson emphasizes the difficulty of obtaining funds for new sugar investments. Sitterson, *Sugar Country*, 291-94. Jaynes, however, notes the importance of Northern capital, in the form of direct purchases of sugar estates by Northern investors after the war. Gerald David Jaynes, *Branches without Roots: Genesis of the Black Working Class in the American South* (New York, 1986), 238.

the level of wages through periodic work stoppages, and individuals and families often moved at the close of the year from one estate to another in search of better pay.[19] Opportunities were not likely to be much better elsewhere, but this modicum of mobility put some pressure on planters. Wages gradually climbed, and production grew, albeit slowly. By 1870, sugar output had reached almost 77,000 metric tons — modest by pre-war standards but impressive compared to the immediate postwar decline.[20]

For planters, however, the problem of access to credit became more severe with the panic of 1873, and the conditions of the world sugar market, combined with the growing power of the sugar refining trusts, forced producers to cut costs in order to compete. Faced with falling prices for their crop, planters engaged in a concerted effort to deal with what they portrayed as a "critical labor shortage," attempting among other things to lower costs by attracting seasonal labor.[21] Some planters also entered into explicit collaboration to set, and in some cases reduce, wages.[22]

Louisiana in the 1870s was a rough and bloody terrain on which to fight battles over the control of the labor process. On the one hand, fragile alliances between white Republicans and newly enfranchised African-American voters provided for the election of

19   A report from the parishes of Jefferson and Orleans in 1866 noted that the freedmen were "delaying to make a permanent contract" in hopes of being offered fifty cents an hour, and suggests that "this idea originated probably among freedmen working on the levee in the city who have recently been 'striking' for the aforesaid wages." Dougherty to Hayden, January 31, 1866. Inspection Report of Plantations, freedmen, &c. in the parishes Jefferson and Orleans, Right Bank, January 1866.

20   See Deerr, *History of Sugar*, 2:250; and Sitterson, *Sugar Country*, 251. Deerr's short tons have been converted to metric tons.

21   This process is described, from a somewhat different vantage point, in Sitterson, *Sugar Country*, chaps. 11-12. Planters also imported modest numbers of Italian workers seasonally to assist with the harvest. Working at the lowest-skill jobs and attempting to save as much from their wages as possible, they seem to have provided competition without much commingling. See Jean Ann Scarpaci, "Immigrants in the New South: Italians in Louisiana's Sugar Parishes, 1880-1910," *Labor History*, 16 (Spring 1975): 165-83.

22   See the discussion of planter collaboration in Taylor, *Louisiana Reconstructed*, 385-86; Sitterson, *Sugar Country*, 247; Thomas Becnel, *Labor, Church, and the Sugar Establishment: Louisiana, 1887-1976* (Baton Rouge, La., 1980), 5-7. Ralph Shlomowitz contrasts sugar and cotton regions, and concludes that effective collusion was short-lived in cotton areas but periodically effective during the 1870s over limited periods of time in cane regions. Shlomowitz, "'Bound' or 'Free'? Black Labor in Cotton and Sugarcane Farming, 1865-1880," *Journal of Southern History*, 50 (November 1984): 570-95.

local and state officials who could on occasion allow room for challenges to planters. On the other hand, explicitly white-supremacist paramilitary and vigilante groups were growing in importance, drawing together planters and other whites to "restore our state to its rightful rulers."[23]

For most rural employers, the struggle for control over labor and the broader quest for authority over people of color were inseparable. But the task was not an easy one. Sugar workers were brought together in large numbers at the workplace; they were often in communication with kin in town and with allies in New Orleans: they had not abandoned the search for land and greater autonomy.

When planters in Terrebonne Parish tried to reduce wages in 1873, the response was swift. Some two hundred laborers met at the Zion church and organized themselves into an association with a double goal: to "form sub-associations and rent land to work by themselves" and to "bind themselves not to work for any planter for less than $20 per month, rations, etc., the payments to be made monthly in cash." A second meeting to ratify these understandings was addressed by W.H. Keys and T.P. Shurbem, the first a member of the Louisiana legislature. The group then paraded behind a fife and drum through the town of Houma, "threatening the citizens but doing no harm," according to the hostile report in the New Orleans Daily Picayune.[24]

The next step was to spread the strike. On Tuesday, January 13, a group of some fifty men led by Alfred Kennedy, apparently armed, came down the bayou and halted, intending to stop work on H.O. Minor's plantation. They were deterred in their first attempt, and Minor sought a sheriff's posse, then militia forces. An unspecified settlement was reached but not without an array of alarmed and alarming reports in the press of murder and burning by rioters, virtually all of which turned out to be false.[25] The pre-

---

23   Several Louisiana sugar planters were active in the formation of White Leagues and Law and Order groups. The passage cited is from Committee White League to Hon. Alexandre DeClouet, St. Martinsville, June 19, 1874, in Folder 16, Box 1, Alexandre E. DeClouet and Family Papers, LLMVC. See also the introductory notes to, and the letters in, the Papers of Donelson Caffery, LLMVC. For a vivid general picture of Reconstruction Louisiana, see Ted Tunnell, *Crucible of Reconstruction: War, Radicalism and Race in Louisiana, 1862-1877* (Baton Rouge, La., 1984).

24   See the accounts in the *Daily Picayune* (New Orleans), January 14, 15, 16, and 20, 1874; and in Shlomowitz, "'Bound' or 'Free.'"

cise content of the settlement is unrecorded, but it seems to have involved wages only, not concessions on the question of leasing.

Workers' resistance to wage cuts, combined with the unavoidable competition among employers, was sufficient to thwart the efforts to impose wage ceilings in the early 1870s. But, as Reconstruction receded in the mid-1870s, and large landowners moved toward more thoroughgoing political control, some planters succeeded in imposing wage withholding and the payment of wages in scrip.[26]

The effort to cut costs also stimulated the development of central mills, which would take advantage of economies of scale by grinding cane from multiple suppliers. Many small-scale planters relinquished the manufacture of sugar and turned to the provision of cane to larger mills. In theory, the opening up of mills to several cane providers created new opportunities for small holders as well. But, instead of opening the way to semi-independent cane farming for former slaves, the growth of the central mills led to the replication of the longstanding racial divide. Planters first sought immigrant colonists, then other white farmers, to collaborate in this transition. Although black farmers were occasionally able to buy plots of cane land from bankrupt estates, or otherwise establish themselves as suppliers, the trend was for planters to seek to establish relations with white tenants or sharecroppers who could provide cane for the mill.[27]

The wage labor force in sugar continued to be composed primarily of African-American workers, although some small-scale white farmers and recent Italian immigrants were employed at harvest time. Relations among large landholders, sharecroppers, and wage workers were thus marked by an overlap of class categories with those of race. At the same time, the relative absence of

25   See *Daily Picayune* (New Orleans), January 14, 15, 16, and 20, 1874.

26   See Jeffrey Gould, "The Strike of 1887: Louisiana Sugar War." *Southern Exposure*, 12 (November-December 1984): 45-55.

27   See Joseph P. Reidy, "Sugar and Freedom: Emancipation in Louisiana's Sugar Parishes," presented at the 1980 American Historical Association Annual Meeting; and Reidy, "The Development of Central Factories and the Rise of Tenancy in Louisiana's Sugar Economy, 1880-1910," prepared for the Social Science History Association Convention, November 1982. I am very grateful to Professor Reidy for allowing me to read these unpublished essays. See also Roger W. Shugg, *Origins of Class Struggle in Louisiana* (Baton Rouge, La., 1972), chap. 8.

land rental and sharecropping among African Americans in the sugar parishes reinforced the old pattern of residence in plantation housing and meant less dispersion of population than in the cotton regions. Estates remained centers of population. Even though women had often withdrawn from full-time wage labor on the estates at the end of the war, for example, they frequently continued to live in "the quarters" and work seasonally in the cane. At the same time, the resident labor force was supplemented when young black men from the cotton parishes traveled to the sugar regions for the harvest.[28]

With racial lines etched into the division of labor and with white supremacy largely triumphant at the level of politics, the situation was hardly propitious for collective action. A recent study of waterfront workers in New Orleans argues that black and white workers initially occupied "separate material and ideological worlds," making any cross-racial alliances very fragile.[29] But, in the cane fields as on the waterfront, such alliances did occasionally emerge. The most dramatic instance was the sugar strike of 1887.

In November of 1887, some 6,000 to 10,000 field laborers, with leadership from local Knights of Labor assemblies, halted work in Terrebonne and Lafourche parishes to protest attempts by planters to cut wages and provide payment in scrip. The majority of the strikers were black, although some white workers were involved both as organizers and participants. Most of the white strikers, however, came from the Lower Lafourche region, where relatively underdeveloped plantations employed white, black, and mulatto workers. Planters there were quick to settle with the strikers. In Upper Lafourche, the strike leadership and rank and file were almost entirely black, and the planters were resolutely opposed to settlement. Black workers there soon found themselves holding the line nearly alone.[30]

28 A detailed — if biased — description of two Louisiana sugar estates can be found in J. Bradford Laws, "The Negroes of Cinclare Central Factory and Calumet Plantation, Louisiana." *Bulletin of the U.S. Department of Labor*, 38 (January 1902): 95-111. Jeffrey Gould, "'Heroic and Vigorous Action': An Analysis of the Sugar Cane Workers' Strike in Lafourche Parish, November, 1887," 1973, unpublished, discusses the employment of women, including some cases in which women were recruited as strikebreakers. I am very grateful to Professor Gould for making this paper available to me.

29 Arnesen, *Waterfront Workers*, 3.

30 This account of the strike draws on the reports in the *Thibodaux Sentinel*, November 5-

Planters persuaded the governor to send in the militia, which set up a Gatling gun in the main square of the parish seat of Thibodaux and assisted with the eviction of strikers from their cabins. Many workers retreated to Thibodaux, where they were taken in by urban black families. With the situation still highly unstable, the militia was withdrawn, and the initiative passed to the planters and local white vigilantes. When two white men were fired on by parties unknown on November 22, the repression began. The local white defense committee began pulling black men suspected of assocation with the strike from the homes in which they had taken refuge and executing them. At last thirty black men were killed in what was later called the Thibodaux massacre. The strike was broken; the Knights of Labor were soon driven from the parish.[31]

Mary Pugh, a planter's wife who witnessed portions of the massacre, wrote: "we have had a horrible three days & Wednesday excelled anything I ever saw even during the war. I am sick with the horror of it, but I know it had to be else we would all have been murdered before a great while. I think this will settle the question of who is to rule the nigger or the white man? for the next 50 years."[32] Her bitter prediction reflected the fusion of labor and racial preoccupations among planters. In subsequent decades, Louisiana sugar workers would indeed be politically silenced. African-American communities survived, but wages were low, opportunities were few, and the workplace itself generally ceased to be a locus for organizing collective action.

The concentration of production accelerated, and by the end of the century only 275 mills were grinding. But the accompanying rise of cane farming drew in very few black agriculturalists: in 1900, 2,964 white farmers listed their principal source of income as sugar, compared to 906 black farmers. (This contrasts dramatically with the state's cotton sector, which had 28,390 white farmers and

December 10, 1887, and on William Ivy Hair, *Bourbonism and Agrarian Protest: Louisiana Politics, 1877-1900* (Baton Rouge, La., 1969), esp. 175-84; Gould, "Strike of 1887"; and Becnel, *Labour, Church*, 7-8. An earlier essay by Gould, "'Heroic and Vigorous Action,'" cited above, analyzes the particular situation of Upper and Lower Lafourche planters in detail and links the regional division to the outcome of the strike.

31   For a fuller discussion of the 1887 strike, see Rebecca Scott, "Building, Bridging, and Breaching the Color Line: Rural Collective Action in Louisiana and Cuba, 1865-1912," forthcoming in Theda Skocpol, Judith Vichniac, George Ross, and Tony Smith, eds., *Democracy, Revolution and History*, a festschrift in honor of Barrington Moore, Jr.

32   Mary Pugh to Edward F. Pugh. November 25, 1887, Folder 1, Mrs. Mary W. Pugh Papers, 1882-1895, LLMVC.

51,078 black.) Wage labor, not tenancy or sharecropping, was the overwhelming pattern for African Americans in the Sugar Bowl. St. Mary Parish, for example, the major sugar-producing parish in the state, had a black population of 20,264 but only 248 farms owned or operated by black farmers.[33]

The denial of access to land consigned most former slaves and their descendants to the role of wage-paid farm laborers, and political defeat blocked the compensating possibility of organizing as workers.[34] The cooperative agriculture pioneered during the war and the union organization attempted in the 1880s gave way under the pressure of a fixed model of wage labor backed by both planters and the state, combined with a growing official hostility to organization of any kind among African Americans. The next phase of successful collective challenge would have to await the reconfiguring of power at the level of the state and the nation.[35]

IN THE ISLAND OF CUBA, THE CONTEST OVER the meaning of freedom took a different form. Louisiana's sugar region was a rich enclave within a powerful nation whose economy was largely focused on other products. Sugar in Cuba, by contrast,

---

33 U.S. Census Office, *Twelfth Census of the United States, Taken in the Year 1900, Census Reports, Vol. V, Agriculture*, Part 1, p. 23. The figures of the 1900 census make it difficult to separate white and black farmers by crop and form of tenantry, so one cannot specify the precise number of white and black tenants in sugar. Overall, there were 3,870 sugar farms, of which 1,871 were operated by owners, 240 by part owners, 18 by owners and tenants, 305 by managers, 544 by cash tenants, and 892 by share-tenants. *Ibid.*, p. 9. For figures on black population, see Vol. 1 of the *Census Reports*, titled *Population*, Part 1, p. 542.

34 Access to land through squatting was more difficult in Lousiana than in Cuba or Brazil. Runaways and squatters had long taken refuge in the swamps and along the bayous, but these regions could not support a significant part of the population, and patterns of land-holding and law left little room for squatters elsewhere in the sugar regions. There was a significant amount of squatting in the "piney woods" region, but it did not directly affect the plantation areas. See Shugg, "Survival of the Plantation System," 322. For a compelling portrait of the world of Louisiana sugar plantations in the first half of the twentieth century, see the fiction of Ernest J. Gaines, including *Bloodline* (New York, 1976).

35 Unions did not effectively organize again in the fields until after World War II. There were, however, occasional small-scale work stoppages in earlier years. *The Louisiana Planter and Sugar Manufacturer* reported on May 24, 1919, that there had been "a strike of field laborers on some of the plantations along the river just above Donaldsonville," and that they had succeeded in obtaining a raise from $1.25 to $1.50 a day. On later union activity, see Becnel, *Labor, Church.*

was the major source of wealth in Spain's last remaining major colony in the New World. The reorganization of production after emancipation would determine the fate of the entire island economy; the linkage between slave emancipation and an emerging Cuban nationalism would shape the political future of the colony.

In the early 1860s, approximately 173,000 slaves lived on about 1,500 sugar estates in Cuba, and average annual production between 1860 and 1864 was 478,000 metric tons. Cuba's largest *ingenios* (plantations combining fields and mill) were technologically advanced, most employing steam power and a significant minority using vacuum pans and centrifuges for processing. Whatever contradictions have been claimed to exist between slavery and technological advancement, Cuba's largest plantations continued to add new machinery even as they added more slaves.[36]

By the late 1860s, however, some form of abolition appeared likely. Spanish liberals increasingly enunciated antislavery principles; the Spanish government finally enforced the longstanding treaties banning the transatlantic slave trade; the victory of the Union Army in the U.S. Civil War increased the possibility of intervention in support of abolition; and anti-colonial rebels in the eastern provinces freed slaves in areas under their control and called for an end to slavery in the whole of the island. Emancipation itself was gradual and conflictual. In the face of half-measures advanced by the Spanish parliament, slaves pressed for more rapid and thoroughgoing change, while planters attempted to limit the speed and constrain the extent of the transition. During the period of formal "apprenticeship," 1880-1886, apprentices (*patrocinados*) accelerated their move toward freedom through self-purchase, flight, lawsuits, and individual negotiations. Over 100,000 of them gained their freedom prior to final abolition in 1886. Although external forces made abolition appear to be a logical step, it was the initiatives and determination of slaves, apprentices, and rebels that made it real and irrevocable.[37]

Planters responded to the end of slavery with what one might characterize as apprehensive innovation. The most successful plant-

---

36 For a full discussion of the Cuban sugar economy at mid-century and detailed figures on production, see Manuel Moreno Fraginals, *El ingenio: Complejo económico social cubano del azúcar,* 3 vols. (Havana, 1978). For figures on slave population, see Rebecca J. Scott, *Slave Emancipation in Cuba: The Transition to Free Labor, 1860-1899* (Princeton, N.J., 1985), chap. 1, esp. tables 4 and 5.

37 See Scott, *Slave Emancipation,* chap. 7.

ers already grew their cane in rich soil, processed the juice with advanced machinery, and sold their sugar to the expanding U.S. market. But the market for Cuban sugar was increasingly oligopolistic, as a small group of North American refiners sought semi-processed sugar at low prices to refine and resell.[38] Expansion was essential to survival, and many planters doubted that former slaves would provide a sufficient labor force for a growing sugar industry.

Planters explored the possibilities for immigration while taking their own steps to build narrow-gauge railways and shift toward an expanded network of cane suppliers.[39] The key to the rapid expansion of Cuban sugar production was the development of a system under which cane farmers (*colonos*) contracted with a central mill (*central*) to provide cane for grinding. The compensation paid to *colonos* reflected the price of sugar in Havana, thus shifting some of the risk of unstable prices from mill owner to grower.

Some landowners allocated small areas of cane land to former slaves to cultivate, as a means of keeping them on the estate. Meanwhile, smallholders, both renters and owners, began to plant a portion of their land in cane as new railway lines brought them within reach of expanded milling facilities, and some rented additional land from the *central*. Mill owners in areas of new development rented lands to immigrants from Spain and the Canary Islands, who then used family labor to supply cane to the mill under contract. Finally, some former estate owners and some new entrepreneurs became large-scale cane farmers, employing substantial numbers of laborers. All of these farmers were referred to as *colonos*, and their cane supplemented that cultivated by wage laborers on lands under the direct administration of the central mills.[40]

The dependence of the *colono* on the mill to transform his crop into a saleable commodity, combined with the perishability of the cane, meant that even when a *colono* owned his own land, he was not an independent farmer. Restrictive clauses and multi-year

38   See Alfred E. Eichner, *The Emergence of Oligopoly: Sugar Refining as a Case Study* (Baltimore, Md., 1969).

39   For examples of these intitiatives, see the petitions for permission to build railways in Leg. 201, Sección de Ultramar, Archivo Histórico Nacional, Madrid (hereafter, Ultramar, AHN).

40   On the *colonos*, see Scott, *Slave Emancipation*, chaps. 9, 10; and Alan Dale Dye, "Tropical Technology and Mass Production: The Expansion of Cuban Sugarmills, 1899-1929" (Ph.D. dissertation, University of Illinois, Urbana-Champaign, 1991).

contracts generally prevented him from seeking other buyers. Delays meant serious losses, for the sucrose content of the cane declines gradually once the peak moment for harvesting is past, and it declines precipitously shortly after the cane is cut. One *colono* charged in the early 1890s that estates habitually contracted for more cane than they could actually grind, thus leaving some of their *colonos* stranded at harvest time.[41] Many *colonos* grew some subsistence crops, affording them a buffer with which to survive periods of low prices or unreliable mills.

Under the *colonato* system, the question of access to the land was in some ways subordinate to the question of access to the mill. Large mills, eager to assure a supply of cane, were willing to rent land for a nominal fee; the terms of the cane contract, not the amount of rent, determined the level of profit. Even when the *colono* paid cash rent, his obligations went beyond those of a conventional cash tenant, since he was obliged by contract to plant cane, and the crucial variable of timing a delivery of his crop was set by the mill.[42] Rather than a form of tenancy, the *colonato* was in many cases a kind of "contract farming," perhaps structurally comparable to modern arrangements in which fryer chickens are raised on contract for a specific purchaser or tomatoes for a specific cannery.[43]

Smallholders not bound by *colono* contracts often tried to diversify their plantings rather than undertake the exclusive cultivation of sugar. Land registers from the municipality of Güines in the province of Havana in the early part of the twentieth century, for example, portray a patchwork of small farms growing a variety of crops, interspersed among larger estates and *colonias*. Small-scale owners, renters, and squatters often planted a bit of cane to sell to a nearby mill, but their holdings were not listed as *colonias*, and they were probably not formally counted as such in the census.[44]

41 Juan Bautista Jiménez. *Los esclavos blancos por un colono de Las Villas* (Havana, 1893), 7.

42 Brian Pollitt has argued that the question of actual ownership of cane land remains flexible in postrevolutionary Cuba and cites the ceding of land from state farms to producer cooperatives. The overarching concern remains that of supplying the mills with sufficient cane, regardless of provenance. See Brian Pollitt, "On Social and Technological Change in the Post-Revolutionary Sugar Industry in Cuba," unpublished, and personal communication, February 1990.

43 I am very grateful to Harold Woodman for suggesting the term "contract farming."

44 In the region of Melena, for example, the land register for 1905 shows the existence of numerous small farms. Many of these smallholdings are listed as *sitios*, not *colonias*, even

These tranformation in patterns of production had multiple implications for those who had been slaves. Former slaves were, in a sense, participants in two simultaneous developments: they were freed people seeking to make something of their new status, and they were rural workers attempting to cope with rapidly changing relations of production in agriculture. For those who remained in the older sugar provinces, where the *colonato* was less developed, the range of alternatives was narrow. In the western province of Matanzas, for example, the acquisition of land was nearly impossible. The census of 1899 counted approximately 26,000 "colored" men and women who worked in agriculture in the province, but there were only 537 farms owned or rented by people of color, and these occupied less than 4 percent of the agricultural land. Most freed people had become wage laborers.[45]

The situation was somewhat different in Santa Clara, a sugar-producing province with a history of some mixed agriculture, in which the *colonato* flourished. There, most people of color labored for wages, but a significant number managed to become renters and owners. The census counted 2,737 farms operated by owners or renters of color. The number of holdings operated by owners or renters of color was about 11 percent of the number of people of color working in agriculture in Santa Clara and 30 percent in Santiago de Cuba. Both were areas with a history of smallholding by free people of color before abolition.[46]

In the island as a whole, however, the majority of the properties formally denominated "sugar plantations" — including both estates that milled and cane farms that did not — were owned or rented by whites. The census of 1899 reported 11,271 such plantations in the island operated by white owners or renters and 3,165

---

though they cultivated some cane. See "Provincia de la Habana, Termino Mpal de Güines, Amillaramiento de 1905. Registro parcial de Fincas Rústicas que segun el resultado de las declaraciones presentadas por sus dueños o poseedores radicanen el Distrito Municipal de Melena," Archivo Nacional de Cuba, Secretaria de Hacienda, Libro 833.

45   See U.S. War Department, *Report on the Census of Cuba, 1899* (Washington, D.C., 1900), 556-57, 443. On tranformations in Matanzas, see Laird W. Bergad, *Cuban Rural Society in the Nineteenth Century: The Social and Economic History of Monoculture in Matanzas* (Princeton, N.J., 1990).

46   The comparable figures for white owners and renters as a percentage of the white population working in agriculture were 23 percent in Santa Clara and 29 percent in Santiago de Cuba. For a fuller discussion of the census evidence, see Scott, *Slave Emancipation*, chap. 11.

(comprising just 4.5 percent of the cane land) operated by "colored" owners or renters. Thus, while a larger absolute number of people of color became cane farmers in Cuba than in Louisiana, they were in both instances outnumbered more than three to one by their white counterparts.[47]

It is difficult to determine precisely how many former slaves obtained access to land, in part because the agricultural census counted holdings rather than people, and the population census grouped together those working in agriculture, without distinguishing between wage workers and farmers. Moreover, the labor of women on family holdings was undoubtedly very significant, but women seem not to have been counted as working in agriculture unless they were engaged in wage labor at the time of the census. Children and other kin of the owner or renter sometimes shared access to the land. Thus what appears in the census as a single holding actually represents the place of employment of several people. At the same time, because the holdings of persons of color were generally very small, some family members, particularly younger sons, also worked as wage laborers.[48]

Although most former slaves in Cuba could not acquire sufficient land to become independent farmers, a substantial minority had enough access to avoid complete proletarianization. In societies such as Barbados, where rights to small provision grounds were made contingent on the provision of labor to the landowner, cultivating such plots in some ways increased dependency, because all modes of subsistence came within the orbit of the plantation.[49] But, in Cuba, the cultivation of subsistence grounds, even by those whose major form of employment was wage labor, seems to have provided a margin for maneuver. A North American observer, writing somewhat later, gave a clear statement of the paradox facing Cuban planters in their dealings with their workers, a

---

47   Cane farms rented or owned by people of color were small in size and were concentrated in two provinces: Santiago de Cuba (with 1,708) and Santa Clara (with 1,003). There were very few *colonias* operated by Agro-Cubans in Havana, Matanzas Puerto Príncipe, or Pinar del Río. U.S. War Department, *Report on the Census of Cuba*, 560.

48   See U.S. War Department, *Report on the Census of Cuba*, 556-60; and the discussion in Scott, *Slave Emancipation*, chap. 11.

49   See Trevor Marshall, "Post-Emancipation Adjustments in Barbados, 1838 to 1876," in Alvin O. Thompson, ed., *Emancipation I: A Series of Lectures to Commemorate the 150th Anniversary of Emancipation* (Cave Hill, Barbados, 1986) 88-108.

paradox rooted in the seasonal fluctuations in the labor needs of the plantation:

> the fact that plantation hands are not assured permanent employment throughout the year leads them to depend upon the products of garden patches and other small holdings for their subsistence and to limit their needs to what these can supply. They thereby become in a measure independent of the landed proprietors in the matter of employment, and so afford a less reliable source of labor.[50]

This "unreliability," along with reduced "needs," was, of course, a reflection of a longstanding survival strategy.

By their refusal to shift en masse from slaves to proletarians, freedmen and freedwomen posed a series of challenges to those who sought to harness their labor for sugar. The Spanish colonial authorities briefly considered anti-vagrancy statues to try to compel rural dwellers to work for wages. But the authorities were reluctant to enact measures that might feed an anti-colonial struggle.[51] The importation of additional workers from the peninsula seemed politically more expedient. Some Spanish immigrants were provided with incentives to become *colonos*, while others were hired on the estates as wage workers. Tens of thousands of Spaniards traveled to Cuba seasonally or permanently, providing additional labor for an expanding sugar industry.[52]

The feared insurgency emerged nonetheless. Cuban nationalists challenged the Spanish state in a series of rebellions in 1868-1878 and 1879-1880, and by 1895 they had found the means to organize a multi-class, island-wide revolt. Political suppression, economic hardship, and direct affronts by the Spanish authorities had nourished resentments, and brilliant émigré leadership had brought together a cross-racial separatist alliance. Although the Spanish government moved quickly to meet the insurgent threat and tried to

---

50   Victor Clark, "Labor Conditions in Cuba," *Bulletin of the Department of Labor,* 41 (July 1902): 694.

51   See the debate, and particularly the advisory opinion of the Consejo de Administración, September 13, 1888, in "Medios de estirpar la vagancia," legajo 4942, expediente 345, Ultramar, AHN.

52   See Jordi Maluquer de Motes, *Nación e immigración: Los españoles en Cuba (ss. xix y xx)*(Gijón, 1992).

garrison both towns and sugar estates, the insurgency picked up steam. The rebels quickly came to dominate much of the countryside.

Thousands of rural Cubans of color joined the struggle, both as enlisted men and as officers. Although many came from the smallholding peasantry, sugar plantations themselves also served as centers for recruitment and as battlegrounds in the struggle for terrain. At the same time, plantation residents who did not join the armed struggle could provide substantial material aid through cultivating food supplies or smuggling out supplies. The central mill was a highly porous institution, with hundreds of workers coming and going in the normal course of events. Moreover, its work force was a loosely joined mix of former slaves, peasants, and immigrant workers. There was no possibility of effectively locking them up as slaves had been locked up in the 1860s and 1870s — although this did not stop the Spanish authorities from trying.[53]

Former slaves who fought in the insurgent ranks seem to have hoped that opportunities denied them after slave emancipation would be realized in a new republic and that the invidious distinctions and privileges of colonial society would be extinguished. But this was not to be. The United States intervened, delivering the *coup de grâce* to Spanish colonialism, occupying the island and opening the way for massive new investment in the sugar industry. The nationalist vision of self-determination — which for Afro-Cubans also implied racial equality — was pushed aside.[54]

Even after the formal withdrawal of U.S. occupying forces, economic involvement continued unabated. The industry expanded through the opening of new lands for sugar cultivation and the construction of new mills. Although some Cuban observers feared a process of proletarianization of *colonos*, the basic pattern of buying cane from *colonos* to mill along with cane from estate continued.

53   The case files of the Spanish Treaty Claims Commission provide an excellent source for understanding the link between plantations and the war effort. See, for example, the account of events on the Triunfo Estate contained in Claim 475 (Whiting), Entry 352, RG 76, USNA. For a further discussion, see Rebecca Scott, "Mobilizing across the Color Line: Race, Class, and Anti-Colonial Insurgency in Cuba, 1895-98," paper presented at the Seminario de Historia de Cuba, Universitat Autònoma de Barcelona, March 25, 26, 1993.

54   Ada Ferrer, "The Black Insurgent and Cuban National Identity, 1895-1898," paper presented at the Seminario de Historia de Cuba, Universitat Autònoma de Barcelona, March 25, 26, 1993.

Small-scale subsistence and market cultivators were indeed threatened by the expansion of sugar, however, and the new American-owned *centrales* in the east often bought up new lands and cultivated them directly with wage labor."[55]

Former slaves faced increased competition when planters recruited cane cutters from Spain, Haiti, and Jamaica. Cuban sugar workers, however, often resisted the burgeoning power of the large estates and attempted to protect themselves against the arbitrary exercise of power by planters. In the municipality of Cruces, located in south central Cuba, the district with the highest concentration of sugar plantations on the island, strikes in the cities in 1902 spread to the countryside. There, the Workers' Guild, led by anarchists, carried the red flag from plantation to plantation, stopping work. Even though the ideology of the Workers' Guild was strongly influenced by Spanish immigrants, its credo repudiated ethnic divisions. One call to a meeting by the guild listed the meeting place as the local Centro Africano; among the signers was Evaristo Landa, a mulatto leader from the 1895-1898 war. Their strategy for mobilization seems to have been to ally with members of older Afro-Cuban cultural and educational societies, recruit veterans who had gained prestige in the War of Independence, and analyze the crisis of wages in the relatively new language of anarchism.[56]

The construction of these cross-ethnic and cross-racial alliances reflected various ideological and social forces. Spanish-born anar-

---

55 For a discussion of land ownership, see Fe Iglesias Garcia, "Algunos aspectos de la distribución de la tierra en 1899," *Santiago*, 40 (December 1980): 119-78. Iglesias (p. 129) cites figures from the U.S. occupation government suggesting that *colonias de caña* occupied some 5.37 percent of the cultivated area in the western and central provinces, with *ingenios de azúcar* occupying 13.38 percent. There were still some 30,000 *colonos* growing cane in the 1930s. For 1919 figures, see Cuba, Dirección general del censo. *Census of the Republic of Cuba, 1919* (Havana, 1922 [?]), 82-85. On the overall fate of Cuban sugar producers and the survival of the *colonos*, see Brian Pollitt, "The Cuban Sugar Economy and the Great Depression," *Bulletin of Latin American Research*, 3 (1984): 3-28; and Dye, "Tropical Technology."

56 See John Dumoulin, "El primer desarrollo del movimiento obrero y la formación del proletariado en el sector azucarero, Cruces 1886-1902," *Islas: Revista de la Universidad de las Villas*, 48 (May-August 1974): 5-66. The initial strike was ended by the intervention of the Rural Guard, on orders from the provincial governor, but other strikes followed. See also John Dumoulin, *El movimiento obrero en Cruces, 1902-1925*, published as a volume of Sonia Aragón García, ed., *Las clases y la lucha de clases en la sociedad neocolonial cubana* (Havana, 1981).

chists, always a numerical minority, had good reasons to repudiate divisions on the basis of nationality; Afro-Cuban veterans of the War of Independence had every reason to try to revive the anti-racism of José Marti and Antonio Maceo. For both, the struggle against slavery could provide a symbolic touchstone. The anarchist journal ¡Tierra!, edited by a Spaniard, described the rallying cry of the movement as "the emancipation of all slaves, the disappearance of all privileges."[57]

At the same time, these strategies reflected the realities of social relations. Wage work in sugar was not associated with a single socioracial grouping. Although Afro-Cubans were probably over-represented in field work, and under-represented in millwork, the concentration of seasonal Spanish workers in cane cutting meant that the field work force was not the highly segregated one that prevailed in Louisiana. A multi-racial work force did not make cross-racial alliances automatic, but it did make them feasible.[58]

The mobilization of resistance was also assisted by the ease of communication between town and country. The seasonality of labor in the mills and fields meant that agricultural workers were often town dwellers for much of the year, and agricultural wage labor was frequently part of a larger family strategy of subsistence. Such family strategies had rural and urban variants, building on a sexual division of labor that varied with the season and the opportunities. Some women moved into full-time urban occupations; others returned to field work at harvest time.[59] For both men and women, the plantation did not generally define the boundaries of existence.

Workers' search for greater control over the pace and pattern of labor had multiple implications. A North American observer, Victor S. Clark, commented in 1902 on the preference of many Cuban workers for contract or piecework rather than "a regular wage," and he attributed the growth of the colonato in part to this preference. His explanations were condescending but nonetheless

---

57 Dumoulin, "El primer desarrollo," 16.

58 Nor did the existence of such a multi-racial work force block the possibility of overtly racist repression, of which the events of 1912 were the most striking example. See Louis A. Pérez, Jr., "Politics, Peasants and People of Color: The 1912 'Race War' in Cuba Reconsidered," *Hispanic American Historical Review*, 66 (August 1986); 509-39; and Aline Helg, "Afro-Cuban Protest: The Partido Independiente de Color, 1908-1912." *Cuban Studies*, 21 (1991): 101-21.

59 For a brief discussion of these family strategies, see Scott, *Slave Emancipation*, 242-44.

astute: "[Piecework] seems to appeal to a speculative tendency in his [the worker's] nature that adds interest to his occupation. It also flatters a certain sentiment of self-esteem. He feels himself more independent, more his own master, in the former instance." For the workers themselves, creating and maintaining a distance from the old patterns of direct oversight was not a mere matter of vanity. It was part of defining the meaning of freedom. Indeed, this assertiveness could go a step further and become a forthright claim of equality. "Cuba is one of the most democratic countries of the world," Clark reported with some hyperbole. "Nowhere else does the least-considered member of a community aspire with more serene confidence to social equality with its most exalted personage." However forcefully occupation by the United States has thwarted the aspiration for full national independence, many Cubans still insist on their own version of republican values.[60]

In Cuba, then, the shift from unpaid sugar worker to wage-paid free worker frequently involved a change in residence, increased physical mobility, a new family division of labor, and incorporation into an ethnically heterogeneous work force. Most former slaves who remained in the sugar zones became wage laborers working by the day, the month, or the task, rather than sharecroppers, tenants, or owners. In this, they resembled to a degree their counterparts in Louisiana. But, in joining the free work force in sugar, former slaves were moving into a group whose numbers were rapidly being increased by European and, later, by West Indian immigration, as well as by the employment of native whites.[61]

Under these circumstances, the transition to free labor had a particular meaning for former slaves and their descendents: they continued to labor without much hope of advancement but often in a changing setting, with new co-workers and new employers. Cuban workers generally insisted on physical mobility and often managed to increase their options through internal migration or through provision ground cultivation. The relative openness of portions of Cuban hinterland in the late nineteenth century helped to make these strategies possible; the presence of a significant free rural population of color provided precedents. At the

60   Clark, "Labor Conditions in Cuba," 694, 780.

61   By 1919, the category "agriculturalist" (encompassing peasants, commercial farmers, and rural wage laborers) included 249,500 native white males, 130,500 "colored" males (including Asians), and 65,100 foreign white males. Cuba, Census . . . 1919, 666.

same time, those who worked on sugar estates tried to shape the terms under which they labored, sometimes contracting to perform a specific task rather than submitting to supervised day wage labor, sometimes uniting in search of higher wages.[62]

While the anarchists of Cruces openly identified themselves as belonging to a class of men who sweated to earn a paltry wage, many Cuban workers were poised somewhere between independence and dependence, having taken sideroads off what planters imagined to be the highway to proletarianization. Their access to productive resources was attenuated, but they resisted, both substantively and symbolically, being relegated to the status of mere hired labor. Lawyers interviewing one Cuban cane hauler, Antonio Matos y Navarro, stumbled on the distinction in his own mind between workman and hireling:

Q4. By whom are you employed at the present time?
A. At present — I work with a cart.
Q5. For whom?
A. For me — for the cart is mine.[63]

Proletarianization may well have been the eventual fate of Antonio Matos y Navarro, who worked on the American-owned Hormiguero estate in central Cuba. But, as of 1904, he had not yet conceded the point. His autonomy, however, was fragile, and would depend on maintaining ownership of the cart (and presumably the ox) and on the state of the market for his services. For many former slaves, with neither cart nor ox, the slide toward dependence on wages would advance even more rapidly.

---

62 Clark, "Labor Conditions in Cuba," 694, commented, "Perhaps there is a prejudice against hired service that has come down from the days of slavery and contract labor." Nonetheless, the records of sugar estates show very extensive use of day wages. One owner described work on the cane land under his ownership: "We do everything by day's work. Hire the men by the day — by the month, rather: and they are ordered to do the different kinds of work by the managers of the colonias, under instructions from the office." Deposition of Elias Ponvert, beginning January 25, 1904, p. 209, Claim 293 (Hormiguero), Pt. 1, Spanish Treaty Claims, Entry 352, RG 76, USNA.

63 Deposition of Antonio Matos y Navarro, beginning February 9, 1904, p. 2, Claim 293 (Hormiguero), Pt. 2, Spanish Treaty Claims, Entry 352, RG 76, USNA.

NORTHEASTERN BRAZIL, WHERE THE LARGE-SCALE production of sugar had been pioneered, presents a very different picture.[64] Although the region contained hundreds of thousands of slaves in the 1870s, it had been eclipsed within the national economy by the rapid expansion of the coffee industry in southern Brazil. After a period of growth at mid-century, the sugar industry found itself in an increasingly insecure position, unable to compete internationally with Cuban cane sugar and European beet sugar. Many slaves were sold from the northeast to the coffee regions; others acquired their freedom from faltering sugar plantations in the last decades of slavery.[65] Nonetheless, most sugar planters did not willingly relinquish the majority of their slaves, and as late as 1887 there were still almost 77,000 slaves in Bahia and another 41,000 in Pernambuco.[66] Owners of sugar plantations worried about the declining numbers of slaves and about the "ferment of indiscipline" that they attributed to emancipationist propaganda.[67]

In May 1888, the institution of slavery finally gave way under the pressure of abolitionist agitation, slave initiatives, and imperial politics. In the Bahian Recôncavo, one exasperated planter and municipal councillor wrote from São Francisco do Conde that everything was in complete confusion. He and several of his

64   The Brazilian Institute of Geography and Statistics uses the term Northeastern Brazil to refer to the states of Maranhão, Piauí, Ceará, Rio Grande do Norte, Paraíba, Pernambuco, Alagoas, Sergipe, Bahia, and the territory of Fernando de Noronha. For the purposes of this discussion of the sugar industry, I will confine my attention primarily to the moist riverine and coastal region, the *zona da mata*, between Rio Grande do Norte and the Recôncavo of Bahia, and I will concentrate on Pernambuco and Bahia. See Manuel Correia de Andrade, *A terra e o homem no nordeste*, 4th edn. (São Paulo, 1980), chap. 2.

65   Robert Slenes gives an estimate of over 400,000 for the slave population of the entire northeast (excluding Maranhao) around 1873. Bahia alone contained over 165,000 slaves. The conventional view is that unprofitability in the northeast caused planters to sell their slaves to the south in the interprovincial trade. Slenes argues, however, that "the available data suggest that the majority of slaves in the internal trade did not come from the sugar or coffee industries but from non-plantation activites." See Robert Wayne Slenes, "The Demography and Economics of Brazilian Slavery: 1850-1888" (Ph.D. dissertation, Stanford University, 1975), 57, 208.

66   The figure for Bahia is from *Falla . . . Presidente da Provincia . . . 1 Outubro de 1887* (Salvador, Bahia, 1887), 129. That for Pernambuco is from Peter L. Eisenberg, *The Sugar Industry in Pernambuco: Modernization without Change, 1840-1910* (Berkeley, Calif., 1974), 147.

67   See the analysis in Henrique August Milet, *A lavoura da canna de assucar* (Recife, 1881), viii.

neighbors had freed their remaining slaves a few days early, hoping to incorporate them into the existing population of resident former slaves and labor tenants. But, he reported, even the best-run plantations were witnessing a response of what he termed "respectful inertia" from the freed people. He predicted that the province would soon see a demand by the freed people to remain on the estates, without providing labor or rent. Although his language echoed the usual elite predictions of laziness on the part of freed people, he also recognized what seems to have been a core desire of former slaves: to gain or retain access to land. Two months later, he reported that the freed people believed that, by virtue of the abolition decree, they should have land and that they expected planters to turn the land over to them.[68]

Northeastern planters had a long tradition of allowing rural folk, some of them former slaves, to occupy plots of land as *moradores*. The word literally meant dwellers; in practice, it referred to labor tenants, or tenants-at-will, who occupied land in return for the provision of labor to the estate. Now some of the newly freed were taking this model one step further and insisting on immediate access to land on their own terms. Granting land might be a bargain for the owner, for it allowed him to pay below-subsistence wages, but the "respectful intertia" of former slaves left no doubt that his formal title to land did not imply uncontested dominion.

A year after abolition, the empire itself fell, and Brazil began its long experiment with elite-dominated republican government. The federal government was willing to subsidize immigration to the expanding coffee regions of the south, but landowners in the rest of the country were left largely to their own devices in the area of labor supply. Thus, while in the coffee regions, work relations were rapidly transformed by the development of new forms of immigrant sharecropping, in the northeast planters fell back on traditional forms of dependent labor. Anti-vagrancy legislation provided a modicum of legal compulsion, and occasional efforts to establish immigrant colonies added a few workers, but each employer was largely responsible for recruiting or retaining his or her own work force.[69]

68 Paço da Câmara Municipal, São Francisco, May 19, 1888, to President of the Province of Bahia: and Paço da Câmara Municipal, São Francisco, July 10, 1888, to President of the Province of Bahia, both in Maço 1436, Seçao Histórica, Arquivo Público do Estado da Bahia, Salvador, Bahia (hereafter APEB).

69 For a discussion of efforts to use vagrancy legislation to assist in labor recruitment in Per-

Brazilian seigneurial power — in politics and in the internecine warfare of the countryside — had long rested on dominance over free dependents as well as slaves. Selected dependents served literally as henchmen, *capangas*, defending the landowner's interests with violence when necessary. The group of people who owed some form of dependent service to the patron included once-autonomous peasants who had been subordinated to the estate as well as former slaves who had achieved freedom during the long process of the decline of slavery. Although they lived on land claimed by the estate, these *moradores* had often avoided wage labor and had grown food crops on shares rather than working steadily in sugar. Consistent with the dispersed pattern of slave holding in northeastern Brazil, some *moradores* had even owned a slave or two. (One *morador* in Bahia, fined for failing to register the child of a slave, explained his oversight as a result of "ignorance, as a rustic man, and poor, and one who has the additional misfortune of living among people who are equally rustic."[70])

In practical terms, *moradores* were neither peasants nor full proletarians — they worked for wages, but they relied heavily on family cultivation of provision and small-scale market crops for survival. They generally grew manioc, the "poor sister" of sugar cane, essential for subsistence and salable at the *feiras* held in nearby towns. In Bahia, for example, *moradores* on sugar estates in the early twentieth century grew both manioc and tobacco for sale, providing them with a small marginal income "to be spent in February in the festivals of Santo Amaro." These *moradores* also performed some unpaid labor services in return for the "favor" of being allowed to cultivate their garden plots (*roçados*) or to receive advances on their wages.[71]

Even with an abundant supply of labor in the plantation zones, planters also drew on migrants from the dry interior, the *sertão*. The extremely harsh conditions of the *sertao* encouraged a seasonal migration of backlanders — known as *corumbás, catingueiros*, or *retirantes* — who arrived famished and in need of work. They re-

nambuco, see Martha Knisely Huggins, *From Slavery to Vagrancy in Brazil: Crime and Social Control in the Third World* (New Brunswick, N.J., 1985).

70   Informe o Senr Inspector da Thesouraria de Fazenda, 3 Maio de 1877, in Escravos (Assuntos 1877-89), Judiciário, Presidencia da Provincia, APEB.

71   S. Fróes Abreu, *Alguns aspectos da Bahia* (Rio de Janeiro, 1926), 71. Santo Amaro is a major town in the sugar region of the Bahian Recôncavo.

mained on the coast, often working as cattle handlers on the estates, until the rains came in the interior. Their presence at harvest time reduced still further the pressure planters might otherwise have been under to raise wages or attempt to institute long-term contracts with their resident laborers.[72]

The Brazilian historian and geographer Manuel Correia de Andrade has argued that wage labor as such only came into general use in the northeast in the early decades of the twentieth century and that it did not predominate in the sugar industry until the 1960s, with the application of the Statute of the Rural Laborer.[73] The transition, in effect, was not one from slavery to wage labor but rather from slavery to hybrid work forms, which in turn evolved slowly toward wage labor, with deviations and reversals along the way.

In effect, seemingly outmoded forms of labor gave considerable flexibility to the sugar industry, permitting enterprises to expand and contract cane production without major outlays of cash, while retaining a reserve force of potential laborers.[74] At the same time, the structure of sugar production itself was changing. The first step was the establishment of the short-lived *engenhos centrais* in the 1870s and 1880s, mills heavily subsidized by the state, which did not grow their own cane but ground cane from a range of suppliers. The next phase was that of the *usina*, a vertically integrated enterprise that both grew cane and processed it, while drawing in additional supplies from other growers. The *usinas* more closely resembled the central mills of Louisiana and Cuba, and they became the dominant form in much of the Brazilian northeast by the end of the century.[75]

---

72 For a discussion of migrant and fixed labor in Pernambuco, see Jaime Reis, "From *Banguê* to *Usina*: Social Aspects of Growth and Modernization in the Sugar Industry of Pernambuco, Brazil, 1850-1920," in Keith Duncan and Ian Rutledge, eds., *Land and Labour in Latin America* (Cambridge, 1977), 369-96. On Bahia, see Abreu, *Alguns aspectos*, 70-73.

73 Manuel Correia de Andrade, "Transiçâo do trabalho escravo para o trabalho livre no nordeste açucareiro: 1850/1888," *Estudos econômicos*, 13 (January-April, 1983): 71-83.

74 This argument is made in Antônio Barros de Castro, *7 ensaios sôbre a economia brasileira*, vol. 2 (Rio de Janeiro, 1971), 28-29.

75 Discussions of modernization in the Brazilian sugar industry include Eisenberg, *Sugar Industry*; Nathaniel H. Leff, *Underdevelopment and Development in Brazil* (London, 1982), 6-40; Gadiel Perruci, *A república das usinas: Um estudo de história social e econômica do nordeste: 1889-1930* (Rio de Janeiro, 1978); Reis, "From *Banguê* to *Usina*"; and Denslow,

The farming of cane for provision to mills owned by others had a long history in Brazil, and *lavradores de cana* (cane farmers) had constituted an important intermediate social group in the colonial and early national periods. These early cane farmers were dependent on the mills, but as slaveholders they shared certain interests and aspirations with the larger planters. Like *colonos* in Cuba, their wealth, status, and racial categorization varied, and the term *lavradores de cana* initially included landowners, renters, and sharecroppers.[76]

The number of cane farmers seems to have remained relatively high through the postemancipation period. Even more so than in Cuba, owners of small estates with primitive mills sold cane to neighboring large mills for grinding. These *fornecedores de cana* (literally, cane furnishers) and the smaller scale *lavradores de cana* (cane farmers, often share-tenants) constituted a rural middle group, some in decline and some in ascent.

Written contracts were generally less common in Brazil than in Cuba, so it is difficult to compare the situation of Cuban and Brazilian cane farmers precisely. But, according to analysts of the postemancipation sugar industry in Pernambuco, large-scale cane suppliers owed a percentage of their output to the mill in exchange for grinding, and they employed substantial numbers of laborers, at wages that at least one group of growers admitted were "miserable."[77] Small-scale *lavradores de cana* generally owed a larger percentage of the value of the cane they produced to the mill as rent, up to between 30 and 50 percent of the total output.[78]

"Sugar Production," 42.

76   On *lavradores* in the colonial period, see Stuart Schwartz, *Sugar Plantations in the Formation of Brazilian Society: Bahia, 1550-1835* (New York, 1985). On *lavradores* in the nineteenth and twentieth centuries, see Reis, "From *Banguê* to *Usina*"; and Gileno Dé Carli, *O processo histórico da usina em Pernambuco* (Rio de Janeiro, 1942).

77   See the petition of cane growers in Pernambuco in 1928 quoted in Dé Carli, *O processo histórico*, 33.

78   See Dé Carli, *O processo histórico*, 20-23. He describes both *rendeiro* and *parceiro* arrangements, with renters paying a percentage of output as rent but guaranteeing a minimum rental payment, and sharecroppers owing no minimum but paying a higher percentage. Eisenberg, discussing the late nineteenth century, translates *lavrador* as sharecropper and cites payments of one half the cane and all the molasses, rum, and waste products. *Sugar Industry*, 191. In terms of the typology for the United States developed by Harold Woodman, these sharecroppers might be described as share renters, for they paid a portion of the crop as rent, rather than receiving the value of a portion of the crop as wages.

In the last decades of the nineteenth century and the first decades of the twentieth, the owners of *usinas* (central mills) sought control over substantial areas of cane and actively pursued the purchase of land from the traditional sugar estates. Particularly in Pernambuco, the attempted monopolization of land by the *usinas* was perceived by the old estate owners as an unwelcome transformation and an act of aggression against their prerogatives. However, periodic falls in sugar prices restrained the *usinas* somewhat.[79] In order to reduce costs, the owners of central mills themselves were often eager to use sharecropping cane farmers on newly purchased land. As in Cuba, cane farmers bought their partial independence at the cost of absorbing the impact of low sugar prices.

The consequences of the development of central mills in Brazil were, however, strikingly different from those in Cuba. Increasing productivity still did not make the region competitive, in part because productivity grew even faster in Cuba. Between 1880 and 1910, exports of sugar from the states of Pernambuco, Alagoas, and Paraíba showed an average annual growth rate of zero, compared to more than 4 percent annually in Cuba.[80] In 1894, Brazil's total production reached less than one-third that of Cuba.[81] Population continued to grow, but demand was weak, output was stag-

The fact that the cane has little value until it is consigned to the mill, however, tends to blur the distinction. See Harold D. Woodman, "Post-Civil War Southern Agriculture and the Law," *Agricultural History*, 53 (January 1979): 319-37.

79   See, in particular, Dé Carli, *O processo*. One might contrast this to the situation in Cuba, where much of the expansion that fueled the central mills was onto lands not previously cultivated in cane.

80   David Denslow concludes, "By 1908 total factor productivity of sugar mills in Cuba was over seventy percent greater than that of mills in the Northeast," due in large part to the use in Cuba of very large mills, which extracted more juice per ton of cane. He emphasizes the role of topography in restricting the area from which cane could profitably be drawn to a central grinding mill in Brazil. See Denslow, "Sugar Production in Northeastern Brazil and Cuba, 1858-1908" (Ph.D. dissertation, Yale University, 1974), chap. 2, table 1, and abstract. Bahian sugar exports suffered an absolute decline. For Bahia in the 1880s, see Francisco Marques de Goes Calmon, *Vida econômico-financeira da Bahia: Elementos para a história de 1808 a 1899* (Salvador, Bahia, 1925), table between 106 and 107. For the period 1911-1920, see Brazil, Ministerio de Agricultura, Industria e Commercio, Directoria do Serviço de Inspecção e Fomento Agricolas, *Aspectos da economia rural brasileira* (Rio de Janeiro, 1922), 440.

81   Barbosa Lima Sobrinho, "O Governo Barbosa Lima e a Industria Açucareira," *Annuario Açucareiro para 1938* (Rio de Janeiro, 1938), 353-67. The comparison between Cuba and Brazil appears on 355-56. See also Deerr, *History of Sugar*, 1: 113, 131.

nant, wages were very low, and the internal reorganization that accompanied abolition was less thoroughgoing than in Cuba and Louisiana.[82] Among other things, no war had accompanied emancipation in northeastern Brazil, as it had in Louisiana and Cuba. Mills were neither burned nor confiscated: transformation was not hastened by the destruction of old equipment. Small estates in Pernambuco, for example, often retained their mills and ground their own cane when they were not satisfied with the prices offered by the *usinas*.[83] In Bahia, as late as the 1920s, there were still some 2,000 little mills, called *engenhocas*, producing sugar and the cruder *rapadura*, a coarse brown sugar for local consumption.[84]

It was this process that Peter Eisenberg called "modernization without change" and that has generally been interpreted as implying a crushing continuity of dependence and poverty for former slaves. While this is in one sense quite accurate — indeed, rural northeasterners may have been even more malnourished after emancipation than before — an overemphasis on continuity may obscure the importance of access to land that many former slaves did achieve.[85] Even for squatters and small-scale cane farmers, subsistence and cash-crop cultivation permitted a sense of identity as peasant or farmer, rather than as mere laborer, and provided a practical means of limiting direct dependence on wages. Access to land made it possible to utilize more fully the labor of family members, including women, and to exhange labor with one's neighbors. These labor exchanges, in turn, strengthened horizontal ties among the poor, providing something of a counterweight to the more asymmetrical obligations inherent in the patron-client bond

82 The evidence for low wages in Pernambuco is clear. See Jaime Reis, "From *Bangué* to *Usina*," 375; Eisenberg, *Sugar Industry*, 190; and Denslow, "Sugar Production," 56. Planters in Bahia, however, continued to speak of a labor shortage, and our evidence on wages in Bahia is thin. An observer in Bahia in 1925 believed that many former slaves had initially ceased working in cane and that, after the initial crisis, "resurgiu a lavoura em novos moldes, pagando caro ao trabalhador e logrando resultados pouco compensadores." Of course, what former slaveholders perceived as "expensive" labor may not have involved very high wages. Abreu, *Alguns aspectos*, 68.

83 See Eisenberg, *Modernization*, 106-07.

84 See Brazil, Ministerio de Agricultura, *Aspectos da economia rural brasileira*, 435.

85 On levels of malnutrition, see Jaime Reis, "Hunger in the Northeast: Some Historical Aspects," in Simon Mitchell, ed., *The Logic of Poverty: The Case of the Brazilian Northeast* (London, 1981), 41-57. &

with the landowner.[86]

Even though the physical work performed by labor tenants might differ little from that performed by slaves, the orbits of their lives now had a somewhat different shape. While slaves had lived in a centralized set of quarters under direct supervision, *moradores* usually built their huts "at scattered points on the estates." An even more general dispersion of the population was probably presented by the development of central mills, but the small-scale dispersion within estates could be of crucial importance to the development of a life oriented toward family and neighbors rather than employer. And, to the extent that freedom of movement could be maintained, it provided some constraint on the exactions that could be imposed on rural dwellers.[87]

The category of *morador*, moreover, represented no fixed "racial" identity. The longstanding incorporation of freed slaves into the rural population continued after abolition, expanding the size of a rural free population that had long been composed of folks of African, European, Indian, and "mixed" descent. Although impoverishment and African ancestry were certainly correlated, plantation labor itself was not segregated by social race.

Much of the coastal region was already occupied, but some former slaves found spaces in which to plant manioc as the economy in sugar faltered, or they moved into tobacco, a cash crop that could be grown on a very small plot of land with relatively modest capital investment. In this respect, tobacco in Bahia may have been comparable to coffee in eastern Cuba or bananas in Jamaica — an area of agriculture in which a smallholding peasantry, including former slaves or their descendants, could produce a cash crop for export.[88] The tobacco factories of towns in the Recôn-

---

86   For a general discussion of forms of labor exchange in the northeast, see Helio Galvao, *O mutirao no nordeste* (Rio de Janeiro, 1959).

87   For a geographer's perspective on this process, see J.H. Galloway, "The Sugar Industry of Pernambuco during the Nineteenth Century," *Annals of the Association of American Geographers*, 58 (June 1968): 285-303. On the effects of freedom of movement, see Reis, "From *Banguê* to *Usina*."

88   Judith Allen has also suggested a parallel between tobacco in Bahia and coffee in Haiti, each providing for a certain amount of what Michel-Rolph Trouillot has called "motion in the system" by offering opportunities to free people of color. Personal communication, 1991. See Trouillot, "Motion in the System: Coffee, Color, and Slavery in Eighteenth-Century Saint-Domingue," *Review*, 5 (Winter 1982): 331-88. On bananas in Jamaica, see Holt, *Problem of Freedom*.

cavo, particularly Cachoeira and São Felix, also afforded possibilities for employment.[89]

To lessen further the web of dependency that seemed inevitable if one remained on the estates, some former slaves in the northeast moved to areas of more open land, particularly the *agreste*, the band of drier but not parched land that lies between the coastal plantations and the drought-prone *sertao*. The cattle-raising, cotton-growing, and food-producing regions of the *agreste* had long been closely linked to the sugar zones, and movement from one to the other was both logical and familiar.[90]

In keeping with the different pattern of life in the interior, seasonal migrants to the coast from the *agreste* and the *sertao* resisted working year-round under the direct supervision of owners and overseers. To modernizing contemporaries, this insistence on the "liberty to wander starving" seemed quixotic. But one need only read a few descriptions of work in the cane or of the twelve-hour shifts in the "devil" of a sugar mill, to understand some of the possible sources of this attitude.[91]

Workers thus asserted fragments of independence from employers and defended certain forms of community. Nevertheless, the rural population as a whole was extraordinarily poor and hungry. Former slaves had a degree of physical mobility, in contrast to the immobility of slavery, and they had greater access to grounds for subsistence or small-scale market production. But they shared with long-free rural Brazilians a sparse and vulnerable existence. Relatively few seem to have become share-tenants in cane, able to attempt to climb the agricultural ladder, and fewer still made it to the next rung.

Concerted efforts to change the structure of power were very rare

89 See Fayette Wimberly, "The African *Liberto* and the Bahian Lower Class: Social Integration in Nineteenth-Century Bahia, Brazil, 1870-1900" (Ph.D. dissertation, University of California, Berkeley, 1988), 120-52.

90 Peter Eisenberg emphasizes the importance of movement to the *agreste* as a form of postemancipation escape from the plantations. Personal communication, 1986.

91 See the discussion of workers' resistance to contracts and their preference for liberty, even to the point of wandering starving (*"o hábito de sua liberdade, e até o de andar faminto"*), from the *Diario de Pernambuco* in 1893, cited in Michael Hall and Paulo Sergio Pinheiro, *A classe operária*, Vol. 2, *Condições de vida e de trabalho, relações com os empresários e o estado* (São Paulo, 1981), 19-23. The image of the "devil" in the sugar mill is from a worker interviewed in the 1970s, cited in José Sérgio Leite Lopes, *O vapor do diabo: O trabalho dos operários do açucar* (Rio de Janeiro, 1978).

in the early decades of the republic. There seems to be no evidence of formal strikes in the sugar areas. No rural unions emerged comparable to the Workers' Guilds in central Cuba or the Knights of Labor in the cane fields of Louisiana. The most dramatic collective action of the period — the mass movement of the followers of Antônio Conselheiro — originated outside the sugar regions, although it doubtless drew in some former plantation slaves as it gained in strength. Its vision of autonomy and redemption was extinguished in a brutal army assault in 1897.[92]

For the most part, the struggle for control over the terms of labor seems to have been carried out through an insistence of rights to land for the production of subsistence and market crops, through a refusal to commit oneself to full-time wage labor, and through forms of labor exchange among smallholders. The struggle continued into the twentieth century, even though the growth of central mills brought the establishment of fixed residences and rules of conduct intended to force the workers to adopt "uma vida regular."[93]

In 1922, a government commission reported that, although wage-paid day labor was common in the rural sector of the state of Bahia, substantial numbers of laborers worked *por empreitada*, at job work. Wages in the coastal regions were paid in money; but, in more isolated areas, payment was sometimes made in food and merchandise (*gêneros e mercadorias*). The report observed coolly, "Wages do not vary with the form of payment and these are generally accepted without complaint by the workers."[94] Wages were somewhat lower in Pernambuco, where migrants from the interior arrived in September to work in the cane and where women and children worked by day. When labor was short, workers could insist on payment by the job rather than the day; some forms of rental and sharecropping were also arranged through oral contracts. The report noted with some puzzlement that there were many workers in Pernambuco who preferred to "live in lib-

---

92   There are many studies of the Conselheiro movement: for a recent examination, and an extensive bibliography, see Robert M. Levine, *Vale of Tears: Revisiting the Canudos Massacre in Northeastern Brazil, 1893-1897* (Berkeley, Calif., 1992).

93   See Leoncio G. Araujo, "A Usina de Açucar na Economia Pernambucana." *Annuario Açucareiro para 1938*, 313-19.

94   Wages in sugar had apparently remained stable for a decade between 1912 and 1921. Brazil, Ministerio de Agricultura, *Aspectos da economia rural brasileira*, 471-72.

erty," even in miserable hovels, rather than work as wage laborers in agriculture under the direction of owners, administrators, or overseers.[95] Continuity, yes: but it was a continuity of complex negotiations and renegotiations, carried out with few resources and great tenacity.

YEARS AFTER EMANCIPATION, IN CUBA, BRAZIL, and Louisiana, impoverished workers still headed into the fields at first light to carry out the backbreaking work of cutting, lifting, and hauling sugar cane. But the mechanisms by which their labor was elicited, and the class relations in which their work was embedded, had changed markedly since the time of slavery. Moreover, depite the physical similarity of their situations, those who grew and cut cane in Cuba, Brazil, and Louisiana were differently situated in terms of access to productive and organizational resources. Equally important, the social relations among workers and between workers and employers reflected very different constructions of race and politics.

It seems clear that the production of sugar does impose certain limits on the kinds of labor systems that can be adopted: cutting and processing must be closely coordinated to prevent loss of sucrose in the cane, and the peak demand for labor during harvest must be met reliably in order to get the cane in before the rains (in Cuba) or frost (in Louisiana).[96] As one economist has noted, a given staple crop, while not determining the socio-political environment, "will imprint certain patterns of its own on whatever environment happens to be around."[97] The variety of labor relations associated with sugar production in the decades after the end of slavery suggests that the "imprinting" process is a complex one. Indeed, however great the temptation to personify sugar itself, it is

95   The same report critcized employers for their failure to offer rural workers a degree of well-being and education and to treat them with a bit of civility, Brazil, Ministerio da Agricultura, *Aspectos da economia rural brasileira*, 347-48. See also Eisenberg, *Sugar Industry*, 183-90, for estimates of wage levels in Pernambuco before and after abolition.

96   Even these exigencies vary somewhat with the geography and climate of the region: in areas with appropriate year-round temperature and rainfall, sugar's marked seasonality is diminished.

97   See Albert O. Hirschman, *Essays in Trespassing: Economics to Politics and Beyond* (Cambridge, 1981), chap. 4, esp. p. 96.

the worker and the planter who remain central to the story.

Within the overall goal of producing sugar, there were multiple means to each end. Thus the coordinating of cutting and processing could be achieved through the compulsion and intense labor of slavery. It could also be met, however, by contractual arrangements between cane farmers and a locally monopolistic central mill. If the cane farmer had no one else to grind his cane, he could ill afford to ignore the deadlines set by the mill. There were costs to the mill associated with the difficulties of weighing individual deliveries and maintaining quality, but there were also savings in managerial expenses and in the tranferring of the risks and tasks of labor control to individual growers. Planters in Cuba were relatively quick to follow this path for a significant fraction of their production.

The need for labor at harvest could be met by maintaining a large number of resident laborers in estate dwellings, as in Louisiana, or by permitting sharecroppers to live on marginal land in exchange for providing labor at harvest, as in Brazil, or by drawing workers out of the towns when needed to supplement a smaller permanent work force, with the migration of young men from the cotton parishes to the sugar parishes in Louisiana, the influx of Spanish and West Indian workers to cut cane in Cuba, and the movement of backlanders down to the coast for the harvest in Brazil. But the proportion of each group in the labor force could vary widely, depending in part on the costs and difficulty of maintaining a resident work force and the degree of seasonality of the need for labor.

The overall labor supply in a given region affected the pattern of work that would emerge but not in a linear fashion. Thus, in Cuba, the expansion of grinding capacity and the departure of some freed people created an apparent "labor shortage," and contract cane farming was quickly expanded to attract immigrants and to draw smallholders into sugar production. In Brazil, the growth of population in the absence of alternative forms of employment created a "surplus population," permitting the use of nearly unpaid labor and strongly discouraging substantial immigration. In Louisiana, planters trying to avoid what they perceived as a labor shortage initially sought to bind their existing workers through year-long contracts and later encouraged seasonal immigration from the cotton parishes.[98]

Larger structures of capital and commodity markets could also narrow or expand the range of strategies available to planters. In northeastern Brazil, weak markets and scarce working capital militated against the widespread adoption of wage labor, thus reinforcing the cultural pattern of patron–clientelism. In Cuba, by contrast, the availability of North American capital helped to open up the possibility of rapid growth and the attraction of workers through wage incentives. In Louisiana, Northern entrepreneurs and Northern capital helped to stimulate economic recovery and technological innovation but did not challenge the political and racial order supported by local planters.[99]

In each area, the state showed differing degrees of willingness and capacity to intervene, as well as different policies on the question of labor control. In Louisiana, the Union Army reinforced early efforts to impose annual contracts, but the turmoil of occupation and Reconstruction opened up some space for the freed people to gain ground in their struggle with former masters. Later, strikebreaking was endorsed by that state militia, and waves of repression and disenfranchisement completed the task of silencing workers in the cane. In Cuba, the colonial state's reluctance to provoke opposition restrained efforts at direct labor control, and its encouragement of Spanish immigration helped to guarantee a multi-ethnic rural labor force. But the authoritarian conduct of Spanish officials in the island strengthened Cuban nationalism, reinforcing the separatist ideology and brought black, white, and mulatto Cubans together to challenge colonial domination.

In northeastern Brazil, landholders were prepared to undertake the disciplining of labor on their own terms. The demand for labor, at least in Pernambuco, was if anything in decline as modern equipment increased productivity in a period of limited markets for Brazilian sugar. Northeastern workers thus did not have the leverage that periodic labor shortages in an expanding sugar industry afforded their Cuban counterparts. Stagnation in output was matched by relative stability in social relations. In moments of crisis, however, like the mass movement under the leadership of Antônio Conselheiro, military force was made available to restore the

---

98   An overview of the factors affecting the reorganization of labor after emancipation can be found in Herbert S. Klein and Stanley L. Engerman, "The Transition from Slave to Free Labor: Notes on a Comparative Economic Model," in Manuel Moreno Fraginals, Frank Moya Pons, and Stanley L. Engerman, eds., *Between Slavery and Free Labor: The Spanish-Speaking Caribbean in the Nineteenth Century* (Baltimore, Md., 1985).

99   See John Alfred Heitmann, *The Modernization of the Louisiana Sugar Industry, 1830-1910* (Baton Rouge, La., 1987), chap. 4.

class power of landowners and eliminate the challenge to established social relations.

Planters thus made choices in response to evolving markets, available technology, and the possibility of employing resources from the state. At the same time, however, they had to contend with the efforts of the newly freed to achieve security, voice, and a degree of proprietorship. There would be no cane planted, weeded, cut, or ground without some form of compliance from the workers themselves. In Louisiana, the freed people's dream of proprietorship was thwarted, but repeated strikes raised wages above their immediate postwar levels. In Cuba, a series of tenacious cross-racial movements encompassing sugar workers made it imprudent for any imperial power — Spain or the United States — to attempt direct coercion on the sugar plantations. Spanish forces attempting to take over estates in 1896 were often met with gunfire; employers hoping to pay in scrip in 1901 often found themselves bereft of workers. Even in Brazil, where the continuities of control seem so thoroughgoing, rights to land and subsistence were deeply entrenched, and the final dispossession of the labor force in sugar awaited the middle of the twentieth century.

Introduction

Nick Tiratsoo and Jim Tomlinson's "Restrictive Practices on the Shopfloor in Britain, 1945-60: Myth and Reality" aims, as they say, to "challenge" a widely held view: namely, that organized labour has been responsible for Britain's "recent poor industrial performance" (215). "Restrictive practices" are those conditions which would enable unions to prevent employers from reducing the workforce or introducing new technology to improve productivity.

So widespread is this view that, although it interprets conditions in Britain, it nevertheless shows up in North American debates about prosperity: the case of Britain is cited as a caution or dire warning of the consequences of letting labour get too much power in the workplace. The commonness of this view leads to two interesting features of Tiratsoo and Tomlinson's article.

First, you might notice that, despite their "challenging" stance, Tiratsoo and Tomlinson express themselves, at crucial points, in a rather non-aggressive way. When they attack the reasoning of a thinker whose work has been called on to support the common view, their wording is tentative.

Olson's work demands to be taken seriously, yet it, too, *seems* to be flawed.

... this choice of approach *can be criticized* because it encourages a misleadingly simplified view of reality. (201, emphasis added)

> It *may be right to conclude* about Olson, therefore, that what
> he has produced is not an explanation, merely an historical
> set of abstractions. His thesis *seems* to provide little more sat-
> isfaction than the offerings of far less sophisticated analysts.
> (203)

Similarly, when they summarize their findings, their wordings
suggest tentativeness rather than decisiveness.

> The picture that emerges from this evidence is, therefore,
> *fairly clear*. Restrictive practices *do not seem* to have been a
> problem for *most* British employers in the period 1945-60.
> Large swathes of industry were, in fact, *apparently virtually*
> unhampered by such problems during these years, this being
> true of such key sectors as engineering and motor vehicle
> manufacturing. Damaging restrictionism, *it may be suggested*,
> was *largely* confined in its impact, and *probably* only badly
> affected shipbuilding, printing and the operation of the
> docks. (212, emphasis added)

And the paragraphs which then (212-14) address possible objections to their evidence also resort to indeterminate wordings: "apparently," "might be argued," "may well be grounds," "quite obviously," "we would argue," "it seems very likely," and so on.

Such wordings are characteristic of scholarly expression: researchers are liable to put their most important claims in just such
uncertain terms, offering their contribution to knowledge in self-
effacing, tentative packages. The density of such expressions in Tiratsoo and Tomlinson's article may be attributable to the commonness of the view they are challenging. When an idea is widespread, and deeply rooted in current thinking, the researchers who
challenge it approach it humbly (even when, as seems to be the
case here, they are in fact impatient with the idea's mistakenness
and its undeserved prestige). From the "Restrictive Practices" example, students can learn the rhetorical use of this politely tentative stance, especially in cases like this, where findings depend on
delicate interpretations and re-interpretations of evidence.

So the commonness of the challenged view may account for
this prominent stylistic feature. It may also have traceable (although more subtle) effects in a second feature of Tiratsoo and
Tomlinson's article. Their last two paragraphs tell about "two-

fold" conclusions. The second is what you might expect from your reading of preceding pages: "What this study does is cast doubt on those interpretations which propose labour inflexibility as the key explanatory variable [in the country's poor industrial performance]" (215). (This part of the conclusion is accompanied by a typical gesture toward the future, where "much remains to be discovered," and knowledge waits to be accounted.) But the first conclusion may surprise you: it is "essentially about methodology" (215). While the criticism of Olson's model of economic behaviour may have slipped from our minds as we were guided through the authors' interpretations of contemporary evidence of the extent and impact of restrictive practices 1945-60, it has not been forgotten by Tiratsoo and Tomlinson. The discrediting of certain kinds of scholarship has been on their minds. So our understanding of the article should include this matter. Moreover, the concern with "methodology" can lead us back to the "commonness" issue. At the start of the article, Tiratsoo and Tomlinson show that political figures and academics alike have shared the view of "labour inflexibility" and its contribution to economic troubles. "[P]olitical prejudice" shows up again in the conclusion, and again in association with (a certain kind of) scholarship. A critical reading of this article could attempt to address these questions:

- What is the relationship between views of "the political right" (200) and certain forms of research and theory? To what degree could this relationship account for the *commonness* of a view which the authors show to be, from their evidence, unfounded?

And a critical reading might attempt to answer this question:

- Why, in the last years of the twentieth century, has this "myth" (a powerful and appealing story) of the post-war years become so popular — so common?

If you write about these matters, you could benefit from the stylistic model Tiratsoo and Tomlinson offer. As they approach highly speculative moments, offering high-risk proposals to the community of readers, their language becomes increasingly tentative.

Restrictive Practices on the Shopfloor in Britain, 1945-60: Myth and Reality

NICK TIRATSOO AND JIM TOMLINSON

*Warwick University and the Business History Unit,
London School of Economics*

*Brunel University and the Business History Unit,
London School of Economics*

> Hidden unemployment is commonly referred to by econo-
> mists in their writing. They deduce that it exists. Those in
> industry must wonder what clinical authority they have for
> their parrot-like repetitions of this suggestion ... Those who
> know industry find it barely conceivable that 'hidden em-
> ployment' of any notable magnitude exists.[1]

MANY COMMENTATORS ON POST-WAR Britain have sug-
gested that the work-force and its unions must accept a large part
of the responsibility for the country's continuing economic ills.[2]
British workers may or may not have been unusually strike prone,
but they have certainly long colluded, it is believed, in a range of
restrictive practices on the shopfloor, thus increasing costs, curtail-
ing output and drastically limiting the scope for necessary industrial modernisation. As the distinguished Anglo-German academic
Ralf Dahrendorf has recently put it, working people in Britain
have tended to 'stretch their work so that it begins to look like leisure'.[3] In this situation, the inevitable consequence has been economic stagnation.

Over the following pages, we aim to challenge this view and
demonstrate that restrictive practices of this type have been nowhere near as common or serious as some have argued. We focus
on private manufacturing industry in the years 1945-60, a period
during which it might be thought, *a priori*, that, with full employment, restrictive practices would be growing in importance.[4] In
the first part of the paper we look at the arguments of those who
have thought that this was in fact the case. Subsequently, we marshall a wide range of contemporary evidence which appears to
substantiate our counter-proposition. Finally, we reflect upon this

evidence and present some general conclusions.

The most strident critics of restrictive practices on the shopfloor have, not surprisingly, usually been associated with the political right. For example, in 1979 G.C. Allen summed up a view often previously promoted by the Institute of Economic Affairs when he suggested that restrictive practices were an intrinsic part of 'the British Disease'.[5] Strikes had been harmful, he noted, but the real problem over the post-war period was the everyday impact of labour's intransigence, which had led to 'chronic over-manning' and 'deterred firms from investing in new equipment'.[6] Inevitably, this refrain has been taken up, too, by politicians, with Mrs Thatcher being particularly forthright on the subject. Restrictive practices, she asserted in 1978, had grown over the previous century, and were now 'encrusted like barnacles on our industrial life'. Indeed, they were quite clearly 'the chief obstacle' to popular prosperity. How could it be otherwise, Mrs Thatcher asked: 'When two men insist on doing the work of one, there is only half as much for each'?[7]

Of course, such claims might easily be dismissed as self-serving, but they gain in plausibility because they have also been advanced by more sober and scholarly authorities. The influential political historian Keith Middlemas has described how governments, unions and employers settled down to a cosy corporatism after 1945, while obvious problems, like labour's Luddism, were simply brushed under the carpet, and this interpretation is also given credence in Correlli Barnett's widely read *The Audit of War*.[8] Moreover, the pernicious influence of restrictive practices has also been emphasised by several leading economists and economic historians, and is stressed particularly by those who, like Broadberry and Crafts, take institutions seriously and wish to understand their impact upon growth.[9] A key reference point in this literature is the work of Mancur Olson.

Olson's writings are so widely cited because they appear to offer a very convincing *explanation* as to why restrictive practices have been a particular problem in Britain. His starting point is a global statement about economic growth and retardation derived from a general theory of collective action.[10] He argues that collective bodies such as cartels, trade unions and employers' associations obstruct efficient resource allocation, because individuals will only participate in such bodies — and thus ensure their survival — if they are able to appropriate private benefits from group actions. The negative effects here will be especially pronounced if the collectivities manage to survive a long time, and are not swept aside by calamities like war, totalitarianism or occupation. A major qualification to this broad proposition occurs if collectivities are highly encompassing since then the potential harm that they can do will be so widespread as to engender self-correcting (and thus self-preserving) actions. Such encompassing organisations may in fact, at the limit, actually benefit society, because they have good reason to raise output in the economy. In Olson's words, the members will 'own so much of the society that they have an important incentive to be actively concerned about how productive it is'.[11]

The implications about Britain that arise from these observations seem to be as follows. The country has been, in effect, a double loser. Collectivities grew up in Britain over a long period and have never been radically disrupted, a situation that contrasts strongly with the experiences of other countries such as France, Italy, Germany and Japan. At the same time, British institutions have rarely, if ever, been fully encompassing, either. Trade unions in particular, have continued to play a fractious and sectional role.[12] All of this has inevitably meant slow growth.

How convincing are these various kinds of literature on restrictive practices? The first point to make is that many of the strongest allegations turn out to be based on very little hard evidence. Some authors present their conclusions as if they are self-evidently true. Where examples are cited, they tend to be drawn (often without any comment) from the same group of industries — usually printing, shipbuilding and the docks. Nor is evidence treated with sensitivity. The Institute of Economic Affairs' enquiry during the mid-1960s, which produced the much-quoted volume *The Restricted Society*, cited a *Sunday Times* investigation of 1956 to support its view that restrictive practices had been long endemic in British industry.[13] However, in reality, the newspaper was far less definite than it was later purported to be. It examined four sectors, and found that restrictive practices were only evident in one or possibly two (shipbuilding and the railways).[14]

Olson's work demands to be taken seriously, yet it, too, seems to be flawed. Olson has attracted considerable support from economists and economic historians because his methodology conforms to the tenets of individual rational action theory inherent in neo-classical economics. However, this choice of approach can be criticised because it encourages a misleadingly simplified view of reality.

Whilst claiming allegiance to methodological individualism, much rational action theory is actually closer to orthodox Marxism in its attachment to structural determinism. Individuals are aggregated according to some location in the economic or political firmaments and their aims and objectives are then neatly 'read off' from that location.[15] In the same way, Olson ascribes objectives to his collective bodies which are simply the consequence of their place in the economic structure. There is no need for any close investigation of how interests are understood or strategies formulated. Indeed, in effect Olson simply inverts Keynes' famous, if unhelpful, dichotomy and asserts the dominance of interests over ideas.

The weakness of this is that it involves far too much determinism in the relationship between structure and action. Interest groups do certainly have structural conditions of existence and these will, of course, always shape patterns of conduct. Nevertheless, the linkages here are above all matters of process, and may be influenced, too, by a whole range of other factors — social, cultural, and political. Disregarding this multiplicity of pressures will necessarily produce misleading conclusions.

A brief illustration of what is at stake here can be provided by looking at the actual situation in Britain during the immediate aftermath of the Second World War.[16] Using Olson's terms, it may be argued that both the Federation of British Industries (FBI) and the Trades Union Congress (TUC) emerged from the hostilities with their encompassing natures greatly enhanced. Indeed, the structural conditions at this time were very similar to those that had generated corporatist arrangements in countries like Sweden at the end of the great depression. The two peak organisations were then confronted by a Labour government which put a high priority on industrial modernisation and spent considerable effort on measures to improve productivity. The interesting point is that the TUC and the FBI reacted to Labour initiatives in very different ways. The unions broadly supported official objectives, for example the incomes policy of 1948-50 and a variety of initiatives aimed at improving productivity. Yet the FBI chose to be as obstructive as possible, and in fact was able to neuter several important measures. What explains these contrasting responses?

The unions, of course, had a clear incentive to co-operate. This was *their* government, but it plainly could not deliver full employment and the welfare state if inflation accelerated or production and exports did not expand. For the employers, however, the situation was very different. Here the major concerns were not just shaped by some economic calculation but also revolved around the explicitly political desire to limit state intervention, whatever it aimed to achieve. Facilitating the transformation of this objective into reality was the coincidence of two other factors. Employers enjoyed a relatively favourable commercial environment at the end of the war, and this allowed a wide range of companies to generate high profits. At the same time, it was clear that Labour's policies would only be pursued through the medium of consultation, since the government continued to emphasise its commitment to maintaining tripartite co-operation.[17] In this context, it was always likely that employers would be able to ignore or actually resist the administration's suggestions. Exhortations to 'become efficient or perish' were met with indifference. Meanwhile, more concrete reforms which the government wanted endorsed by the consultative machinery could be easily sabotaged by those with a different agenda.

What all of this strongly indicates is that Olson's model cannot really aid understanding of a significant episode in recent British history. Important 'actors' were actually behaving in very different ways from the pattern suggested by his approach. Most obviously, the employers' responses to Labour initiatives cannot be understood in terms either of their structural position or allegedly encompassing nature. Theirs were political objectives, given potency by the particular character of the post-war years. It may be right to conclude about Olson, therefore, that what he has produced is not an explanation, merely an ahistorical set of abstractions. His thesis seems to provide little more satisfaction than the offerings of far less sophisticated analysts.[18]

At this point, it appears wise to turn from the current literature and re-examine the contemporary evidence. Many recent authorities have argued, as we have shown, that restrictionism was strongly evident on Britain's shopfloors after 1945, but not much of what has been written, it seems fair to conclude, is very persuasive. Can some new insights on the whole issue be generated by a detailed search through the archives?

Looking at the press in the 1940s and 1950s, it is certainly easy to find vivid exposures of restrictive practices.[19] Some more substantial enquiries came to similar conclusions. In pulling together the Anglo-American Productivity Council findings, Graham Hutton emphasised that restrictionism of all kinds occurred in Britain, and was one reason why this country lagged behind the United States when it came to productivity growth.[20] Nor were such impressions simply confined to outsiders. Lewis and Stewart's 1958 study *The Boss* reported that, next to high taxation, 'the cussedness of labour' was the businessman's greatest grievance. As the ordinary employer saw it, they noted, labour expected 'the annual increase in the standard of living as advertised' but would make no real contribution to get it. In this situation, according to Lewis and

Stewart, most business leaders had become quite jaundiced about their workers: 'Perhaps some indication of business gossip about labour behind the scenes is furnished by the remark "probably half those engaged in industry are redundant; they do not work, they are merely employed"'.[21]

Taken together, these various accounts appear to constitute a formidable indictment, yet closer inspection once again exposes flaws. Some industrial correspondents did, of course, have good contacts in business and may have accurately reported what they were told. Nevertheless, it is not certain what employer's complaints really added up to: grumbles from the boardroom were, of course, nothing new. Moreover, some of the press accounts have a fomulatory ring and may well have been shaped more by the pressure to grab the reader's attention than the desire to present accurate facts. In these pieces, restrictive practices are always being 'exclusively exposed' after having remained 'hidden' behind a 'conspiracy of silence'. Finally, it is also worth noting that, even in the more substantial pieces, hard examples of restrictionism do not occur with any frequency. Little wonder, then, that when a Conservative MP asked his party's Research Department for a brief on restrictive practices in 1956, he was told by an official with access to the more obvious published sources that 'no worthwhile research [had been] done into the matter since the 1930s'.[22]

The latter comment might suggest that little more can be said about restrictive practices in post-war Britain. However, such a conclusion would be premature. For looking into the matter more closely reveals that there is, in fact, a rich vein of further evidence on the subject. Much of this comes from academic studies or various semi-official enquiries. And, interestingly, most of it supports the view that restrictive practices were much less of a problem than so many have continued to allege.

One important body of data emerges from various journalistic and academic enquiries which involved serious questioning of those in the business world. The social investigator Ferdinand Zweig was an early exponent of this approach, interviewing some 400 people in industry during 1947 and 1948.[23] His aim was to discover what factors were shaping productivity performance and how the trade unions were behaving on this question. He concentrated on five main sectors (building and civil engineering, cotton, engineering, iron and steel, and printing) and found that restrictive practices of various kinds were certainly sometimes evident. However, he also emphasised that the incidence and severity of restrictionism varied considerably. Printing employers seemed to be badly hemmed in by custom and practice, but in the other four sectors the situation was not nearly as bad. Moreover, Zweig was careful to record his belief that the overall position was gradually improving. As he explained:

> I tried to see whether restrictive practices are on the increase or decline. When I started my inquiry I was under the impression that restrictive practices were increasing, because of the strengthened bargaining power of the Unions. But fortunately the reverse is true.[24]

P.W.S. Andrews and E. Brunner conducted their research at roughly the same time as Zweig. They were part of R.F. Harrod's circle at Oxford and attended a regular series of discussions with senior businessmen that ran for almost two years.[25] Amongst other things, Andrews and Brunner wanted to discover what influenced decision-making over the introduction of new machinery. Was anticipation of resistance from labour a significant factor or were the really important determinants finance and the tax structure? Putting these points to their contacts revealed that, whatever the position with the other variables, the fear that labour would be an important impediment was not uppermost in businessmen's minds. In fact, only three of the 18 interviewed felt that labour hostility might be influential. In these circumstances, Andrews and Brunner confidently concluded that there was 'little evidence that resistance of labour to new machinery was important in preventing investment in a firm'.[26]

Addressing the question as to whether restrictive practices were harming output, the authors found that their contacts' views were somewhat equivocal. Most of those questioned felt that production was being deliberately constrained, with seven being definite about this and five being rather less certain. However, as Andrews and Brunner noticed, when it came to substantiating these opinions, the businessmen themselves became rather more cautious. 'Although a majority of our witnesses', they wrote, 'were convinced of the existence and importance of restrictive practices, a number stressed how difficult it was to make a rational assessment of their effect.'[27]

Similar findings emerged from a *Future* survey of 1951.[28] The journal had asked Social Surveys Ltd to find out about a wide range of management attitudes and this had led the company to circulate a detailed questionnaire to 'a random sample of manufacturers'. The number replying constituted what the journal called 'an adequate sample to represent business views,' though one that was 'somewhat weighted in favour of firms with more than 100 employees'.[29] The findings reported were revealing on a number of issues, not least the question of restrictive practices. The sample was asked, 'Do you find trade union practices or trade customs restrict output or keep up costs?' In all, only 19 per cent agreed that union actions were damaging, while only 14 per cent said the same about trade customs. *Future* admitted that some might well find these figures surprising, and was resigned to the fact that 'economists of the Right and the Left' would probably not believe what they were reading. Nevertheless, the journal stood by its survey. The position was quite clear: 'In management's view, restrictive practices of all kinds have little effect on British industrial efficiency'.[30]

Finally, reference needs to be made to Carter and Williams' work, which appeared towards the end of the 1945-60 period.[31] These authors were primarily interested in how technical progress could be speeded up but their findings hardly reinforced the idea that restrictive practices were of great significance. There could be no doubt that some resistance to new techniques had occurred, though where good management existed, this had remained virtually unknown. However, Carter and Williams continued, it was necessary to put the whole question in context, and doing so greatly deflated its real importance. As they underlined: 'Our general conclusion is that the hindrances caused by labour . . . cannot be regarded as a major determinant of the speed of scientific and technological advance . . . in the period 1945-56.'[32]

These studies are certainly indicative and do much to place the problem of restrictionism in a more realistic perspective. What makes them particularly believable is the fact that other solid evidence points in a similar direction. Most important, here, is the information that was uncovered on the three occasions when various state bodies became concerned with restrictive practices. The first time that this happened was at the beginning of our period, after the Labour government started to consider what to do about the Restoration of Pre-War Trade Practices Act.

This piece of legislation had been passed by Parliament in 1942. Its aim was to protect those unions that had made significant concessions on working arrangements because of the war emergency. The Act guaranteed that pre-war trade practices would be restored and maintained for at least 18 months after the cessation of hostilities. During this time, it was hoped, collective bargaining would determine what new conditions were to prevail. The specific moment for restoration was a matter for the Minister of Labour, though it could not be later than the expiry date of the 1939 Emergency Powers (Defence) Act.[33]

The conditions enshrined in this legislation induced some nervousness in official circles, and during the course of the war there were a number of attempts to determine just how many pre-war trade practices came within the ambit of the legislation. Regional Controllers reported that 'a mass of trade practices' had been changed during the early years of the war. On the other hand, the Ministry of Labour Statistical Department provided a more reassuring picture. It had knowledge of over 200 dilution agreements, but felt that concessions elsewhere had not made a great deal of difference. Of course, a crucial factor, civil servants recognised, was the attitude of the trades unions. Few practices that had been surrendered were registered at local Ministry of Labour offices. Nevertheless, the official worry was substantially increased by the rumour that the Engineering Union had 'notified their intention of recording thousands, possibly tens of thousands of such changes, presumably with a view to challenge at the first convenient opportunity'.[34]

At the end of the war, no immediate problems were raised from this quarter, but the Labour government had, clearly, to decide what it should do about the legislation. Accordingly, Isaacs, the Minister of Labour, approached the TUC to sound out its views. He argued that, given the country's precarious economic predicament, it would be highly dangerous to re-introduce any practices which might constrain production. Accordingly, what the government wanted was a postponement of the restoration date central to the wartime Act. This, the Minister proposed, could be achieved by inserting a relevant clause in the Emergency Laws (Transitional Provisions) Bill which was to be put before Parliament.[35]

The TUC recognised that this request had serious implications. It had already been pressurised by one union (the Birmingham and Midland's [sic] Sheet Metal Workers Society) which had members allegedly suffering unemployment because of continuing dilution. Nevertheless, the TUC in the end accepted Isaacs' logic and agreed that pre-war practices should not be resurrected for the foreseeable future.[36]

The reinstatement date was postponed by new temporary legislation every year until 1950, but during that session the government decided that a more permanent solution to the Pre-War Trade Practices Act was necessary. Isaacs therefore approached the two major peak organisations for their views and discovered that there was 'absolutely no desire or intention on either side to go back to the pre-war trade practices'. Given this information, he then prepared legislation which in effect permanently suspended the 1942 Act, or, as one backbencher expressed it, 'put . . . restoration into cold storage'. This was passed by Parliament, with numerous references to the sacrifices that had been made by the trade unions.[37]

The significance of this whole episode is obvious. First, it indicates that many trade unionists fully accepted that modernisation on the shopfloor was essential for the country's survival. Second, there is a clear implication about the extent of restrictive practices in post-war Britain. There can be no certainty about what exactly the 1950 Act legislated away, but it cannot be doubted that a significant number of restrictive practices in operation before the war never reappeared after 1945. This is confirmed by Zweig's 1951 judgement (already referred to) that in 'many industries restrictive practices were relaxed or partially suspended' during the hostilities, 'and this position still obtains at present'.[38]

While debate about the Restoration of Pre-War Trade Practices Act was underway, another official enquiry began which also cast light on the issue. One trigger here was the government's Monopoly Bill of 1948. This aroused opposition amongst the Conservatives, who argued that, if business restrictionism was to be subject to legislation, so should that enforced by labour. The government was not in agreement here, but Morrison did promise that the National Joint Advisory Council (NJAC) would consider the point further.[39]

The NJAC enquiry, which proceeded over the next couple of years, in fact came up with very little, largely because the two sides of industry on the Council could not agree about how a restrictive practice should be defined.[40] Nevertheless, during the course of deliberations, valuable information on restrictionism was collected by the British Employers' Confederation (BEC) and this is worth presenting in some detail since it constitutes what amounts to a snapshot of the problem, revealing something of its true dimensions.[41]

The BEC wanted to show that restrictive practices were very common in British industry in order to strengthen its negotiating position on the NJAC, and it invited its members (all trade associations) to provide private and completely confidential assessments of the situation in their particular sectors. The response to this request was disappointing. In fact, only 22 of the 66 member organisations bothered to reply. Moreover, the picture of restrictive practices that emerged from these replies hardly measured up to the BEC's hopes: only 11 of the trade associations reported significant problems of this type. As a result, the BEC decided to circulate a further questionnaire, again on a confidential basis, asking for more detailed information, in the hope that this would be taken somewhat more seriously.

In all, some 35 of the member organisations responded to this second initiative. Twelve trade associations reported that they had no difficulties with restrictive practices, but as many as 23, this time, agreed that they did. However, careful scrutiny of the information received indicates that 'serious impediments to production' were only evident in 18 of these 23 cases. Moreover, within this group distributions tended to be highly skewed. Thus, half of the 18 complained of only one or two of the 15 possible types of restrictive practice, which meant that some important sectors (for example, engineering and iron and steel) remained virtually trouble-free. Similarly, some kinds of restrictive practice were comparatively unusual: eight of the 15 categories appeared four or fewer times in the 18 questionnaires. The picture revealed, in other words, is of a small number of afflicted industries — cotton, shipbuilding, bleaching and printing — and a relatively limited group of recurring restrictions.

The third and final episode of state involvement over the question of restrictive practices occurred during the late 1950s. Once again, the initial impetus stemmed from a tangential issue. In 1956, the Conservative government introduced the Restrictive Trade Practices Act to deal with, amongst other things, price-fixing amongst businesses. It found that this measure was not popular amongst all shades of Conservative opinion, and sought to conciliate its critics by promising an enquiry into labour restrictionism as a *quid pro quo*.[42]

The resulting investigation was carried out under the aegis, once again, of the NJAC. In effect, this meant that the BEC was put in charge, as before, of collecting information from its constituent organisations. In fact, events repeated themselves all round, since employers no more leapt at the chance to unburden themselves about restrictive practices this time than they had on previous occasions, so that a final report could not be put together until early 1959.[443]

This document divided British industry into three sub-groups:

Category I — Industries which had reported that they had no problems in regard to the efficient use of manpower.
Category II — Industries which had set up machinery to deal

with any problems or which appeared to be in the process of doing so.

Category III — Industries which needed more time, including those which, because of various difficulties, had been unable to undertake a joint examination.

In all, some 112 industries had provided information for the investigation, and of these, the NJAC felt that 64 could be allotted to Category I, 42 to Category II and six to Category III. Looked at in a different way, it was possible to estimate that 29 per cent of those in civilian employment were in Category I industries, 39 per cent in Category II industries and seven per cent in Category III industries.[44]

Commenting on these figures, the NJAC felt that 'some encouragement' could be gained from its deliberations. It had often been said, the Council noted, that industry was 'riddled' with restrictive practices. However, it had been a source of some satisfaction to those involved 'to learn that so many industries . . . felt able to report that they were meeting no real difficulties in their efforts to ensure that manpower was efficiently used'.[45]

At the same time, the NJAC was also forthright about what it saw as a weakness of its classification, namely the ambiguity of Category II. As the report put it, whilst the existence of satisfactory joint machinery could give 'some measure of reassurance', much would depend on the use which was made of it. To deal with this problem, the Council had agreed to re-approach Category II industries in the later stages of its enquiries, to see 'whether the machinery referred to in the original replies was functioning satisfactorily'.[46]

The collection of this supplementary information allowed a more complete picture of the restrictive practices to emerge. Of the original 42 Category II industries, it was now revealed that only about four had any real complaints.[47] However, it was also clear that all of this group — jute spinning, building, chemical and allied industries, and printing — were faced with problems on very limited fronts. For example, the master printers were hardly overwhelmed by their difficulties, grumbling only of 'some opposition . . . to certain method study schemes'.[48]

These revelations acted to re-focus attention on the original 'black sheep' Category III industries — electrical contracting; heating, ventilating and domestic engineering; painting and decorating in Scotland; paper bag manufacture; road haulage; and shipbuilding and ship repairing. Some of these clearly belonged where they had been consigned, but in other cases the situation was far less clear-cut. For example, the Heating, Ventilating and Domestic Engineering Employers' Association reported that it had bad relations with one union in the industry, but got on with the other very well.[49]

Taken together, the information uncovered by the NJAC enquiry constituted the most accurate and comprehensive survey of restrictive practices in Britain that had ever been completed. As such, it attracted a good deal of attention from various interested parties. Private responses were particularly revealing. The Minister of Labour (and Chairman of the NJAC), Ian Macleod, noted during the enquiry that 'the nature and extent' of the restrictive practices' problem 'were frequently misconceived'. Robert Carr, his Parliamentary Secretary, came to a similar conclusion:

> That there are difficulties in some industries is undeniable, but the replies to the enquiries made by the Council have shown quite clearly that, over much of industry, the two sides are willing to tackle jointly any problems caused by restrictive practices and have already taken a great deal of useful action.[50]

Most indicative of all were some paragraphs that appeared in the Industrial Management Research Association's 'Confidential Bulletin'. This organisation had long provided a network for large companies to talk to each other privately, and it naturally took a considerable interest in the NJAC enquiry. However, there was no surprise here about the Council's eventual findings, nor any belief that they were misleading:

> As might be expected it [the report] shows that restrictive practices relate in any serious sense only to some 7 per cent of employees of the country. At the time of the introduction of the Monopolies Bill, the T.U.C. privately pressed I.M.R.A. on a number of occasions, asking members to state the restrictive practices which were of concern to them . . . The moment was ripe to raise the matter and the T.U.C. was willing. In no case did any member have any serious allegation to make, nor did they make any allegation.

Of course, the 'Confidential Bulletin' recognised, some trade unions had tried to impose restrictions, but 'in actual working, the foreman and workers winked . . . or else . . . got around them in one way or another without undue effort'.[51]

The picture that emerges from this evidence is, therefore, fairly clear. Restrictive practices do not seem to have been a problem for most British employers in the period 1945-60. Large swathes of industry were, in fact, apparently virtually unhampered by such problems during these years, this being true of such key sectors as engineering and motor vehicle manufacture. Damaging restrictionism, it may be suggested, was largely confined in its impact, and probably only badly affected shipbuilding, printing and the operation of the docks.

However, close scrutiny of the sources reveals that, even in these spheres, the situation was not as straightforward as it has sometimes been made to appear. Firstly, it is important not to exaggerate what the extent of the problems were. Press reports presented a picture of all-pervasive and unchanging restrictionism, but this is very misleading. Thus, demarcation difficulties in shipbuilding varied considerably from yard to yard. Moreover, even in the so-called 'print jungle', unions and employers' associations were co-operating throughout these years in an effort to curb the most damaging practices. Secondly, it was certainly often true that, where restrictive practices did persist, this had as much to do with the employers in question as the workforce. Some kinds of restrictionism had actually been originally introduced by employers, or, alternatively, had got out of hand because of management negligence. At the same time, several of the afflicted employers' associations continued to prove highly inept at trying to alleviate their predicaments, preferring long-drawn-out guerilla warfare to constructive initiative. Finally, it is worth emphasising that even where labour obstructionism did seem to be an intractable problem, the motives of those involved could easily be shaped by a complex of factors, and were rarely reducable to irrational anti-modernism or greedy self-interest.[52]

Our survey has, therefore, uncovered a good deal of evidence on restrictive practices, much of it pointing in one direction and apparently supporting a revisionist case. However, before moving to any firm conclusions, it will be prudent to pause for a moment and speculate briefly on the nature of the evidence we have presented.[53] Can the various surveys cited really be accepted at face value? It might be argued, for example, that their validity is fatally compromised by definitional vagueness: in this situation, one employer's irritating restrictive practice could be easily another's unremarkable (and unremarked upon) long-standing custom. Moreover, there may well be grounds for believing that most employers would have automatically played down their labour problems to outside enquiries during this period: they did not want in any way to jeopardise output given the ease with which goods could be moved in the post-war seller's market. Finally, there is, surely, a sharp and instructive comparison between the evidence dealt with here and the voluminous literature on restrictive practices in the 1970s and 1980s, much of which underlines the salience of restrictionism. Should not the conclusions which emerge from the later and seemingly more rigorous studies alert us to the dangers of putting too much faith in, for example, the *Future* enquiry of 1951?

On the first point, we can agree, straight away, that many of the surveys we cite do not contain very much about what actually constitutes a restrictive practice. In fact, only the BEC investigation of the late 1940s casts light on this subject in any detailed way. Furthermore, we have not, quite obviously, tried to rectify this situation by providing a definition of our own to act as a measuring rod. Nevertheless, it is not clear than any of this really raises great problems. Rumination about the definition of restrictive practices may be helpful in certain circumstances but this will by no means always be the case: the whole area is highly contentious, making any 'objective' criteria very hard to construct. On the other hand, it is reasonable to believe that when employers spoke of restrictive practices in the 1940s and 1950s, they knew what they were talking about. After all, it was they who had to deal with the problem from day to day. In fact, we would argue that the fairly fluid methodology employed in these surveys adds to, rather than detracts from, their significance. If employers were asked somewhat open-ended questions about restrictive practices, and still came up with the answers we have referred to, surely this, as much as anything, underlines the fact that the incidence of restrictionism was not great. Put another way, it is likely that by relying upon subjective assessments the contemporary surveys went a long way towards establishing an upper bound estimate of the problem. Given what this actually constituted, it seems very likely that more rigorous definitions would only have reinforced the overall conclusion, that restrictive practices were not of great importance in most sectors.

What of the somewhat different argument which sees the context rather than the methodology as the key factor promoting inaccuracy in our surveys? Were employers deliberately under-reporting their problems with restrictive practices, because they feared trouble from the unions, and thus costly interruptions to output in the post-war seller's market? A number of points can be made here. First, it is clear that some managers *were* adopting a somewhat conciliatory stance in industrial relations bargaining at this time in order to safeguard production.[54] Nevertheless, it would be wrong to assume that such behaviour was either typical or equally likely to occur at any time across the two decades. The seller's market existed for varying lengths of time according to sector. *The Economist*, to give one example, was always warning that British car exports were insecurely based in the 1940s, and dated the end of the 'post-war boom' in the motor industry to 1952, when '[all] the leading manufacturers' had suffered from 'keener competition by foreign manufacturers in markets where consumer resistance is growing'.[55] Indeed, profit figures for British industry as a whole tell a similar story, rising to the early 1950s but then stagnating until 1958.[56] It is by no means clear, therefore, that all managers were simple output-maximisers during these years; many clearly remained acutely aware of their precarious market position even in the 1940s, a fact that would hardly have blinded them when thinking about labour costs and practices.

However, leaving the question of motive aside, there are other good reasons why the under-reporting thesis hardly convinces. All of the enquiries we have cited, bar the NJAC investigation of the late 1950s, guaranteed respondents either complete confidentiality or at least anonymity.[57] Each was designed to find out what employers were really thinking, but all recognised (more or less explicitly) that such an aim would be compromised if information was attributable. In the light of this, to argue that there was some kind of conspiracy of silence when the subject of restrictive practices came up is unconvincing. It is surely stretching credibility, for example, to assert that businessmen who had built up a trusting relationship over a number of meetings with the anyway sympathetic Harrod group should suddenly lie when the subject of restrictionism was raised, especially since they would have known that their opinions were only likely to reach the public domain in anonymous form between the covers of an academic journal.

What of the apparent contrast between the surveys we have referred to and the investigations of the 1970s and 1980s? An authoritative evaluation of the later literature is obviously impossible within the confines of the present article, but it is worth pointing out that recent studies are rather less in agreement about the extent of restrictive practices than has sometimes been imagined. Metcalf's work, emphasising the importance of restrictionism, remains influential, but it has also been widely criticised.[58] On the other hand, there are a number of investigations which suggest that the whole problem has been greatly exaggerated.[59] In this situation, it may be correct to call for further work on all of the post-war period, but there can be no question of damning the earlier studies simply because they are at odds with a later and better established consensus.

The conclusions that emerge from the foregoing survey are, therefore, twofold. The first is essentially about methodology. The whole issue of restrictive practices has often been clouded by political prejudice. Yet some academics have also produced misleading conclusions, and here the problem has been an over-reliance on abstract theories and a lack of interest in actual events. 'Positive economics', for example, announces that it seeks neither to praise nor blame but its assumptions in fact produce a highly oversimplified and thus misleading depiction of reality. *Homo economicus* may look fine in the lecture theatre, but such a construct is of little use as a guide to the past. For in real life, as we have shown, 'economic agents' had (and have) a very much more complex set of motivations, informed as much by social, cultural and political influences as by structural positioning.

Secondly, our findings have clear implications in terms of the literature on Britain's post-war economic decline. Much remains to be discovered about the reasons for the country's recent poor industrial performance.[60] What this study does is cast doubt on those interpretations which propose labour inflexibility as the key explanatory variable.

NOTES

1   London School of Economics, Management Research Group Papers, Box Four, IMRA Confidential Bulletin No. 352, 9 Sept. 1959, p. 5.

2   The research upon which this paper is based was completed while both authors were visitors at the Business History Unit of the London School of Economics. We would like to thank Dr. Terry Gourvish (Director of the BHU) for inviting us to become part of the Unit and for his support and encouragement while we were there. We would also like to express our gratitude to Dr. Richard Storey and the staff at the Modern Records Centre, the University of Warwick, for their help in locating sources.

3   R. Dahrendorf, *On Britain* (1982), p. 46.

4   Studies of restrictive practices in preceding and succeeding periods which adopt a broadly similar perspective to the one employed here include J. Hilton *et al.* (eds.), *Are Trade Unions Obstructive?* (1935); T. Nichols, *The British Worker Question* (1986); and P.J. Hilditch and A.J. Read, *Trade Unions and Labor Productivity: The British Shipbuilding Industry, 1870-1950* (DAE Working Papers No.

8907, 1989).

5   G.C. Allen, The British Disease (Hobart Paper 67, 1979).

6   Ibid., pp. 61-2.

7   M. Thatcher, *Speeches to the Conservative Party Conference, 1975-1988* (1989), p. 43.

8   K. Middlemas, Power, Competition and the State, Volume One: Britain in Search of Balance, 1940-61 (1986), passim; and C. Barnett, The Audit of War (1986), p. 274.

9   S. Broadberry and N.F.R. Crafts, 'Explaining Anglo-American Productivity Differences in the Mid-Twentieth Century', *Oxford Bulletin of Economics and Statistics*, Vol. 52 (1990), pp. 375-402; N.F.R. Crafts 'The Assessment: British Economic Growth over the Long-Run', *Oxford Review of Economic Policy*, No. 4 (1988), pp. i-xxi; and idem, 'Economic Growth', in N.F.R. Crafts and N. Woodward (eds.), *The British Economy Since 1945* (Oxford, 1991), pp. 261-90.

10   The following is based upon M. Olson, The Logic of Collective Action (Cambridge, MA, 1965); idem. *The Rise and Decline of Nations* (New Haven, CN, 1982); and idem, 'A Theory of the Incentives Facing Political Organisations: Neo-Corporatism and the Hegemonic State', *International Political Science Review*, Vol. 7 (1986), pp. 176-87.

11   Olson, *Rise and Decline of Nations*, p. 48.

12   Ibid., p. 144.

13   J.A. Lincoln, *The Restrictive Society* (1967), p. 172.

14   *Sunday Times*, 29 Jan. 1956; 5 Feb. 1956; 19 Feb. 1956; 26 Feb. 1956 and 4 March 1956.

15   B. Hindess, *Choice, Rationality and Social Theory* (1988), Ch. 6.

16   The following is based on material in N. Tiratsoo and J. Tomlinson, *Industrial Efficiency and State Intervention: Labour, 1939-51* (1993).

17   J. Tomlinson, 'Mr. Attlee's Supply-side Socialism', Economic History Review, Vol. 46 (1993), pp. 1-22.

18   See also, for other critiques of Olson, various contributions to D. Mueller (ed.), *The Political Economy of Growth* (New Haven, MA, 1983).

19   See, for example, *Daily Express*, 11 April 1947; *News Chronicle*, 20 Jan. 1953; and *Listener*, 2 May 1957.

20   G. Hutton, *We Too Can Prosper* (1953).

21   R. Lewis and M. Stewart, *The Boss* (1958), pp. 166-8. See also, for example, A. Flanders, *The Fawley Productivity Agreements* (1964).

22   Bodleian Library, Oxford, Conservative Party Archive, CRD 2/7/8, Letter J. Douglas to E.S.T. Johnson, 23 Jan. 1956.

23   F. Zweig, *Productivity and Trade Unions* (Oxford, 1951), p. 8.

24   Ibid., p. 21.

25   P.W.S. Andrews and E. Brunner, 'Productivity and the Business Man', *Oxford Economic Papers*, Vol. 2 (1950), pp. 197-225.

26   Ibid., p. 209.

27   Ibid., p. 218.

28   Anon, 'Management Looks at Labour', *Future*, Vol. VI (1951), pp. 54-8.

29   Ibid., pp. 54-5.

30   Ibid., pp. 56-7.

31   C.F. Carter and B.R. Williams, *Industry and Technical Progress* (1957).

32   Ibid., p. 173.

33   Background information on this Act can be found in PRO, LAB 9, 52 and *Economist*, 7 Feb. 1942.

34   PRO, LAB 10, 271, Note of 23 Dec. 1943; PRO, LAB 10, 433, Min. of Labour Statistics Dept. Memo. 'War Time Relaxations', Sept. 1943, pp. 1-5.

35   TUC, *78th Annual Report, Brighton 1946* (1946), p. 180.

36   Ibid. and PRO, LAB 10, 604, Letter G. Isaacs to E. Bevin, 26 June 1946.

37   *Hansard* (Commons), 5th series, Vol. 480, 10 Nov. 1950 and 15 Nov. 1950.

38   Zweig. *Productivity and Trade Unions*, p. 30.

39   *Hansard* (Commons), 5th series. Vol. 449, 22 April 1948.

40   Modern Records Centre, University of Warwick, CBI Predecessor Archive, MSS 200/B/3/2/821 Pt. 1, passim.

41   The following paragraphs are based on ibid., N.C. 10487, BEC Memo, 'Trade Union Restrictions' [nd. but 1948] and MSS 200/B/3/2/C 821 Pt.2, BEC Memo, 'Restrictive Practices . . . Summary of replies' [nd. but 1950].

42   *Hansard* (Commons), 5th series, Vol. 549, 6 March, 1956.

43   Ministry of Labour, *Practices Impeding the Full and Efficient Use of Manpower* (1959), p. 6.

44   Ibid., p. 7.

45   Ibid., pp. 7 and 10.

46   Ibid., pp. 6-8.

47   PRO, LAB 10, 1453, NJC 276, Memo, 'The Efficient Use of Manpower' (April 1959), p. 4. Four of the 41 Category II industries re-approached did not bother to send 'substantive replies'.

48   Ibid.

49   Ibid., pp. 1-3.

50   PRO, LAB 10, 1452, Minutes of NJAC, 22 Jan. 1958; and ibid., Letter R. Carr to T.L. Iremonger, 3 Feb. 1958.

51   London School of Economics, Management Research Group Papers, Box Four, IMRA Confidential Bulletin No. 360, 24 Feb. 1959, pp. 8-9.

52   See, for example, J.R. Parkinson, *The Economics of Shipbuilding in the United Kingdom* (Cambridge, 1960), p. 165; material in the British Productivity Council, *A Review of Productivity in the Printing Industry* (1950), D.P. Wilson, *Dockers* (1972), p. 215; H. Clegg, 'Restrictive Practices', *Socialist Commentary* (Dec. 1964), pp. 9-11; and H. Gospel, *Markets, Firms and the Management of Labour in Modern Britain* (1992), Ch. 6.

53   In compiling the following paragraphs, we acknowledge helpful comments by three anonymous referees and various participants at the 1993 Economic History Conference.

54   See, for example, H.A. Turner, G. Clack and G. Roberts. *Labour Relations in the Motor Industry* (1967), p. 82.

55 *Economist*, 20 March 1948 and 15 Nov. 1952.

56 J.C.R. Dow, *The Management of the British Economy, 1945-60* [Cambridge, 1964], p. 348.

57 However, the late 1950s NJAC enquiry was only very marginally less opaque in these terms than its predecessors: individual trade associations were named, but there was no question of revealing either details of trade association viewpoints or any information about individual firms.

58 See, for example, D. Metcalf 'Water Notes Dry Up', *British Journal of Industrial Relations*, Vol. 27 (1989), pp. 1-31 and P. Nolan 'Walking on Water?', *Industrial Relations Journal*, Vol. 20 (1989), pp. 81-92.

59 See, for example, W.W. Daniel. *Workplace Industrial Relations and Technical Change* (1987).

60 For an excellent summary of the state of the literature, see M. Dintenfass, *The Decline of Industrial Britain, 1870-1980* (1992).

Introduction

A classic persuasive strategy is for speakers to link their cause with an idea everybody likes. Somebody could link higher taxes with *safety*: pay more taxes and get better highways or more policing, and be safer. Everybody likes safety. Nobody is against it. The rhetorical effectiveness of appeal to a common value has been observed since ancient times, when Aristotle called it an appeal to "ethos," an ethical appeal: that is, a strategic reference to widely held (if not necessarily widely practised) values to substantiate a particular position. Verkuyten, de Jong, and Masson's research into "racist and anti-racist discourse" throws some light on this phenomenon.

They examine not the speech of orators or political leaders, or even of corporate advertisers, but the speech of "Dutch residents of an ethnically mixed, inner-city neighbourhood in Rotterdam." (The section called "The Study" explains their method — tells how they captured this speech.) They find that "in the context of debate the same values and notions are used in a more racist as well as a more anti-racist discourse, for interpreting, justifying and criticizing the views on the neighbourhood in which the discussants live" (222). In other words, *both* racists and anti-racists (implicitly) refer to, for example, the principle of "equality" to support their interpretations of life in this setting which daily confronts them with ways different from theirs. Is this a counterintuitive finding? That is, does it contradict what common sense would lead us to expect? Or

- Can you trace this finding to the nature of the ethical appeal it-self, with its gestures to compelling but very broad abstractions?

(Note that, while the ethical stance appeals to widely held values, they are not necessarily universal ones. As Verkuyten, de Jong, and Masson repeatedly remark, the values of "equality," "rights," "freedom," and "rationality" [as opposed to "prejudice"] are those of "western liberal-democratic culture," arising from particular sociohistorical conditions.)

- What are the implications for anti-racist campaigns?

Like Kabeer's article on decision-making among Bangladeshi garment workers, this one offers substantial portions of inform-ants' speech, each portion interpreted by the researchers. And, like Kabeer, Verkuyten, de Jong, and Masson consult a theoretical model of human behaviour to guide their interpretations. This model is summarized in the section headed "Theoretical Back-ground" (223). Don't be alarmed if the theory is not entirely clear to you at this stage of reading. The authors' interpretations of the speech they have collected will exemplify the conditions the the-ory predicts. At the same time, be prepared for the complexity of their analyses. They are looking at argument in its everyday form, which, perhaps paradoxically, may be more elusive and confound-ing than professional argument in scholarly forms. And, despite their preference for anti-racist views (they are, after all, trying to add to our knowledge of racism in the interests of getting rid of it), their analyses do not aim to prove the rightness or wrongness of any of the speakers' views. Instead, they are looking for the rea-soning that supports these views in the exchanges of everyday life, and they respect the contribution of everyday life itself to "[e]ve-ryday ideology" (255). All these informants are daily confronted with *difference*.

To test your understanding of Verkuyten, de Jong, and Mas-son's analyses, plan how you would explain to someone who had not read this article

- how *both* a racist and an anti-racist could invoke the positive value "rationality" and the negative value "prejudice";

- how a racist could support the human right to seek refuge.

Similarities in anti-racist and racist discourse: Dutch local residents talking about ethnic minorities

MAYKEL VERKUYTEN, WIEBE DE JONG AND
KEES MASSON

Abstract: This article discusses the way central liberal-democratic values and notions are used in anti-racist as well as a more racist discourse. Eleven ethnic Dutch adults living in an old inner-city quarter of Rotterdam spent four evenings discussing the situation of their neighbourhood. Transcripts of the discussions were analyzed focusing on the commonplaces used in arguing about ethnic minority groups. The principle aim is to show how values such as freedom, equality, rationality and human rights are used and applied to fit the argument in both an anti-racist and a more racist discourse. Considering the shared values it is concluded that anti-racist strategies should be sensitive to actual living conditions in old neighbourhoods.

TO COMBAT RACISM effectively it is necessary to understand its complex features and underlying themes. In Britain it has recently been argued that such understanding is lacking in many anti-racism strategies (see Gilroy 1990; Rattansi 1992). Anti-racist understanding of racist thinking and arguing is not very sophisticated. Cohen (1992), for instance, typifies anti-racism as the disavowal of complexity for the sake of pursuing moral certainties. Anti-racism appears to be lacking in effectiveness because of its doctrinaire form and its lack of powerful arguments which go beyond a moral appeal to tolerance. What seems to be required is a more complex understanding of the nature of racism and critical reflection on the ideas and approaches used in anti-racist work.

A similar argument is made outside Britain. For instance Blommaert and Verschueren (1992), in analysing the public debate on ethnic minorities in Belgium, concluded that anti-racist discourse hardly differs from racist discourse in terms of underlying notions and conceptual framework. In particular they criticised the idea of homogeneity which everyone involved in the debate would share. This idea takes as its point of departure the necessity of homogenisation with the result that pluriformity as such is considered problematic. Blommaert and Verschueren speak about a rhetoric of tolerance which is based on views that actually imply intolerance.

Another example outside Britain is France where Memmi (1982) had criticised the easy and effective indignation of what he calls the sentimental anti-racism. Anti-racism would also disregard and deny real existing differences between ethnic groups, which could be seen as a strategy for evading difficult community problems.

Anti-racist strategies which avoid moralistic and doctrinaire forms are needed. This is especially necessary in relation to everyday situations in old neighbourhoods in the inner cities. It is one thing to discuss and condemn racism publicly in the media, but quite another to actually live in situations where there are people from many different ethnic and cultural backgrounds. In these situations an appeal to tolerance is often considered moralistic by the indigenous population. It is also seen as disregarding everyday reality which, to a certain extent, involves living among culturally different groups, and the more or less inevitable tensions and conflicts associated with it.

In order to combat racist views effectively it is necessary to understand the nature and structure of these views. Studying the way indigenous people think and talk about minority groups living in the same neighbourhood can provide direction for the development of more adequate anti-racist practices. In the present study, discussions held among some Dutch inhabitants of an old neighbourhood in the city of Rotterdam will be analysed. Our aim is to identify underlying ideological themes which the discussants used in arguing about ethnic minority groups living in the same neighbourhood. We will focus on the implicit values and notions which were being articulated and which were not disputed since they are considered commonplaces. We will try to show how in the context of debate the same values and notions are used in a more racist as well as a more anti-raicst discourse, for interpreting, justifying, and criticising the views on the neighbourhood in which the discussants live. The notions and values we will focus on concern core principles of the liberal-democratic society. We will argue that these principles are used in the production of anti-racist and racist discourse. On this level of basic principles there seems to be no difference in argumentation which helps explain why anti-racist arguments are often not very effective, and may even be counter-productive. Before discussing the present study some remarks on theoretical background are necessary.

Billig (1987) discusses the role of commonplaces extensively in his rhetorical approach to social psychology. Commonplaces are principles which speak for themselves and are not questioned as such. They are the foundations or basic instruments which people (implicity) use in the argumentation. One of the consequences is that a real discussion is precluded. After all, legitimising specific views or arguments in terms of generally accepted notions and values, implies that these views are being represented and accepted as self-evident and obvious. Billig (1987) points out that commonplaces can also be used to start and pursue discussions. Not by bringing the generally accepted notions and values up for discussion but because first, the interpretation of a value can differ, and secondly because there can be disagreement about which value is appropriate for a specific case in hand.

Considering the former, there can be disagreement about the meaning and importance of a specific notion or value. This would manifest itself in that the same abstract notion or value can be used for two opposing arguments. For instance not only an anti-racist discourse can draw upon the principle of equality but also a racist discourse (see below; see Wetherell and Potter 1992).

The second aspect is linked to the idea that common sense is inherently dilemmatic. Everyday thinking is assumed to be organised on the basis of contrasting themes which in fact would make thinking and arguing possible (Billig et al. 1988). Ideological dilemmas and controversies are in other words inherent in social life where almost every principle has an opposite principle, such as rights being linked to obligations and freedom to equality. Billig et al. (1988) make a distinction between lived and intellectual ideology. Intellectual ideology refers to a formalised or systematic philosophy of professional theorists, while lived ideology refers to the non-formalised values and beliefs typical of everyday thinking in a particular culture. Everyday ideology or common sense contains elements of intellectual ideology but is not a reflection of it. People use these elements in combination with everyday knowledge and in relation to their actual experiences to give meaning to their world.

THE STUDY

Discussion sessions were held with 11 indigenous Dutch adults living in an old neighbourhood in the centre of the city of Rotterdam. Around 40 per cent of the people who live in this neighbourhood are considered (also by themselves) to belong to an ethnic minority group and in some parts of the neighbourhood the proportion is around 75 per cent. In total 61 different nationalities are represented. The neighbourhood can be characterised as having a high level of un-employment (33 per cent of the working population) and a relatively high crime rate. In general it is a typical poor inner-city quarter of one of the major Dutch cities.

The participants were asked to take part in a study on 'social renewal' which is a government policy to revitalise old urban areas. The discussion was introduced under this heading and it was explained that we wanted to hear what inhabitants of these old quarters thought about social renewal. In the introduction and during the sessions we made no references to ethnic groups and inter-ethnic relations. It was also made clear to the participants that we were conducting an independent study and that there were no links with the city council or other governmental institutions, i.e. the study would have no policy implications.

There were two discussion groups (six and five participants respectively) and each group met once a week for four weeks in a row. All eight sessions were taped and transcribed and each session lasted approximately two and a half hours. The participants in both discussion groups varied in age (between 30 and 70 years of age) and sex (four women and two men in one discussion group and three women and two men in the other). The participants either had no paid job (three housewives and two retired skilled labourers) or were employed in low-skilled jobs. Most of the participants were either currently or previously involved in different kinds of community activities on a non-professional basis.

We opted for an intensive form of research among relatively few people because we wanted to create a situation where residents discussed their neighbourhood first of all among each other rather than with us as researchers. There are relatively few studies which focus on people's actual conversation or everyday discourse. Studies which do analyse people's conversation have been concerned mainly with material collected during interviews (e.g. Van Dijk 1987; Essed 1991; Wetherell and Potter 1992). Such a research context might have an effect since part of what people say is probably linked to the fact that they are communicating with social scientists. In the present study we tried to create a more 'natural' situation where Dutch inhabitants talked and argued primarily among themselves. In order to do so, it was important that the participants got to know each other and felt free to say whatever they wanted. This required an intensive form of research where people met more than once.

The discussions were largely unstructured and two of the authors were present. The prime task of one of the two was to inaugurate the discussion and to raise some general issues ('living in the neighbourhood, education, neighbourhood provisions, crime'). Few interventions were made so that the discussions could run their own course. The second researcher observed the sessions and afterwards discussed the proceedings with the 'interviewer'.

The participants in both groups indicated that they appreciated and valued the sessions very much. They were enthusiastic and all of them participated actively in the four evenings. Take, for example, one of the participants who said to us at the end of the fourth session, 'I: Well, I wanted to thank you both for the evenings you sacrificed, we ourselves found them very enjoyable evenings (Yes, Yes)'. There were two main reasons for this positive evaluation of the sessions. First, it was stated that it was always interesting to hear what other people experience and think about living in the neighbourhood. People were said to have hardly any time or opportunity to talk to each other about these matters, despite it being considered everybody's concern. Second, it was especially appreciated that they could say their piece and could be open and honest about what they thought and felt. This evaluation of the sessions is important as it indicates that the discussions were not restricted because of the existing social taboo on racism and discrimination. The participants felt free to say what they thought, which is illustrated in the excerpts which will be given in the subsequent text.

During the discussions there were four participants who presented themselves in a specific way and who held quite strong values on ethnic minority issues. Two of them presented themselves explicitly anti-racist. One of the two was involved in an anti-racist committee on a voluntary basis, and the other stressed her humanistic orientation (see Verkuyten, de Jong and Masson 1993). The other two participants described themselves as being more or less racist. For instance the first utterance in the first session of one of the two was, 'K: Well, I'll second a number of things, erm, I'v been getting quite racist the last couple of years. I can't help saying it'. In general both these participants described ethnic minorities very negatively. They saw minority groups as the main reason for problems in the neighbourhood and they favoured a policy of repatriation. The following excerpt of discussion illustrates their views.

(1) G: 'I'm not the only one who thinks that way, because that's what I meant the first time — those are the kinds of things you're gonna start hearing, that all the Dutch, at least all the ones you talk to about it, also the ones in this community centre, erm, they also say to kick the foreigners out of the country. Let them go to their country, what are they doing here? They devour everything and now unemployment is rising. I say kick em all out the country, let 'em clean up their own mess'. K: 'No, but it's a logical consequence, if you just look, through, erm, through the budget cuts. We cut back because the national income, uh, is decreasing because, erm, erm, at least people have less to spend because we haul more foreigners into the Netherlands who keep working less and who produce more kids than we do, and these kids, erm, they either stray from the straight and narrow or they don't find any work either. So it's just all a logical consequence (Yeah)(Yeah) that's why, *that's why* they have to cut back. They have to cut back because there are more and more unemployed people. Why are there more unemployed? Because we keep hauling in all these foreigners and that's why we have less and less to spend. Well, yeah. yeah, it all just keeps adding up, and then I think, well, in one way or another it has to be more normal, it just keeps going further and further. The more they haul in the more we've got to cut back'.

In the subsequent sections, other sizeable tracts of text and details of our analyses of them will be presented. This serves the purpose of providing readers with a critical understanding of our process and thus to meet some of the requirements of reflexive practice (Potter 1987).

It may be argued that our sample is too small to merit any firm conclusions. Our principal aim, however, is not to prove the generality of our findings but to describe and analyse in detail some of the ways that common values are used in racist and anti-racist discourse. As such, the present study corresponds to other discourse approaches to the analysis of racism (Condor 1988; Potter and Wetherell 1988; Reeves 1983; Wetherell and Potter 1992), which are also being conducted in the Netherlands (van Dijk 1987, 1992; Essed 1991). These studies, however, focus primarily on official documents, papers and other printed material, or use material collected during interviews, and are not concerned with more 'spontaneous' conversation. These studies also do not compare racist and anti-racist conversation from within the same social context.

EQUALITY: EQUAL TREATMENT

Discrimination is obviously an important argument to condemn the attitudes and behaviour of indigenous people as well as to explain and justify the behaviour of ethnic minorities. One could argue that the existence of discrimination, which is irreconcilable with the goal of equal treatment, is at the heart of anti-racism approaches and constitutes one of its major arguments.

The existence of discrimination is not denied by the participatns who hold more racist views. Dutch people 'haven't always been angels themselves, that's for sure, because they've certainly discriminated against people', and; 'foreigners are certainly discriminated against, if only because their skin's a different colour' (participants 'K' and 'L' respectively). Several times during the discussions, however, it is pointed out that it is not so much ethnic minorities who are discriminated against, but Dutch local residents (K: 'I feel now like I'm discriminated against instead of them'). Community and social workers, housing corporations, schools, and also municipality officials were accused of favouring ethnic minorities and of only standing up for minority groups. It was held, for instance, that Dutch children would receive less attention in schools and might even be left behind. The following excerpt illustrates this position:

> (2) I: 'The school, the school board is totally directed toward foreigners. They simply take priority over the other children, they get extra lessons, they get this, they get that. Where are *our* children?'

The proposition that it is the Dutch who are being discriminated against is important because it endorses the moral condemnation of discrimination, and places oneself within the moral community. The fact that discrimination is considered unjust is not questioned but the question of whom is discriminated agaisnt is disputed. The rejection of discrimination as such implies the recognition of the value of equal treatment. This also manifests itself in another way.

In the discussions, racist views were not considered self-evident and requiring no justification. On the contrary, the participants tried to make their views understood and they accounted for their views not only of others but also of themselves. This indicates that the moral value of not discriminating and being unprejudiced is internally acknowledged. The construction of racist views as understandable and acceptable is achieved by presenting them as more or less inevitable and logical. It would be the circumstances in the neighbourhood and not so much one's own personal biases that are responsible for racist views. In the discussions there were many references to reality as it was claimed to be, and the negative attitude towards ethnic minority groups was presented as the logical consequence of this reality. An example is participant 'K' who said to us after a litany of complaints about foreigners and stories about criminality in the neighbourhood; 'I think you'll also be racists when you leave this evening'. Racist views were justified by means of externalisation. It is not so much the person who is to blame, but especially the living conditions in the neighbourhood which would turn almost everybody into a racist.

In other words, racism and discrimination do not seem to be a matter of taking no notice of or rejecting existing moral views. On the contrary, the value of equal treatment is endorsed and used to justify one's own position. With respect to the underlying basic principle there is no difference between a more racist and an anti-racist discourse. The differences exist in the employment of the principle in representing the living conditions in the neighbourhood.

It could be argued that the acknowledgement of the value of equal treatment should be treated as an expression of impression management rather than as a genuine attitude. There may be strategical motives involved whereby the speaker wants to present a favourable image of him or herself (van Dijk 1987). Such an acknowledgement might also function as a disclaimer: a verbal device employed to ward off potential accusations of attributes which attract social disapproval (Hewitt and Stokes 1975). Elsewhere we have tried to show that in the discussion sessions, where the participants explicitly stated that they felt they could really say what they thought, the statements were not so much relative to the goal of making a good impression or deflecting criticism, but were genuine themes reflecting the dilemmatic character of common sense (Verkuyten, de Jong and Masson 1993). For the participants who presented themselves as holding racist views, equal treatment was a meaningful and important principle, not merely used for strategical or rhetorical ends. The genuineness of these principles is also stressed in what is called symbolic and aversive racism (McConahay 1986; Gaertner and Dovidio 1986). Both kinds of racism would be the result of psychological conflict between negative feelings toward minority groups and democratic values such as freedom and equality.

In the discussion there were not only references to the principle of equal treatment, equality was also conceived of as equal opportunities. This more liberal notion of equality stresses the idea that a society needs to assure that everybody has the opportunity to develop and improve him- or herself. Inequality then becomes a matter of not making the most of one's opportunities. The consequences of this principle is that the arrears of specific groups can be blamed on the groups themselves, rather than be a product of discrimination.

The idea that everybody can 'make it' if he or she wants to, was a recurring theme in the discussions and one which is used in the argumentation. The claimed reality of equal opportunities is constructed by referring to successful people from ethnic minorities who are presented as examples of the fact that people can improve themselves if they want to. Being successful socio-economically is hereby linked to being assimilated to the Dutch society. This representation clearly places the responsibility for socio-economic success within the ethnic minority groups. It would be a question of willing and the right mentality. An example is the next excerpt from the discussion about the importance of a command of the Dutch language for finding a job.

(3) D: 'erm, A Turkish man comes to you (C: 'Yes') who speaks Dutch quite well, and he writes it too, and you know him and you know him personally from somewhere, you know he's diligent and wants to work'.

C: 'Then he can start tomorrow at 7 am'.

D: 'But then comes a Dutchman who isn't so diligent, who do you take then?'

C: 'The Turk'.

D: 'Look, that's what I mean and that's what I wanted to hear, because it all has to do purely with practical considerations'

E: 'But there are also a lot of foreign kids who don't speak standard Dutch, but they have spent a number of years in Dutch schools ('Yes') they speak Dutch, but still, the unemployment rate among these young people is a lot higher than for Dutch young people'.

C: 'And for good reason'.

D: 'Now what do you mean, for good reason'.

E: 'You can say that again'.

C: 'That's inherent in the environment they come from, and then, they probably don't speak Dutch that well, than, than the start that the boy with the Dutch parents had, because it's the same. It's also the mentality of the parents among each other. It's a damn shame if your little Jhonny quits school at 16 and you say, then go and get welfare payments of 800 guilders [a month]. You'd think, if I'd ever have done that with my father, then he'd have . . . well, he didn't really deal out blows, but I think he would have hit me once or twice. That's the mentality you have to get through to these people'.

In the first part of the discussion it is said that an industrious Turkish man who speaks Dutch would be preferred to a Dutchmen. Confronted with the fact that many minority young people speak reasonable Dutch but nevertheless are unemployed, another explanation is introduced: the lack of the proper mentality. This reaffirms on the one hand the principle of equal opportunities, but at the same time the cause of unemployment is situated among the minority groups themselves. Another example can be found in the fourth excerpt below where the attitude of people from ethnic minority groups is questioned.

MERIT

Those who make the most of their (equal) opportunities and in that way contribute to society deserve to be rewarded and can make a legitimate claim to existing provisions. Making a contribution implies an entitlement to rewards and this is an important principle of social justice in contemporary thinking. In general it is considered fair that people who contribute to society can claim specific rights. In the discussions this principle is acknowledged by all participants and used in the argumentation. It is for instance a central argument in the discourse of one of the two participants who present themselves as anti-racist. The heavy and unhealthy work that many 'guest workers' have done and still do is considered an important contribution to society which justifies their entitlement to benefit from social security provisions. In the next excerpt from the discussion participant 'A' reacts to the suggestion that ethnic minorities only take advantage of existing provisions and hardly contribute.

(4) C: 'It's just that all of the Dutch social legislation is put together in such a way that you can easily spend your whole life falling asleep, and then you keep it up until your hundredth birthday, and that's how it works with everyone, and thankfully so, but erm, that's then one of the nasty side-effects of the system. Because if they don't say anything then they don't hear from anyone else, like come on, as long as I don't say anything it's all ok. Three months per year I go to my homeland and let them work it out for themselves. Now, I think that a large portion has to do with that, that nobody thinks about those cultural differences that exist. In their own environment, where they're originally from, they had to fight for every crust of bread, and here the roasted chickens are flying into their mouths, to use an extreme expression. Well, then it's logical that a large group of them says something like, I like having chickens like that once in while, so I'll stick to it'.

A: 'A whole bunch of Turkish men have become ill *from the work they had to do in the 1960s*. They've got bad backs, they had to do all the dirty work, and they've landed, among other things, in the Disablement Insurance Act'.

(Later in the discussion)

A: 'They had to work with their hands to clean ships and they've become ill from all the misery'.

C: 'Yea, but why do you apply that to migrants. I've also cleaned ships before'.

A: 'Yes, now by change, well, erm, do you mean, ok, but that isn't pleasant (C: 'You just do it'). It certainly isn't *pleasant work* if you have to do it for years'.

C: 'Some things simply aren't pleasant, but what matters is the attitude. One person will do it and the other won't, and that's a big point, erm, but of course if you don't speak Dutch or write it, well, we've already talked about that, then it gets a lot more difficult'.

The principle of deserts is not disputed by both participants but the discussion about whether this principle is applicable to ethnic minorities. According to participant 'C' this is not the case since ethnic minority people are claimed only to take advantage. Confronted with a concrete example, about the cleaning of ships in the docks, which is hard to refute, the working conditions of ethnic minorities are normalised by comparing them with Dutch people who 'just do the job'. Every argument allocating minority people a special position is rejected so no specific rights can be claimed. This notion of rights will be explored below.

RIGHTS

In western liberal-democratic societies tolerance and individual rights are core principles. The implicit appeal to the indivisible and universal human rights are especially stressed in anti-racist discourse. Also in the discussions it is frequently pointed out that people from minority groups have, for instance, the right to keep their cultural identity, practice their own religion, and to found their own (Islamic) schools. These rights are acknowledged by all participants and not questioned as such. They form a major foundation of modern thinking and are used (implicitly) in the argumentation. For instance, human rights define the willingness to accept into one's own affluent society those people who live under deplorable conditions in their country of origin. In anti-racist discourse, the bad and poor living conditions in the country of origin are seen as a valid argument why ethnic minorities (especially Turks and Moroccans) have the right to come to the Netherlands. In addition it is pointed out that Dutch society has recruited those people as 'guest workers' and that they have helped to make the society prosperous. The consequences of this policy should be accepted. One of the participants, in discussing Islamic schools, expressed this idea as follows.

(5) D: 'Freedom is happiness, I mean, if you haul all these Moslims here in large numbers then these people also have a right to their own schools'.

Human rights are also a valid argument in more racist discourse, for instance in relation to the reception of political refugees. The next excerpt follows a litany of complaints about ethnic minorities.

(6) G: '. . . and with these Vietnamese hunger strikes — now that's practically daily news — let them starve (K: 'Yeah I think so too') what does it matter to me (K: 'Just let them all starve to death'), go back to your island. People that are really and truly in danger in their own country, that's only reasonable that they're taken in, but not everybody. The Turks that are waiting for a hand-out and the Surinamese and the Moroccans'.

These statements do not question the general willingness to accept others but dispute when this hospitality should be extended. It is not considered appropriate for people who have come to the Netherlands of their own volition and who it is claimed are merely taking advantage of Dutch prosperity. In this way the value of tolerance is subscribed to, but at the same time the limits of tolerance are made clear. In other words, the acknowledgement of human rights does not lead automatically to an attitude of acceptance and tolerance. For one thing the rights of immigrants should not affect the rights of indigenous people. A way to prevent this from happening is to draw a clear distinction between the private and public sphere of life. The next excerpt illustrates this approach.

(7) G: 'That they keep their own culture, fine. In the Mosque, fine. But just like 'K' says, that we're not bothered by it. We don't have to carry the burden of their religion'.

Ethnic minorities are not denied their right to cultural identity but this right is restricted to the private sphere. In public life they should adapt to the Dutch norms and habits. This view presents the culture of minority groups as something which can be significant only in a restricted sphere of life and not as something which constitutes a way of thinking, feeling and behaving. By contrast Dutch culture is represented in the discussions as something which can not be detached from what and who people are, and which is more or less the touchstone of cultural value.

In the excerpt above it is stated that effectuating the right to keep one's own religion should not burden Dutch inhabitants.

This utterance is taken from a discussion where participant 'L' says that the religion of ethnic minority groups should be respected, as should that of strict Calvinists in the Netherlands. In a reaction to this participant 'K' puts forward that respect for others can lead to the situation that, 'our people here are the dupe, because they have to maintain their culture here'. Participant 'L' acknowledges this objection, which forms a dilemma for her as the next excerpt shows.

> (8) L: 'Yes, I find it really difficult. I mean, we respect people's religion here, from the Dutch anyway, let me put it that way, and then I have a feeling like, well then you have to respect their culture, but if I hear her, uh, then she's also right'.

This statement is a good example of the way people are confronted with the ideological dilemmas of common sense. There is not only a reference to the value of tolerance but also to the limits involved, and this is explicity formulated as a dilemma.

In the public sphere of life, the existing rights and rules may not be attacked or questioned. In the next excerpt, the indivisible right to one's own identity and religion is acknowledged, but it is stated that this right should not affect one's own position.

> (9) A: 'of course they can keep their own identity ('Yes')'.

> D: 'erm, the faiths that doesn't do anything to me. I have the most widespread faith there is; atheism'.

> C: 'It's so confusing. They can keep their own identity, of course, everybody has their own identity and they've got to keep that, whatever they do or wherever they come from, but it seems to be like the roles are reversed'.

And in another session participant 'C' said:

> (10) C: 'because look, what I don't understand is the tolerance is so elastic that at a certain point you take your whole culture with you and after that you, erm, push another culture in a corner in order to put your own culture on top. Yeah, that's what I call reversing the roles'.

The roles of majority and minority and the issue of which of these two groups has the most rights is not questioned, but the division of these roles over ethnic majority and minority groups is.

FREEDOM

In our modern society freedom is an important principle rooted in the liberal tradition. Freedom for everyone is considered one of the major principles in liberal thinking. This notion of freedom is closely linked to human rights. These rights can be seen as formalised freedom demands and requirements. However, in the discussions the notion of freedom has also a more direct meaning. It implies that people should not be obliged to do what they do not want to. Compulsion is contrary to individual freedom
    and formulating something as compulsory is defining it negatively within a discourse of freedom.
    In anti-racist discourse the notion of freedom is a central argument. People from ethnic minorities should decide for themselves how they want to live their lives, and if for instance they want to integrate or not. The two participants with anti-racist views express this notion in the next two excerpts.

> (11) A: 'erm, attending the Dutch language lessons for adults, that actually could be demanded from migrants. We can tell them they have to, but they also have to want to, in my opinion'.

> (12) E: 'Yes, we're talking about integration, but the question is whether the Turks and the Moroccans want to integrate'. [...] 'not that they have to integrate'.

Another participant reacted to the latter comment with:

> (13) D: 'I agree with 'E', it isn't good that they have to integrate. There are people who don't feel any need for it, well ok, freedom is happiness, huh'.

In more racist discourse the value of freedom is not disputed but is interpreted in a specific way. Freedom does not only imply self-determination but also responsibility. If people determine for themselves what they want to do than they are also themselves responsible. The view that ethnic minority people should integrate is mainly argued on the basis of this notion of responsibility. Ethnic minorities have chosen themselves to come to the Netherlands and as a corollary have to accept the responsibilities of their own choice: integration.

(14) M: 'As difficult as it is, they just have to adapt, because they came here, indeed, by their own free will, so they just have to adapt'.

Since this is a powerful argument, the anti-racist participants tried to deal with this representation of one's own responsibility by pointing out that 'guest workers' have been recruited, lived under very bad conditions in their land of origin, and were sometimes politically persecuted.

In contrast to the emphasis on freedom as responsibility when talking about minority groups, the relation between freedom and self-determination is stressed when the participants talked about their own situation. Especially, it was pointed out that the large number of people from ethnic minority groups living in the neighbourhood severely restricts and unacceptably affects, one's own way of living.

The fact that compulsion is at odds with the principle of freedom and is accordingly rejected in relation to the indigenous Dutch, constitutes no obstacle to restricting the freedom of ethnic minorities. The rights which ethnic minority people have is linked to obligations. In other words, freedom is not only interpreted in terms of responsibility but also is limited by other notions and values. It concerns freedom under the condition of accepting the Dutch norms and values: freedom within the existing normative framework. In excerpt 5 it is stated that minority groups have the right to found their own schools because 'freedom is happiness'. In the discussions, however, this right appears to be limited because the assumed necessity of integration also holds. Integration can be the prime consideration as in the next quotation.

(15) C: 'By change, to remain really up-to-date, now you again get more Islamic schools, etc., etc. If you don't think any further and you just keep it simple, and you say, well, now these people want an Islamic this and an Islamic that, then at a certain point I get this feeling, then they have everything here that they didn't have in Morocco, to name a Moroccan, I could have just as well said Cape Verdian, it doesn't matter, and then I say, except for the sun, yes, but that isn't integrating into Dutch society'.

The freedom to found one's own schools or other institutions is measured along the necessity of integration; C: 'but if you're going to found an Islamic school then there'll never ever be any integration'. Prioritising one's values provides a solution to the dilemma posed by the juxtaposition of these two principles.

RATIONALITY

Billig (1988) has shown that the concept of prejudice came to be regarded negatively during the period of Enlightenment as prejudice was associated with the maligned notion of irrationality. Prejudice became seen as an opinion lacking rational judgement and unsupported by reality. It was the result of a psychological disposition or of preferences of the self. According to Billig the present-day use of the prejudice concept shows that the belief in reason has pervaded in common sense. The association with rationality and reality still pervades and both aspects form an ideological basis in anti-racist discourse for criticising prejudice and racism. This can be seen for instance in those approaches which see prejudices as generalisations based on faulty or incomplete knowledge. As a corollary it is assumed that racism must be redressed by providing facts and adequate explanations. Cohen gives an example of this line of anti-racist thought: 'When they are cited in the context of discussion or debate, arguments about irrationality and its cultural transmission are frequently used as a strategy of professional empowerment on the part of teachers, who define racism in such a way to privilege their own role, as guardians of reason and enlightenment, in combatting it' (Cohen 1992: 76).

So the appeal to reason and accurate representation of reality seems a useful strategy in the verbal combat against racism. However, a problem is that in a racist discourse the value of rationality is acknowledged, and along with a realist conception, is used to justify one's own views, and also to discredit the views of those who stand up for minority groups.

An example has already been discussed. One's own more racist views are made understandable and as more or less inevitable by referring to reality as it is claimed to be. It is the factual conditions in the neighbourhood and not one's own preoccupations which determine one's views. The negative attitude towards ethnic minorities is presented as logical, as something every right-minded individual would agree with. In the discussions there were more examples where the speaker's own racist views were justified by referring to reality and down-to-earth view.

Firstly, in the sessions many real life descriptions were given of events in the neighbourhood. These examples make a specific claim literal, solid and independent of the speaker. The examples are hard to question because of their vivid and suggestive descriptions which are rich in contextual detail and incident. In this way a version of events is made factual, as something that really happened or exists, and is independent of the person's own concerns and (prejudicial) views.

Secondly, very often the value of a down-to-earth and sensible approach is emphasised, and the assumed logic ('it's a logical fact') of all kinds of situations is pointed out (I: 'If you just look at it objectively, you can see that those kids are really brought up completely differently, then, our kids'). Such an approach is contrasted with a judgement which is determined by xenophobic feelings, but also in contrast to biased attitudes in favour of minority groups. This bias is attributed to those people who stand up for ethnic minority groups such as community workers. So the value of a down-to-earth, sensible view is not only used to criticise ethnic minorities and to present oneself as unprejudiced, but also to present the approach of others as irrational and unrealistic. The reproach to the anti-racist position is clear. It would be based insufficiently on the complex and multi-faceted reality with the result that one is unable to respond adequately. In addition, an adequate approach would be impossible because of their biased attitude which prevents a sensible and realistic view of the situation.

CONCLUSIONS

We have tried to show that there are basic principles which are being shared and used in an anti-racist as well as a more racist discourse. Notions such as equality, freedom, human rights and rationality are used by Dutch local residents in their daily thinking and arguing about ethnic minorities living in the same inner-city quarter. In the discussions these principles are acknowledged and used by all participants: those who present themselves as anti-racists as well as those who describe themselves as racists.

These general principles are central elements of modern liberal-democratic thinking. This does not mean that the participants simply reproduce the intellectual ideology of the modern western state. It illustrates, however, that elements of this ideology are used in common sense. This shows that in order to express racist views no specific racist ideology is necessary. The local residents in the present study did not articulate a systematic philosophy which derogates specific ethnic or racial groups. Instead, different generally accepted principles were used and interpreted in view of one's own situation and experiences. These general principles themselves are not questioned, but what gives rise to debate are the interpretations of these principles as well as the question if and when such a principle is applicable to a specific case. The result is that the same principle can be used in an anti-racist as well as a more racist discourse. For example, equality can be interpreted in such a way that it justifies a racial view or conversely criticises such a view. Also a principle can be considered differentially applicable. For example, a claim on social security provisions can be rejected by referring to the proposition that no contribution to society has been made. And more generally, practical considerations can be mobilised in order to question an argumentation based on values.

The fact that both in an anti-racist as well as a racist discourse the same principles are used implies that an appeal to these principles is not a very effective strategy for combatting prejudice and racism. Stressing the moral unacceptability of discrimination and calling on tolerance, is not effective when almost everybody accepts these principles. Such an appeal can even be counterproductive because these principles are used to justify one's own racist views and position, and to question the position of minority groups and the people who stand up for them.

This raises the question how prejudice and racism should be approached in an old inner-city centre. A pre-requisite would appear to be a more sophisticated understanding of the complexity and many-sidedness of racism whereby attention is paid to its contradictory and ambivalent character. The interpretation of shared values and the reasons why they are considered appropriate have to become the object of study. The question seems to be how these general principles are being interpreted and used in justifying and criticising one's own views and those of others.

This question, however, should not only be studied on the level of discourse, but especially in relation to the living conditions and daily experiences of the people involved. It is necessary to gain insight into the way everyday experiences and events are described and interpreted. What people in interaction with each other define as reality in their everyday lives, constitutes the interpretive frameworks for the organisation of their experiences and defines their situation. In this, both the ideological content and common sense play an important role, but there is also what people actually see and go through. Of course, experiences are always interpreted facts, but that does not mean that any interpretation is possible (Bader 1991). The fact that every experience is not a direct reflection of reality does not mean that there is only a linguistic reality and that every experience only becomes meaningful in and through language. If people experience inconveniences this has also to do with what actually happens. In other words, reality as it is represented is constructed out of interpretations of factual experiences. This implies that in order to change racist interpretations effectively it is necessary to treat the experiences of (ethnic minority and majority) local residents seriously so that concrete daily conflicts and problems can be addressed.

General principles should not be applied stereotypically to reality as if there are no other realities for people. The task is to interpret these principles in view of the specific situation in old neighbourhoods so that the tensions and conflicts in these neighbourhoods can be addressed. On the one hand local residents can struggle with what they define as intolerable living conditions becuase ethnic minority people do not want to integrate, and on the other hand they struggle with the moral value of not being prejudiced. General principles have to be applied to concrete situations in relation to the complexity of these situations, and not applied rigidly. However, a more tailored employment of general principles should not lead to ignoring real problems, trying to respond to concrete situations should not lead to sacrificing principal considerations. The task is always to interpret and apply basic principles in view of concrete situations. In this way it is possible to be in keeping with the everyday experiences and living conditions of local residents and to try to develop a redefinition of their situation (see de Jong 1989).

In this respect, the finding that values such as freedom, equality and rationality are shared is a welcome one. This means that there is no difference of opinion concerning underlying principles. These principles present a platform for the discussion of opinions and interpretations through which events, processes, and experiences are racialised.

REFERENCES

Bader, V.M. (1991) *Sociale Ongelijkheid en Collectief Handelen: Collectief Handelen,* Groningen: Wolters-Noordhoff
Billig, M. (1987) *Arguing and Thinking,* Cambridge: Cambridge University Press.
Billig, M. (1988) 'The Notion of Prejudice': Some Rhetorical and Ideological Aspects', *Text* 8:91-110.
Billig, M., Condor, S., Edwards, D., Gane, M., Middleton, D. and Radley, A.

(1988) *Ideological Dilemmas: A Social Psychology of Everyday Thinking*, London: Sage

Blommaert, J. and Verschueren, J. (1992) *Het Belgische Migrantendebat*, Antwerpen: International Pragmatics Association

Cohen, P. (1992) 'It's Racism What Dunnit: Hidden Narratives in Theories of Racism', in J. Donald and A. Rattansi (Eds.) *Race, Culture and Difference*, London: Sage: 62-103

Condor, S. (1988) 'Race, Stereotypes and racist Discourse', *Text* 8:69-89

Dijk, T. van (1987) *Communicating Racism: Ethnic Prejudice in Thought and Talk*, London: Sage

Essed, P. (1991) *Understanding Everyday Racism: An Interdisciplinary Theory*, London: Sage

Gaertner, S. and Dovidio, J. (1986) 'The Aversive Form of Racism', in J.F. Dovidio and S. L. Gaertner (Eds.), *Prejudice, Discrimination and Racism*, Orlanda: Academic Press:61-89

Gilroy, P. (1990) 'The End of Anti-Racism', *New Community* 17:71-83

Hewitt, J. P. and Stokes, R. (1975) 'Disclaimers', *American Sociological Review* 40:1-11

Jong, W. de (1989) 'The Development of Inter-Ethnic Relations in an Old District of Rotterdam between 1970 and 1985', *Ethnic and Racial Studies* 12:257-78

McConahay, J. B. (1986) 'Modern Racism, Ambivalence, and the Modern Racism Scale', in J.F. Dovidio and S.L. Gaertner (Eds.), *Prejudice, Discrimination and Racism*, Orlanda: Academic Press: 91-125

Memmi, A. (1982) *Le Racisme*, Paris: Gallimard

Potter, J. (1987) 'Discourse Analysis and the Turn of the Reflexive Screw: A Reponse to Furhman and Ochler', *Social Studies of Science* 17:171-77

Potter, J. and Wetherell, M. (1988) 'Accomplishing Attitudes: Fact and Evaluation in Racist Discourse', *Text* 8:51-68

Rattansi, A. (1992) 'Changing the subject? Racism, Culture and Education', in J. Donald and A. Rattansi (Eds.), *'Race', Culture and Difference*, London: Sage: 23-45

Reeves, W. (1983) *British Racial Discourse: A Study of British Political Discourse about Race and Race-Related Matters*, Cambridge: Cambridge University Press

Verkuyten, M., De Jong, W. and Masson, C.N. (1993) 'Discourse, Strong Views and Rhetorical Manoeuvres: Race Talk in the Netherlands', (manuscript submitted)

Wetherell, M. and Potter, J. (1992) *Mapping the Language of Racism: Discourse and the Legitimation of Exploitation*, London: Harvester-Wheatsheaf

8

Introduction

Like other articles collected in this volume, Harriet Baber's "The Market for Feminist Epistemology" may give you the feeling that you have wandered into an ongoing discussion — one part of an exchange between people who share familiarity with contested points and established positions. For example, there is, apparently, such a thing as "feminist epistemology"; there is, apparently, a "villain of the feminist epistemologists' story," and it is Descartes (256).

This is indeed an ongoing discussion — a current debate about gender differences. But it is not recent in its origins. It stretches back millennia. And it is by no means confined to scholarly circles (as this article points out, in its mentions of folk wisdoms): it is a traditional and popular topic. Yet its current form, in scholarly circles, may be less familiar than its enduring folk forms. Despite the perennial schedule of this topic, you may come up against some assumptions that feel like impediments to your understanding of Baber's argument.

In its current form, discussion of gender difference has snagged a troublesome paradox: if we overturn "patriarchal" notions (see Calhoun for summary of feminist analyses of patriarchy) of women's lesser value, and embrace women's ways as worthy, or even as better than men's ways, we redeem women from disparagement and from rationalizations of their subjugation. However, if we embrace the notion of "women's ways" involved in this redemption, we are also in danger of confirming an essential and significant difference between men and women, the idea of which has historically been the basis of patriarchy itself. Although she does not put the case in quite these terms, Baber tackles this paradox, by focussing on "feminist epistemology" ("epistemology" is defined in the article's third paragraph; in the fourth paragraph "feminist epistemology" is outlined, but more loosely). What are the implications of "women's ways of knowing"? (After you have read the article, you will be in a position to return to the question in Baber's first heading: "*Is 'feminist epistemology' feminist?*")

Baber's focus on epistemology is appropriate to her discipline — philosophy. And her discipline also determines the style of her argument. You will see that she depends on substantial *summary* of writers who describe historical and contemporary conditions in the world of men and women: Christian sects, corporate preferences, behaviours in psychology experiments. Sometimes, passages are even summaries of summaries. So, in the section which reviews evidence for different "ways of knowing," Baber quotes lengthily from Carol Tavris, who summarizes Carol Gilligan, who summarizes Nancy Chodorow (250-51). In her role as a researcher in philosophy, Baber does not venture into the empirical realm, but, rather, receives and evaluates news from it. (By way of contrast, consider Dorothy Counts and David Counts, who spent two and a half months travelling with RVers to gather materials for their study of RV culture.) Even this arms-length contact with the world of empirical studies and historical accounts may be somewhat uncharacteristic of writing in philosophy.

More characteristic are two patches of sustained reasoning by which Baber seeks to clarify assumptions involved in feminist epistemology. In the first (247-48), she uses deductive logic to loosen our grip on reasoning "we are inclined to accept." In the second, much longer passage of argument (261 *ff.*), she defines and applies a concept whose name comes from everyday speech: "vicious circle." While other types of scholarly expression might leave "vicious circle" unanalyzed, allowing it to capture a shared sense of a recognizable kind of impasse, Baber's argument proceeds in a characteristically philosophical manner, looking first to establish the *form* of the situation ('P's and 'C's and 'G's) and then applying the form to actual situations – that is, filling the form with content. To measure your grasp of the concept "vicious circle," you might try to answer these questions:

- What is the basis for comparing the development of "home economics" to the development of "feminist epistemology"? Why do both present instances of "vicious circles"?

- How do we *know*, in matters of feminist concern, that "Pursuing P' under C' is preferable to pursuing P under C" (261)? (Note that "C" represents actual conditions — things the way they are — whereas "C'" represents unrealized conditions — things as they are not.)

And, in the interests of developing an overview of the many parts of Baber's complex argument, try to explain to yourself

- the relation of the theory of markets of "increasing returns" to "vicious circle" (how is IBM like mother-infant bonding?);

- the relation of the account of mind-body "dualism" to feminist epistemology.

However challenging you find Baber's account, keep in mind that she is actually working in territory adjacent to the conversation of everyday life — a discourse that has produced concepts such as "woman's intuition," and that has more recently produced best-selling popularizations of concepts of men's and women's different ways of talking and relating to others.

The Market for Feminist Epistemology

HARRIET BABER
UNIVERSITY OF SAN DIEGO

HARRIET BABER
UNIVERSITY OF SAN DIEGO

IS FEMINIST EPISTEMOLOGY FEMINIST?

AT FIRST BLUSH, the notion of a "feminist epistemology" appears, at best, peculiar — not, as Sandra Harding suggests, because "'woman the knower' (like 'woman the scientist') appears to be a contradiction in terms"[1] but because it is hard to see how an epistemology, a philosophical theory of knowledge, can be either feminist or anti-feminist since it is not clear how such a theory might benefit or harm women.

Advocates of feminist epistemologies however suggest that traditional theories of knowledge are male-biased insofar as they fail to account for features of women's experience which are different from the characteristic experiences of males.

"Epistemology," writes John Pollock, "is 'the theory of knowledge' and would seem most naturally to have knowledge as its principal focus.

> But that is not entirely accurate. The theory of knowledge is an attempt to answer the question, 'How do you know?', but this is a question about how one knows, and not about knowing per se. In asking how a person knows something we are typically asking for his grounds for believing it. We want to know what justifies him in holding his belief. Thus epistemology has traditionally focused on epistemic justification more than on knowledge. . . .
>
> Epistemic justification is a normative notion. It pertains to what you should or should not believe.[2]

A number of writers in the Continental tradition have rejected this paradigm of epistemology for a variety of reasons. Advocates of feminist epistemology however reject it specifically on the grounds that the norms it embodies are male norms and hence that their acceptance sets standards which women find it difficult, or impossible, to meet. In particular, they hold that the traditional epistemic ideal of an objective, detached observer, conducting his investigations in isolation from any historical or social context, is alien to women's engaged, concrete, contextual way of knowing:

> The female construction of self in relation to others, leads. . . toward opposition to dualisms of any sort, valuation of concrete, everyday life, sense of variety of connectedness and continuities both with other women's relationally defined existence, bodily experience of boundary challenges, and activity of transforming both physical objects and human beings must be expected to result in a world view to which dichotomies are foreign.[3]

The popular acceptance of traditional epistemological views, according to which this mode of reasoning is defective, they suggest, is bad for women insofar as it results in their being assessed adversely as knowers. The popular acceptance of epistemologies which recognize the legitimacy of women's way of knowing is good for women because it results in women being more highly valued. To this extent, presumably, such epistemologies are "feminist."

There are a great many different theories which purport to be feminist epistemologies and it may be a mistake to look for essential characteristics as distinct from family resemblances. Nevertheless advocates of feminist epistemology by and large seem to make two assumptions which are highly questionable.

First, they commonly assume that there are deeply entrenched differences in the ways in which men and women see the world which arise either from biological differences or from early developmental history and so are, at best, difficult to alter. Thus Jaggar notes,

> Growing empirical evidence shows that women tend to conceive the world differently from men and have different attitudes towards it. The discovery of the precise nature and causes of these differences is a task for feminist psychologists and sociologists of knowledge. The task for feminist scientists and political theorists is to build on women's experience and insights in order to develop a systematic account of the world, together with its potentialities for change, as it appears from the standpoint of women.[4]

"Growing empirical evidence," it will be shown, suggests no such thing. Thus, for example, the thesis of gender differences in moral reasoning hypothesized by Carol Gilligan who, according to Jaggar, "*demonstrated* that the categories used to describe the moral development of children in fact fit the development only of boys"[5] [emphasis added] was early shown to be false on empirical grounds. Nevertheless, like a number of other "scientific fictions," including the myth of mother-infant bonding to be considered presently, the myth of women's way of knowing took on a life of its own within the literature, in which feminist theoreticians cited other feminist theoreticians and the highly speculative work of feminist psychoanalysts in support of claims about gender differences which had little or no empirical basis.[6]

Secondly, many advocates of feminist epistemology make a number of normative assumptions which are questionable and, in any case, in need of explication since they are largely tacit. Arguably, even if all the assumptions about women's distinctive way of viewing the world were correct, it would still not follow that we ought to reject traditional "androcentric" theories of knowledge, according to which women are assessed as epistemically defective, in favor of theories which legitimate and value women's way of knowing.

On the face of it, it seems reasonable that the acceptance of such accounts would benefit women. Presumably, if a trait which women possess (or are thought to possess) is valued, women benefit. This seems plausible because, more generally, we are inclined to accept the following argument:

(1) Members of Group G have trait X

(2) People benefit when traits that they possess are highly valued

(3) Therefore, members of Group G benefit when trait X is highly valued

(2) and (3) are however ambiguous since it is not clear whether the suggestion is that people benefit *ceteris paribus* when traits they possess are highly valued or whether the claim is that people actually benefit *on net* when traits they possess are highly valued. The former claim is plausible but is not adequate for the feminist epistemologist's purposes; the latter claim is, however, plainly false for it is not the case that people invariably benefit *on net* when

traits they possess are highly valued. Consider the following argument:

(1) Epileptics have fits

(2) People benefit on net when traits they possess are highly valued

(3) Epileptics benefit on net when having fits is highly valued

Some societies in fact have valued having fits along with other manifestations of altered states of consciousness as signs of divine favor and, presumably, in such societies epileptics gained a certain amount of prestige from their condition. Arguably however the prestige they gained in such circumstances was outweighed by the costs and epileptics are, on net, better off in circumstances where fits are not valued and where, as a consequence, researchers make aggressive and ultimately successful efforts to find means to control seizures.

Similarly, assuming (falsely as it happens) women really do "think differently" from men and speak in a different moral voice, to make the case that women would benefit by the acceptance of theories that value these modes of reasoning, we should have to show that the benefits of being recognized as being epistemically and morally competent outweigh any costs associated with women's epistemic strategies and modes of moral reasoning. After all, it might turn out when the costs are weighed against the benefits, that it was very much better for women to cure them of their "non-linear" thinking about proclivity for "caring," by psychotherapy, neurosurgery or, best of all, a solid course in logic, than to exalt women's way of knowing.

EMPIRICAL CONSIDERATIONS:
FLAWED DATA AND BOGUS EXPLANATIONS

Even if their empirical assumptions about gender differences were correct, advocates of feminist epistemology would still have to make a case for the benefit to women of their theories of knowledge. Their case however is all the more difficult to make because in fact many of the empirical claims about gender differences which they cite are false and the explanations given for those differences which do exist are implausible.

Consider Carol Gilligan's highly influential study of moral reasoning in boys and girls which Jaggar cites as not merely having *demonstrated* that boys and girls follow radically different courses of moral development but even as having shown that "basic categories of western moral philosophy such as rationality, autonomy and justice, are drawn from and reflect the moral experience of men rather than that of women."[7] These would be apocalyptic results indeed if it were not for the fact that Gilligan's research methods were flawed and her results were disconfirmed in subsequent research.

Thus Carol Tavris, citing an extensive body of empirical studies, notes

> Research in recent years casts considerable doubt on the notion that men and women differ appreciably in their moral reasoning, or that women have a permanently different voice because of their early closeness to their mothers. . . .
>
> When subsequent research directly compared men's and women's reasoning about moral dilemmas, Gilligan's ideas have rarely been supported. In study after study, men and women used both care-based reasoning . . . and justice-based reasoning. In study after study, researchers reported no average differences in the kind of moral reasoning that men and women apply. . . . results confirm Gilligan's argument that people make moral decisions not only according to abstract principles of justice, but also according to principles of compassion and care. But they fail to support her notion that women have any special corner on that compassion. . . . [cites Stephen J. Thoma. "Estimating gender differences in the comprehension and preference of moral issues." *Developmental Review*, 6, (1986), pp. 165-80].
>
> Two other psychologists in the field of moral development, Anne Colby and William Damon, likewise found little scientific support for Gilligan's claims. 'While her portrayal of general, sex-linked life-orientations is intuitively appealing,' they concluded, 'the research evidence at this point does not support such a generalized distinction.'
>
> Similar efforts to pin down differences between males and females in the value they place on 'autonomy' versus 'attachment' have been unsuccessful. In one study of 130 college students — who were of an age where we might expect the most exaggerated sex differences — psychologists Susan Co-

chran and Letitia Anne Peplau found no average difference in students' desire for attachment. . . . [8]

If the task of feminist theorists in sociology, psychology, political science and the hard sciences is, as Jaggar suggests in the passage cited above, "to build on women's experience and insights in order to develop a systematic account of the world, together with it potentialities for change, as it appears from the standpoint of women" these feminists are out of a job.

Similarly, Tavris cites additional empirical data which undermines what have become commonplace assumptions about gender differences as regards attachment/connection, cognitive abilities, dependency, emotions, empathy, moods and 'moodiness', need for achievement, need for love and attachment, need for power, nurturance, pacifism/belligerence, sexual capacity, verbal aggressiveness and hostility.[9] At the very least, the theses about psychological differences between men and women which Jaggar and others believe to have been "demonstrated" and which have become commonplace in pop psychology and self-help literature, have not been established.

To explain male-female differences which she thought she had discovered, Gilligan invoked speculative theories of development espoused by feminist psychoanalysts including Nancy Chodorow and Jean Baker Miller.

Gilligan's work was, at first, an important correction of bias in the study of psychological development, which had been based almost entirely on men's lives. In particular, she showed that earlier psychologists, finding that women did not seem to reason like men in evaluating moral dilemmas, concluded that women were somehow morally deficient, lacking in moral reasoning skills, and developmentally retarded. 'I cannot evade the notion,' Freud had written, 'that for women the level of what is ethically normal is different from what it is in men.'

Gilligan agreed with Freud that women and men differ in what they regard as 'ethically normal,' but she maintained that women's ways are just as moral. . . .

The origin of women's different voice, according to feminist psychoanalysts such as Nancy Chodorow and Jean Baker Miller, lies in the psychodynamic consequences of being raised primarily by mothers. Girls may continue to stay attached to their mothers as they form their identities, but boys, in order to develop a male identity, must separate themselves psychologically at an early age. The result in this view, is that adult women find comfort and solace in connection and are frightened of separation; adult men find security in independence and are frightened of attachments, which they fear will swallow them up and obliterate their identity as males. 'Since masculinity is defined through separation while femininity is defined through attachment,' Gilligan summarized, 'male gender identity is threatened by intimacy while female gender identity is threatened by separation.' . . .

As Chodorow put it, 'The basic feminine sense of self is connected to the world, the basic masculine sense of self is separate.'[10]

Such theories, however, are highly speculative and do not appear to be confirmed by empirical data which suggest that those psychological and behavioral differences which do exist are explained not by early development and relations with one's primary care-taker so much as by one's current situation in life — and that, far from being deeply entrenched and virtually ineradicable, they are subject to modification.

New studies find that the behavior that we link to gender depends more on what an individual is doing and needs to do than on his or her biological sex. For example, sociologist Barbara Risman compared the personality traits of single fathers, single mothers, and married parents. If biological predispositions or childhood socialization create stable personality differences between women and men, she reasoned, then fathers should differ from mothers in their babycare skills and nurturing talents in general, regardless of marital status. Instead, Risman found that having responsibility for child care was strongly related to 'feminine' traits, such as nurturance and sympathy, as being female was. The single men who were caring for children were more like mothers than like married fathers. These men were not an atypical group of especially nurturant men, either. They had custody of their children through circumstances beyond their control — widowhood, the wife's desertion, or the wife's lack of interest in shared custody.

Similarly, a study of 150 men who were spending up to sixty hours a week caring for their ailing parents or spouses found that the men provided just as much emotional support as women traditionally do. . . .

In the 1970s, the sociologist and business consultant Rosabeth Moss Kanter, in studies of men and women in corporations, showed conclusively that *conditions of employment, not qualities of the individual*, determine what most people value about their work. . . . When men and women hold the same prestigious jobs, their values and behavior are similar.[11]

In addition to doctrines about psychological differences between men and women which allegedly make it difficult for women to meet the requirements of traditional theories of knowledge, and psychoanalytic accounts of their origin, most advocates of feminist epistemology hold also that such epistemologies are male-biased to the extent that they assume a mind-body dualism of some sort and denigrate the body in favor of the mind. According to the received view women are "associated with nature . . . and the body" in such a way that what Jaggar calls "normative dualism, the excessive value placed on the 'mind' at the expense of the body," is detrimental to women's interests.

Of course, both men and women have both minds and bodies but, through the western philosophical tradition, women have been seen consistently with (or entangled in) their bodies in a more intimate way than men are with theirs. . . . The traditional view, in short, is that women are more closely associated with nature and men with culture; women with the body and men with the mind.

The association of women with body and men with mind has been reinforced if not generated by a sexual division of labor in which (some) men have dominated the 'intellectual' fields of politics, science, culture and religion while women have been assigned the primary responsibility for many day-to-day tasks necessary for physical survival.[12]

The suggestion that women are, in this sense, archetypally and universally associated with the body is simply implausible. The association of women with the body does indeed seem to be a feature of Greek culture which, as a consequence, found its way into the philosophical literature.[13] The Victorians, however, whose attitudes are far more influential on the general public than the opinions of Greek philosophers, associated men with the body and brute nature and regarded "culture" as the domain of ladies. Men, indeed, monopolized the high-prestige leadership roles in religious, literary, and artistic activities, but even such men were regarded as perhaps a trifle effeminate, not truly men's men. Religion and culture then, as now, were regarded as feminine domains.

In addition, the suggestion that women by and large do "physical labor" which men ("at least men of a certain class") monopolize "mental" work is plainly false — unless we gerrymander the distinction between "mental" and "physical" work in such a way that all low-prestige jobs typically done by women count as "physical." Otherwise it is hard to see how, e.g., clerical work, which occupies almost one-third of all women who work outside the home, counts as "physical labor." Indeed, arguably, one of the most egregious injustices against women which feminists ought to work to rectify is women's *de facto* exclusion from most jobs which are ordinarily understood as "physical work" — from carpentry, plumbing, and other construction work, from house painting, from mining, from auto mechanics and other skilled trades, from ditch-digging and the operation of heavy machinery, and generally from work that is mobile, involves physical exertion or is done out of doors.[14]

In addition to questionable claims about the association of women with the body, Jaggar suggests women fare better in societies where the importance of the body and of natural, mutualistic relationships are recognized, than in those which embody ideologies that trivialize or denigrate the body and conceive of society as an "atomistic" association of rational egoists. Women, writes Jaggar, would be unlikely to have developed ideologies like the liberal theory of human nature which regard "mental" activity more highly than physical work, embody an atomistic conception of society and place the highest value on individual autonomy.

It is easy to see how certain features of the liberal theory of human nature are far more likely to have been produced by men than by women. For instance, it is easy to see how men, at least men of a certain class, would be likely to place supreme value on 'mental' activity and to ignore the fact that such activity would be impossible without the daily physical labor necessary for survival, especially the physical labor of women. It is even harder to imagine women developing a political theory that presupposed political solipsism, ignoring human interdependence and especially the long dependence of human young. Nor would women be likely to formulate a conception of rationality that stressed individual autonomy and contained such a strong element of egoism as the liberal conception.[15]

As a matter of fact, despite highly speculative accounts of primitive matriarchy, historically women appear to have done better in communities where the body, the family and the material world were regarded as suspect or positively evil.[16] Thus, in his account of sexual practices and sex roles in the ancient world, Richard Posner suggests that women were better off in early Christian communities, whose members were more distrustful of the body and material nature than pagans, than in Greek society generally.

> Companionate marriage . . . signified marriage between at least approximate equals, based on mutual respect and affection, and involving close and continuous association in child rearing, household management, and other activities, rather than merely the occasional copulation that was the principal contact between spouses in the typical Greek marriage. . . .
>
> Despite its fulminations against woman the temptress and the devil's helper, Christianity seems to have been, on balance, more solicitous of women's interests than the pagan religions had been. By praising celibacy, the Church gave women other options besides marriage. . . . In forbidding divorce, the Church protected married women from being cast off by husbands who had tired of them — and losing their children in the process, since, under both Greek and Roman law, in the event of divorce the children remained with their father. And by insisting that marriage should be consensual — that a man and woman should be free to reject the family's choice of mate — the Church not only prompted companionate marriage but made indissoluble marriage more tolerable.[17]

Women did still better in communities that were even more hostile to the body and to natural, mutualistic relationships than the Church at large, such as monastic movements within the church and gnostic communities without. Thus Ross Shepard Kraemer in her history of women's religious practice in the ancient world notes grudgingly that dualistic cosmologies benefited women:

> The specific belief systems that provided women in antiquity with autonomy and alternatives are enormously prob-

lematic. Ascetic and monastic women from the Therapeutics to Thecla to the desert mothers found it necessary to repudiate the boy and its female associations, becoming male both in theory and in aspects of appearance in order to achieve self-determination. Splitting the body from the soul, dualist cosmologies such as those advocated by gnostics frequently provided women with alternatives denied them by those (men) who insisted on the integral connection of body and spirit. Conversely, cosmologies that value embodiment seem then to need to constrain and confine women as a necessary corollary. The notion that self-determination for women is only available at the cost of psychic self-destruction, at the cost of the repudiation of the feminine, is hardly comforting.[18]

In general, women have been attracted to movements that have been anti-nomian, gnostic, individualistic and distrustful both of sexuality and of the body. In *The Pursuit of the Millennium*, a history of "revolutionary millenarians and mystical anarchists of the Middle Ages," for example, Norman Cohn documents the participation of women in such movements as the highly individualistic, anarchistic and dualistic heresy of the Free Spirit. More recent religious movements founded by women have rejected sexuality and denigrated materiality, e.g., the Shakers, who were celibate, and Christian Science and Theosophy, based on the assumption that material reality is, in some sense, "unreal." More generally it has been in just those religious groups that were the most distrustful of materiality, the Quakers for example, where women first exercised leadership roles; by contrast, within Christianity, it has been those traditions which are the most sacramental and "incarnational," and to that extent, most "materialistic" — the Roman Catholic, Eastern Orthodox and Anglican Churches — which have been slowest to accept women in leadership roles.

There is good reason for this. To the extent that disabilities and constraints attach to being female, ideologies which denigrate the body trivialize gender differences and so liberate women from the disadvantages that have traditionally attached to the condition of being female, as Kraemer suggests. It is hard to see, however, why this "repudiation of the feminine" represents an act of "psychic self-destruction" for women. It may be that for some, if not most women, femininity itself, quite apart from any social, economic or political disabilities attached to it, is itself oppressive, is something which women *happily* repudiate. In any case, whether the repudiation of "femininity" is intrinsically beneficial or costly to women, dualistic ideologies which enable women to detach themselves from it appear to benefit women.

In short, although the thesis that women are "connected with (or entangled in) their bodies in a more intimate way than men are with theirs" is too woolly to be conclusively refuted, and unless one relies quite heavily on sociological data about the ancient Greeks (mediated through the philosophical tradition), there is little reason to believe that this connection — whatever it may come to — holds universally. Moreover an historical survey of the position of women in the West beginning with the Greeks of antiquity strongly suggests that dualism is good for women. Is it any wonder that Descartes, the villain of the feminist epistemologists' story, was sponsored by Queen Christina?

On the face of it, it may be puzzling how a large body of academic work could be built around claim, like Gilligan's thesis of women's "different voice" or Jaggar's suggestion that "women have been seen consistently as being connected with (or entangled in) their bodies in a more intimate way than men are with theirs" which were simply false. And yet books and articles in support of the views considered above boast extensive bibliographies of academic work by like-minded authors. Surely, one wishes to object, where there is so much smoke there must be some fire.

This is however to underestimate the power of scientific fictions which can be put to service in support of entrenched ideologies and institutional policies. Consider, for example, research during the past 20 years on the supposed phenomenon of mother-infant bonding among humans. "By the early 1980s," writes Diane Eyer in her recent study *Mother-Infant Bonding: A Scientific Fiction*, "research on the bonding of mothers and their newborns has been dismissed by much of the scientific community as having been poorly conceived and executed."[19] Yet in the decade prior to this an extensive academic literature had been generated in an attempt to examine and explain this bogus phenomenon. Moreover, even when the scientific community had largely dismissed this body of research, at the popular level, doctors, nurses and social workers continued to accept it as factually accurate. In materials given to pregnant women, by doctors and Lamaze educators, bonding was described as if it were an uncontroversial, plain fact like the dilation of the cervix during labor.[20] Bonding, in spite of its lack of empirical support, became widely accepted because it had been "pulled into the maëlstrom of popular belief and the institutional goals that inspire science."

The research on bonding was inspired by the popular belief that women, one and all, are inherently suited for motherhood. This belief coincided with a number of institutional goals, including the needs of the psychological and medical professions. . . . New mothers, whether feminist or traditional, also embraced the ideology of motherhood at a time when their sex role was being challenged. Bonding promised insurance against the psychological damage that might be caused by women's increasing involvement in work outside the home. . . .

Bonding appeared to give women more control over their birth experience, and it supported their wish to have their newborn infants and other family members with them in what had previously been a lonely and often demeaning experience.[21]

The myth of mother-infant bonding is by no means the only scientific fiction that has enjoyed undeserved success in virtue of its apparent confirmation of popular assumptions about gender and gender differences. Relatively shoddy research which purported to demonstrate a neurological basis for psychological differences between the sexes has also been given undue favorable attention. Why?

Because the study of sex differences is not like the rest of psychology. Under pressure from the gathering momentum of feminism, and perhaps in backlash to it, many investigators seem determined to discover that men and women 'really' are different. It seems that if sex differences (e.g., lateralization) do not exist, then they had to be invented.[22]

THE COST OF FEMINIST EPISTEMOLOGY

Similarly, in spite of a lack of empirical support, Gilligan's book and other works which constructed and elaborated scientific fictions about psychological differences between men and women became popular among both academics and the general public. Tavris suggests that their appeal was due to the apparent confirmation of folk wisdom about gender differences: they embodied claims which many people found "intuitive." Nevertheless, she notes,

One problem with intuitions, of course, is that what feels right to one person may feel entirely wrong to another. A friend of mine, a professor in a law school, was discussing Gilligan's theory with her class and met vociferous resistance from the students, male and female. Many of the males felt resentful that their very real affections and attachments were being overlooked or disparaged. Many of the females felt resentful that their professional abilities were being compromised or questioned. 'These women are planning to be litigators,' said my friend, 'and they don't consider themselves "naturally" soft or pliable, or less capable of a justice-based form of moral reasoning.'[23]

In addition to being unintuitive and offensive to men and women who have, to a great extent, broken free from traditional sex roles, giving the academic seal of approval to folk wisdom about male-female differences seems to provide justification for policies which reinforce traditional sex roles.

The idea that women operate on a different moral wavelength and speak in a different voice has made its way into many fields and into common consciousness. In business, many employers and managers are using Gilligan's theory to account for sex differences they observe in the workplace. Clinical psychologist Harriet Goldhor Lerner, describing her experiences as a consultant to organizations, says, 'I frequently hear Gilligan's research interpreted as demonstrating that women on the job care primarily about people's feelings and personalities, whereas men, in contrast, think in rational, logical, and abstract terms and are primarily oriented toward the task at hand.[24]

The popular acceptance of such doctrines, particularly by management consultants and managers involved in personnel decisions, may be highly detrimental to women's interests. So, for example, the author of a popular journalistic account of the achievements of female executives in her introduction cautions readers aspiring to emulate them to "beware of 'experts' on working women":

The legitimation of the notion of the schizophrenic working woman, torn between career and kids — or what we call 'safe sexism' practised by so-called experts on the workplace —

has probably done more to sully the positive image of women in business than any backward attitude manifested by a male manager. . . .

The practitioners of 'safe sexism' whether in the form of management consultants or advice-book authors, also defame women by legitimizing the notion of women as the second sex, that they have a distinct 'management style' that emphasizes 'nurturing,' 'building consensus,' and 'empowerment' while men are better at being leaders.

Not surprisingly, it's this very simple-minded stereotyping of women that has relegated them to the soft, fluffy pink ghettos of human resources and public relations instead of being put in charge of running factories, leading sales teams, and heading up mergers and acquisitions departments.[25]

While the myth of women's peculiarly feminine "management styles" may, to some extent, have benefitted women in business — to the extent that it provided some women with a way out of the typing pool and into what were at least nominally management positions — the overall result of myth was harmful to women in business.

Similarly, during a period when women were entering the sciences, while myths about women's "unique skills" and "special talents" opened doors, as Margaret Rossiter suggests in her study of women scientists in America, the creation of "women's work" within the sciences, the justification of which was grounded in such myths, was ultimately detrimental to the interests of women in the sciences.

Even though women could claim by 1920 that they had 'opened the doors' of science, it was quite clear that they would be limited to positions just inside the entryway. . . .

Henceforth when better-educated and more qualified women tried to move beyond this territorial demarcation or up the hierarchy, they were met with strong resistance. . . . In their attempts to get around these artificial barriers and inconsistencies early women scientists developed a great many strategies. These tended to be of two sorts. One was the idealistic, liberal-to-radical, and often confrontational strategy of demanding that society reject all stereotypes and work for the feminist goal of full equality. . . .

The alternative strategy was the less strident and more conservative and 'realistic' tactic of accepting the prevailing inequality and sexual stereotypes but using them for short-term gains such as establishing areas of 'women's work' for women. Strategists for this approach emphasized that women had 'unique skills' and 'special talents' that justified reserving certain kinds of work for them. . . .

If success can be judged in numbers, women scientists had done very well indeed, for by 1940 there were thousands of such women working a variety of fields and institutions. . . . This great growth, however, had occurred at the price of accepting a pattern of segregated employment and underrecognition, which, try as they might, most women could not escape.[26]

If this is correct then the doctrine that there are profound and deeply entrenched psychological differences along the lines suggested by advocates of feminist epistemology is neither true nor beneficial to women. It is therefore, on the face of it, puzzling why a great many feminists eagerly accepted and promoted this view.

THE MARKET FOR SCIENTIFIC FICTIONS

The answer, I think, is that while in the long run the doctrine of La Différence was detrimental to the interests of women as a group, in the short run invoking the doctrine (and so entrenching it all the more deeply in the popular imagination) was beneficial to the individual women. Thus, for example, women having babies could invoke the myth of "bonding" and other dogmas of the natural childbirth movement to secure more humane treatment in hospitals and a greater measure of autonomy during the birth process and immediately afterward. Most women who bought into these views did not recognize their role in promoting traditional views about the nature and duties of women which were detrimental to women's interests.

Similarly, women in business and in the sciences stood to gain by promoting the idea that there were uniquely feminine talents and "management styles" since these were an entré into management and the professions that they would not otherwise have had: better to be a manager in a "fluffy pink ghetto" (where "feminine management styles" were deemed appropriate) than a secretary; better 'women's work' in a scientific area in which one had been trained than no work at all. The suggestion that women had "special talents" to offer businesses which would benefit their employers opened doors for women that appeals to fairness could not budge. Rhetorically, it was effective to promote the idea that hiring women was "good business."

The difficulty with such a strategy however is that in many cases using gender stereotypes for short-term gains generates vicious circles which lock in policies that are detrimental to women's interests. Arguably, the promotion of feminist epistemology is pernicious because it helps to generate such vicious circles. To make this out, however, we need first to provide a brief account of how vicious circles are generated.

A vicious circle of the sort with which we are concerned arises when the following state of affairs obtains:

(1) Conditions, C, actually obtain.

(2) Under conditions, C, the best policy for members of group G, is P.

(3) Under conditions, C^1, the best policy for members of group, G, is P^1

(4) Pursuing P^1 under C is preferable to pursuing P^1 under C^1

(5) Pursuing P contributes to the persistence of C

Consider, for example, the plight of computer buyers in the mid-80s when IBM and compatibles dominated the market and the newly emergent Macintosh was seen as little more than an expensive toy. Because it was advantageous to own a computer that was compatible with as many other computers as possible, all other things being equal, it was to the advantage of computer buyers to buy the computer that most other computer buyers had bought: Within the computer market, success bred more success. Apple, because it entered the market with the Mac relatively late, was almost caught in a vicious circle since conditions (1) to (5) obtained and, arguably, the Mac was only saved from extinction by fierce, uncompromising and, in many respects, irrational and obnoxious loyalty of its fans.

(1) In the mid-80s, IBM dominated the market. There was relatively little software available for the Macintosh and no convenient way to transfer data created under DOS to a format that the Macintosh could digest. Moreover, while IBM-compatible users could easily upgrade, with cheap cards and chips available at local computer-users

groups, the Mac was a closed box, upgrading was expensive, and hardware was monopolized by Apply. Finally, IBM-compatible users did not take Macintosh users seriously.

(2) Under the conditions described in (1), the best policy for computer buyers was to go IBM.

(3) Under different conditions, in a more Mac-friendly environment, going Mac would have been preferable. If the Mac had been competitively priced, if there had been a wide range of software available for it, and if it, and not IBM had been the "industry standard," going Mac would have been the best policy for computer buyers.

(4) Since (as all Macintosh users know) the Mac is intrinsically far superior to IBM and compatibles, buying a Mac in a Mac-friendly environment is preferable to buying an IBM in an IBM- friendly environment.

(5) But, the fact that IBM and compatibles dominated the market, contributed heavily to making IBM and compatibles desirable from the consumer's point of view and to perpetuating the Mac-hostile conditions described in (1). Indeed, when the Mac first came out, potential consumers worried that it might be orphaned or abandoned like the Osborne and other early CPM machines, or like Apple's own Apple III and Lisa. So consumers continued to favor IBM and compatibles and by buying them further contributed to the IBM-friendliness of the environment.

The Apple/IBM competition in fact is a classic example of the phenomenon of increasing returns which operates in some parts of the economy, particularly where high technology products are involved. In such systems, economists suggest, "small chance events early in the history of an industry or technology can tilt the competitive balance" in many cases toward products that are intrinsically inferior. Markets where increasing returns operate are not efficient.

> Conventional economic theory is built on the assumption of diminishing returns. Economic actions engender a negative feedback that leads to a predictable equilibrium for prices and market shares. Such feedback tends to stabilize the economy because any major changes will be offset by the very reactions they generate. . . .
>
> Such an agreeable picture often does violence to reality. In many parts of the economy, stabilizing forces appear not to operate. Instead positive feedback magnifies the effects of small economic shifts . . . [which] makes for many possible equilibrium points. There is no guarantee that the particular

economic outcome selected from among the many alternatives will be the 'best' one. Furthermore, once random economic events select a particular path, the choice may become locked-in regardless of the advantages of the alternatives.[27]

The labor market for women is another market in which increasing returns operate and where, arguably, sex-segregated employment, a sub-optimal equilibrium, has become locked-in as a consequence of the vicious circle in which most female employees are caught.

Consider the situation of women who work outside the home.

(1) The overwhelming majority of women in the labor force are still employed in traditionally female occupations which are boring and underpaid. In addition, as most women know, such positions offer little chance for advancement. Women still make on the average 71¢ to every dollar earned by their male counterparts. Discrimination against women in hiring and promotion is the norm and sex segregation in the labor force is the rule rather than the exception.

(2) In such circumstances, it does not pay women to invest too heavily in their careers: It is advantageous to opt for the Mommy Track. Men's earning potential and prospects are more promising than women's; hence, where resources are limited, a rational woman will invest in marriage and in her husband's career in preference to her own because this strategy is likely to have a better payoff for her as well as for him. Moreover, a rational, self-interested woman in a boring pink-collar job who recognizes that her chances of advancement are negligible will take full advantage of the questionable features of the Mommy Track — extended maternity leave, part-time work, job-sharing schemes and other arrangements which provide immediate benefits to working women at the cost of undermining their value as workers.

(3) If women had the same opportunities as men in the labor market, it would not be advantageous to opt for the Mommy Track.

(4) Being off the Mommy Track under conditions of male/female equity in the labor market is preferable to being on the Mommy Track under conditions of inequality.

(5) Opting for the Mommy Track promotes inequality. Notoriously, women don't invest in work because employers don't invest in women, but employers don't invest in women because women don't invest in work — thus women's rational, self-inter-

ested choices help to perpetuate discrimination, which is ultimately detrimental to women's interests.

It is just because women's situation in the labor market is viciously circular in this respect that feminists disagree about the desirability of the Mommy Track. Whatever the long-term costs, the Mommy Track *does* benefit women who take advantage of it. As many feminists have recognized, expecting women to behave like men in the workplace is, in most cases, actually demanding more of them than of their male counterparts and is, to that extent, unfair. Unlike men, most women cannot count on their spouses to take on the responsibility of child care; unlike men, women cannot count on their spouses to take care of entertaining or day-to-day domestic responsibilities. Women in the labor force, unlike men, notoriously work a "second shift" in the home. On balance, however, one would hope that women would behave nobly rather than rationally and reject the benefits of the Mommy Track.

Similarly, the promotion of feminist epistemology benefits women, particularly academic women who gain from the acceptance of it and other areas of "feminist scholarship" at the cost of re-enforcing stereotypes of women and policies that are ultimately detrimental to women's interests. Women in the general population also benefit because, under conditions in which myths about gender differences are deeply entrenched and where men and women as a rule play different roles in social and economic transactions, women benefit to the extent that the traits they are thought to possess and the roles they play are valued as equal to, or even superior to, what are perceived as characteristics and roles appropriate to men. So, Tavris notes,

> In generating public reaction, Gilligan clearly struck a nerve: Thousands of women have seen themselves in her book. . . . One reason for this enthusiasm, I believe, is that Gilligan and others finally recognized and validated the long-disparaged, unpaid work that women do: the work of day-to-day caring for children, the work of keeping extended families together with calls, letters and gifts, the work of worrying about everyone's feelings, the work of monitoring relationships to make sure they are going well. . . .
>
> It was encouraging and life-affirming to read that intimacy and an ethic of care are as valuable as, indeed more valuable than, typical male aloofness and men's ethic of justice.[28]

Similarly, in circumstances where most people believe that "men and women think differently," in particular that women are "intuitive" and prone to "non-linear thinking" that defies the canons of conventional logic, it was "encouraging and life-affirming" for women to be told, by feminist epistemologists, that this special women's way of knowing was equal or superior to men's way of knowing which had been taken to be normative by traditional epistemology.

Nevertheless the market for feminist epistemology, like other markets where increasing returns operate, is inefficient insofar as it creates a vicious circle.

(1) It is generally believed that women "think differently" from men.

(2) Under conditions in which it is believed that women think differently from men the best policy for women is to promote the idea that women's way of thinking is equal or superior to men's way of thinking, that is, to promote feminist epistemology.

(3) Under conditions in which it is not believed that women think differently from men the best policy for women is not to promote this idea: feminist epistemology is at best pointless and potentially harmful.

(4) A state of affairs in which people reject the view that women think differently from men is preferable to one in which people accept this view. For one thing, all other things being equal perhaps, a state of affairs in which people hold true beliefs is better than one in which they accept superstitions, myths and falsehoods.

(5) Promoting feminist epistemology contributes to the persistence of the myth that men and women "think differently."

Thus women gain some benefits from the popularity of feminist epistemology, given prevailing myths about gender differences. Ultimately, however, the wide-spread acceptance of feminist epistemology is detrimental to women's interests since women suffer when myths of gender difference are rehearsed and given the academic imprimatur.

Academic women in particular lose insofar as the growing industry of "feminist scholarship" facilitates the construction of academic pink-collar ghettos. To see how and why academic pink-collar ghettos are constructed it may be instructive to compare the rise of feminist scholarship during the past two decades with the invention and development of home economics, perhaps the quintessential academic pink-collar ghetto, a hundred years earlier.

The founder of 'home economics,' and one whose leadership and character touched her contemporaries deeply, was Ellen Swallow Richards, Vassar 1870 and MIT 1873 . . . As a student at MIT she had learned how to make a place for herself (and other women) by capitalizing on women's traditional role or, as she put it in 1871, 'Perhaps the fact that I am not a Radical or a believer in the all powerful ballot for women to right her wrongs and that I do not scorn womanly duties, but claim it as a privilege to clean up and sort of supervise the room and sew things, etc., is winning me stronger allies than anything else.' . . .

By 1911 many [agricultural colleges of the Midwest and West] . . . had already formed programs and even departments of home economics and others were eager to do so. . . . Yet the very success of this kind of 'women's work' on major campuses helped to harden the sexual segregation for future generations still further. Rather than being accepted for other scientific employment once the pioneers had shown women could handle this employment, the women found themselves more restricted to 'women's work' than ever. Since women were finding such good opportunities in this field, many persons (including the first vocational guidance counselors, a new specialty around 1910) urged ambitious young women interested in science to head for home economics. It was the only field where a woman scientist could hope to be a full professor, department chairman or even a dean in the 1920s and 1930s.[29]

Unlike many contemporary feminist philosophers, Ellen Swallow Richards never claimed that her acceptance of traditional views about gender differences on her creation of a separate sphere within Academe for women was "Radical." Nevertheless, as the above considerations suggest, the popularity of home economics in the early part of this century benefited academic women in the sciences in much the way that the current popularity of feminist philosophy benefits women in philosophy. And, of course, in light of these benefits it has not been unknown for graduate school faculty to advise female grad students in philosophy to "do feminism" so that they can put it on their vitae. Arguably, however, the association of women in philosophy with "feminism" thus understood is harmful to all women in the profession, including those who do "do feminism."

Shortly after I had successfully defended my dissertation, which included a rousing defense of Relative Identity, I attended an APA function wearing a tee shirt I had made in honour of the occasion which proclaimed, "Repeal Leibniz' Law." An earnest male philosopher approached me and asked whether that motto "had something to do with feminism." When I expressed bewilderment he explained that he assumed that it had something to do with feminists' rejection of "Western male logic." Mercifully, once I began expounding the virtues of Relative Identity and explaining the more interesting logical moves in my dissertation he went away.

Grant that, even if "doing feminism" is merely a temptation for women in the profession and no woman is forced into the academic pink-collar ghetto, the visibility of "feminist philosophy," including "feminist epistemology," makes it difficult for women in the profession to avoid guilt by association unless they actively distance themselves from this enterprise by ignoring issues that concern women, remaining aloof from women's organizations in the profession and even denying that they are feminists. These seem to me to be some of the worst consequences of the rise of "feminist philosophy." Even if "doing feminist philosophy" is, at best, a questionable business, doing a philosophy as a feminist, in particular bringing analytic expertise to bear in the discussion of ethical and political issues that concern women, and exposing misconceptions about women, is extremely important. Worst of all, "feminist philosophy" has provided grist for the mill of conservatives in the profession — including some who claim to be feminists — who lampoon it in order to exploit anti-feminist backlash.

For these reasons, I suggest that, on balance, quite apart from the intrinsic intellectual merits of what are currently understood as "feminist epistemologies," the identification of these theories as "feminist" motivated by unsubstantiated assumptions about the psychological differences between men and women, is detrimental to women's interests.

NOTES

1   Harding, p. 47.
2   Pollock, p. 7.
3   Hartstock, "The Feminist Standpoint," p. 23 cited by Jaggar, p. 376.
4   Jaggar, p. 376.
5   Jaggar, p. 372.
6   For an empirically based summary of gender differences see Tavris, p. 296.
7   Jaggar, p. 372.

8   Tavris, pp. 83-86.

9   Tavris, p. 296. This is Tavris's list of "where the differences aren't."

10   Tavris, pp. 80-81.

11   Tavris, pp. 63, 88-89. Numerous studies by Arrow, Blau, Bergman and other economists confirm Kanter's result. In general, labor-force attachment and behavior on the job, including most notably absenteeism and quit behavior, are a function of the nature of the job and not the sex or race of the worker. Although women in the aggregate behave differently from men in the labor force, the differences are accounted for by the differences in the work that men and women in the aggregate do.

12   Jaggar, 46.

13   See Posner, esp. pp. 38-45 for a discussion of sexual mores and sex roles in the Mediterranean world during the period.

14   For a discussion of the characteristics of women's work, see, e.g., Game and Pringle, esp. ch. 1, "Masculinity and Machines." Taking as representative the sexual division of labor in the whiteware (appliance) industry, the authors suggest that, at least in manufacturing, women's work is characteristically unskilled, "light," perceived as "less dangerous" than men's work, "clean" rather than dirty, boring, and immobile. Although women's work within this context is less prestigious than men's work, it is also insofar as it is light, clean and immobile, less "physical."

15   Jaggar, p. 46.

16   See Tavris's account of "the search for the feminist Eden," pp. 71-79.

17   Posner, pp. 45, 47.

18   Kraemer, p. 208. It should be noted that neither Posner nor Kraemer is sympathetic to Christianity. Thus Kraemer writes:

> Those preoccupied with Christianity might do well to reflect on the differences between a religion whose central myth is that of the separation and ultimate reunion of mother and daughter beloved of one another, and that of a religion whose central myth is of a father who requires the painful sacrificial death of his only son.

19   Eyer, p. 3.

20   As the mother of three children born during this period, I can vouch for this.

21   Eyer, pp. 1-2.

22   Marcel Kinsbourne. "If sex differences in brain lateralization exist, they have yet to be discovered" in The Behavioral and Brain Sciences, 3, p. 242 cited by Tavris, p. 53.

23   Tavris, p. 83.

24   Tavris, pp. 81-82.

25   Jane White. A Few Good Women. (Englewood Cliffs, NJ: Prentice-Hall, 1992), p. 26.

26   Rossiter, pp. xvii-xviii.

27   Arthur, p. 92.

28   Tavris, p. 82.

29   Rossiter, pp. 68-70.

REFERENCES

Arthur, W. Brian. "Positive Feedbacks in the Economy" in *Scientific American* (February 1990), 92-99.

Bergman, Barbara. "Does the Market for Women's Labor Need Fixing?" in *Journal of Economic Perspectives*, vol. 3, no. 1 (Winter 1989), 43-60.

Cohn, Norman. *The Pursuit of the Millenium*. New York: Oxford University Press, 1961.

Duran, Jane. *Toward a Feminist Epistemology*. Savage, MD: Rowman & Littlefield, 1991.

Eyer, Diane E. *Mother-Infant Bonding: A Scientific Fiction*. New Haven, CT: Yale University Press, 1992.

Faludi, Susan. *Backlash*. New York: Crown, 1991.

Game, A. and R. Pringle. *Gender at Work*. Boston: George Allen & Unwin, 1983.

Gergen, Mary McCanney. *Feminist Thought and the Structure of Knowledge*. New York: New York University Press, 1988.

Harding, Sandra. *Whose Science? Whose Knowledge?* Ithaca, NY: Cornell University Press, 1991.

Harman, Joan E. and Ellen Messer-Davidow. *(En)Gendering Knowledge: Feminists in Academe*. Knoxville, TN: The University of Tennessee Press, 1991.

Jaggar, Alison M. and Susan R. Bordo, eds., *Gender/Body/Knowledge*. New Brunswick, NJ: Rutgers University Press, 1989.

Jaggar, Alison M. *Feminist Politics and Human Nature*. Totowa, NJ: Rowman and Allanheld, 1983.

Keller, Evelyn Fox. *Reflections of Gender and Science*. New Haven, CT: Yale University Press, 1985.

Kraemer, Ross Shepard. *Her Share of the Blessings*. Oxford University Press, 1992.

Pollock, John L. *Contemporary Theories of Knowledge*. Totowa, NJ: Rowman & Littlefield, 1986.

Posner, Richard. *Sex and Reason*. Cambridge, MA: Harvard University Press, 1992.

Rossiter, Margaret W. *Women Scientists in America*. Baltimore, MD: Johns Hopkins University Press, 1982.

Tavris, Carol. *The Mismeasure of Woman*. New York: Touchstone, 1992.

White, Jane. *A Few Good Women*. Englewood Cliffs, NJ: Prentice-Hall, 1992.

9

Introduction

In "Protecting Infants: The French Campaign for Maternity
Leaves, 1890s-1913," Mary Lynn McDougall asks why it took so
long – twenty-five years — for French legislators to agree on provisions for women to take time off work before and after childbirth. After all, these legislators had no such trouble agreeing to
pass seemingly related legislation regarding work, women, and
children. She answers the question by "analyzing the arguments
and tactics of the proponents of maternity leaves in the context of
contemporary political and medical debates about social legislation" (274).

The form of the answer is mainly narrative: that is, the political
story of bills, discussion, disagreement, votes, publicity. Once the
story is under way, footnotes refer almost exclusively to documents of the time — parliamentary records and medical publications, including academic theses — rather than to the work of
other historians. This is how McDougall found out about these
episodes: she read these archival documents.

And, once the story is under way, it proceeds year by year,
these years divided into two sessions of parliamentary activity
(1886-1892 and 1903-1913) and the period of lobbying between
them. But you will find that several pages intervene between
McDougall's forecast of the organization of her discussion — "I
will consider the three phases of the campaign sequentially" (274)
— and the beginning of the story (278). These pages summarize
and interpret principal features of the story which is to follow.

You should take these preliminaries to the narrative of political activity as a guide to the subsequent details and intricacies. Like most historians, McDougall understates rather than over-emphasizes her large claims. Interpretation and generality are laminated into the narration of the past, that narration secured by scrupulous accounting of the evidence available.

Accordingly, you will find that the end of the article, at first glance, is not a "conclusion" in the sense of culminating generalizations, not a conclusion like those you will find in selections in this volume from other disciplines. Rather, it is yet another legislative episode, another instalment in the *story*. But a closer look will reveal that the end of the article reinvokes terms with which the article began: the "social and fiscal conservatism" of the first paragraph appears in the second-to-last paragraph in a statement about the relation between these two forces: "The controversy over the purpose of the legislation and related disputes over the population to be protected, as much as fiscal conservatism, stalled the enactment of even this limited protection for mothers and infants" (300). (Consider how the *extent* of the legislation — who is to be affected? — is an issue for debate between social reformers and social conservatives.) And, more important, the article's last sentence, summing up the issue's appearance during the war years —

> Although their efforts were only partially successful, they indicate that the more positive, if in the short run more expensive, approach to work and maternity was possible, when there was a need for women workers (300)

— invokes matters that have been of concern throughout the article: whose interests are served by legislation enforcing maternity-leave provisions and by the assumptions and discourse that accompany such legislation? (Consider in this regard McDougall's observation on "the displacement of mothers": an 1892 report marked "a transition from the humanitarian to the utilitarian rationale and simultaneously, a transfer of focus from mothers to babies and the nation as principal beneficiaries" (282).)

The article also gives us a chance to reflect on relations between politics and science. (You might try to estimate the function of quotation marks around *science*, for example, "they devised a 'scientific' rationale for intervention in childbearing" (274):

- What circumstances would induce us to put *science* in quotation marks?

While "Protecting Infants" directs our attention to connections between political definitions of babies and nationalist — even militarist — interest and policy, it also directs our attention to the way science — expert, specialist knowledge — can be involved in configurations of control and authority. At the turn of the century, medical knowledge of women and childbearing produced advisory pamphlets, instruction in childcare, supervision of feeding, regimes of measurement, and unconditional claims about how long women should be immobilized before and after childbirth. We might ask

- Who produced this knowledge?

- Who benefitted from its practical enforcement?

- How are women defined by this knowledge?

Another article in this volume, Harriet Baber's "The Market for a Feminist Epistemology," also summarizes ideologies of childbirth — modern ones:

- How do current conceptualizations of women's ideal birthing and mothering behaviour compare with those McDougall describes as arising from turn-of-the-century French science?

And, still keeping Baber's article in mind,

- To what degree would you consider McDougall's research "feminist"?

Protecting Infants:
The French Campaign for Maternity
Leaves, 1890s-1913

MARY LYNN MCDOUGALL

In the last quarter of the nineteenth century, most major European states passed laws prohibiting women from industrial work for four to eight weeks before and/or after childbirth. Only France and Russia did not legislate mandatory maternity leaves. French inaction seems puzzling, because the French birth rate was declining and French politicians were concerned about depopulation. Moreover, spokesmen for maternity leaves skillfully associated their cause with the issue of repopulation. The apparent solution to the puzzle is that French legislators refused to vote for maternity leaves without the financial benefits that would make them feasible for working women,[1] then could not agree on financing the program. This solution fits the familiar interpretation of the immobilism of the Third Republic in social and fiscal affairs. Yet the idea of immobilism ignores the laws regulating child labor and wetnursing in the 1870s,[2] the divorce and education acts of the 1880s,[3] and the considerable body of protective labor legislation

---

1   AN, F^{12} 422, Repos des femmes en couches, dossier labelled "Législation étrangère." A review of European legislation can be found in H. Harris (U.S. Department of Labor, Children's Bureau), *Maternity Benefit Systems in Certain Foreign Countries* (Washington, 1919).

2   L.S. Weissback, "*Qu'on ne coupe le blé en herbe;* A History of Child Labor Legislation in Nineteenth Century France," doctoral dissertation (Harvard University, 1975), pp. 220ff.; and J. Bonson, *Cents ans de lutte sociale, La Législation de l'enfance, 1789-1894* (Paris, 1894) pp. 41ff.

3   E.S. Kanipe, "The Family, Private Property and the State in France, 1870-1914," doctoral dissertation (University of Wisconsin-Madison, 1976).

for women and children in the 1890s.[4] Late nineteenth century legislators were fairly active in "policing" the family[5] and the workworld. Since the French Parliament did not enact maternity leaves until 1913, the germane question is why the social and fiscal conservatism of French parliamentarians retarded this *kind* of family and labor reform. This article will answer the question by analyzing the arguments and tactics of the proponents of maternity leaves in the context of contemporary political and medical debates about social legislation.

Parliamentary deliberations about maternity leaves occurred in two distinct stages, from 1886 to 1892, then from 1903 to 1913; extraparliamentary lobbying spanned the two stages but peaked between 1895 and 1905. I will consider the three phases of the campaign sequentially, because the extraparliamentary propaganda altered the nature of the two parliamentary debates. Chronology also helps account for confusion about the purpose of maternity legislation, a confusion that delayed its passage. When the original proposal for maternity leaves emerged in a prolonged debate over restricting women's work day, politicians resisted humanitarian appeals for the protection of working mothers. Subsequently, obstetricians, demographers, and charitable organizations defined infant mortality as a major social problem, one that could be solved by maternity leaves. Furthermore, they devised a "scientific" rationale for intervention in childbearing, which policy makers could use to create a consensus. Unfortunately, they did so by shifting the focus from helping working mothers *per se* to the more utilitarian but also more costly concept of public assistance for needy mothers to encourage "repopulation." The senator who sponsored the successful bill combined elements of a limited labor law with a more comprehensive public assistance program and parallels to the new social insurance system to gain leaves and benefits.

Compounding differences over whether maternity leave was a component of labor, welfare, or social insurance legislation were related disagreements about coverage and compensation, as well as financing. As long as the measure was attached to factory bills

---

4   M. L. McDougall, "Protecting Women or Preserving the Family: The French Campaign for Protective Legislation, 1874-1914," paper presented at Yale University, February 26, 1981.

5   J. Donzelot, *The Policing of Families* (New York, 1979).

confined to industrial workers, critics asked why agricultural working women were excluded. Even after a separate bill encompassed nonindustrial workers, amendments to extend assistance to homemakers threatened the bill. Similarly, advocates of industrial leaves preferred compensation in the form of "indemnities" based on wages lost; spokesmen for broader coverage favored allowances or insurance benefits without reference to wage levels.

A cursory look at French population trends will clarify the change in the character of the two parliamentary debates. The birth rate had been falling longer than in any other major country; as a consequence, natality was noticeably lower than in neighboring countries, especially Germany. Exacerbating the low birth rate was a relatively high infant mortality rate of over 135 per 1000 live births in the 1890s. Published reports of an excess of deaths over births in 1890, 1891, 1892 and 1895 aroused anxieties about depopulation.[6] As in England, where evidence of a decline in population growth gave an impetus to the infant welfare movement,[7] the reports fostered demands to reduce infant mortality by improved infant care. The first report appeared too late in the first legislative debate to help supporters of maternity leaves build a political consensus about leaves as a remedy for depopulation. Instead the reports were cited by extraparliamentary lobbies to obtain prenatal rest homes, postnatal convalescent homes, baby clinics, and maternity leaves. These lobbies contributed to a precipitous drop in the infant mortality rate, to 100 per 1000 births in 1910. During the second legislative discussion, advocates admitted the drop but argued that leaves would enhance population *growth* and close the widening gap between the German and French armies.[8] Nationalistic and militaristic appeals did build a political consensus in the tense pre-World War I years.

The case for postnatal leaves as a way of saving infant lives was relatively solid. In the 1890s, systematic demographic studies confirmed that up to 45 per cent of the deaths between one day and one year occurred in the vulnerable first month of life. Medi-

6   Bureau de la Statistique Générale, *Annuaire statistique de la France, 1892,* p. 42, *1893,* p. 39, *1898,* p.21.

7   C. Dyhouse, "Working-Class Mothers and Infant Mortality in England, 1840-1940," in C. Webster, *Biology, Medicine and Society* (Cambridge, 1981) pp. 77ff.

8   *Annales de Sénat* (hereafter *AS*), *Débats,* December 3, 1912, p. 145, and *Annales de la Chambre des Députés* (hereafter *ACD*), *Débats,* June 5, 1913, pp. 513-15.

cal reports in the 1880s and 1890s proved that the neonates fed animal milk suffered more gastroenteritis and succumbed in far higher proportions than breast-fed babies. Although French demographers and doctors did not link infant mortality to maternal occupation (save a few "dangerous" trades), geographic comparisons suggested a positive correlation between high infant death rates, especially from diarrhea, and concentrations of women workers, particularly textile workers. Strangely, researchers did not connect the incidence of infant diarrhea to the feeding practices of working mothers. Instead, they analyzed maternity hospital records to show that most *poor* women left the hospital earlier than recommended to return to work and interviewed working women who had lost many babies to learn that most had stopped nursing early to resume work. Given this indirect evidence,[9] and new information about the large proportion of women of childbearing age in the labor force,[10] many policy makers inferred that postnatal leaves would significantly lower the infant mortality rate. The case for prenatal leaves to prevent infant deaths rested on more speculative statistics about maternal rest reducing the number of premature deliveries and underdeveloped, unviable newborns.

Because politicians and "scientists" emphasized that leaves would mean healthy infants and a larger population, they generated very little data on the actual practices of, and provisions for, childbirth and infant care among working women. The three maternal breast-feeding charities established in the 1870s and 1880s suggest many working-class women left childbed within two weeks and resorted to bottle feeding. However, few charities provided for hospitalization, as opposed to midwives and home-births, while the largest charity, the Society for the Propagation of Maternal Nursing, only aided fifteen hundred to two thousand mothers a year in the first decade of the twentieth century.[11] As

9   These studies are reviewed in D. Bernson, *Nécessité d'une loi protectrice pour la femme avant et après ses couches* (Paris, 1899).

10   Direction du Travail, *Résultats statistiques du recensement des industries et professions, 1896*, IV, *Résultats généraux* (Paris, 1901) pp. XCII-XCV. Sixty-two per cent of the women in industry were between 18 and 44 years of age.

11   E. Bertin, *De la protection légale des ouvrières pendant leur grossesse et après leur accouchement* (Paris, 1906) p. 52; A. Goirand, *De la protection et de l'assistance légales des femmes salariées avant et après leur accouchement* (Paris, 1906), pp. 120-21, notes that only three charities

early as the 1860s, the Dollfus family had introduced maternity leaves and benefits to encourage new mothers among their textile workers to rest, nurse, and develop "an attachment" to their babies. Despite publicity about their success in lowering the infant death rate in their workforce,[12] few employers followed their example. A 1905 investigation into the protection accorded pregnant and parturient women in industry found that only one factory offered "organized protection for pregnant women." This textile factory in Rouen provided medical and pharmacological assistance and unemployment benefits if a doctor prescribed rest. Elsewhere pregnant women depended on the good will of foremen to reassign them to less taxing work stations or on the custom of workmates easing their task, or, if they had to quit work, they resorted to charity. For new mothers, there were approximately 150 maternity plans, mainly in the textile, clothing, and watchmaking trades, the department stores, and the state tobacco monopoly. Most plans were partially funded by working women's payments into an insurance scheme which paid monetary benefits in the form of a fixed sum or a portion of wages. Some also gave relief in kind (e.g. layettes). Most plans were in the South, with a few in Paris, Rouen and Lille. The divisional inspector in Lille estimated that 0.25 per cent of the firms in his area offered insurance that covered about 5 per cent of the female labor force.[13]

In the absence of systematic charitable or paternalistic maternity schemes, some feminine (largely female) trades tried self-help. In 1891, Felix Poissineaux and other (male) leaders of clothing unions founded a maternity insurance association composed of clothing workers who paid annual premiums of 6 francs in return for benefits at childbirth. The membership peaked at 1,912 in 1896, then fell until the premiums were halved in 1905. State subsidies more than compensated for the loss. Honorary members' donations and union contributions always supplemented regular members' payments; after 1906, external sources provided four-fifths

for unwed mothers provided hospitalization; and A. Vallin, *La Femme salariée et la maternité* (Paris, 1911) p. 137, reported that the Oeuvre de l'allaitement maternel only aided fifteen hundred to two thousand mothers per year.

12 G. Dollfus, "Statistique des résultats de l'Association des femmes en couches," *Bulletin de la Société industrielle de Mulhouse*, September 1888, pp. 501-02.

13 AN, F^{22} 445, Repos des femmes en couches, Correspondence March 11, 27, 29, and September 14, 1905, "Enquête du Service d'Inspection. . . ."

the total revenue. By 1909 the association had 17,202 members and helped finance 2,667 births.[14] After the infusion of state monies, the number of maternity insurance schemes shot up to 129. But politicians and scientists insisted self-help was inadequate, for young workers would not put away money for future pregnancies, the poorest workers could not afford even modest premiums, and women past child-bearing ceased to contribute. Aside from having too small a population at risk able to make payments, many of these plans imposed moralistic conditions that excluded many needy women.[15]

One general observation must precede the analysis of the first parliamentary debate. Attempts to identify political support beyond social Catholics, Socialists, and outspoken individuals in the radical republican tradition have proved unsatisfactory, partly because few parties took a formal position on the issue, partly because individuals often voted for the principle, or motherhood, in the first reading, then sent bills back to committee in the crucial second reading. Nevertheless, a pattern is apparent. The loose coalition of the Left and Center, which succeeded in passing factory acts, splintered over maternity leave. Early efforts to broaden the base of support by presenting maternity leave as a remedy for depopulation failed. Later efforts succeeded, because new advocates, with new medical and demographic data, convinced Parliament that leaves contributed to national military strength.

In 1886, when the social Catholic and monarchist deputy, Count Albert de Mun, proposed pre- and postnatal leaves, the Chamber of Deputies was discussing a bill to reduce women's workday and bar them from night work. De Mun considered leaves humane complements to these measures to lighten women's work load (and revive family life). After he abandoned prenatal breaks because of objection about when they would begin, the Work Committee revising the already complicated factory bill added an article prescribing a four-week postpartum leave. Although the article survived the first reading, it was hastily dropped after an amendment to permit an earlier return to work on presentation of a medical certificate evoked criticism about possible fraud. When the Work Committee reincorporated the article in

---

14   Goirand, *De la protection*, pp. 129-31, and Vallin, *La femme salariée*, pp. 150-63.

15   *AS, Débats*, December 3, 1912, p. 145, and *ACD, Débats*, June 5, 1913, pp. 513-15.

the 1890 version of the factory bill, conservative complaints about excluding nonindustrial women forced the article back to committee.[16] Doctor Dron, a Radical member of the committee, tried to salvage the measure as a separate bill, and Emile Brousse, a reform socialist not on the committee, called for universal leaves *and* assistance. The committee compromised on a bill prohibiting industrial work after childbirth but providing relief to all needy new mothers. Differences about coverage and financing buried that bill in November, 1892.[17]

Introducing the concept of mandatory maternity leave in a debate on protective labor legislation for women was logical if problematical. Experience with previous factory acts for children and the new consciousness of childhood as an essential stage of development had made it possible to justify banning young children from the workplace for their physical and intellectual development. To Albert de Mun, barring new mothers from factories so they could care for vulnerable infants was the obvious corollary. Nevertheless, *laissez faire* liberals formally opposed restricting women's freedom to work. At first, the fight over women's workday diverted attention from the issue of leaves and lulled the Work Committee into false complacence. Once liberals lost the battle over the workday, they turned their critical attention to leaves. Only then did the committee, through Doctor Dron, offer a systematic defense.

Surprisingly few liberals or conservatives made purely ideological objections. Because liberals were not really committed to women's right to work, and because they knew about the custom of long confinements, few protested that mandatory leave was an infringement on individual liberty.[18] Instead they emphasized individual differences between women and therefore the tyranny of a fixed rest period for all. The point was temporarily blunted by the amendment authorizing earlier returns to work with medical approval, then discredited when a critic, Doctor Després, failed to submit promised evidence that some women could resume work on the third day after giving birth. Després, a specialist in venereal

16   *Ibid.*, December 13, 1886, June 18, 1888, and July 8, 1890.

17   *ACD, Documents*, 1891, nos. 1187 and 1191, and 1892, no. 2027, and *ACD, Débats*, February 5, 1891, October 19, and November 3 and 4, 1892.

18   *Ibid.*, February 5, 1891, p. 285.

diseases, trivialized the issue with inappropriate references to "all husbands' knowledge" that women had to be "spared" three days a month. His tasteless remarks amused many deputies but offended others.[19] Both the laughter and the indignation leave the impression that politicians felt uncomfortable discussing a subject that reminded them of sexual intercourse and "unmentionable" bodily functions. To counteract Després' self-proclaimed expertise, Dron belatedly consulted the Obstetrical Society, which obligingly confirmed the need for four weeks rest after childbirth.[20] Dron also denied liberal and conservative charges that the committee was trying to initiate change in personal life and argued that the committee was trying to "generalize" the practice of "responsible" employers.[21]

In 1891 a liberal, François Deloncle, noted that supporters of leaves treated "maternity" (pregnancy and delivery) as an infirmity, but no one, including Deloncle, elaborated on the disturbing implications of this conceptual framework, so endemic was the notion of childbirth as illness.[22] Deloncle further observed that leaves without pay would throw working women into poverty precisely when they needed extra income. Deloncle's insight inspired Emile Brousse to move that mothers be compensated for wages lost on leave. Fearful that the principle of compensation could be applied to, and thereby destroy, provisions for a weekly holiday in the factory bill, the Work Committee refused to consider the motion. When the Chamber of Deputies welcomed it, the committee insisted on detaching leaves from the factory bill.[23] Then Brousse tabled a bill calling for leaves and "indemnities" of 1 franc per day for *all* working women. Deputies, worried about the inequity of protection only one category of workers, rallied behind the bill, and obstructionists, who reasoned that a more expensive program would prove politically unpalatable, joined them to vote the bill back to committee.[24]

19   *Ibid.*, p. 284.

20   AN, C5515, Commission chargé de considérer . . . des femmes en couches, July 16, 1891; and *ACD, Documents*, 1892, no. 2027, pp. 10, 13-14.

21   *Ibid.*, pp. 11-12; and *ACD, Débats*, June 18, 1889, pp. 670-71.

22   See, for instance, A. Oakley, "A Case of Maternity: Paradigms of Women as Maternity Cases," *Signs*, IV (1979).

23   *ACD, Débats*, February 5, 1891, pp. 186 and 285.

By the time the Work Committee considered maternity leaves as a separate measure, the French delegation's report on the International Conference on Labor Legislation, written by the respected liberal, Jules Simon, was available. At the Berlin conference, the new Kaiser's representatives had proposed several ways of "protecting" working women and children. The French delegation, which voted with the minority opposing restrictions on women's day or night work, voted with the majority favoring limitations on children's work, as well as forbidding work for four weeks after giving birth. To justify the negative votes, Simon referred to reservations about regulating adult labor, given the French "cult of individual liberty," as well as the fact that France had not yet intervened in women's work. Just as he accepted limits on child labor as a state "obligation" to safeguard children's health and intellectual development, he accepted maternity leaves as protection due "persons whose health and safety can only be safeguarded by the state." More significantly, he characterized maternity leave as a restraint on freedom "done in the name of the evident and superior interest of the human race." He even admitted that mandatory leaves would "create a new public assistance responsibility for the state."[25]

The Berlin conference, the Simon report, and the new rationale about higher interests profoundly influenced Dron's report, released in 1892. The report responded to objections that maternity leaves would make French industry noncompetitive by citing the resolutions of the Berlin conference and maternity legislation in Austria, Belgium, Germany, and four other European countries. The report also replied to assumed, if largely unexpressed, concern about infringing on individual liberty by quoting Jules Simon and noting he could not be "suspected of socialism." More specifically, Dron contended that enforced leaves were in the best interests of the mother, the child, and the nation. Mothers would benefit from better health; babies would be breast-fed and avoid gastroenteritis, the major cause of infant mortality; lower infant mortality would halt the natural decrease in population revealed in the last census and insure "the future and even the very existence of the

24 *Ibid.*, pp. 286-87; AN, C5515, Commission . . . March 11, 1891; and *ACD, Documents,* 1891, no. 1087.

25 Ministère des Affaires Etrangères, *Conférence internationale de Berlin* (Paris, 1890) Rapport . . . par M. Jules Simon, pp. 17-24.

race." Although Dron quoted the Bible on forty days' confinement and a variety of homilies on "the maternal instinct," he stressed that he intended to base his report on "medical treatises, the authorities in this matter." He cited the opinion of the Obstetrical Society and called it "exclusively scientific, leaving nothing equivocal," footnoted one medical report, appended another, and reproduced mortality statistics.[26] This report marks a transition from the humanitarian to the utilitarian rationale and simultaneously, a transfer of focus from mothers to babies and the nation as principal beneficiaries. No one questioned the rationale or lamented the displacement of mothers.

Opponents did attack and amend the details about coverage. Dron defended the limitation of leaves to women employed in the industrial sector on grounds of their long, uninterrupted work away from home and the pragmatic consideration that the work inspectors could not enforce leaves in family workshops or on farms. Pursuing his distinction between industrial women and poor women, he offered the former indemnities of half their daily wages from a minimum of 50 centimes to a ceiling of 2 francs and the latter daily "aids" of 50 centimes to 1 franc.[27] In the final debates of October-November 1892, opponents made moving appeals about field laborers who put in long hours of heavy physical labor away from home and added their practical assessment that Dron's paltry aids would hardly prevent poor women from working. After the committee refused an amendment to forbid new mothers agricultural labor, the Chamber adopted it by an overwhelming majority of 431 to 31.[28] However just and therefore hard to reject in first reading, the amendment pushed the bill beyond the realm of existing labor legislation and effective enforcement. Consequently, as the committee realized, it would lose support from the essential but fragile coalition of interests that had just passed the factory act of 1892. The amendment dealt a mortal blow to the bill.

Further complications came in the form of questions about Dron's estimates about eligibility and expenses. Using national

26   ACD, Documents, 1892, no. 2027, pp. 8-41.

27   Ibid., pp. 43-73.

28   ACD, Débats, October 29, 1892, p. 261; November 3, 1892, pp. 167-68, 172-73, and 187 (vote).

figures on natality and women of child-bearing age, Dron established an annual ratio of one birth per nine women and applied this ratio to the number of industrial and indigent women to estimate that 223,918 births would be eligible for assistance. Assuming an average payment of 30 francs per birth, he calculated an annual cost of 6,417,704 francs.[29] In the debate other advocates used different figures, and the opposition ridiculed the idea of predicting the number of eligible births. Paul Doumer, another Radical, argued by analogy to the operation of the system of relief for poor army reservists' families that only half the new mothers would apply for assistance. By multiplying half the total annual births by 28 francs, he nearly doubled Dron's cost estimate. When the finance minister dismissed both men's calculations, Andre Castelin, a Boulangist deputy, offered more speculative statistics. Starting with the number of women of childbearing age, he subtracted those who were single or presumed infertile and computed a net birth rate of 132 per 1000 fertile women (and expenses of 8,064,000 francs). His contention that his estimate was "rigorously determined by statistics that cannot be contested because they are official" evoked derision.[30]

Dron's financial provisions also drew fire. Although he divided the financial burden equally among the three levels of government, he only arranged for the communes and departments to raise their revenues to cover expenses. Further, he did not consult the budget committee or the finance minister, ostensibly because the charges would not devolve on the next budget but more likely because he expected a negative reaction. Indeed, the finance minister, Maurice Rouvier, preached and practiced liberal financial orthodoxy. After the requisite statement in favor of the principle, Rouvier flatly declared that the state did not have the funds for such an expensive subsidy and suggested that the communes assume the entire burden since they were, "in effect, extensions of the family." The committee had resisted passing along the costs because they knew that small, poor communes had the highest natality and that conservatives, who posed as defenders of the communes, would accuse them of fiscal irresponsibility. In debate, both the committee and the conservatives opposed the suggestion. Meanwhile, counterproposals came from

29   *ACD, Documents*, 1892, no. 2027, pp.63-64 and 73.

30   *ACD, Débats*, November 3, 1892, p. 172.

right and left. Protesting that government financing undermined self-help, de Mun proposed that working women and employers of women pay premiums into a maternity insurance scheme.[31] The same day, Paul Lafargue of the *Parti Ouvrier* introduced a bill to indemnify *all* working women 3 to 6 francs a day, depending on the cost of living in their area, from the fourth month of pregnancy to the end of the first year after childbirth. The bill included a tax on *all* employers to pay for this radically enlarged program. The preamble explained that childbirth was "a social function" and it was the state's "duty" to intervene as long as capitalism "pulls women and children out of the domestic sphere to transform them into instruments of production...."[32]

At this stage in the discourse, the concept of childbearing as a social function to be rewarded elicited laughter in the Chamber. Indeed the only acceptable feature of the bill was the idea women belonged in the home. The original sponsor complained that Lafargue's proposal fundamentally altered the bill from an attempt to regulate work into an effort "to encourage population." De Mun also initiated a purely ideological exchange about state socialism. Dron, who was preparing a new instalment of labor legislation, wearily recommended that the Chamber await the bill on men's hours to debate the state's role in relations between capital and labor. Lafargue's bill did not come to a vote, but less radical amendments passed on the understanding that they would be revised between readings. When the government warned the committee to return to the "restraint" of their first bill and ignore amendments which would "compromise the final vote,"[33] the committee abandoned the bill and ended parliamentary consideration of the issue for over a decade. With de Mun diverted into more conventional conservative politics, and Dron dedicated to more universal labor standards, no influential member of the Assembly pressed for leaves.

Outside Parliament, however, medical scientists continued to investigate the relationship between maternal work and childbirth and to make a case for maternity leave as a deterrent to infant mortality. In the late 1880s, industrial hygienists studied how early re-

---

31   *Ibid.*, October 29, 1892, pp. 159-60; and November 3, 1892, pp. 169-74.

32   *ACD, Documents*, 1892, No. 2369.

33   *ACD, Débats*, November 3, 1892, pp. 168-70, 174-75; and November 4, 1892, pp. 200-03.

turn to a job affected the reproductive organs. When this line of inquiry ran into controversy, obstetricians and the emerging specialists, pediatricians, turned to correlations between bottle feeding and infant diarrhea. If the Work Committee had queried the reputation of the Obstetrical Society in 1890,[34] no one questioned the authority of this and like professional groups a decade later. In the interval, many doctors became crusaders for maternal breast feeding and postpartum rests to reduce infant mortality. Similarly, obstetricians and pediatricians proselytized for prenatal rests in order to reduce the number of premature deliveries. Both types of researcher joined philanthropic organizations and pressure groups promoting various measures to enhance population growth. These lobbies mobilized public opinion in favor of legal maternity leaves.

In the late 1880s, Doctor Henri Napias of the Society for Public Medicine reported in the *Revue d'hygiène* that most poor mothers left the charity hospitals or midwives' rooms provided by Public Assistance nine to twelve days after delivery. Citing four prominent obstetricians who held that the uterus took three to four weeks to recover, Napias argued that resuming work in less than four weeks could cause prolapse and chronic inflammation of the uterus, which would make the next pregnancy difficult, even impossible. He concluded that "hygienists of a country with as feeble natality as France should not be indifferent to future fecundity."[35] Even then, at least one medical text advised only one week's rest, and medical anthropologists claimed that "primitive" women who promptly returned to their tasks experienced less puerperal infection.[36] In the ensuing decade, German and French experiments found that standing and walking days after birth helped drain the uterus and therefore lowered the risk of infection. The Parisian obstetrical establishment retorted that "civilized" women were "deformed," patients could sit up in bed for drainage, and "brisk movements" caused fallen wombs.[37] Despite mounting evidence to

34   AN, C5515, Commission . . . July 16, 1891.

35   H. Napias, "Note sur un point d'hygiène et d'assistance. . . . " *Revue d'hygiène*, X (December 1888), 1063-69.

36   A. Corre, *La Mère et l'enfant dans les races humaines* (Paris, 1886) pp. 133-34; and G. J. Engleman, translated by J. Rodet, *La pratique des accouchements chez les peuples primitifs* (Paris, 1886) pp. 172ff.

37   Dr. Audebert, "Du sejour au lit des accouchées," *Archives médicales de Toulouse*, May 15, 1899.

the contrary, most obstetricians prescribed eighteen to twenty-five days bed rest into the twentieth century. As late as 1912, Doctor Louis Pierra had to deny he was a revolutionary for getting new mothers up progressively between the fifth and fourteenth days.[38]

While the controversy continued, Doctor Napias disseminated a questionnaire about the "legislative, administrative, and medical remedies" for infant mortality. Although the alleged experts disagreed, Napias' report to the 1889 Congress on Hygiene and Demography recommended a "rigorous inquiry" into infant feeding practices as well as measures to encourage maternal breast feeding and limit women's workday. The Congress adopted his recommendations with little discussion.[39] The emphasis on infant feeding was clearly more acceptable to the public health lobby.

Research into infant feeding practices was already underway. Doctor Comby, among others, documented that most infants dying from gastroenteritis had been fed animal milk. Recognizing that maternal breast feeding, the obvious preventative measure, posed economic problems for working women, Comby suggested that they come home once a day to nurse, then nurse six to eight times at night. He was satisfied that this would ensure babies of enough food and sleep; he did not, however, explain when the mothers would sleep.[40] Chemical analysis of different milks proved that cow's milk, which was chemically closest to human milk, was harder to digest. Bacteriological counts showed that cow's milk had more harmful microbes, especially after dilution, adulteration, and standing for several hours without refrigeration, as happened in working class shops and homes.[41] After publicity through the Society for the Protection of Children,[42] these studies were used in campaigns to promote maternal nursing and impose sanitary standards on dairies.

---

38   L. Pierra, "De la mobilisation précoce des accouchées, . . ." *Revue mensuelle de gynécologie, d'obstétrique et de pédiatrie*, 1912, pp. 1-41.

39   Napias and Landouzy, "Mésures d'ordre législatif, administratif et médical . . . pour la protection de la santé et de la vie de la première enfance," *Congrès International d'hygiène et de démographie à Paris en 1889* (Paris, 1890), pp. 35-90.

40   J. Comby, "La diarrhée infantile," *Bulletin médicale*, I, May 1887, pp. 299-300.

41   For example, Dr. H. Rothschild, *L'Allaitement mixte et l'allaitement artificiale* (Paris, 1898).

42   Dr. M. Rivière, "De l'alimentation des enfants, . . ." *Congrés international de la protection de l'enfance* (Bordeaux, 1895), pp. 58-99.

The indefatigable propagandist of maternal nursing and postpartum rests was Doctor Pierre Budin, a professor of obstetrics at the Paris Medical School and chief obstetrician at two maternity hospitals. In the course of his work with premature babies, Budin developed theories about how much milk to feed babies based on their weights, and consequently insisted on supervising feedings and weighing babies during and after confinement. With the help of Paris City Councillor Paul Strauss and funds from the municipal welfare bureau, Budin established the first free baby clinic. To gather evidence for a nationwide drive for public and private financing of clinics, Budin asked a doctor and a public health statistician to undertake a survey of the extent and etiology of infant mortality.[43] The Balestre and Gilletta study, published in 1901, confirmed that infant diarrhea accounted for one quarter of all infant deaths, 44 per cent of infant deaths in large cities, and over half of the high infant mortality rates in industrial cities like Amiens, Lille, and Rouen. Balestre and Gilletta calculated that infant diarrhea and other "preventable" infant diseases killed thirty-six thousand per year, predicted that one-fifth the infants would not have survived to the age of twenty, and inferred that this would have left thirty thousand or fifteen thousand youths eligible for armed service. Drawing the obvious conclusion, they claimed that France lost one army corps a year to preventable infant disease. To stop this drain on France's armed strength, they advised the state to fund baby clinics and fight premature return to work after childbirth. They did not say how to keep mothers from going back to work, since this was "a delicate point in social science."[44]

Professor Budin had links with Solidarist Radicals, who believed that the state had social obligations, the "most pressing" of which was the protection of human life. In a series of political speeches and academic conferences all over France, and in a major report to the Extra-Parliamentary Commission on Depopulation set up in 1902, Budin promoted a new bill on maternity leaves and assistance, rest homes for pregnant women, convalescence homes for parturient women, breast feeding allowances, and baby clin-

43   Reviewed in Dr. A. P. Robesco, *La mortalité infantile, essai critique des moyens employés pour la combattre* (Thesis, Faculty of Medicine, 1908) pp. 31-33.

44   A. Balestre and A. Gilletta de Saint-Joseph, *Etude sur la mortalité de la première enfance dans la population urbaine de la France de 1892 à 1897* (Paris, 1901).

ics.[46] Paul Strauss, who had been elected to the Senate in the interval, had tabled the bill. Although France's preeminent demographer, Jacques Bertillon, questioned Budin's stress on industrial cities, noting that Balestre and Gilletta found the highest infant mortality in a fishing village, Budin's answer about mill women in the village satisfied the Commission on Depopulation. The commission, which included Doctor Dron, Senator Strauss, and other supporters of maternity leaves, quoted Budin's report for a decade as the definitive statement on infant mortality.[47]

Budin was also a founding member of the League Against Infant Mortality composed of obstetricians, pediatricians, public health administrators, and philanthropists from the maternal and infant charities. Many of the philanthropists were women, who were virtually the only women involved in the entire campaign. The league tried to sustain private charities and "where necessary, appeal for public intervention" for maternity insurance plans, breast feeding allowances, baby clinics, sterilized milk dispensaries, and créches. In concert with dozens of maternal and infant charities, the league seconded Senator Strauss' efforts to obtain leaves and benefits.[48]

Professor Budin also sponsored doctoral theses on maternal nursing. One of his doctoral candidates, A. L. D. Binet, was inspired by Budin's belief that doctors should go beyond individual pathology "to discover and cure social ills." He interviewed 479 working-class mothers who had cumulatively lost two-fifths of their children by the age of two, and learned that almost all had stopped nursing early to go back to work. Citing another thesis showing that most new mothers did not know Budin's theory about fixed nursing schedules, Binet deduced that mothers must be taught "maternal science" in baby clinics, "veritable schools of motherhood." Since staying home to nurse on schedule would

46   For instance, Budin, *Etude sur la mortalité de la première enfance, rapport sur un mémoire de MM. Balestre et Gilletta* (Melun, 1904); "La Mortalité infantile," in L. Bourgeois, ed., *Applications sociales de la solidarité* (Paris, 1904), and "Rapport sur la mortalité infantile . . ." in Commission de la Dépopulation, Sous-Commision de la Mortalité, *Rapports . . . 1902* (Melun, 1903).

47   *Ibid.*, December 3, 1902, pp. 10-17, and December 9, 1902, p. 18; and P. Strauss, *Rapport général sur les causes de la mortalité présenté à la Commission de la dépopulation* (Melun, 1911) pp. 68-69.

48   Ligue contre la mortalité infantile, Assemblée générale du 7 juin 1901 (Paris, 1909).

mean financial hardship for working-class households, he endorsed Senator Strauss' bill. But Binet went further. Stating it was "more profitable for society to exploit women . . . as producers of children" and "the mother's milk is the child's property," he advocated a legal obligation to breast feed.[49] If no one repeated his blatant remarks about exploiting women as reproducers or pursued his bizarre notion of a legal duty to breast feed, many supporters of maternity leaves agreed that the breast belonged to the baby.

The old medical practice of advising working-class women on infant care was changing by broadening the media and narrowing the message. Earlier advice came in pamphlets disseminated, at birth, by maternal charities and Public Assistance. In the early 1900s Budin's disciples offered personal instruction in baby clinics, and Professor Adolph Pinard of the Paris Medical School introduced preparatory education in a course and textbook in a new subject called *puériculture*, designed for the intermediate girls' schools. In the clinics and classrooms, the previous acceptance that some women had to work and therefore supplement their milk,[50] ceded to insistence on regularly spaced, daytime nursing. Pinard and Budin did concede that some 2 per cent of women were physiologically incapable of breast feeding. For these women, they provided minute instructions on sterilizing animal milk and the one type of bottle judged safe.[51] Pinard influenced women's groups and journals, including the equal-rights feminist journal, *La Fronde*, to campaign for girls' school training in infant care. However, *puériculture* did not enter the regular curriculum until the postwar period.[52] After Budin died, Pinard, who also sat on the Commission on Depopulation, become the most effective medical

49 A. L. D. Binet, *L'Allaitement maternal considéré spécialement au point de vue de ses difficultés sociales* (Thesis, Faculty of Medicine, 1904).

50 Dr. Brochard, *L'Ouvriére, mère de famille* (Lyon, 1874); Dr. E. Picard, *Conseils aux mères de famille ou Quelques considérations pratiques sur la mortalité des nouveau-nés* . . . (Nancy, 1877) and *La Mére de famille ou la maitresse de maison* (Lyon, 1886).

51 Dr. A. Pinard, *Education morale et pratique dans les écoles de filles. La Puériculture* (Paris, 1904).

52 K. Offen, "Depopulation, Nationalism and French Feminism during the Belle Epoque," paper presented to the Society for French Historical Studies, March, 1981, and L. Clark, "Educating Girls to Combat French Depopulation: *Puériculture* in the Primary Schools of the Third Republic," paper presented to the Duquesne History Conference, October 1981. See also *La Puériculture, Revue de la femme, la mère et l'enfant*, 1906.

spokesman for leaves.

Pinard had specialized in prenatal care. As early as 1890 he had publicly condemned the popular opinion of pregnancy as a "nine month illness" and called it a "physiological state" characterized by "physical and moral depression," "languor and despair." If his definition was less pathological, his description of the symptoms reaffirmed the popular view of pregnancy as travail. Furthermore, his assertion that pregnant women "forced to work" suffered a "special functional impotence" which often led to "incurable infirmities" reinforced bourgeois prejudice. In 1891 he decried the treatment of unwed mothers-to-be and joined a charity drive for refuges for abandoned pregnant women. After the opening of two refuges (with the support of Paul Strauss and the Paris City Council),[53] he compared the weights of neonates whose mothers had rested in refuges with those whose mothers had worked to term. In 1895 he reported to the Academy of Medicine that neonates whose mothers had rested weighed, on average, ten to twelve ounces more. He also calculated the length of gestation — measured from the last day of the last menstrual period — to find that women working to term were slightly more liable to deliver prematurely. Oblivious to problems of comparing two different populations, to concepts of statistical significance, or to the common sense explanation that women delivering prematurely would more likely be at work, he used these figures to prove the need for prenatal rest.[54]

When other members of the Academy of Medicine objected that parental physique and birth order determined neonatal weight, Pinard put his doctoral candidates to work studying the relationships between maternal work, neonatal weight, and length of gestation. An 1897 dissertation examined the effects of "tiring" versus "non-tiring" occupations — very subjectively classified by the amount of physical exertion — and of prenatal breaks for both occupational categories. Discovering an insignificant weight difference between babies born to the two types of working women, Doctor Letourneau rationalized that most subjects in the nontiring category were seamstresses, who were "frail, elegant and

53   A. Pinard, "De l'assistance des femmes enceintes, des femmes en couches et des femmes accouchées," *Revue d'hygiène*, XII, December, 1890, pp. 1098-1110, and *De l'assistance des femmes enceintes, Conférence* (Paris, 1891).

54   Pinard, "note pour servir à l'histoire de la puériculture intrauterine," *Bulletin de l'Académie de Médicine*, 1895, pp. 593-97.

gracious, but incapable of carrying large foetuses," while most in the tiring category were domestics, who were bigger, stronger and "capable of carrying superb foetuses in their flanks." Since Letourneau had conceded the critics' point about physique and raised the problem of different populations, Pinard did not publicize his thesis.[55]

Two other dissertations confirmed Pinard's theory. First, Doctor F. C. Bachimont tabulated the weights of 4,445 neonates according to birth order and whether or not their mothers had rested before childbirth. The tables revealed that babies of rested mothers weighed four and a half to twelve ounces more than babies *in the same birth order* whose mothers had worked to term. Contending his tables proved "with mathematical rigor" the beneficial effects of prenatal rest, Bachimont concluded it was necessary "to intervene to protect the pregnant woman in the final three months of her pregnancy."[56] Pinard publicized this thesis and explained that standing in the final months precipitated the descent of the uterus, which induced premature deliveries.[57] One of Budin's students made the complementary study of the length of gestation in women in refuges versus those coming directly to hospitals. Like Bachimont, Madame Sarraute-Lourié controlled for birth order, but not for occupation or physique. (Information on physique was not recorded on the hospital forms that served as their major source.) On average, women in refuges carried twenty days longer. Noting that the foetus gained the most weight in the final three weeks, Sarraute-Lourié demanded more "sanatoria for pregnancy."[58]

The number of subjects, the introduction of intervening variables (however insufficient by present-day standards), and the handy tables in these essentially statistical studies impressed lobbyists and publicists, who quoted figures from them and similarly "scientific" theses in the reviving parliamentary campaign. Politicians who cited the same figures apparently drew them from

55   Letourneau, *De l'influence de la profession de la mère sur le poids de l'enfant* (Thesis, Faculty of Medicine, Paris, 1897).

56   F. C. Bachimont, *Documents pour servir à l'histoire de la puériculture intra-uterine* (Thesis, Faculty of Medicine, Paris, 1898).

57   Pinard, "Note pour servir à l'histoire de la puériculture pendant la grossesse," *Annales de gynécologie,* L. August 1898, pp. 81-89.

58   Sarraute-Lourié. *De l'influence du repos sur la durée de la gestation* (Thesis, Faculty of Medicine, Paris, 1899).

popularizations of these rather dry theses.

By 1899 there were enough medical studies on work and maternity to warrant a more popular survey of the literature. Doctor Deborah Bernson advertised her political purpose in her title, *The Necessity of a Law Protecting Working Women before and after Giving Birth.* Perhaps because she was one of the few French women in the medical profession, her book differs from other medical studies in paying some attention to the impact of wage work on *all* women's health. Still, Bernson only devoted three pages to the impact on *pregnant* women's health, and most of that section consists of commonsensical observations, such as that women close to term are prone to work accidents. The bulk of the book reviews the previously mentioned theses, introduces more specialized research done in other countries, and presents infant mortality data graphically. While English and German doctors had monitored infant mortality among specific occupational groups, including factory women, French doctors had only isolated the notorious lead trades and otherwise relied on mortality statistics compiled by cities. When these statistics showed high infant mortality in textile towns, the doctors, including Bernson, blamed women's work without bothering to consider the high natality and environmental conditions in industrial cities.[59]

After Bernson's widely read book, doctoral candidates did analyze infant mortality by *quartiers* and consider explanatory factors such as poverty. Since one of their indices of poverty was the number of women in low-paying jobs, they continued to advocate restricting pregnant and parturient women's work.[60] Many theses became explicitly political. A 1900 thesis began by acknowledging that the issue of maternity leaves was "agitating" France, politicians were asking doctors for "practical advice," and doctors needed "preconceived solutions." After assessing the services provided by private rest homes, Doctor Thiroux decided that private solutions were insufficient and restrictive, notably along moralistic lines. Consequently, he evaluated foreign legislation and opted, pragmatically, for a mandatory leave of six weeks before and six weeks after birth. His advisor, Pinard, insisted that he increase the time to two months before and two months after birth.[61]

59   Bernson, *Necessité d'une loi.*

60   E.g., Doctor H. Cury, *Hygiène sociale de la grossesse chex les femmes de la classe ouvrière à Paris* (Thesis, Faculty of Medicine, 1898).

Practicing physicians associated themselves with overtly political pressure groups. In 1903 Doctor Fauquet outlined the medical and legislative case for maternity leaves before the Association for the Legal Protection of Workers. This lobby, which included labor lawyers and philanthropic industrialists, voted unanimously for leaves and benefits. They also adopted resolutions in favor of nursing facilities in the workplace. A decade later, when Senator Strauss spoke to the association, the membership endorsed his bill. The association always publicized its conferences and resolutions.[62]

In the hiatus between the two parliamentary debates, municipalities and private agencies did extend welfare and charity to needy mothers. In addition to a handful of refuges and clinics jointly funded by municipalities and philanthropists,[63] Paul Strauss arranged for the Paris welfare bureau to provide "pregnancy relief,"[64] and Doctor Dron, in his capacity as mayor of Tourcoing, started an aid program for new mothers.[65] The 1893 law on free medical assistance assimilated childbirth to illness so that needy women could get "free medical and pharmacological assistance" from municipal welfare bureaus. Although this law encouraged the development of maternity clinics in the provinces, most of these facilities only admitted married mothers-to-be. The Council on Public Assistance, which had recommended more comprehensive maternity aid, later backed Senator Strauss' bill.[66]

The medical and philanthropic interest groups and the election of Strauss to the Senate in 1897 transformed the campaign. Strauss was a more tenacious parliamentary advocate of leaves than de Mun or Dron, although, like them, he had other goals. Because he was primarily interested in compulsory social insurance or, failing that, public assistance for the young and aged,[67] the second phase

61   Dr. H. Thiroux, *La Protection légale des femmes enceintes et accouchées dans la classe ouvrière* (Thesis, Faculty of Medicine, 1900).

62   Fauquet, *La Protection légale des femmes avant et après l'accouchement* (Paris, 1903); P. Strauss and L. Marin, *La Protection de la maternité ouvrière* (Paris, 1912).

63   F. Saporte, *Assistance et maternité* (Bordeaux, 1910) pp. 34ff.

64   *Bulletin Municipal officiel*, December 19, 1893.

65   *ACD, Débats,* June 5, 1913, p. 517.

66   Conseil Supérieur de l'Assistance Publique, Session de janvier 1892, *Création des maternités départmentales* (Paris, 1892), *L'Assistance maternelle* (Paris, 1902).

of the parliamentary debate interacted less with stalled efforts to extend labor legislation than with the newer movement for social security. Strauss argued for pre- and postnatal leaves for industrial women alone but never asked for indemnities based on wages. Instead, he called for assistance as an interim measure until France accepted "the cycle of insurance."[68]

In this second round of debates, proponents of leaves made fewer appeals to humanitarian sentiments and more arguments about "the grave national peril" of depopulation. As Senator Strauss wrote, "A utilitarian preoccupation has come to double and reinforce the humanitarian concern. Patriots and philanthropists must therefore cooperate. . . ." Since the *patrie* needed babies "for its defense and maintenance," maternity leave was presented as a way "to save" infant lives "for national advantage."[69] Once the idea of childbirth as a social function was connected to the more acceptable concept of birth as a "patriotic duty" — and separated from utopian schemes for long-term financial support — it ceased to be an outrageous proposition. Particularly after the Agadir Crisis of 1906, concern about military weakness made social policy on maternity leaves more respectable. The connection to military affairs was most overt in a 1906 bill to guarantee women who *chose* to take leaves of absence for childbirth, of jobs on their return to work; Engerand, the deputy who tabled the bill, borrowed the language from a law guaranteeing army reservists their civilian jobs on their return from active duty. Throughout the debates, Engerand and Strauss delighted in drawing parallels between men called up for army service and women called upon for maternal service to their country.[70]

By the early twentieth century, Engerand, Strauss, and other spokesmen could quote extensively from medical and demographic studies. Although they oversimplified and overstated the implications of this literature, almost no one challenged their scientific and statistical evidence. An early critic, Doctor Alcide

67   E.g., P. Strauss, *Assistance sociale: Pauvres et mendiants* (Paris, 1901).

68   *AS, Documents*, 1899, No. 234; *AS, Débats*, December 3, 1903, p. 233.

69   *Ibid.*, p. 235 and October 30, 1908, p. 38; *AS, Documents*, 1906, 1899, no. 235, p. 449, and 1906, no. 124; *ACD, Documents*, 1906, no. 199, pp. 13 and 62; and Strauss, *Dépopulation et puériculture* (Paris, 1901) p. 1.

70   *ACD, Documents*, 1908, no. 1651, p. 4; and *AS, Débats*, October 30, 1908, p. 44.

Treille, did point out that much of the evidence was based on pathological cases, because it came from hospitals, which mainly admitted difficult deliveries. Senator Treille, who had some qualifications in the field as an editor of a book on lead poisoning, correctly characterized Pinard's publications as propaganda. He added that doctors were not unanimous on the need for leaves and consulted the forty doctors in or recently in the Assembly on how they would determine when a woman was two weeks away from delivery, so she could start her prenatal rest. Treille's informal survey raised enough doubts to remove the prenatal portion of the leave from the 1906 version of the bill. Beyond this, though, Treille preferred to make irrelevant remarks about the greater necessity for conjugal separation throughout pregnancy — and "the delicate time of the month." Deciding too late in his speech that it would be "indecent" to continue, he concluded by asking his laughing audience if the state intended to assign gendarmes to the bedrooms of the nation.[71] With the exception of this sarcastic reference to the prospect of infringing on individual liberty in the bedroom, no one raised objections on the grounds of individual rights or differences. Given a consensus on the principle of state intervention, the obstacles to leaves and benefits were finally tactical, technical, and financial.

Tactically, Senator Strauss erred by embedding leaves and assistance in an "entire program of preventive maternal assistance." His 1899 bill included a nation-wide network of refuges for pregnant women, separate maternity wings, arrangements for home births, convalescence homes for parturient women, breast-feeding allowances or free sterilized milk for all needy mothers, supervision of feeding practices in the family, and stricter regulation of dairies![72] When the bill finally came to debate four years later, Doctor Treille wittily complained that the "noble project . . . embraced mothers, babies, and cows at the same time." Although the omnibus bill passed the first reading intact, the Senate Committee on Assistance promised to pare it between readings.[73] Next, Senator Strauss was absorbed for two years in preparing laws on children's aid and old age pensions. When he returned to the bill in

---

71   *Ibid.,* December 3, 1903, pp. 236–37.

72   *AS, Documents,* 1899, no. 235.

73   *AS, Débats,* December 3, 1903, p. 236 and 241 (vote).

1906, he removed the medical, milk, and dairy clauses "to ensure the adoption of the essential measures from which," he felt, "all the others will follow."[74]

By the time a practical bill emerged, another tactical problem surfaced. In essence, Strauss was hobbled by being in the Senate, which normally did not initiate legislative proposals. By 1906 Engerand and other deputies who despaired of an early resolution in the slow-paced Senate, introduced a compromise proposal to guarantee jobs after voluntary maternity leaves and to increase subsidies to private maternity insurance schemes. A 1908 version of the bill only retained the guarantees, because the state had increased its subsidy to maternity plans.[75] Strauss agreed to advance this bill, which had the advantages of being presented as a correction of a rare but scandalous abuse of authority and of costing the taxpayers — and therefore the politicians — very little. Despite hopes of rapid progress, senators with industrial connections delayed passage by inserting superfluous clauses to safeguard an employer's right to fire a pregnant or parturient woman for "just cause." After the bill bounced between the Chambers for three years, the Senate abandoned the safeguards and it passed into law.[76]

Another tactical problem was Strauss' failure to generate or utilize nonmedical evidence. In 1903 the Chamber's Work Committee instigated an inquiry into the textile industry which included questions about provisions for maternity breaks. Their 1905 report revealed the abuses that motivated Engerand's bill[77] and made it easier to defend. The report also stirred another deputy, René Renould, to demand the investigation into protection for pregnant and parturient women mentioned above. These two surveys were the only efforts made to ascertain the general condition of pregnant and parturient working women. Only the textile investigators interviewed working women to find out their attitudes (and discovered, not surprisingly, that they were dissatisfied). Even more than

74 *AS, Documents*, 1906, no. 124.

75 *ACD, Documents*, 1906, no. 199, and 1908, no. 1651.

76 *Ibid.*, 1909, no. 2823; *ACD, Débats*, November 24, 1909; *AS, Documents*, 1908, no. 156, and 1909, no. 129; *AS, Débats*, October 20 and 30, 1908, pp. 7-8, 36-47; June 11, 1909, pp. 518-21; October 26 and 28, 1909, pp. 6-11 and 17-18.

77 AN, C 7318-7320, Chambre des Députés, Enquête sur l'industrie textile. See *ACD, Documents*, 1906, no. 199.

the advocates of sex-specific labor laws, Strauss ignored working women's opinions and preferred, like Dron, to quote "the authorities in this matter." While the medical "authorities" were more respected sources, their aggregate data might have been more evocative in combination with touching illustrations of how pre- and postnatal employment contributed to infant mortality.

Furthermore, Strauss was slow to mobilize support for economic interest groups. Engerand, whose voluntaristic approach was more congenial to employers, quickly gained an ally in the paternalistic textile magnate, Bonnier. After Engerand accepted his advice to limit the prenatal break to one month, Bonnier, who was president of the Vienne Chamber of Commerce, orchestrated a barrage of Chamber of Commerce petitions in favor of an eight-week break.[78] Strauss' approach was inherently less attractive, but there were signs that large "benevolent" employers would have welcomed more comprehensive, compulsory programs.[79] Secondly, as a deputy reporting on Engerand's bill observed, maternity assistance did not charge employers for actions "foreign to working conditions," from which they "derived no special profit." State assistance would cost employers very little.[80] Nevertheless, Strauss did not get significant support from employers until 1913 in the final push for the passage of his bill.[81]

Although Radical ministers displayed interest by instituting leaves and benefits for female post office employees and civilian personnel in military establishments, Strauss, a Solidarist Radical, did not seek government assistance until 1906, when a Radical government formally committed to social reform came to power. Initially, he only asked the Labor Office for copies of relevant foreign legislation and advice on editing his text to conform to complementary bills in the chamber and existing labor legislation.[82]

---

78 AN, F²² 445, Repos des femmes en couches, petitions dated April 10, 1907 to July 7, 1908.

79 *Ibid.,* letter from the divisional inspector in the Vosges, November 12, 1904.

80 *ACD, Documents*, 1908, no. 1651, pp. 2-3.

81 AN, F²² 224, petitions from the "Union des Syndicats Professionnels Patronaux" and the Chambers of Commerce of Amiens, Marseilles and Rochefort-sur-Mer, January-June, 1913.

82 *Ibid.,* correspondence dated February 26, and March 17, 1906; March 15 and 17, May 7, and June 8, 1907, and September 17, and October 27, 1909. See also *ACD, Documents*, 1906, Durand bill annexed to session of December 12.

Since he did not consult the finance committee or finance minister, he encountered their skepticism in debates. The first finance committee report on his bill, released in 1907, took a dim view of imposing over 80 per cent of the expenses on the departments and communes (a formula borrowed from the 1893 law on free medical assistance). The finance minister, Joseph Caillaux, also challenged the cost estimates. Using different figures from Dron's, Strauss calculated a lower cost of 4,650,000 francs; the Ministry of Finance countered with 6,272,000 to 9,408,000 francs, depending on the average daily payment. Even after Strauss made some adjustments, Caillaux expressed his preference for maternity insurance. Insisting that state assistance did not rule out maternity insurance, Strauss publicly asked Caillaux to collaborate on a revision of the bill.[83] Even then, real cooperation awaited the appointment of a more sympathetic (pronatalist) finance minister in Aristide Briand's first cabinet (1909-1910).[84]

Just as Strauss approached an accord with the Finance Ministry, a spokesman for large industry, Eugène Touron, disingenuously complained about the exclusion of nonindustrial women. Recognizing an old threat, Strauss pleaded with the Senate not to "overextend" and render the bill unacceptable. Nevertheless, a pronatalist (and women's rights advocate) moved in good faith that leaves apply to all women "who habitually do wage work." Although Caillaux unequivocally rejected the motion, the labor minister, a former Socialist, René Vivani, secured the bill's return to committee.[85] With the cooperation of Briand's first and second cabinets, Strauss' committee arrived at a compromise whereby industrial and commercial workers would get leaves and all mothers working away from home would get assistance. They justified limiting leaves by the familiar argument that only industrial, since 1901, commercial workers were under the jurisdiction of the work inspectors, who alone could enforce leaves. When the revised bill came to debate in 1912, pronatalists offered amendments to include domestic workers, homemakers, and "all women of French nationality." The principal critic, Emile Rey, derided "the

83   *AS, Documents,* 1906, no. 422; *AS, Débats,* March 21, 1907, p. 631, and October 30, 1908, pp. 39-42, and October 28, 1909, p. 18.

84   AN, F22 445, notes re financing, September 13, and November 1909, February 17 and April 1911.

85   *AS, Débats,* October 30, 1908, pp. 42ff.

narrow, artificial, and arbitrary terrain of labor regulation," which restricted coverage to one-third of the births. Rey, who had sponsored the law on free medical assistance, drew attention to the replacement of indemnities, implying compensation for wages lost, with assistance, signifying relief for needy mothers. The new finance minister, Klotz, reminded the Senators that they had already voted (noncontroversial) parts of the bill into the Labor Code and managed to detach the amendments so the bill could pass.[86]

The final negotiations with the Chamber of Deputies produced a few revisions, but the Chamber debate was similar. Both the Work Committee and the Assistance Committee considered the bill, which still included elements of labor and social welfare legislation. When pronatalists suggested including homemakers and needy mothers, the reporter for the Work Committee, which sponsored the bill in the Chamber, responded with the need to enforce leaves. In a speech reminiscent of one he had delivered twenty-two years before, Doctor Dron admonished the deputies that it was this admittedly imperfect measure or nothing. He also promised to table a bill extending assistance to all needy mothers. After a rather listless debate, the eighth version of the bill passed in June, 1913.[87]

The final text accorded to any women "in an apparent state of pregnancy" the right to take a break from paid employment without penalties. This prenatal break of up to four weeks was optional. The postpartum leave of four weeks was obligatory for women in "all industrial and commercial establishments . . ." The law established a daily allowance for eight weeks before and after birth, for "all women of French nationality who habitually work for wages outside the home, whether as a worker, an employee, or a domestic . . ." Although prenatal aid was predicated on medical verification that the recipient could not work without endangering herself or "her baby," there were no medical conditions for postpartum allowances.[88]

In the end, then, French legislators did resolve the problem of

---

86 *AS, Documents,* 1910, no. 42; 1911, no. 45; *AS Débats,* March 8, 1912, pp. 605ff, and December 3 and 5, 1912, pp. 1424ff and 1441ff.

87 *ACD, Documents,* 1912, no. 2421, and 1913, no. 2669; and *ACD, Débats,* June 6 and 13, 1913, pp. 1725ff and 1864ff.

88 *Journal officiel,* June 19, 1913.

whether the measure was to be a limited labor law or a broader welfare or social security law. If they expanded the original conception by extending leaves to employees and allowances to all wage workers outside the home (and soon to wage workers in the home),[89] they never covered the large contingent of nonwage workers, including peasant wives. The act went beyond previous labor legislation, but never to the point of becoming a comprehensive welfare or social security law. The controversy over the purpose of the legislation and related disputes over the population to be protected, as much as fiscal conservatism, stalled the enactment of even this limited protection for mothers and infants.

The renewed debate about maternity leaves during World War I will illuminate the uneasy mix of humane and utilitarian/patriotic motives behind maternity legislation. By the winter of 1916-17, Professor Pinard publicly protested "the natality crisis," defined as rising rates of stillbirths, premature deliveries, infant deaths from infectious diseases, and (in a rare recognition of maternal health) maternal mortality. Together with Mme. Siegfried of the Society for the Protection of Maternity, Pinard lobbied to have women banned from war production for six months before and six months after childbirth. Senator Strauss objected, correctly if rather inconsistently, that factory work was only one factor in the natality crisis and reactivated his Consultative Committee on Women's Work (composed of industrialists, workers of both sexes, and relevant civil servants) to get "practical advice" on measures to protect pregnant and parturient women *at work*. After an inquiry which found that few women in war production quit work before the final month of pregnancy (indeed, only one quarter took leave in the final month, as entitled by law), the committee recommended regular consultations with midwives *at the factory* and guidelines about jobs that posed "a manifest risk to the safety of the pregnancy," so women could be transferred to safer posts. Later the committee urged nursing rooms and *créches* in the factories. The Minstry of War, satisfied these measures were "inspired by concern not to hinder the recruitment of the female labor force," cooperated with the committee and the League Against Infant Mortality in efforts to implement them. Although

89   *Ibid.*, July 30, 1913 (article 74 of the Finance Act).

their efforts were only partially successful,[90] they indicate that the more positive, if in the short run more expensive, approach to work and maternity was possible, when there was a need for women workers.

90 AN, F22 448, Ouvrières employées dans les usines de guerre. See especially Rapport de M. le Docteur Pinard and inderdepartmental memos of November 20, 1916 through May 1, 1917 and January 22, 1918.

10

Introduction

To claim for a book or a film, or other cultural item, a "universal" appeal is to praise it. Writers who win Nobel Prizes are often celebrated for their "universal" appeal. They are said to reach diverse audiences, spanning national, historical, or ethnic differences. So they get a prize. Reed Way Dasenbrock's "Intelligibility and Meaningfulness in Multicultural Literature in English" summarizes arguments which analyze such praise — when it comes from "mainstream" Anglo-American critics and is applied to literature from cultures other than the globally dominant ones — as only a new form of colonialism. Since we are accustomed to hearing "universal" as a term of approval, and perhaps even at some deeper level conditioned to respond positively to implications of unity ("brotherhood," "humankind") and commonality, it may be hard to get in a position to see such praise as a case of appropriation or domination. Perhaps a generalized example would help: consider the "universal" motives of Christian missionaries in the New World. Claiming all peoples as equally and similarly God's children, missionaries' work in the New World and elsewhere enforced a unity that recognized only the values and attitudes that conformed to European cultural categories and ignored, deplored or erased other values and attitudes. This "universality" was a ready servant of European political and economic expansion. Those who are antagonistic to "universalist" accounts of literature from Africa or Asia, or from first-nations or ethnic communities in the white settler countries (Australia and New Zealand, for example, Canada and the United States) observe similar political motivations in Western or mainstream response to non-Western or minority literatures: "... the supposedly universal standards the critics appeal to are simply white, European ones ..." (11). It may be worthwhile to compare the universalist stance, and opposition to it, to Lu's account of the philosophies which support "Basic Writing" pedagogy.

- How does the "acculturation" model of education, as Lu describes it, compare with the "universalist" notion of literary value, as Dasenbrock describes it?

Dasenbrock accepts the reasoning which attacks the universalist standard — attacks the position, that is, that would lead people to say, "this is a very good book because everybody can relate to it." But he also disallows reasoning which proposes "localist" rather than universalist criteria for evaluating literature. Your reading of the article should prepare you to account not only for the political problems with universalist readings but also the problems with "localist" ones. As it turns out, it may be easier to let go of universalist positions than to oppose localist ones, which have a political prestige that is hard to resist. So you may notice that Dasenbrock's head-on rejection of "localism" is less sophisticated than his dismantling of universalism: "... surely it is foolish to confine each reader in a prison of only the literature that can be read expertly and surely. There is something wrong with a critical position that deprives a literature of much of its potential readership" (12).

- What is "foolish" and "wrong" about "localist" evaluations of literary texts?

But there is more to Dasenbrock's argument than just his rejection of both universalist and localist positions. He is also concerned to establish an alternative — a place from which we can appreciate *failure to understand* as not only a worthwhile but also a *meaningful* reading experience, and as not just a rhetorical accident — the wrong readers wandering into a book not intended for them — but as a strategic device, more or less consciously used by writers producing works he defines as "multicultural." (You might investigate this definition:

- Is it only works with certain preoccupations and rhetorical devices that are "multicultural?" Or would all works written in English by writers not living in the "Anglo-American" mainstream be "multicultural?"

Dasenbrock often repeats this idea which dissociates *understanding* and *meaning*. You will get several chances to grasp it. But you may welcome these repeated chances to absorb this idea for it is not such an easy one. We may be inclined to stick understanding and meaning together: if we don't understand something, how can we know what it means?

The idea first shows up in the introduction (12), after both universalist and localist positions are shown to be inadequate to explain the phenomenon of multicultural literature, and liable to produce errors. The idea is then demonstrated in each of four multicultural novels. These novels are Dasenbrock's *research site*: just as, for Verkuyten, de Jong, and Masson, Rotterdam residents' evening conversations were a site for researching the discourse of racism, and for Apter et al. the test scores of eleven groups of young Israeli women were a site for researching the effects of culture on eating disorders, these books are for Dasenbrock a place to go and find out about "intelligibility" in multicultural literature.

Chances are you will not have read all of these four novels — or maybe any of them. Each is introduced by a brief summary. So, for example, we get a two-paragraph, guided overview of Witi Ihimaera's *Tangi* — "guided" in that the summary does not account for all aspects of the book but, rather, sketches a portrait of the book which brings into focus those features which are relevant to the present argument. (So these summaries are — like any summary, to some degree — an *interpretation* of the work referred to. For example, *Tangi* is described as being a novel "about arrivals and departures and the greetings and partings that accompany them" (16). Perhaps not everyone would say that this is what the novel is "about," but this interpretation is plausible, and leads to Dasenbrock's main concern: the language at the borders between cultures.) If you haven't read these books, the summaries will enable you to understand the points Dasenbrock is making. But, at the same time, readers who *have* read these books will not find these summaries tedious or unnecessary: they bring the books in question onto the stage for discussion *in light of* present concerns. The don't tell the whole story; they don't provide any irrelevant information. It is possible that even widely known works like *Jane Eyre* or *King Lear* could be summarized in this quick, deft, interpretive way without offending readers by telling them what they already know. Dasenbrock's brief summaries would never be condemned as "plot summary," and offer a good model for students who are writing papers for literature courses and don't want to upset their instructors/readers by "telling the story."

Intelligibility and Meaningfulness in Multicultural Literature in English

REED WAY DASENBROCK
New Mexico State University, Las Cruces

LITERATURE IN ENGLISH IS AN increasingly international, even global, phenomenon. Writers all over the world, from the Pacific, Asia, Africa, and the West Indies as well as from the traditional centres in the British Isles and the United States, use English as a medium for fiction and poetry. One consequence has been that literature in English has become increasingly cross- or multicultural, as writing about a given culture is destined — because of its language, English, and its place of publication, usually London or New York — to have readers of many other cultures. This is not simply a matter of readers in the traditional centers of the English language struggling to understand work rooted in other cultural traditions; a Kenyan reader of a Nigerian or Guyanese or Indian novel is caught up in the same multicultural dynamic as the American reader of that novel. Admittedly, previous writers in English have found themselves in similar situations: Sir Walter Scott, writing about Scotland for an audience of the English as well as his compatriots, offers an interesting parallel. But Scott's situation was hardly typical at the time; in contrast, over the last generation there has been such an explosion in writing from a global range of cultures that, arguably, multicultural literature dominates literature in English today. I use the term *multicultural literature* to include works that are explicitly about multicultural societies and those that are implicitly multicultural in the sense of inscribing readers from other cultures inside their own textual dynamics. By examining aspects of four such multicultural narratives written in the last fifteen years — R. K. Narayan's *The Painter of Signs*, Maxine Hong Kingston's *The Woman Warrior*, Rudolfo Anaya's *Bless Me, Ultima*, and Witi Ihimaera's *Tangi* — I hope to show that explicitly multicultural texts are also implicitly multicultural.

The multiculturalism of contemporary world literature in English raises crucial issues that have not been dealt with by critics working with this body of material. As many linguists and discourse analysts argue, all units of language are necessarily incomplete or open. No utterance or written text is ever fully explicit, completely freestanding. To be understood, any text must be read in light of prior knowledge, background information, expectations about genre and about sequence — all the aspects often considered together as "context."[1] Many of these factors are culturally specific, varying across languages and even within the various English-speaking communities and nations of the world. Oscar Wilde once called England and the United States "two countries divided by a common language," and any American who has even been asked by an English host or hostess when he or she would like to be "knocked up in the morning" knows that the common language can divide and lead to some potentially disastrous misunderstandings. We expect problems when communicating with speakers of other languages; more startling, however, is that such problems often occur between speakers of the same language.

These problems grow more acute when one is dealing with written texts since the opportunity for clarifying discussion disappears, and they grow yet more acute with literary texts, which tend to lack some of the specifying contexts that head off misunderstandings in nonliterary forms of discourse. Thus, the multicultural writer and his or her audience may indeed be divided by a common language, and the greater gap between the two, the more open to misconstrual the multicultural work of literature becomes. This should not be ignored, for while some of the greatest writing being done in English today is coming from outside the traditional Anglo-American mainstream, there would seem to be real barriers to a broad understanding and appreciation of that literature.

The criticism that has responded to the issue has overwhelmingly tended to concentrate on the criterion of intelligibility. This emphasis is a little surprising, since poststructuralists might be expected to find such literature interesting precisely because of its potential undecidability and unintelligibility. But most deconstructive criticism has stayed within the confines of a traditional canon, and the Nigerian Sunday O. Anozie, in his work on African literature in English, is the only prominent critic attempting to argue for a deconstructive reading of any of the new literatures in English (but see Appiah). Virtually every other critic working in this field has seen misunderstanding or unintelligibility as the danger to be avoided at all costs. I argue, in contrast, that intelligibility cannot be made the sole criterion in our understanding and evaluation of multicultural texts. Ready intelligibility is not always what the writer is striving for; it therefore cannot be what the critic always demands.

Two critical approaches that use the criterion of intelligibility can be differentiated both according to how they use it and according to the body of literature each approach champions. On one side are the so-called universalist critics, who argue that writers should appeal to a universal audience — or, more precisely, a global audience in English — and that therefore barriers to ready intelligibility are flaws. John Updike, in reviewing *Petals of Blood*, by the Kenyan novelist Ngugi, complains of the profusion of untranslated Swahili and Kikuyu words in the novel, obviously preferring a novel without any such barriers to intelligibility for a non-East African audience. A number of academic critics, such as M. M. Mahood and Charles Larson, have given a more sophisticated formulation to this view, praising those "Third World" writers who have addressed a "universal" audience. Mahood writes, "I should be very happy if my juxtapositions did something to persuade the guardians of the pure English tradition of fiction that we do not need to change our criteria in approaching Third World novels" (2). Analogously, Larson praises the work of the African novelist Lenrie Peters for "its universality, its very limited concern with Africa itself" (229). Unlike Updike, these critics tend to commend works for avoiding barriers to intelligibility, like Ngugi's use of Swahili, instead of criticizing works for having them, but implicit in their praise is a stance that is one with Updike's.

This view has not passed without comment or indeed without counterattack. And though the issue of universality is one faced — implicitly or explicitly — in the criticism of all the new literatures in English, it has inspired the most controversy in the criticism of African literature. African writers and critics have argued that the supposedly universal standards the critics appeal to are simply white, European ones, stands and values that Africans deliberately reject. As Chinua Achebe puts it, "I should like to see the word *universal* banned altogether from discussions of African literature until such a time as people cease to use it as a synonym for the narrow, self-serving parochialism of Europe" (11). The criticism of Charles Larson has come under particular attack, the Ghanaian novelist Ayi Kwei Armah describing it as "Larsony" (14). Ironically, Larson praised Armah highly, and in fact was attacked by Achebe for that praise. Achebe in turn has cited Larson as one of a number of "colonialist critics" who, he says, are doing the same thing to African literature that the colonizing whites earlier did to African society (7, 10-12).[2] Other European and American critics have also been taken to task by Africans for their "Eurocentric" and colonialist approaches to African literature.[3]

This African critical position insists therefore on African literature's being African first and universal only second, if at all. In rejecting the tenets of "universalist" criticism, Achebe calls his vision "necessarily local and particular" (69). This stance determines a very different attitude toward the barriers to global intelligibility that Updike complains about. To understand African literature, readers need to be informed so that they can come to the texts with at least some of the necessary context of expectations. The reader who is interested in a work should expect to do some work to appreciate it. In an article entitled "The Limitations of Universal Critical Criteria," the Nigerian critic Donatus Nwoga argues that "there is not much of Soyinka that can be understood without a deep knowledge of Yoruba mythology and oral tradition literature" (627).[4] Similarly, the Ghanaian writer Kofi Awoonor comments that the Nigerian novelist Tutuola "is a writer whose art rests and has meaning only within the larger world construct of Yoruba thought and ontology" (667). These critics imply that Soyinka and Tutuola are not to be faulted because their work is rooted in their traditional culture.[5] On the contrary, the use they make of that tradition is part of their strength as artists. Consequently, one must know something about Yoruba culture to understand their work, and from this one can draw the general proposition that one must know something about the culture of any African writer to understand his or her work. It is therefore up to the reader, not the author, to do the work necessary to make the literature intelligible.

Nwoga's "localist" or contextualist position is more fruitful for a critic than the universalist or acontextualist one, if only because it makes the critic's role must more interesting and powerful. Both approaches are deeply prescriptive: the universalist praises works without a density of local reference difficult for outsiders to follow; the localist praises precisely the opposite. But if readers need to know about Yoruba culture to understand Soyinka, then critics have a job to do beyond simply praising or attacking him: they can provide the uninformed with the needed contextual background. Some of the best criticism of the new literatures in English has been of this explanatory kind, filling in the gaps between author and reader and offering information that makes the text intelligible.[6] Thus an informed guide helps the foreign reader open a door that had previously seemed closed and enter into the world of the text. In the localist view, however, the door still seems firmly closed against foreign critics, who can presumably never have the local competence needed for elucidation.

But the localist and universalist approaches to these new literatures in English share a great deal more than they recognize. Both feel that a work must be readily intelligible to be of value, that Ngugi's use of Swahili in *Petals of Blood* or Soyinka's use of Yoruba mythology is a problem if it is not understood. The difference is that they assign blame differently, the one blaming the writer who will not explain, the other the reader who thinks everything should be made easy to understand. But they are one in their dislike of, and desire to head off, any moments of openness in the text, in their denial of any value to difficult passages or failures in understanding. The reader, they seem to say, must have everything understood: if the author does not make everything clear, that simply defines the task of the critic.

In such an uncritical acceptance of intelligibility as an absolute value, these different (or not so different) approaches are not proving adequate to the literature they purport to describe. The universalist approach seems an unworkable ideal for a writer, for only a writer of allegory such as J. M. Coetzee can successfully avoid specific, local references of the kind that fill any novel. But if the universalist position is unworkable for the writer, the localist position is equally unworkable for the reader. If we must be or become expert in the culture of any book we read, then we will tend to limit ourselves to our own literature. This would probably suit many African critics perfectly, since they seem to resent any outside interest in African literature. But surely it is foolish to confine each reader in a prison of only the literature that can be read expertly and surely. There is something wrong with a critical position that deprives a literature of much of its potential readership.

What these critics have failed to grasp is that intelligible and meaningful are not completely overlapping, synonymous terms. Indeed, the meaningfulness of multicultural works is in large measure a function of their unintelligibility for part of their audience. Multicultural literature offers us above all an experience of multiculturalism, in which not everything is likely to be wholly understood by every reader. The texts often only mirror the misunderstanding and failures of intelligibility in the multicultural situations they depict, as I hope to show by analyzing four works, each set in a different cultural milieu. My examples deliberately come from a range of cultures, none of them African, so as to indicate how the issues I have traced in African criticism are an integral part of all multicultural literatures in English.

Ready intelligibility, then, is far from crucial to the understanding of a multicultural text; in fact, the reader's ready assumption of understanding can itself be misleading, in just the way that American guests in Britain can be disconcerted because they think they know what "knocked up" means. Readers of multicultural literature can miss the point precisely where they think they get it (or fail to notice anything "to get" at all). In this case, the writer must disturb that assumption in order to be read correctly. The Indian novelist R. K. Narayan provides a good, concise example of this strategy in one of his later novels, *The Painter of Signs*.

The Painter of Signs is an understated comedy about a sign painter, Raman, who falls in love with a family-planning official named Daisy. Now in a forest of strange Indian names like Raman and Veerappa, the Western reader, consciously or unconsciously, will feel more at home with a name like Daisy. "Ah, finally a name I know," such a reader is likely to think. But this assumption of cross-cultural understanding would itself lead to a misunderstanding, since in an Indian context the name Daisy carries a very different weight or meaning from what it does in an American one. Narayan, aware of this potential misunderstanding, goes out of his way to impede any overconfident possessing of the text by the Western reader. When the name is first mentioned in the novel, Rama muses to himself, "Daisy! What a name for someone who looked so very Indian, traditional and gentle!" (31). This passage should make readers who are unaware of anything unusual about the name stop and wonder, which is to say, begin to doubt the appropriateness of their own cultural frames of reference. What is unusual about the name is, of course, precisely that it is a Western name, so that its possessor is probably a Christian and is in any case outside the Hindu caste system. This implication is spelled out in a much later conversation between Raman and his devout and traditional Hindu aunt:

> "That girl! What is her caste? Who is she?"
> "Who is she? It is immaterial. She is going to be my wife, that's all that need be known."
> "Isn't she a Christian or something—a name which is . . ."
> "Nothing more than the name of a flower, that's all. Daisy is a flower." He realized that he was not sure what flower it was. "It's a most lovely flower grown in America, England, and so forth. What is wrong with that name?"
> "A Christian! How can you bring in a Christian . . ."
> (146-147; Narayan's ellipses)

None of this dialogue is necessary for the Indian reader, for whom the name alone would suffice, and Narayan has indeed been criticized in India for his "pandering" to a Western audience.[7] But note what shape this pandering takes. He does not explain the unfamiliar; he makes the familiar itself unfamiliar so that Western readers can see how a name unremarkable to them can be a meaningful and richly evocative name in a different context, meaningful, Narayan makes one aware, without anyone's quite knowing what a daisy is.

This small example of the ways different cultural perspectives can be allowed for in a multicultural text can be seen as a classic example of what the Russian formalist Viktor Shklovsky calls *ostranenie* 'making strange' or "defamiliarization," as it is usually rendered in English.[8] But instead of Shklovsky's generalized defamiliarization capable of working on any reader of the text, Narayan's use of the name Daisy is a culturally coded defamiliarization that works on only a specific part of the audience, those readers who otherwise would have felt familiar with the name. Narayan's novel thus provides its differing audiences with differing experiences, since what will seem an excrescence to an Indian reader (or a reader informed about the novel's contextual background) may prove revelatory to a less informed or non-Indian one. Narayan does not choose between writing for a "universal" and a local audience; he writes to two audiences simultaneously and structures his text accordingly. But there is nothing unstable or undecided about this duality, no confusion about the meaning, because the defamiliarization makes the less informed reader more informed, moves that reader closer to being an informed reader of the novel. The reader has to do some work, work that is an important locus of the novel's meaning.

The matter of Daisy's name is, however, rather easily understood and explained, so I would like to test that suggestion by looking at some further examples. Maxine Hong Kingston's *The Woman Warrior*, an autobiographical account of growing up Chinese American in Stockton, California, is subtitled *Memoir of a Childhood among Ghosts*. In the third chapter, "Shame," we hear a good deal about ghosts, in particular about a ghost that plagued the author's mother in medical school. A few pages later, the author herself seems to live among ghosts:

But America has always been full of machines and ghosts —
Taxi Ghosts, Bus Ghosts, Police Ghosts, Meter Reader
Ghosts, Tree Trimming Ghosts, Five-and-Dime Ghosts.

Once upon a time the world was so thick with ghosts, I could hardly breathe; I could hardly walk, limping my way around the White Ghosts in their cars. There were Black Ghosts too, but they were open eyes and full of laughter, more distinct than White Ghosts. (113)

Thereafter the book is littered with references to "Grocery Ghosts," "Social Worker Ghosts," "Jesus Ghosts," "Mail Ghosts," "Druggist Ghosts," and so on. Now a reader quickly figures out that *ghost* here doesn't mean what it does to most English speakers; instead, it means non-Chinese or non-Oriental. Indeed, before *ghost* is used in this sense, we are told: "The Japanese, though 'little,' were not ghosts, the only foreigners considered not ghosts by the Chinese" (109). But just as we think we have a firm criterion for distinguishing ghosts from ghosts, we encounter passages where it is genuinely difficult to tell: "But how can I have that memory when I couldn't talk? My mother say that we, like the ghosts, have no memories" (194). Or, "That ghost! That dead ghost! How dare he come to the wrong house" (196). Or again, "They would not tell us children because we had been born among ghosts, were taught by ghosts, and were ourselves ghost-like. They call us a kind of ghost. Ghosts are noisy and full of air; they talk during meals" (213-214).

If one insists that the word *ghost* must mean either a spirit ("our" meaning) or a non-Oriental ("their" meaning), in all these passages it is possible to decide that the second meaning is intended, that the object referred to by the word *ghost* is indeed an animate, corporeal one. But the effect of these passages, reinforced by the constant reiteration of the tag *ghost* ("Hobo Ghosts," "Delivery Ghosts," "Sales Ghosts") is to show the reader a way of using the word and of seeing the world in which that distinction is not made. The "Delivery Ghost" is indeed a ghost for the author's mother, and he takes on a spectral quality in these pages, even for "ghost" readers of *The Woman Warrior*. My point is that we cannot decide which meaning of the word *ghost* is intended; my point is that after a while, we do not bother to decide, as we enter into the semantic world of the book.

Again, like the meaning of the name Daisy, the meaning of the word *ghost* as Kingston uses it is not hard to figure out and is not a serious or insuperable barrier to intelligibility (though the number of students who have asked me, "What are all these ghosts doing in the book?" indicates that a significant percentage of the book's readers may be confused longer than a careful reader might think probable). But it is worth inquiring for a moment why Kingston might want to make non-Chinese readers do that work.

One motive is simply a realistic one, for the Chinese do refer to outsiders by a word most closely translated as ghost, even though, as we have seen, the English word does not have quite the same semantic field. But the second, more important reason is that the reiteration of *ghost* confronts those of us who are not Chinese with the different way of using the word and hence with a different way of seeing the world. To understand *ghost* in *The Woman Warrior*, non-Chinese readers need to understand the Chinese use of the word, which means that we must, momentarily at least, learn to see ourselves as ghosts. As we experience the word, we also experience a perception and a category of thought, and in so doing we learn a good deal about Chinese perceptions of us.

Even if the task is not that difficult, it is still something we have to work at. The writer has deliberately made her text more difficult, blocking automatic intelligibility by using *ghost* in a less broadly available sense, in a way that makes a "ghost" reader pause and think. This again is a Shklovskian defamiliarization, not so much of the word as of our self-concept. And again, it is a culturally specific defamiliarization, one that would not take effect on a Chinese or Chinese American reader. Yet this split effect, like the split effect of the name Daisy in *The Painter of Signs*, leads ultimately to a reconciliation, since the net effect is that a non-Chinese reader can understand Chinese cultural horizons more expertly than before.

This effect is of course a major theme of the book itself, which is multicultural in that it deals with multiculturalism, addresses a multicultural audience, both Chinese and non-Chinese, and above all imbues that audience with at least a measure of multiculturalism, making non-Chinese readers more aware of, and sensitive to, Chinese and Chinese American culture.

Writers can therefore choose to make moments of their work more difficult to understand, less immediately intelligible, because they know that the reader will work for their meaning. One could say, adapting the language of Paul Grice, that there is implicit in any act of reading a maxim of intelligibility, which is that readers — like speakers and listeners — will work to make texts as intelligible as possible.[9] Assuming that a work makes sense and has significance, the reader will try to find that sense and significance even when they are not readily apparent. Obviously writers also work most of the time to maximize the intelligibility of their texts. But aware that readers will go on obeying the maxim even if writers do not, an author may flout the maxim so as to exploit it, to make the reader work harder at certain moments. This principle can be abused, but a skillful writer will make the reader work hard only at those moments where the work is meaningful. If we are not already informed about Chinese culture, we work to understand the meaning of *ghost* in *The Woman Warrior* and thus come to understand the book's subtitle and a great deal about the form of life the book seeks to represent. Only by doing that work, by striving to understand a different mode of expression, are we brought up against the fact of cultural difference. If everything is translated into our terms and made readily intelligible, then our cultural categories will be reinforced, not challenged. So the work the reader does when encountering a different mode of expression can be a crucial part of a book's meaning, since the book may have been designed to make the reader do that work.

This principle holds true for works over a range of difficulty, from the relatively easy texts we have examined so far to much more difficult ones. It was Ngugi's use of Swahili that particularly irritated John Updike, we remember, because the incorporation of words from another language into a work of literature makes that work partially unintelligible to those who do not know that language. But to make it unintelligible is not to make it unmeaningful; the use of opaque foreign words can be part of a deliberate artistic strategy. Rudolfo Anaya's *Bless Me, Ultima*, a novel about a young Hispanic growing up in bilingual New Mexico in the 1940s, exemplifies this technique. Though the novel is in English, it includes a substantial amount of Spanish, for which there is very little covert or overt translation. One critic has referred to Anaya's "aggressively bilingual mode of presentation" (Gingerich 215-16), and certainly a reader who knows no Spanish will encounter a barrier to intelligibility. But critical discussion of the use of Spanish in *Bless Me, Ultima* should not be allowed to stop there.

The book represents a bilingual society, but not one whose bilingualism is stable. As the narrator and protagonist Antonio himself tells us early on, "All of the older people spoke only in Spanish, and I myself understood only Spanish. It was only after one went to school that one learned English" (9). But those who do learn English tend to come to prefer it because, in the world of the novel, it is higher-status language. Antonio's slightly older sisters speak English in preference to Spanish, and the English dialogue in the scenes at school is rendered colloquially enough that we understand it as a transcription of conversations in English, not — as in the scenes set at home — translations of conversations in Spanish.

One exception to this pattern is that all the school scenes are full of swearing that is almost entirely in Spanish and never translated. The reasons for Anaya's refusal to translate and its effect on a monolingual reader are worth consideration. One good reason lies in the situation Anaya is depicting. Students can get away with saying things in Spanish at school (that they could never say in Spanish at home) because the teachers, all Anglo, do not know what the words mean. "'A la veca!' 'What does that mean?' Miss Violet asked. 'It means okay'" (145). In such a situation bilinguals have expressive resources that give them an enormous advantage over monolinguals, the ability to speak a language closed to the listeners one wishes to exclude, to tap a natural code that yet has the capabilities of a secret code.

The dynamics of the audience's response reflect the dynamics of the situation depicted in the novel. In *Bless Me, Ultima*, the characters are divided into two groups, the bilinguals who know fully what is going on and the monolinguals on either side who do not completely grasp what is being said; and the audience of *Bless Me, Ultima* is divided in exactly the same way. On one side, monolingual Spanish readers cannot understand the book at all; though important in the society depicted in the novel, they are marginalized by the novel just as they are marginalized in the world of the novel. On the other, monolingual English readers are in Miss Violet's situation, reduced to grasping from the context what "a la veca" might mean.

"A la veca" may be unintelligible to most of the book's readers, just as it is to Miss Violet, at least if she accepts its gloss as "okay." But unintelligibility does not preclude meaningfulness. For the very situation of Anaya's novel is a bicultural-bilingual society in which almost no one is adequately bilingual. Antonio (before he goes to school) and his parents and adult relatives experience in their everyday life a good deal of English they do not understand; Anglos such as Miss Violet are surrounded by a largely Hispanophone community that they find unintelligible. Only the young like Antonio can speak to both worlds. Difficulties in communication and understanding are thus built into the texture of this society, just as they are in the working of Anaya's novel. If in his bilingualism some of us encounter the unintelligible, that merely allows us to share for a moment the day-to-day experience of many members of the society the book is about.

But Antonio does learn to talk with both worlds, and his ability to put together home and school, Spanish and English, is an image of what the book can do for the reader as well. The reader is never told the referential meaning of "a la veca," and Miss Violet presumably never learned it either. But by the end of the novel anyone attentive to the way the untranslated profanity has been used could swear with fair proficiency in Spanish. And, after all, the meaning of profanity is to be found in its use, in what J. L. Austin would call its illocutionary and perlocutionary force, not in its referential or locutionary content. In reading *Bless Me, Ultima*, one learns how these words are used, which perfectly illustrates how meaning and meaningfulness are not entirely functions of intelligibility.

Thus, the voyage of the reader through the book mirrors Antonio's experience. No one translates for Antonio. no one cushions his transition into English. He is thrown into the school world of English and forced to find his way in it. By the end, he is moving toward becoming someone who could write the book in which he appears. In the same way, though less violently, the reader is thrown into a world of Spanish without translation or cushioning, and even the monolingual reader moves toward a functional bilingualism, an ability to understand the world of the novel. Antonio moves toward being able to write the novel; the reader moves toward being able to read it.

In this respect at least, though their means might differ considerably, there is a strong similarity between Kingston's *Woman Warrior* and Anaya's *Bless Me, Ultima*. Both works are curiously bifurcated: the bilingual-bicultural reader has an easy time, reexperiencing an already known and familiar world; the monolingual reader has a more difficult time (especially in Anaya's novel), experiencing biculturalism and, in Anaya's work, a bilingualism that provide some barriers to intelligibility. But it does not follow that one reading is right, the other wrong. Both are simply places to start from. Each work is set up with that dual or split reading in mind. No matter where one starts, the difference between the two reading experiences should be eliminated or at least reduced by the books' ends, as the monocultural reader should be that much less monocultural than at the start. The bicultural reading is the "right" one in the sense that biculturalism is clearly where the author wants to lead the reader, but by not beginning there, the monocultural reader may have a richer experience of the work, richer because he or she has had to do that much more work.

So far my examples have been isolated lexical units, names or words or, at most, phrases or sentences. These are ultimately not that difficult for the reader to negotiate, since the immediate textual context provides most of what is necessary for understanding. Such devices can also work on a larger scale, however. A novel by a Maori writer from New Zealand, Witi Ihimaera's *Tangi*, shows how a strategic refusal to accommodate the reader can stand at the very core of a work's meaning.

The story of a young man's coming to terms with the death of his father, *Tangi* revolves around the Maori extended funeral service that gives the book its title. Tama has left the small Maori community in which he was born, gone to the "big city" (Wellington), and found a *pakeha* (white) girlfriend, but by the end of the novel he has decided to come home to take care of the family farm. Though the point is not spelled out, this return, a return to the Maori values represented by Tama's father, entails leaving his *pakeha* girlfriend and, in a larger sense, the *pakeha* world he has entered in Wellington.

The novel thus is about arrivals and departures and the greetings and partings that accompany them. It is not told chronologically but is structured around Tama's trips from Wellington to the *tangi* and back to Wellington to close out his affairs there, so scenes and images from these trips pervade, indeed organize, the novel. This structure gives Ihimaera an opportunity to contrast Maori and *pakeha* ways of saying hello and especially goodbye. On a train platform, Ihimaera will cut from his Maori family group saying goodbye to Tama in rich, emotional, sentimental, and ceremonial fashion to the understated and stiff goodbyes of *pakeha* families. These scenes are too long to quote in full, but notice the juxtaposition of the two cultures in this conclusion to a parting scene between Tama and his family:

> The farewells are ended. My mother waits, alone. Silently we embrace each other.
> — Heare ra, Son.
> — E noho ra, e ma.
> My mother, don't weep. I'm only going away for a short while. I'm coming back.
> — What a tangiweto you are, Mum.
> — What's those then, ay? Mum says, pointing at my own tears. I suppose you call that rain.
> — Hone, Marama, look at Mum. She's the crybaby, not me. She . . .
> I look at my mother. One last embrace. Our love is expressed in the soft, moist pressing of our noses together.
> — Tama, you come back soon.

— Ae, e ma. E noho ra.

The train whistle blows a final blast. The porter hastens along the platform.

— All aboard. Move away from the train please.

I step onto the train. All around me, other goodbyes are being said.

— Give our love to Jim.

— Thanks for having me, Uncle.

— Bye bye Susan.

— Don't forget to write, dear.

— Goodbye

— Goodbye. Goodbye.　　　(31; Ihimaera's ellipses)

Elsewhere Tama observes or experiences similar contrasts. On the train, he sees a young Maori girl parting from her family, seemingly for the first time, to go to the city. Tama himself — the figure who, like Antonio, can negotiate the cultural divide — has goodbyes to make to his *pakeha* friends and colleagues. His goodbye to his boss at the airport, as understated as those we observe among *pakehas*, offers a sharp contrast to his meeting with his cousin inside the airport, a contrast reiterated when his girlfriend later calls him in the midst of the *tangi* and when *pakeha* acquaintances of his father briefly come to the *tangi*. Thus, we are not only given an initial contrast between Maori and *pakeha* greetings and partings, we see Tama enact that contrast. With *pakehas*, one greets in *pakeha* fashion. The biculturalism of Tama's world is not a balanced biculturalism: *pakeha* ways and values are the dominant norm, Maori ways a marginalized exception.

The novel as a whole, however, refuses to make that concession to a *pakeha* norm. Written in the *pakeha* language and with *pakeha* readers in mind (though not exclusively so), *Tangi* nonetheless does not endorse *pakeha* ways and values, choosing instead to celebrate those of the Maori. This orientation can be seen in a number of respects. First, as in the passage already quoted, Ihimaera leaves a great deal of Maori untranslated. We are given the full greetings and farewells in Maori, not English versions of them. Like the other writers discussed in this essay, Ihimaera undoubtedly has a realistic motive: he is trying to represent the actual language use of his characters, bicultural but no longer fully bilingual, who though using certain Maori phrases would speak mostly in English. In addition, however, the way those greetings and farewells stand out from their English language context draws our attention. Here, too, what the outside reader can grasp is their illocutionary force rather than their referential meaning. The use of Maori gives these speakers a dimension of community and intimacy, and it marks the importance of these forms of greeting and parting, again in contrast to the antiformal (and hence, in another sense, more formal) *pakeha* world. Ihimaera does not translate these words because their meaning derives from their being in Maori.

What Ihimaera leaves untranslated are primarily these greetings and farewells. Toward the end of the novel, at the high point of the *tangi*, as much as a third of the text is in Maori, as Ihimaera includes the songs of lament and mourning that are being sung. Aware of the limits to how hard he can make non-Maori readers work, he translates some of the songs and explains the meaning of others. But the Maori always precedes the English, so that we experience the unfamiliar first. Ihamaera's reluctance to translate or explain the Maori phrases gives the outside reader precisely the same experience as Anaya gives the reader in *Bless Me, Ultima*. We are like the *pakeha* friends of Tama's father who come to the *tangi* "ill at ease," "hesitant" (166). At the *tangi*, and in the novel *Tangi*, we are on Maori ground, and, for a change, we have to do the accommodating and adapting. As we do so, we experience the kind of shifting and adapting a Tama undergoes every day in his life.

Moreover, just as in *Bless Me, Ultima*, a bridge of understanding is created, at least for the sympathetic reader. Ihimaera's refusal to give us, his *pakeha* readers, everything on our own terms means that we learn something about his terms and about the extent to which we have not made that effort before. And I expect reading *Tangi* makes New Zealand readers reflect on the extent of their biculturalism in a bicultural situation in exactly the same way *Bless Me, Ultima* makes New Mexican readers reflect. The Anglo or *pakeha* reader is inscribed into the novel as Miss Violet or as Tama's boss or his father's friends, and each book makes that reader wonder about the desirability of being like that character. Interestingly, *Tangi* has been criticized in New Zealand for its "sentimentality."[10] This response judges *Tangi* by *pakeha* norms of restraint and understatement the novel seeks to call into question. And though the judgement can be seen either as a failure of the book to persuade readers of its values or as a failure of criticism to shed its prejudices, in one sense it is a sign that the critics are getting the book right. Aware that *Tangi* challenges their values, *pakeha* critics respond on that level of their values, underscoring Ihimaera's point that the biculturalism of New Zealand is not balanced, that *pakeha* values are taken as the norm.

The refusal to translate does something else as well. A refusal to translate generally indicates difficulty in translation. No ready equivalent of *dharma* or *karma* exists in English, so translators of Sanskrit philosophical texts have tended to use these and other Sanskrit words with explanatory glosses attached. As a result, the words have across time become less foreign in English and now appear in English dictionaries. Anaya does something similar in *Bless Me, Ultima* when he refuses to translate words such as *llano* 'plain,' *curandera* 'good witch,' and *bruja* 'bad witch.' He keeps the Spanish words where their English equivalents would seem odd (as in *good witch* or *curer*) or where they would not carry the emotional force of the original (as in *llano*). Ihimaera uses the same technique, making it more prominent by leaving the title of the novel itself untranslated. Early on, the word *tangi* is used, followed by the parenthetical phrase "or funeral rites," but that gloss far from exhausts the full implications of the word. The translation of the title is really to be found across the entire book; in a sense, it is the book. Farewells are given such a large place in the novel because the whole novel is a long farewell to Tama's father. *Tangi* can be translated as "funeral," but the two words are as far apart as the Maori and *pakeha* family partings at the railway station. The full resonances of the words differ because of different attitudes toward life, toward death, and toward ceremony. It would be grotesquely inappropriate to call the novel *Funeral*, and this is clearly one of the things the book should make the reader grasp.

What Ihimaera does with the title of his book encapsulates what I have tried to show in this discussion. Multicultural works of literature are multicultural, not only in having multiculturalism as part of their subject matter and theme, but also in allowing for readers from a range of cultures. Ihimaera, in representing Maori culture, structures his work with Maori and non-Maori readers in mind, and we have seen how differently informed and less informed readers experience all such multicultural works. But critics of these works have erred in thinking that one of these experiences must be the right one. The difficulty experienced by a less informed reader, far from preventing the reader from experiencing the work justly, is what creates meaning for that reader. A full or even adequate understanding of another culture is never to be gained by translating it entirely into one's own terms. It is different and that difference must be respected. In multicultural literature in English today, that difference is primarily established by barriers to intelligibility being strategically and selectively raised for the less informed reader, forcing the reader to do work that then becomes part of the book's meaning. It is not as if the author could have made things easy but refused. Making things easy would have denied the reader the experience needed to come to an understanding of the culture. By the end of *Tangi*, we have experienced a tangi; we know something of its importance and richness; we know something of its importance and richness; we know, in short, something of what the word means. But to know that is to know that it cannot be translated, and we would not have arrived at that knowledge if it had been.

Difficulties in a text cannot simply be attacked as destroying the "universality" of a work or celebrated as establishing its "localism," as closing the text to outsiders. The critic needs to decide whether unintelligibility exists merely for its own sake or for the sake of the work the reader must do to make the text intelligible. Writers accommodate themselves to their readers' horizons as much as they can; where they honestly cannot, the reader must take over. Attention paid to moments where the reader must work to broaden his or her horizon of understanding tells us more than anything else does about a work's locus of meaning and values.[11]

NOTES

1 A great deal of work could be cited here, including J. L. Austin's on speech acts and Paul Grice's on "conversational implicatures." Many scholars have tried to carry on the work of Austin and Grice; for the initial attempt to apply Gricean pragmatics to literary theory, see Mary Louise Pratt (152-200).

2 Achebe's charge seems unfair in the sense that Larson does attempt to identify distinctively African characteristics of the novels he studies. But Larson has a disconcerting habit of viewing these differences as elements of the European novel that the African novel lacks rather than as positive elements in their own right, and he posits that the African novel of the future will be less and less distinctively African. He likes the fiction of Armah because he considers that it represents this trend; Achebe dislikes it for the same reason and dislikes Larson's singling it out for praise; and Armah himself disagrees with Larson's praise, disdaining the critics' "obsessive, blind need to annihilate whatever is African in me and my work" (9).

3 For a typical attack on non-African critics of African literature, particularly Bernth Lindfors, see Emenyonu. See Lindfors for his response to attacks on his criticism by Emenyonu and others.

4 Nwoga's words are closely echoed by the European critic Albert Gerard: "Likewise no one can hope to have anything truly meaningful to say about Wole Soyinka, even when he is adapting Euripides or Gay or Brecht, unless the analyst is aware of the particulars of Yoruba culture" (20).

5   In fact, Soyinka has been widely attacked for not being "African" enough, for being a "eurocentric modernist." See Chinweizu et al., but also see Soyinka's response to an earlier version of these critics' attacks on him.

6   E.g., see A. Afolayan, who compares Tutuola's syntax to the syntactic structures of the novelist's native language, Yoruba.

7   For a discussion of this and other failures of the Indian criticism of Narayan, see Feroza Jussawalla (70-84).

8   For a good exposition of Shklovsky's concept, see Fredric Jameson (50-64, 70-79).

9   See Grice (45-46). My maxim combines aspects of two separate maxims in Grice's taxonomy: the maxim of quantity, that one should make one's contribution as informative as is required, and the maxim of manner, that one should avoid obscurity of expression.

10   Paul Sharrad discusses the criticism and attempts to defend Ihimaera's work against such charges.

11   I should like to thank first of all the National Endowment for the Humanities for granting me a Fellowship for College Teachers, during which this essay was written; second, Andy Wiget, my colleague at New Mexico State, for a helpful reading of an earlier draft; finally and most important, my wife, Feroza Jussawalla, for, among many other things, reading and criticizing successive drafts of this essay, lending me the Paul Sharrad essay that initially drew the work of Ihimaera to my attention, and teaching me most of what I know about multilingualism, multiculturalism, and Indian writing in English.

WORKS CITED

Achebe, Chinua. *Morning Yet on Creation Day*. Garden City: Doubleday, 1976.
Afolayan, A. "Language and Sources of Amos Tutuola." *Perspectives on African Literature: Selections from the Proceedings of the Conference on African Literature held at the University of Ife, 1968*. Ed. Christopher Heywood. London: Heinemann, 1971. 49-63.
Anaya, Rudolfo. *Bless Me, Ultima*. Berkeley: Tonatiuh, 1972.
Anozie, Sunday O. "Negritude, Structuralism, Deconstruction." *Black Literature and Literary Theory*. Ed. Henry Louis Gates. New York: Methuen, 1984. 105-25.
Appiah, Anthony. "Strictures on Structures: The Prospects for a Structuralist Poetics of African Fiction." *Black Literature and Literary Theory*. Ed. Henry Louis Gates. New York: Methuen, 1984. 127-150.
Armah, Ayi Kwei. "Larsony: Or, Fiction as Criticism of Fiction." *Asemka* 4 (1976): 1-14.
Austin, J. L. *How to Do Things with Words*. 1962. Ed. J. O. Urmson. New York: Oxford UP, 1965.
Awoonor, Kofi. "Tradition and Continuity in African Literature." *Dalhousie Review* 53 (1973-1974): 665-71.
Chinweizu, Onwuchekwa Jemie, and Ihechukwu Madubuike. *Toward the Decolonization of African Literature*. 1980. Washington: Howard UP, 1984.
Emenyonu, Ernest. "African Literature: What Does it Take to Be Its Critic?"

African Literature Today 5. New York: Africana, 1971. 1-11.

Gerard, Albert. "Is Anything Wrong with African Literary Studies?" *African Literature Studies: The Present State/ L'état présent.* Ed. Stephen Arnold. Washington: Three Continents, 1985. 17-26.

Gingerich, Willard. "Aspects of Prose Style in Three Chicano Novels: *Pocho; Bless Me, Ultima*; and *The Road to Tamazunchale.*" *Form and Function in Chicano English.* Ed. Jacob Ornstein-Galicia. Rowley: Newbury, 1984. 206-28.

Grice, Paul. "Logic and Conversation." *Speech Acts: Syntax and Semantics.* Ed. Peter Cole and Jerry L. Morgan. New York: Academic, 1975. 41-58.

Ihimaera, Witi. *Tangi.* 1973. Auckland: Heinemann NZ, 1984.

Jameson, Fredric. *The Prison-House of Language.* Princeton: Princeton UP, 1972.

Jussawalla, Feroza. *Family Quarrels: Towards a Criticism of Indian Writing in English.* Berne: Lang, 1985.

Kingston, Maxine Hong. *The Woman Warrior.* 1976. New York: Vintage, 1977.

Larson, Charles. *The Emergence of African Fiction.* 1971. Bloomington: Indiana UP, 1972.

Lindfors, Bernth. "The Blind Men and the Elephant." *African Literature Today* 7. New York: Africana, 1975. 53-64.

Mahood, M. M. *The Colonial Encounter: A Reading of Six Novels.* Totowa: Rowman, 1977.

Narayan, R. K. *The Painter of Signs.* New York: Viking, 1976.

Nwoga, D. Ibe. "The Limitations of Universal Critical Criteria." *Dalhousie Review* 53 (1973-74): 608-30.

Pratt, Mary Louise. *Toward a Speech Act Theory of Literary Discourse.* Bloomington: Indiana UP, 1977.

Sharrad, Paul. "A Rhetoric of Sentiment: Thoughts on Maori Writing with Reference to the Short-Stories of Witi Ihimaera." Unpublished ms., 1985.

Soyinka, Wole. "Neo-Tarzanism: The Poetics of Pseudo Tradition." *Transition* 48 (1975): 38-44.

Updike, John. Rev. of *Petals of Blood*, by Ngugi. *Hugging the Shore: Essays and Criticism.* New York: Knopf, 1983. 697-701.

II

Introduction

Some specialist, technical terms enjoy big careers not only in research discourse but also in popular discourse. *Anorexia nervosa* is such a term, a wording shared by journalists and highly trained specialists and everyday conversationalists alike. (This transfer of a specialist term from scholarly enclaves to the public domain may alert us to the way social preoccupations — in this case, the preoccupation with women's bodies and psychological fallibilities — can seize the terms of science to elaborate on matters of widespread interest.) Even if you have never read a research account of anorexia nervosa before, you probably don't need the definition/description of the disorder which appears in the first two paragraphs of this article. (Note that, even though these writers are addressing other specialists, they still explain the term, constructing common ground for the advance of the discussion.)

However, despite seemingly widespread public knowledge of this disorder, professional knowledge of it is incomplete — for one thing, knowledge of successful treatments seems to be incomplete. The particular knowledge deficit the authors of "Cultural Effects on Eating Attitudes in Israeli Subpopulations and Hospitalized Anorectics" mention concerns "Arab populations" (they are "rarely studied" [331]) and, more broadly, sociocultural influences on eating attitudes and behaviours. They say that "Israel is a multicultural country, and psychiatrists here must be aware of sociocultural factors in psychopathology" (331). Their concerns locate these researchers a few steps away from a universal model of the human psyche — which would assume that all people share essential psychological characteristics — and closer to a model which pays more attention to sociohistorical determinants of psychological characteristics. (Since psychology has been principally a Western science, its models of the human personality may tend to be models of Western personalities.) Anorexia nervosa seems a particularly appropriate site for this kind of inquiry, since it has regularly been associated with the images and ideals of femininity which twentieth-century Western culture has developed.

This study selects a group of people (783 young Israeli women) to investigate, in the interests of testing the authors' hypothesis about social change, role conflict, and anorexia. In this it is like other studies collected in this volume. Counts and Counts study more than 81 RVers; Kabeer 90 Bangladeshi Londoners; Verkuyten, de Jong, and Masson 11 residents of Rotterdam. But, despite the fact that this article resembles the others in studying a selected population of human subjects, it differs from them in important respects.

At a glance, you can see that the system of division and headings differs from those in the other articles. Here we find

Method
    Subjects
    Procedure
Results
Discussion

In the other articles, we find more complex and variable headings. Counts and Counts, for example, do use

Research Method

to head one section, but their other headings are qualitatively different:

They Speak With Many Voices: Alternative Versions of the RV Lifestyle
Equality, Community and the Good Life
Community and Reciprocity

One way of distinguishing between these two styles of headings is to say that the psychologists studying anorexia use ready-made headings: you will find these headings (or something very like them) over and over again in psychology journals, and in journals which publish research in the "hard" sciences. Beyond that distinction, we may note that, while the headings used by Counts and Counts not only title what follows but also present a guide to interpreting what follows ("you will find evidence of ideas of 'reciprocity' in what follows, and reciprocity will be related to 'community'"), the headings used by Apter et al. only tell you that you are entering a particular stage of the discussion.

And you will see that this non-interpretive stance is reflected in other features of the article. In some respects the "Results" and "Discussion" section of "Cultural Effects on Eating Disorders" resembles major sections of the other articles. Kabeer, for example, also systematically elicited response from her subjects, and transforms these responses in her article, presenting collated fragments of interviews. Similarly, Apter et al. transform the responses of their subjects, presenting eight Tables in the "Results" section. Both Kabeer and Apter et al. draw their readers' attention to these representations of responses. But Apter et al. do no more than describe overall statistical patterns in each of the small paragraphs that accompany the Tables. In other words, in the "Results" section they *refrain from interpreting* their findings. In your reading of "Results," you may find this restraint very pronounced: as you go through pages 334–340, you may find yourself struggling to calculate what all this adds up to, and you may be aware of the surface repetitiveness of these paragraphs. Although you are specifically guided in how to look at each Table, you get no help in constructing the overall picture — until the last sentence of the "Results" section, when you may have your own calculations confirmed: "The anoretics had significantly higher scores (in total eating pathology) than all the ethnic groups, $F = 5.19$, $p<.0001$, apart from the kibbutz subjects, again indicating the high proportion of disturbed eating attitudes among the kibbutz population" (340).

What motivates this interpretive restraint? Possibly, the separation of "Results" and "Discussion" in psychology, and in other disciplines "harder" than the social sciences, is a discursive replication of the separation of "facts" from speculation. "Results" are facts; "Discussion" is interpretation. So in the "Discussion" section you will find signs of inference and indeterminacy, as in these sentences from its first paragraph:

> The one factor that most clearly differentiated anorectics
> was the oral control factor — an indicator of impulsivity

and *presumably* of sexuality. This finding *suggests* that oral control *may be* the pivotal element in anorexia nervosa. (340, emphasis added)

Except for formulaic expressions of statistical probability, the "Results" section contains no such expressions of indeterminacy. This difference may represent, in psychology, a valued distinction between data and their interpretation. Perhaps not all disciplines are in a position to make such a clear distinction.

Still keeping in mind the resemblances between this article and others which investigate human groups, we might also observe differences in the representation of the relationship between the investigators and the objects of study. For example, we find in Counts and Counts' Method section, before we encounter report of informants' answers to questions, report of informants' attitude towards being asked questions.

- What element of "Cultural Effects on Eating Attitudes" compares to this part of the article on RVing? That is, where do you get an idea of the social relationship between investigators and objects of investigation?

In the "Procedure" section of "Method," Apter et al. describe the "EAT-26."

- Is there anything equivalent to this instrument of inquiry in Counts and Counts, Kabeer, and Verkuyten, de Jong and Masson? (Think carefully before saying "no.")

Finally, although the research presented by Apter et al. may seem a far cry from some articles in this volume which address feminist issues, from a certain perspective we could see it as a concerned with gender issues. It refers to social constructions of femaleness both in its hypothesis —

[adolescent girls most exposed to Western values but residing in affluent, non-Western cultural-ethnic settings] would likely suffer from acute conflict between Western expectations to perform successfully at work and be sexually attractive 'new-wave women' and their traditional role as nurturant wives and mothers (330-31)

— and in the interpretation of findings (340-43). Other researchers — Calhoun, Baber, Kabeer, Eckert — also refer to women's traditional roles, Kabeer including, as these writers do, "ethnic" dimensions to these roles.

- How do assumptions about these roles differ amongst these writers?

Cultural Effects on Eating Attitudes in Israeli Subpopulations and Hospitalized Anorectics

ALAN APTER
MOHAMMED ABU SHAH
IULIAN IANCU
Department of Child and Adolescent Psychiatry Geha Psychiatric Hospital

HENRY ABRAMOVITCH
Department of Behavioral Science Tel Aviv University

ABRAHAM WEIZMAN
SAMUEL TYANO
Department of Child and Adolescent Psychiatry Geha Psychiatric Hospital

ABSTRACT: We assessed eating attitudes and body image using Eating Attitudes Test-26 (EAT: Garner & Garfinkel, 1979) and a 17-item body image scale in Israeli Jewish female high school populations in five distinct residential settings (kibbutz, moshav, city, and 2 different boarding schools); in five ethnically distinct Arab female high school populations (Muslim, Christian, Druze, Circassian, and Bedouin); and in a group of hospitalized adolescent girls with anorexia nervosa. We hypothesized that the attitudes of the adolescent females most exposed to Western body shape ideals and simultaneously undergoing role conflict between traditional and modern images of the female role would most resemble attitudes of anorectics. This was partly supported by the findings. Ethnic differences also emerged in attitude toward food. All the Arab populations except the Circassian showed strong Western influences in the attitudes toward eating and body image and thus may well be prone to epidemics of anorexia and similar eating disorders in the near future. Kibbutz girls were most similar to the anorectic group.

upper & middle class adolescent

wealthy Western countries

publically visible

↑ in disorders in last 2 decades

ANOREXIA NERVOSA most often occurs in upper and middle-class adolescents and young women in affluent Western countries (Prince, 1985; Szmulker, 1985). In her recent review of the literature, Yates (1989) summarized the situation as follows: "The association of anorexia and class commences at age 15 and the incidence increases with economic strata. For these women, thinness and scrupulousness about food, eating and exercise become prime goals around which they may organize their lives."

Ballet dancers, models, gymnasts, and cheerleaders, who may serve as role models, are all the more likely to have an eating disorder (Garner & Garfinkel, 1980; Yates, 1989). Most clinicians and researchers agree that eating disorders have increased dramatically in the Western world over the past two decades as the fashionable figure has become thinner and more tubular (Szmulker, McCance, McCrone, & Hunter, 1986). Most Western surveys establish the prevalence of anorexia at about 1 of every 100 adolescent girls (Yates, 1989).

In non-Western countries, anorexia nervosa is relatively rare (Al-Issa, 1966; Dolan, Lacy, & Evans, 1990; El-Sarrag, 1968; Neki, 1973; Nwaefuna, 1981). This may be due to different attitudes toward beauty in those countries and cultures where plumpness is considered attractive and a symbol of feminine nurturance (Dolan, 1991; Nasser, 1986). The pressure on women to succeed outside the home, which has recently increased in the West (Russel, 1979), may not be a factor in other cultures. And in societies subjected to periodic food shortages, thinness is usually associated with low socioeconomic status and the corresponding inability to get enough to eat. Although such undernourished individuals may often resemble victims of anorexia, from an evolutionary perspective they appear to use an anorexia-like syndrome as an "adaptive emergency strategy of reproductive suppression" (Voland & Voland, 1989).

In contrast, in societies with a reliable oversupply of food, body ideals have undergone a radical transformation. There is a newly established association between thinness (in women) and level of education and vocational achievement (Sobal and Stunkard, 1989). Thinness symbolizes the feminine ideal, combining qualities of self-discipline, control, and sexual liberation with attractiveness and fashionability (Nasser, 1988a, 1988b).

adol. girls exposed to W. values in affluent non-W. ethnic settings w/ attitude towards anorectic

We hypothesized that adolescent girls most exposed to Western values but residing in affluent, non-Western culture-ethnic settings would have an attitude toward food similar to that of anorectics. These subjects would likely suffer from acute conflict between Western expectations to perform successfully at work and be sexually attractive "new-wave women" and their traditional roles as nurturant wives and mothers. We also hypothesized that adolescent girls residing in ethnic environments with little exposure to Western values would have a more complacent attitude toward food and would be less prone to eating disorders.

To test our hypothesis, we surveyed adolescent girls in 10 Israeli subpopulations, 5 Jewish and 5 non-Jewish, as well as a group of hospitalized anorectics deliberately selected from a wide ethnic and class range. The study was part of a series of surveys intended to examine attitudes to various problems related to mental health among the different populations living in Israel. Israel is a multicultural country, and psychiatrists here must be aware of sociocultural factors in psychopathology; it is also a country that provides unique opportunities for studying ethnic differences in relation to public health issues (Aviram & Levav, 1975).

We were especially interested in Arabic populations, which are rarely studied and generally considered to have low incidences of eating disorders (Al-Issa, 1966; El-Sarrag, 1968; Nasser, 1986, 1988a, 1988b). We assumed that the major risk factors for anorexia are emerging role conflict and cultural dissonance coupled with increasing economic affluence. We also hoped to gain insight into the sociocultural factors that form the background for the development of eating disorder epidemics. This knowledge may help in the determination of public health policy and in the establishment of preventative measures.

METHOD

Subjects

Adolescent schoolgirls ($N = 783$) between the ages of 15 and 18 years took part in the study in 1986. Five groups of Jewish girls and five groups of Arabic girls were assessed, as well as a group of girls suffering from anorexia nervosa. The Jewish groups were as follows:

1. High school students ($n = 67$) from Tel Aviv, Israel's largest city.

2. Students living on a <u>kibbutz</u> ($n = 33$), a communal settlement based originally on socialist principles, with no private ownership of property. In recent years, the kibbutz population has come to represent an elite society, showing high levels of achievement, especially with regard to standard of living and public services.

3. Students living on a <u>moshav</u> ($n = 26$), a rural settlement also dedicated to socialist principles but allowing private ownership of property.

4. Middle-class students ($n = 37$) attending a regular agricultural boarding school.

5. Students of Eastern European origin ($n = 107$) attending an agricultural boarding school for new immigrants.

The Arabic groups were as follows:

1. Muslim students ($n = 204$) from a <u>very small town</u>. Muslim Arabs in Israel are very conscious of their culture and religion and do not socialize with the Jewish population; most adhere to the Sunni rite.

2. Christian students ($n = 91$) from a <u>small</u> Christian <u>town</u>. The Christian society in Israel is somewhat closer to the Jewish one, compared with the Muslim settlements, although there remain sharp distinctions between Christian Arabs and Jews in many spheres of life.

3. Druze students ($n = 77$). The Druze live in villages in the Galilee and maintain excellent relations with the Jewish majority. They have, since 1957, constituted a separate Arabic-speaking minority. Most of the Druze are agriculturalists who preserve their traditional way of life. They pay homage to Jethro (Moses' father-in-law). The Druze take an active part in national political life and serve in the Israeli army.

4. Bedouin students ($n = 67$). The Bedouin are Arabic-speaking tribesmen of the Middle Eastern deserts. The subjects in our sample lived in <u>small</u> settlements in the Negev and attended a central high <u>school</u> run by the Israeli government. Thus, they differ from their nomadic grandparents and represent a society in transition.

332 APTER ET AL

5. Circassian students (n = 50). The Circassians, who are Sunni Muslims, emigrated to Israel from the Caucasus mountains in the vicinity of the Black Sea in the 1870s. They live in small villages in the Galilee, preserving their language and traditions. The men serve in the Israeli army.

Health records, including height and weight, were available for all Jewish and Arabic subjects. None had been diagnosed as suffering from an eating disorder. Complete confidentiality was guaranteed regarding the respondents' answers.

A third group consisted of 24 patients under active treatment for anorexia nervosa. The girls were at different stages of disease, but all were far from complete recovery. All met the DSM-III-R criteria (American Psychiatric Association, 1987) for anorexia nervosa.

Procedure

All subjects completed an abbreviated version of the 40-item Eating Attitudes Test (EAT-40) in addition to 17 questions, rated on a 3-point scale, dealing specifically with body image (Are your thighs too fat? Do your friends think you are fat?). The EAT-40 is an objective self-report measure that has been validated for use in Western populations (Garner & Garfinkel, 1979; Mann et al., 1983). It had been used to detect undiagnosed cases of anorexia nervosa in high-risk populations (Garner & Garfinkel, 1980), although some authors have reported a high false-positive rate with the test in college students (Carter and Moss, 1984). The EAT was proved valid for Arab university students in London (Nasser, 1986) and for Jewish Israelis (Iancu, 1990).

The shortened form of the EAT-40, the EAT-26, was used in the present study. The EAT-26 has been shown to be as valid as the original for clinical and research purposes (Garner & Garfinkel, 1980). It was translated into Hebrew and Arabic and then retranslated into English. This process was repeated several times, until the final translated version closely approximated the original English version.

In addition to a total score, the EAT-26 give three subscores: a dieting factor (I don't eat high-calorie food); a bulimia and food preoccupation factor; and an oral control factor. A cut-off score of 20/21 was used to distinguish between EAT-positive and EAT-negative subjects. The scores of all groups were examined for statistically significant differences by a one-way analysis of variance (ANOVA)

and a Scheffe pair-wise comparison. The body image factor score
was calculated by summing the positive answers to the items on
the questionnaire.

All rural subgroups represented the total population of 16-year-
olds in the particular settlement. In collaboration with the local
educational authorities, the subjects were told that they were participating in a survey of eating habits. The test was administered
and explained by the local school nurse who lived in the community. The urban students attended a school that is considered representative of the Tel Aviv catchment area.

RESULTS

Table 1 contains the age, height, and weight distributions of the
eleven subgroups. It also shows how much weight participants in
each subgroup desired to gain or lose. All the Arabic and Jewish

---

Table 1

Mean and (SD) Age, Height, and Weight Statistics of Israeli Subpopulations and Anorectics

Group	N	Age (yrs)	Height (cm)	Weight (kg)	Y (kg)
Jewish schoolgirls					
City	67	16.1 (0.05)	163 (4.41)	52.6 (1)	2.9 (0.8)
Kibbutz	33	16.3 (0.25)	162 (6.2)	51.4 (1.4)	3.7 (1)
Moshav	26	16.6 (0.16)	165 (8)	51.8 (1.4)	1.8 (1.2)
Boarding school	37	16.0 (0)	165 (6)	53.6 (1)	2.3 (0.8)
Youth immigration	107	16.0 (012)	160 (7.3)	50.4 (0.9)	2.1 (0.7)
Arabic schoolgirls					
Muslim	204	16.5 (0.07)	160 (8)	53.8 (0.5)	2.1 (0.4)
Druze	77	16.0 (0.1)	156 (7.1)	46.4 (0.7)	1.0 (0.6)
Bedouin	67	16.5 (0.12)	145 (10)	41.3 (1)	1.5 (1)
Christian	91	16.4 (0.15)	160 (9.5)	50.7 (0.9)	2.4 (0.7)
Circassian	50	16.7 (0.07)	160 (4.8)	45.4 (1)	1.1 (1)
Anorectics	24	16.8 (0.3)	160 (8.9)	40.4 (0.7)	-3.7 (0.9)
All groups	783	16.4 (0.06)	159 (8.5)	50.0 (0.3)	1.9 (0.3)

Note. Y = weight subjects desired to gain or lose.

Table 2

Eat-26 Scores of Israeli Subpopulations and Anorectics

Group	N	M	SD
Jewish schoolgirls			
City	67	10.8	1.2
Kibbutz	33	14.1	1.7
Moshav	26	11.7	1.4
Boarding school	37	10.2	1.5
Youth immigration	107	11.2	0.9
Arabic schoolgirls			
Muslim	204	13.0	0.7
Druze	77	11.7	1.2
Bedouin	67	13.1	1.1
Christian	91	11.6	0.9
Circassian	50	8.2	1
Anorectics	24	26.3	3.5
All groups	783	12.2	0.4

(handwritten annotations in margins: "standard deviation", "adds weight", "and a weight")

girls expressed the wish to lose weight. Only the anorectic girls wished to gain weight, probably because they were under treatment at the time.

Table 2 contains the mean total EAT-26 scores of all 11 subgroups. The scores ranged from 8.2 ± 1 in the Circassian subjects to 14.1 ± 1.7 in the kibbutz subjects. The anorectic patients had a mean of 26.3 ± 3.5. ANOVA results showed that the EAT-26 significantly differentiated between subgroups, $F = 3.61$, $p < .005$, and a pair-wise test showed that the anorectic group ($p < .05$) achieved significantly higher scores on the EAT-26 than the other groups did except for the kibbutz girls and the Muslim and Bedouin subjects, who did not differ from the anorectics.

Table 3 contains the percentage of EAT-positive (score > 20) subjects in each group. Again, the kibbutz group had the highest percentage (27.3%) and the Circassians the lowest (8%). Of the anorectics, 62.5% had EAT-positive scores. On the chi-square test, the kibbutz members had significantly more positive scores than the other healthy groups, X^2 (1, N = 783) = 4.30, p < .05.

Table 3

Percentage of Eat-Positive (Score > 20) Subjects in Israeli Subpopulations and Anorectics

Group	N	(%)
Jewish schoolgirls		
City	67	19.4
Kibbutz	33	27.3
Moshav	26	19.2
Boarding school	37	16.2
Youth immigration	107	16.8
Arabic schoolgirls		
Muslim	204	18.6
Druze	77	14.3
Bedouin	67	19.4
Christian	91	15.4
Circassian	50	8.0
Anorectics	24	62.5

Table 4

Eat-26 Dieting Factor Scores in Israeli Subpopulations and Anorectics

Group	N	M	SD
Jewish schoolgirls			
City	67	8.00	1.07
Kibbutz	33	11.39	1.50
Moshav	26	7.65	1.32
Boarding school	37	6.81	1.23
Youth immigration	107	7.76	0.75
Arabic schoolgirls			
Muslim	204	8.37	0.56
Druze	77	7.48	0.82
Bedouin	67	7.42	0.77
Christian	91	7.83	0.65
Circassian	50	4.38	0.91
Anorectics	24	13.33	2.24
All groups	783	7.95	0.2

Table 5

Eat-26 Bulimia and Food Preoccupation Factor Scores in Israeli Su-populations and Anorectics

Group	N	M	SD
Jewish schoolgirls			
City	67	0.80	0.15
Kibbutz	33	1.18	0.21
Moshav	26	0.84	0.27
Boarding school	37	1.32	0.32
Youth immigration	107	1.13	0.19
Arabic schoolgirls			
Muslim	204	1.50	0.17
Druze	77	1.08	0.27
Bedouin	67	1.64	0.28
Christian	91	1.06	0.23
Circassian	50	0.66	0.17
Anorectics	24	4.33	0.75
All groups	783	1.30	0.08

Table 4 contains the distribution of scores on the dieting factor of the EAT-26. The highest scores for the ethnic groups were shown by the kibbutz subjects (11.39 ± 1.5) and the lowest by the Circassians (4.38 ± 0.91). The anorectic girls had a mean score of 13.33 ± 2.24. ANOVA results showed the dieting factor to significantly distinguish among the subgroups, $F = 2.70$, $p < .005$. A pair-wise test showed that the Circassians had significantly lower scores ($p < .05$ level) that the kibbutz, Muslim, and anorectic individuals.

Table 5 contains the distribution of the bulimia and food preoccupation factor scores. Scores for ethnic groups ranged from 0.66 ± 0.17 for the Circassians to 1.64 ± 0.28 for the Bedouins. The anorectics had a mean score of 4.33 ± 0.75. ANOVA results showed that the bulimia-food preoccupation factor differentiated among the subgroups, $F = 3.82$, $p < .0001$, and a pair-wise comparison showed that the anorectics had significantly higher scores ($p < .05$) than all groups except Bedouins and Muslims; the Muslims scored significantly higher on this factor than the Circassians.

Table 6 contains the distribution of scores on the oral control factor across the groups. Scores ranged from 2.01 ± 0.34 for the

Table 6

Eat-26 Oral Control Factor Scores in Israeli Subpopulations and Anorectics

Group	N	M	SD
Jewish schoolgirls			
City	67	2.01	0.34
Kibbutz	33	1.54	0.39
Moshav	26	3.19	0.66
Boarding school	37	2.02	0.46
Youth immigration	107	2.20	0.25
Arabic schoolgirls			
Muslim	204	3.13	0.24
Druze	77	3.14	0.38
Bedouin	67	4.07	0.39
Christian	91	2.71	0.31
Circassian	50	3.12	0.37
Anorectics	24	8.66	1
All groups	783	2.99	0.12

Jewish city girls to 4.07 ± 0.39 for the Bedouin group. Anorectic patients had mean scores of 8.66 ± 1. ANOVA results showed this factor to significantly distinguish among subgroups, $F = 7.05$, $p < .0001$. The pair-wise comparison showed the following differences: The anorectic group had significantly higher scores than all the other groups ($p < .01$ for moshav members and Bedouins, $p < .001$ for all other groups); the Bedouin group had significantly higher scores than subjects from the city ($p < .01$), the kibbutz ($p < .001$), and the boarding school ($p < .01$).

Table 7 contains the distribution of the body image score across the groups. Scores in the ethnic populations ranged from 2.94 ± 0.37 in the Jewish city group to 8.21 ± 0.68 in the kibbutz group. The anorectics scored 13.29 ± 1.7. ANOVA results showed this scale to distinguish among subgroups, $F = 10.81$, $p < .0001$. The following pair-wise comparisons were significantly different, $p < .01$: The kibbutz girls had higher scores than Muslims and Circassians;

Table 7

Body Image Scores in Israeli Subpopulations and Anorectics

Group	N	M	SD
Jewish schoolgirls			
City	67	2.94	0.37
Kibbutz	33	8.21	0.68
Moshav	26	6.96	0.68
Boarding school	37	6.13	0.47
Youth immigration	107	6.73	0.47
Arabic schoolgirls			
Muslim	204	5.36	0.33
Druze	77	5.56	0.54
Bedouin	67	7.15	0.55
Christian	91	5.40	0.47
Circassian	50	4.26	0.53
Anorectics	24	13.29	1.70
All groups	783	5.90	0.17

Table 8

Total Eating Pathology Score (Eat-26 + Body Image Factor) in 10 Israeli Subpopulations and a Group of Anorectics

Group	N	M	SD
Jewish schoolgirls			
City	67	13.74	1.34
Kibbutz	33	22.33	2.19
Moshav	26	18.65	1.78
Boarding school	37	16.29	1.98
Youth immigration	107	17.82	1.22
Arabic schoolgirls			
Muslim	204	18.37	0.94
Druze	77	17.26	1.44
Bedouin	67	20.28	1.36
Christian	91	17.02	1.20
Circassian	50	12.42	1.31
Anorectics	24	39.62	4.99
All groups	783	18.14	0.47

the anorectics had higher scores than the boarding school group and the Muslims, Druze, Christians, and Circassians.

Table 8 contains the total eating pathology score derived from combining the EAT-26 and the body image test scores. The scores for ethnic groups ranged from 12.42 ± 1.31 in the Circassian subjects to 22.33 ± 2.19 in the kibbutz subjects. The anorectics scored 39.62 ± 4.99. The anorectics had significantly higher scores than all the ethnic groups, $F = 5.19$, $p < .0001$, apart from the kibbutz subjects, again indicating the high proportion of disturbed eating attitudes among the kibbutz population.

DISCUSSION

The results support the use of the EAT-26 for the detection (and primary prevention) of anorexia nervosa in cross-cultural contexts, although further validation is required (Button & Whitehouse, 1981; Leichner, Arnett, Rallo, Srikameswaran, & Vulcano, 1980; Toro, Castro, Garcia, Perez, & Cuesta, 1989; Vandereycken & Meerman, 1984). On all measures and subscales (EAT-positive, dieting factor, bulimia and food preoccupation, oral control, body image, and total eating pathology), the anorectic group scored highest, and in most cases significantly so, compared with the 10 healthy populations. The one factor that most clearly differentiated anorectics was the oral control factor — an indicator of impulsivity concerning oral gratification and presumably of sexuality. This finding suggests that oral control may be the pivotal element in anorexia nervosa.

We hypothesized that the ethnic subpopulations most exposed to Western values and body ideals — and therefore having the highest degree of internal conflict between traditional and modern female roles — would have the highest eating pathology scores, and that the groups with the least exposure and minimal female role stress would have the lowest overall scores. This prediction was borne out only for the kibbutz and Circassian adolescents, who had the highest and lowest scores, respectively, for total eating pathology, EAT-26, and most subscales.

Circassian adolescents live in small, relatively self-contained, endogenous communities (Eisenstadt, 1989); Krausz, 1980). Of all the groups in our sample, the Circassians most often maintain the traditional nurturing female roles as daughters / sisters / wives / mothers, subordinating career aspirations. As yet the mass media have had relatively little impact on the norms and values of village life. There is no recorded case of anorexia nervosa among this ethnic group. We suggest that their relative unconcern with dieting and thinness reflects their own preexisting feminine ideal.

In contrast, kibbutz adolescents are under the most severe role stress and conflict between being the traditional nurturant female and the self-disciplined, controlled, and sexually liberated "new woman" (Krausz, 1980; Spiro, 1980; Talmon, 1972; Tiger & Shepher, 1975). The kibbutz movement was founded on, and still formally embraces, an ideology of sexual equality and liberation of women from their traditional subordinate roles as dependent daughters and mothers. Women originally won this equality at the cost of becoming more masculine and doing men's work.

In recent years, however, a majority of women on the kibbutz have gravitated toward low-status traditional female occupations, such as kitchen service, day care, and education (Sprio, 1983; Tiger & Shepher, 1975), ostensibly to leave themselves more time for their own children, homes, and spouses. In a real sense, however, the role of housewife is not available to kibbutz women, who must first work up to eight hours daily at their kibbutz-approved occupations. In addition, the kibbutz, formerly fairly isolated from outside influences, is today very open to the mass media, foreign volunteers, and so on. At least one study has suggested that kibbutz women are more feminine than urban women, and for a woman to remain unmarried on a kibbutz is considered an almost unbearable tragedy (Spiro, 1980). The result is that the elite kibbutz woman, like her Western counterpart, is expected to succeed at work (if not necessarily in a career), as a homemaker, and as an attractive, sexually desirable object.

We suggest that this strong exposure to Western norms and a high level of female role stress are expressed in the high eating pathology scores, indicating that kibbutz adolescents, of all the Israeli groups studied, are most at risk of anorexia-bulimia type disorders. (There is a small amount of epidemiological evidence confirming that kibbutz members are highly over-represented among hospitalized anorectics.) This hypothesis is supported by a recent in-depth study of patients with eating disorders treated at a kibbutz clinic, where the referral rate has increased by 400% over the past 20 years (Kaffman & Sadeh, 1989).

The majority of the other subgroups fell midway between the two extreme groups and were not significantly different from each other. An unexpected result was the eating pathology scores of two of the Arab populations, Bedouins and village Muslims, whose scores were higher than the scores of all the other groups except kibbutz members.

The Bedouin group, in particular, most resembled the kibbutz group in total eating pathology and body image factor. Although Bedouins would be expected to fall squarely into the "periodic famine — plump female body ideal type," Bedouin society is currently undergoing rapid social change (George, 1973; Marx, 1973). In a single generation, most Israeli Bedouins have moved from an isolated, pastoral, nomadic lifestyle to a sedentary, urban existence in new towns in the south of the country. Bedouin women, formerly isolated, protected, and often veiled, are now entering mainstream Israeli society, studying in universities and working in white- and blue-collar occupations.

The Bedouin group differed significantly from the kibbutz group with regard to only one factor: oral control. Suprisingly, here, the kibbutz scores were lowest, and the Bedouin scores were highest ($p < .001$). Although it is difficult to interpret such a result in cross-cultural research, we suggest that different cultures have distinguishable patterns of food concerns and body image pathology. Oral control, as noted earlier, best distinguished anorectics from all the other subgroups, but specifically reflects a preoccupation with impulsivity. Given the buffet style of most kibbutz communal dining rooms, there is, in practice, an unlimited access to food. This social arrangement may serve to diminish the degree of oral control.

Moreover, it has been suggested that concern with food and dieting is reflective of a specific attitude toward sexuality, and this attitude is strikingly contrasted in kibbutz members and Bedouins. On the kibbutz, premarital sex and extramarital affairs are very common, and the divorce rate is high (Spiro, 1980; 1983). No special value is placed on virginity. In Bedouin society, virginity and sexual fidelity remain supreme values. Open violation of the family honor is rigorously condemned, to the point that a transgressor's life may be in serious danger.

Contrary to our prediction were the relatively high scores of the village Muslims. Unlike Bedouins, this population is undergoing only very gradual social change and is less exposed to Western ideals than most of the other groups. However, here, too, breakdown of the total eating pathology revealed a culturally specific concern with food. The Muslims had overall EAT-26 scores similar to those of the Bedouins, but they scored significantly lower on body image pathology and significantly higher on the dieting factor. The Muslim group had the highest average weight (53.8 kg), so that their concern with dieting may reveal a desire to lose weight rather than an insidious "slenderness culture." We suggest that village Muslims, despite their total eating pathology scores, are not at high risk for eating disorders, but this unexpected finding deserves further investigation.

In Arab village society, food has strong cultural significance; that is, missing a meal may be association with illicit love: "When food starts to disappear from a house, an affair is always expected" (Bar Gal, 1975; Hoffman, Hoffman, & Roohana, 1976; Muhawi & Kanaana, 1989). Although the association of food and affection is widespread, the link between food and illicit sexuality is apparently culture-specific. In traditional Jewish culture, there is a strong association between food and maternal affection, but not with sexuality.

Based on our findings using the EAT-26 and body image scale, healthy adolescents have attitudes toward food most resembling those of anorectics when they reside in affluent ethnic-cultural settings that are exposed to Western body ideals. This places them in a role of conflict between traditional and modern female images. Different ethnic groups, however, have culture-specific patterns of food concerns. The kibbutz population was most similar to the anorectics but scored very low on oral control; Bedouins scored very high on oral control; Muslims were concerned with dieting but not with body image. Nevertheless it is noteworthy that all the healthy adolescents in this study wished to lose weight.

We expect that the ever increasing infiltration of Western values of slimness, self-control, and female independence in non-Western societies will render these societies succeptible to epidemics of anorexia nervosa and similar eating disorders. The connotations of food, body shape, and femininity within a cultural context clearly require further study.

REFERENCES

Al-Issa, M. (1966). Psychiatry in Iraq. *British Journal of Psychiatry*, 112, 827-832.

American Psychiatric Association (1987). *Diagnostic and statistical manual of mental disorders* (3rd ed., rev.) Washington, DC: Author.

Aviram, U., & Levav, I. (1975). Psychiatric epidemiology in Israel: An analysis of community studies. *Acta Psychiatrica Scandinavica*, 52(5), 295-311.

Bar-Gal, Y. (1975). Changes in the structure of minority villages in Israel — Outlines and reasons. *Sociologia Ruralis*, 15(3), 173-188.

Button, E.J., & Whitehouse, A. (1981). Subclinical anorexia nervosa. *Psychobiological Medicine*, 11, 509-516.

Carter, P.I., & Moss, R.A. (1984). Screening for anorexia and bulimia nervosa in a college population. *ADD Behavior*, 9, 417-419.

Dolan, B.J. (1991). Cross-cultural aspects of anorexia nervosa and bulimia: A review. *International Journal of Eating Disorders*, 10, 67-78.

Dolan, B.J., Lacey, J.H., & Evans, H. (1990). Eating behavior and attitudes to weight and shape in British women from three ethnic groups. *British Journal of Psychiatry*, 157, 523-528.

Eisenstadt, S. (1989). *Israeli society* (2nd ed.). New York: Stockten.

El-Sarrag, A. (1968). Psychiatry in the northern Sudan: A study in comparative psychiatry. *British Journal of Psychiatry*, 114, 946-948.

Garner, D.M. & Garfinkel, P.E. (1979). The Eating Attitudes Test, an index of symptoms of anorexia nervosa. *Psychological Medicine*, 47, 483-491.

Garner, D.M. & Garfinkel, P.E. (1980). Sociocultural factors in the development of anorexia nervosa. *Psychological Medicine*, 10, 647-654.

George, A.R. (1973). Processes of sedentorization of nomads in Egypt, Israel and Syria: A comparison. *Geography*, 58(259), 161-165.

Hoffman, R., Hoffman, J.E., & Roohana, N. (1976). Young Arabs in Israel: Some aspects of a conflicted social identity. *Journal of the Society of Psychology*, 99(1): 75-86.

Iancu, I. (1990). *Validation of the EAT in Israel*. Unpublished doctoral dissertation, Sackler School of Medicine, Tel Aviv University, Israel.

Kaffman, M., & Sadeh, T. (1989). Anorexia nervosa in the kibbutz: Factors influencing the development of a monoideistic fixation. *International Journal of Eating Disorders*, 8, 33-53.

Krausz, E. (Ed). (1980). *Studies of Israeli society: Migration, ethnicity and community*. New Brunswick, NJ: Transaction Press.

Leichner, P., Arnett, J., Rallo, J.S., Srikameswaran, S., & Vulcano, B. (1980). An epidemiological study of maladaptive eating attitudes in a Canadian school age population. *International Journal of Eating Disorders*, 5(5), 969-982.

Mann, A.H., Wakeling, A., Wood, K., Monec, E., Dobbs, R., & Szmulker, G. (1983). Screening for abnormal eating attitudes and psychiatric morbidity in an unselected population of 15-year-old schoolgirls. *Psychological Medicine*, 13, 573-580.

Marx, E. (1973). Circumcision feasts among Negev Bedouins. *Journal of Middle Eastern Studies*, 4, 411-427.

Muhawi, I., & Kanaana, S. (1989). *Speak bird, speak again: Palestinian Arab folktales*. Berkeley, CA: University of California Press.

Nasser, M. (1986). Comparative study of the prevalence of abnormal eating attitudes among Arab female students at both London and Cairo universities. *Psychological Medicine, 16,* 621-625.

Nasser, M. (1988a). Culture and weight consciousness. *Journal of Psychosomatic Research, 32,* 573-577.

Nasser, M. (1988b). Eating disorders: The cultural dimension. *Social Psychiatry and Psychiatric Epidemiology*, 23, 184-187.

Neki, J.S. (1973). Psychiatry in South East Asia. *British Journal of Psychiatry*, 123, 257-269.

Nwaefuna, A. (1981). Amnorexia nervosa in a developing country. *British Journal of Psychiatry*, 138, 270-271.

Prince, R. (1985).1 The concept of culture-bound syndromes: Anorexia nervosa and brain fatigue. *Social Science and Medicine*, 21(2), 197-203.

Russel, G.F.M. (1979). Bulimia nervosa: An ominous variant of anorexia nervosa. *Psychological Medicine*, 9, 429-448.

Sobal, J., & Stunkard, A.J. (1989). Socioeconomic status and obesity: A review of the literature. *Psychological Bulletin*, 105, 260-276.

Spiro, M.E. (1980). *Gender and culture: Kibbutz women revisited*. New York: Schocken.

Spiro, M.E. (1983). Introduction: Thirty years of kibbutz research. In E. Krausz (Ed.), *The sociology of the kibbutz: Studies in Israeli society II*. New Brunswick, NJ: Transaction Books.

Szmulker, G.I. (1985). The epidemiology of anorexia nervosa and bulimia. *Journal of Psychiatric Research*, 19, 143-145.

Szmulker, G.I., McCance, C., McCrone, L., & Hunter D. (1986). Anorexia nervosa: A case register from Aberdeen. *Psychological Medicine*, 16, 49-58.

Talmon, Y. (1972). *Family and community in the kibbutz*. Cambridge, MA: Harvard University Press.

Tiger, L., & Shepher, J. (1975). *Women in the kibbutz*. New York: Harcourt Brace Jovanovich.

Toro, J., Castro, J., Garcia, M., Perez, P., & Cuesta, L. (1989). Eating attitudes, sociodemographic factors, and body shape evaluation in adolescence. *British Journal of Medical Psychology*, 62, 61-70.

Vandereycken, W., & Meerman, R. (1984). *Anorexia nervosa: Clinician's guide to treatment*. Berlin: de Gruyter.

Voland, E., & Voland, R. (1989). Evolutionary biology & psychiatry: the case of anorexia nervosa. *Etiology and Sociobiology*, 10, 223-240.

Yates, A. (1989). Current perspectives on the eating disorders: I. History, psychological and biological aspects. *Journal of American Academy of Child and Adolescent Psychiatry*, 19, 143-145.

12

Introduction

Leo R. Chavez's "The Power of Imagined Community: The Settlement of Undocumented Mexicans and Central Americans in the United States" is epistemologically complex: that is, it resorts to more than one technique for making knowledge. First, it invokes theory, principally Benedict Anderson's concept of the "imagined community." Anderson's explanations of how we get the idea that we belong to something that could be called a "nation" have been influential in the last decade in a number of scholarly disciplines. Anderson's work is, in turn, historically located by Chavez as a recent step in a long tradition of scholarly interest in what "community" is. For scholars, "community" is not a self-evident concept. Chavez sets this complex concept in the current context of human migration: what happens to "community" when large numbers of people leave their homes and go to new places?

Second, Chavez's research uses quantitative methods: large-scale surveys whose results are reported in five Tables. His concern for quantitative validity is reflected in his account (360) of the character and limits of the research population: for various reasons, his sample is not "random" but "snowball." And to his data he applies the analytic technique of "logistic regression" — a technique which, he argues, helps to achieve quantifiable interpretations of data which inherently tend to resist such interpretation.

But, third, he also uses knowledge-making methods that are qualitative: that is, local and specific rather than broad and general.

You will find (364-366) a mix of Tables and quotations from particular informants ("Hector Gomez" is one). So, in these sections at least, the article resembles on the one hand the "Findings" section of Apter et al. — an example of research in psychology — and on the other hand the extensive middle sections of Counts and Counts — an example of ethnography. (While Apter et al. provide no quotations from the young women they studied, Counts and Counts offer us no Tables.) Chavez, then, works at substantiating Anderson's concept on two empirical levels: statistical and ethnographic.

He also situates his work amongst other researchers on the settlement of Latin American immigrants in the United States, finding that "[l]ess attention has been paid to how perceiving themselves to be part of a local community influences immigrants' desire to stay in that community" (350) than to factors more typically regarded as influential. Especially, he observes deficiency in research that overemphasizes migrants' attachment to their place of origin, and that characterizes immigrant families as "perpetual outsiders" (355).

Chavez's ostensible reservations about this finding are that it is based on insufficient evidence (his own work, in contrast, involves 600 structured interviews and "scores" more unstructured interviews and encounters). But his criticisms are in fact more comprehensive than this. Chavez leads us to consider the serious political implications of assumptions about the outsider status of undocumented immigrants. (On our own, we might also wonder whether, in an intellectual climate like the present one, which nourishes interest in the "margins" and the "marginalized," the idea of "perpetual outsiders" could be very attractive, and could therefore be accepted too uncritically.)

As a researcher, Chavez investigates an area of modern life which he himself says has been a "hot" issue not just for researchers but for the public generally. He quotes politicians and commentators on immigration (356-357), and suggests that "some segments of the larger society may like to imagine undocumented immigrants to be rootless, unattached, and temporary residents in U.S. society ..." (374).

- Why is this image of the undocumented immigrant useful to "some segments" of political culture? What are the political implications of this view?

- How does this image of the migrant contribute to arguments supporting the North American Free Trade Agreement (NAFTA) ([357])?

Chavez devotes most of his attention to immigrants' imagination of community, inquiring into their perceptions of belonging to and participating in U.S. settings. But he also describes "the larger society" as "imagining" (374) — constructing an image of immigrants.

- How does the phenomenon of "imagined community" work when those who imagine focus not on themselves but on others?

Finally, consider the word "power" in the article's title: "The Power of the Imagined Community." It turns up again, in the article's last sentence, when Chavez gestures beyond immigrant groups in San Diego and Dallas, to global levels — "the many displaced and mobile populations in the world" (376).

- What is the "power" he is talking about? How does it work in relation to another form of power — the force of law, which denies certain residents status and makes them "illegal"?

As a last step, you might consider the connection between these "powers" and Chavez's summary of Anderson's ideas, which emphasize "deep, horizontal comradeship" and people's sense of "[sharing] equally in their fundamental membership in the community" (353).

The Power of the Imagined Community: The Settlement of Undocumented Mexicans and Central Americans in the United States

LEO R. CHAVEZ
University of California, Irvine

Using logistic regression, this article tests the relative importance of the "imagined community" on the intentions of undocumented immigrants to stay in the United States. The argument is that, everything else being equal, imagining oneself as part of a local community is a powerful influence on settlement. If, for whatever reason, an undocumented immigrant comes to this self-reflection, then he or she is likely to desire to stay in the community. The results clearly underscore the importance of feeling part of the community. Not only is the influence on the dependent variable statistically significant, but the odds ratio indicates that those who feel part of the local community are almost four times (Mexicans) or almost five times (Central Americans) as likely to intend to stay permanently in the United States as those who do not.

CONTEMPORARY LARGE-SCALE HUMAN migrations across national borders have affected every continent on the planet. Not surprisingly, anthropologists have sought to understand the significance of these movements for notions of community, nationalism, and identity. Anderson's (1983) notion of the "imagined community" has received particular attention in recent literature. The purposes of this article are to examine contemporary notions of community in relation to international migration; to suggest ethnographically how undocumented Mexicans and Central Americans in the group studied perceive their relationships to the communities in which they live; and finally, to test, using logistic regression, the relative importance of the imagined community on the intentions of undocumented immigrants to stay in the United States.

The settlement of undocumented immigrants in the United States is of broad academic and public interest (Piore 1986). Popularly called "illegal aliens," these undocumented immigrants to the United States often stay for relatively brief periods of time. Some, however, do settle and add to the existing population. Because undocumented immigrants are a clandestine population, making accurate estimates of their numbers is problematic. Despite these difficulties, some reasonable assessments of the number who settle in the United States are available.

The number of undocumented immigrants who settle permanently in the United States, rather than staying for a short time and then returning home, appears to be about the same at the end of the 1980s as it was at the beginning. Based on the 1980 Census, Passel and Woodrow (1984) estimated that between 200,000 and 300,000 undocumented immigrants settled in the United States each year. Later, they examined data from the Current Population Survey and estimated that, during the late 1980s, about 200,000 undocumented immigrants settled annually in the United States (Woodrow and Passel 1990:57). The similarity between the two estimates suggests that the monumental 1986 immigration law (the Immigration Reform and Control Act), which was designed to stem the flow of undocumented immigrants, had little effect on the number who settle in the United States each year (U.S. House of Representatives 1986).

Studies among Latin American immigrants to the United States suggest that settlement is influenced by a number of factors, including length of stay in the United States, family formation, network development, work, and changing gender roles (Browning and Rodriguez 1982; Chavez 1985, 1988; Chavez, Flores, and Lopez-Garza 1990; Lamphere 1987; Marmora 1988; Massey 1987; Massey et al. 1987; Melville 1978; Montes and Garcia Vasquez 1988; Papademetriou and DiMarzio 1986; Pessar 1982, 1986; Rodriguez 1987). Less attention has been paid to how perceiving themselves to be part of a local community influences immigrants' desire to stay in that community. The argument made here is that, in addition to the factors typically used to explain settlement, imagining oneself as part of a local community also has a powerful influence on settlement. If, for whatever reason, an undocumented immigrant comes to this self-perception, then he or she is likely to desire to stay in the community. These assertions are tested below. But first, what directions have anthropological notions of community taken that help us to understand international migration?

Classical theorists wrestled with the notion of community, particularly the forces that hold together complex societies. For Marx (1967[1867]), the community or society was the arena within which interest groups, defined by their relationship to the means of production, competed. History was tantamount to the struggle for power among these interest groups or classes, and society was in a constant state of tension as a result of the competition. For Durkheim (1984[1893]), on the other hand, complex societies developed their solidarity precisely because of the division of labor within their social and economic systems. The mutual interdependence of individuals meant they had to rely on the skills and abilities of others in the society, which increased social solidarity and cohesion. For Weber (1978[1947], the community or society was the locus of expanding bureaucratic power in place of decreasing individual autonomy. But for Weber (1978[1947]:40), "community" itself refers simply to "a subjective feeling of the parties, whether affectual or traditional, that they belong together," which Brow (1990:1) argues combines both a feeling of solidarity and an understanding of shared identity.

Whether or not we emphasize class conflict, solidarity, or bureaucratic power, or even accept that all three play some role in understanding communities, community members have something in common; they share membership in the corporate group. Early anthropological work on tribal societies, the "classic" ethnographies of Malinowski (1961[1922]), Evans-Pritchard (1972[1940]), and others, were concerned with issues of social solidarity and village life, social structure, and organization. Tribal, lineage, and clan memberships were of paramount interest. It was Redfield (1956) who, while perhaps not the first anthropologist to examine the concept of community, nevertheless brought the notion of the "little community" into full anthropological gaze.

Redfield was particularly suited to channel attention to communities, rather than tribes or lineages, because of his interest in the lives of peasants in a class-stratified society and his relationship to the Chicago "School of Sociology," where Robert Park, Louis Wirth, and their colleagues raised questions about the nature of urban life. Redfield chose as his task to understand not life in large, heterogeneous urban centers but life in "little communities" characterized by their "distinctiveness, smallness, homogeneity, and all-providing self-sufficiency" (Redfield 1956:4). In the type of little communities Redfield was interested in, community membership was a given, something "felt by everyone who is brought up in it and as a part of it" (Redfield 1956:10). Because the intellectual territory he staked out was the polar opposite of that focused on by his sociological colleagues in Chicago, Redfield was less concerned with the contested nature of community membership in more heterogeneous communities. The theoretical issues concerning community membership raised by the Chicago sociologists, however, have also influenced contemporary anthropology.

Park and his colleagues raised fundamental questions concerning community membership and social marginality. Park's work on "migration and the marginal man" focused on the question of community membership, and he emphasized two points of interest here. First, "Migration as a social phenomenon must be studied not merely in its grosser effects, as manifested in changes in custom and in the mores, but it may be envisaged in its subjective aspects as manifested in the changed type of personality it produces" (Park 1969[1928]:136). Second, Park, building on the work of Georg Simmel, viewed migrants as "strangers" who enter into a new community, where their experiences change them. Moreover, "The stranger stays, but he is not settled. He is a potential wanderer" (Park 1969:137).

Following Park, Siu (1987[1953]) examined the lives of Chinese immigrants in Chicago in the 1930s. He delineated the concept of the "sojourner" as a way to understand the personal struggle immigrants engage in as they constantly reevaluate whether to stay in their new communities or return to their communities of origin. The tension between the two choices forces immigrants to reflect on their personal goals, the circumstances of their lives, their family values and social relationships, and how the larger society perceives them. The sojourner, for Siu, is the immigrant who maintains an orientation to the home country. He or she has little contact with the larger society and lives for the moment of return migration. In contrast, settlers were those whose orientation had shifted from their places of origin to their new communities. Even if they ultimately desired to return to their place of origin late in life, or to be buried there after death, settlers went about the business of establishing their lives in their new communities.

Since the 1950s, the notion of community has become one of those all-encompassing concepts in anthropology. "Community studies" are driven by the idea, dating back to Redfield, that we can understand communities in holistic terms (Arensberg and

Kimball 1965). The subfield of human anthropology, drawing on both Redfield and the Chicago School, has produced a wealth of interesting research on communities around the world (Hannerz 1980). The exposition of this vast array of research would take us well beyond the purposes of this discussion.

Suffice it to say that despite all the work that has been carried out on communities, the question still remains: What underlies a sense of community? Anderson (1983) examined this question and suggested that communities are "imagined." Members of modern nations cannot possibly know all their fellow-members, and yet "in the minds of each lives the image of their communion. . . . It is imagined as a *community* because, regardless of the actual inequality and exploitation that may prevail in each, the nation is always conceived as a deep, horizontal comradeship" (Anderson 1983:15-16). In this view, members of a community internalize an image of the community not as a group of anomic individuals but as interconnected members who share equally in their fundamental membership in the community. The internalization of the image and a sense of connectedness to the community is as important as actual physical presence in the community.

Such a view allows for a redefinition of *community*. Since it is imagined, a sense of community is not limited to a specific geographic locale (Gupta and Ferguson 1992). Immigrants are said to live in "binational communities" (Baca and Bryan 1980), "extended communities" (Whiteford 1979), "transnational communities" in "hyperspace" (Rouse 1991), and "transnational families" (Chavez 1992). These concepts highlight the connections migrants maintain with life in their home communities; living dislocated on the other side of a political border does not necessarily mean withdrawing from community life or membership.

As accurate as these characterizations may be, we must be careful to also capture the changes migrants experience as a result of life in a new community. By overemphasizing migrants' linkages to their home communities, we run the risk of underemphasizing the changes they undergo and the linkages, both perceived and material, that they develop to their new communities. Mobile people are less fixed and static than one would think from the image often presented in anthropological research. They change geographic locations, change identities, and defy limited characterizations of which communities they belong to. As Appadurai (1991:93) has noted, the contemporary landscape consists of deterritorialized "ethnoscapes" in which "the homeland is partly invented, existing only in the imagination of the deterritorialized groups." Gupta and Ferguson (1992) make this point well in "Beyond 'Culture'":

> But today, the rapidly expanding and quickening mobility of people combines with the refusal of cultural products and practices to "stay put" to give a profound sense of loss of territorial roots, of an erosion of the cultural distinctiveness of places, and of ferment in anthropological theory. The apparent deterritorialization of identity that accompanies such processes has made Clifford's question (1988:275) a key one for recent anthropological inquiry: "What does it mean, at the end of the twentieth century, to speak . . . of a 'native land'? What processes rather than essences are involved in present experiences of cultural identity?" [1992:9]

Their point is also well taken in regard to the concept of community. A migrant is not limited to membership in one community; sentiments and connections for one community do not categorically restrict feelings of membership in another. The desire for discrete categories of community membership is a product of academic needs, I suspect, rather than the ambiguous, changing, and pragmatic perceptions of migrants themselves.

Anthropologists — and others examining international labor migration — who do not appreciate the ability of migrants to develop feelings of belonging to multiple communities run the risk of over-emphasizing the view that migrants can maintain allegiance to only one community, the community of origin. This point is perhaps best made through example. Although many examples exist, a recent example was presented by Rouse (1991), who carried out ethnographic research among immigrants from the Mexican community of Aguililla living in Redwood City, California. In developing the notion of "transnational communities," Rouse presents a novel challenge to spatial images, highlighting the social nature of postmodern space. He points out that members of a "transnational migrant circuit" can be part of two communities simultaneously. However, he argues that migration is "principally a circular process in which people remain oriented to the places from which they have come." In other words, Rouse posits that Mexican immigrants in the United States are essentially "sojourners," using Siu's conceptualization.

Rouse's argument stands on the following points. First, "various factors have discouraged most Mexicans from staying permanently [in the United States]. In the case of Aguilillans, their cultural emphasis on creating and maintaining independent operations has led them to have deep-seated reservations about many aspects of life in the United States, prominent among them the obligation of proletarian workers to submit to the constant regulation of supervisors and the clock" (1991:13). As a result, he argues, Mexican immigrants "send their children back to Mexico to complete their education" (1991:14).

Unfortunately, Rouse presents very little supporting evidence for these arguments. For example, it is not clear how many Mexicans he interviewed and what proportion actually sent their children back to Mexico for education. That this is probably not a widespread phenomenon is suggested by the large numbers of Mexican immigrant children in public schools in California and elsewhere.

Rouse's argument that Mexican immigrants send their children to Mexico for education reinforces the perception that Mexican immigrant families are sojourners, and because of their orientation "back home" they remain perpetual outsiders. Although his argument is couched in the discourse of contemporary theory, Rouse's characterization of Mexican immigrants is not new. Rather, the idea that Mexicans are tied to their families and communities in Mexico, that they are "homing pigeons" who have no desire to become "real" members of U.S. society, has had a wide currency for most of this century. For example, this view was clearly and explicitly expressed by the 1911 Dillingham Commission on immigration issues, where it was argued that Mexicans made for the ideal labor force because of their supposed "homing pigeon" mentality (Portes and Bach 1985:80). And yet, may Mexican immigrants did stay and settle in the United States during the first two decades of this century.

Moreover, while much contemporary Mexican migration is circular, as Rouse and others assert, many Mexican migrants, including undocumented immigrants, do settle in the United States, as the data provided above suggest. And while many Mexican immigrants retain ties with their home families and communities, this does not necessarily undermine their experiences in their new communities, experiences that may isolate them from the larger society or lead to a change, sometimes well thought out and other times unconscious, in their orientation from sojourners to settlers. Because of various experiences, some immigrants may even develop feelings of belonging to their local communities, which does not necessarily imply a loss of sentiment for a geographically distant community.

Ultimately, to generalize from interviews with some members of one community that Mexican immigrants remain static in orientation because they retain significant linkages to their home communities is not convincing. And yet, such conclusions follow from an initial assumption that immigrants cannot develop a sense of belonging to more than one community.

In contrast to such a restricted notion of community membership, I would assert that undocumented immigrants can have multiple senses of community membership. In particular, I argue that undocumented Mexicans and Central Americans can, and often do, develop social linkages, cultural sentiments, and economic ties that result in many of them imagining themselves to be part of their communities in the United States (Chavez 1991). And interestingly enough, this imagined belonging does not necessarily include a profound sense of shared identity with the larger society; the imagined community is not Redfield's "little community."

UNDOCUMENTED IMMIGRANTS AND AMERICAN SOCIETY

Immigration tests the limits of Anderson's notion of the imagined community. Immigrants, as newcomers to a community and society, may not readily be imagined to be part of the community by those already living there, nor is shared identity necessarily extended to them. In fact, they are often viewed as outsiders, strangers, aliens, and even a threat to the well-being of the community and larger society. Undocumented immigrants, in particular, are often characterized as a drain on public resources (health, education, welfare, police, etc.) as displacing citizen workers from jobs, and as having a deteriorative affect on American culture (Chavez 1986; Cornelius 1980). The comments of the exgovernor of Colorado, Richard Lamm, and Gary Imhoff are illustrative of such views:

At today's massive levels, immigration has had major negative consequences — economic, social, and demographic — that overwhelm its advantages. . . . To solve the immigration crisis, we Americans have to face our limitations. We have to face the necessity of passing laws to restrict immigration and the necessity of enforcing those laws. If we fail to do so, we shall leave a legacy of strife, violence, and joblessness to our children. [Lamm and Imhoff 1985:3]

As an issue of concern for the American public, immigration rarely goes cold; rather, it simmers most of the time and boils over occasionally, typically around periods of economic downturn (Simon 1985). In 1992, the "immigration problem" was hot. In a time of entrenched economic recession and rising unemployment rates, as well as a presidential election year, it is not surprising that Americans were asked to "rethink immigration" (Brimelow 1992). Not only was it suggested that we again take steps to limit immigration but the underlying desire was for many of those already here, especially undocumented immigrants, to return to their countries of origin.

Blaming immigrants for many of our social problems has contributed to anti-immigrant positions. In California, the governor blamed immigrants for the state's economic problems, fueling public sentiment "to narrow the gates to the Golden State" (Reinhold 1991:A1). At the national level, Pat Buchanan, a 1992 Republican presidential candidate, regularly cited immigration as one of our biggest problems (*Newsweek* 1992:33). In particular, Buchanan has warned that undocumented immigration puts the United States at risk of "not being a nation anymore" (Jehl 1992:A1). Such rhetoric resembles past anti-immigrant discourse, which placed immigration high on the list of threats to national security (Cornelius 1980).

Some pundits have also blamed Latin American immigrants for the riots that ravaged Los Angeles after the acquittal of the police officers accused of beating Rodney King. As two columnists in the *Los Angeles Times* argued:

> Weary conservatives and liberals have no shortage of explanations for the devastating Los Angeles riots. Yet a major factor has escaped serious discussion. It is immigration, currently running at unprecedented levels, that exacerbates the economic and social forces behind the riots. [Graham and Beck 1992:B11]

On the other hand, recent events suggest that Mexico and Central America may be on the precipice of a period of relative stabilization and economic growth. Mexico's gross domestic product (GNP) reached its highest level in ten years in the first quarter of 1992, and investment in Mexico is on the upswing, a pattern sure to be given even greater impetus as a result of the signing of the North American Free Trade Agreement (NAFTA) (El Financiero 1992:1). One of the implicit arguments for NAFTA is the possible affect it would have on keeping Mexicans in Mexico and luring Mexican emigrants back home.

In El Salvador, the government and rebel forces have reached an historic agreement to work toward peace. Nicaragua and Guatemala have experienced democratic elections. Although it is perhaps too early to predict a genuine period of peace and stability in the region, changes are occurring that may reduce the pressures for out-migration as well as the barriers to possible return migration. As one scholar has noted: "Hundreds of thousands of migrants — some refugees, some illegally abroad, and some now with resident status elsewhere — will be seeking to return to their home countries [in Central America] as the strife of the 1980s gives way to genuine peace in the 1990s" (Palmer 1992; see also Diaz-Briquets 1989).

The predictive validity of these views is dubious. However, the perspectives of both those who would like to see undocumented immigrants leave and those who believe conditions "back home" will lure undocumented immigrants into returning miss an important factor: undocumented immigrants themselves may view things differently. Even though they may have emigrated for specific economic or political reasons, neither of which may have entailed settling, their perceptions are subject to change.

Let me provide an example of what I am asserting. I raised this issue of return migration at a meeting a Salvadoran community group called to discuss the options and strategies available to Salvadorans who had applied for Temporary Protected Status (TPS) once the original TPS time period had terminated. After the meeting, I asked a Salvadoran who had been in Southern California for about seven years if he thought the peace negotiations would mean that he and others would be returning to El Salvador. He replied, "I don't think so. We are here now. Too much has changed. Most of us will stay."

His response underscored the issue of concern here: What can we learn from the experiences of undocumented Mexicans and Central Americans in the United States that will help us to understand why some might choose to settle in this country rather than return to their countries of origin?

RESEARCH AMONG UNDOCUMENTED IMMIGRANTS

The research reported on here focused on the San Diego area, where the economy is based on a mixture of tourism, the aerospace industry, computer-related businesses, and agriculture. Latinos, or individuals of Spanish origin as designated by the U.S. Census Bureau, accounted for 14.8 percent of the county's 1.8 million inhabitants in 1980 and 20 percent of the 2,498,016 inhabitants in 1990. Among Latinos, persons of Mexican origin were the largest single group, comprising 12 percent of the population in 1980 and 17.4 percent in 1990. The 1990 census counted 64,870 Latinos other than of Mexican descent, of which 9,062 were from Central America (U.S. Bureau of the Census 1984:6-1206, 1990, 1991). Of course, these figures do not include those who were missed by census-takers. About 50,000 undocumented immigrants were counted in the 1980 census, of which about 34,000 (68 percent) were from Mexico (Passel 1985:18).

During the summer of 1986, I, along with some research assistants, interviewed close to 300 undocumented immigrants in the San Diego area, about half of whom were from Central America. Interviews followed a set schedule, combining closed questions, for which answers are anticipated, with open-ended ones. Most closed questions were followed by open-ended questions that would give the interviewee an opportunity to explain his or her answer. (A typical open-ended question was "Why do you believe that?") Responses to open-ended questions were recorded verbatim, which resulted in a large number of qualitative data. This method provided for a much greater depth of understanding to be brought to bear on the responses than would a standard survey.

For comparative purposes, the same structured interview was used in Dallas, Texas, with about three hundred interviewees, about half of them Mexican and half, Central American. Dallas is comparable to San Diego in size and ethnic breakdown, and it too has experienced significant levels of immigration.

All of the interviews were conducted in Spanish in the safety of the interviewee's home or in a location where the interviewee felt comfortable. Before each interview we carefully explained the purpose of the research and the precautions taken to protect the informant. In order to ensure anonymity, the interviewee's names, addresses, and phone numbers were not recorded. The interviews averaged an hour in duration, but two-hour interviews were not uncommon; if the interviewee enjoyed talking, the interview would take even longer.

During and after 1986, I personally conducted scores of in-depth, unstructured interviews with undocumented immigrants living throughout San Diego county. Informal interviews with undocumented immigrants did not follow a schedule, but covered similar questions and were tape-recorded when possible. Many informal discussions also took place in completely social situations in which I participated. These interviews and discussions provided me with additional ethnographic information to be used in gauging the reliability of the responses to the structured interview schedule.

Because of the clandestine nature of the population, which does not allow for the development of a known population from which to draw a random sample, undocumented interviewees were found using a "snowball" sampling technique (Biernacki and Waldorf 1981; Cornelius 1982). This technique uses the informant's own kinship and friendship networks as the basis for drawing a sample. A number of initial contacts are made with as many undocumented immigrants as possible, in as many different settings as possible. These people are then interviewed and asked to introduce the interviewer to a relative or friend who might be willing to participate in the study. This method, although time-consuming, helps to develop a measure of rapport, since contact is made through an established and trusted personal relation.

Because snowball sampling is based on social networks, it tends to produce a sample biased toward individuals who have lived in the United States for a relatively long time. I did not view this inherent bias as a detriment, since a key objective of my research was to examine the factors leading to settlement in the United States. In line with this objective, interviewees had to have lived in the United States for at least one and a half years to participate in the survey. Informal interviews included more recent arrivals.

As is the case with most anthropological samples that do not rely on a strict random sample, the methodology employed here allows for results that provide insight into this group of interviewees' perceptions and behaviors only. I do not claim to speak about undocumented immigrants in general. Any statistical tests presented here must be viewed as suggestive only — as hypothesis generating. Despite such limitations, I believe that the data examined here contribute important information on otherwise clandestine populations, and help to provide data against which other case studies can be compared.

CHARACTERISTICS OF THE INTERVIEWEES

In San Diego, 146 Mexicans and 92 Salvadorans were interviewed, as well as 24 Hondurans, 15 Nicaraguans, 11 Guatemalans, and 3 Costa Ricans. In Dallas, 154 Mexicans and 86 Salvadorans were interviewed, along with 47 Guatemalans, 6 Hondurans, 6 Nicara-

Table 1

Characteristics of Interviewees

Characteristic (median)	San Diego			Dallas		
	Mexicans (N—146)	Salvadorans (N—92)	Other Central Americans (N—53)	Mexicans (N—154)	Salvadorans (N—86)	Other Central Americans (N—60)
Age	30	30	36	33	30	35
Range	18–56	17–69	19–57	16–60	17–63	18–56
Years of schooling	7	8	7	6	6	7
Range	0–18	0–16	0–14	0–19	0–19	3–14
Years in U.S.	4	3	2	9	4	4
Range	1.5–30	1.5–16	1.5–11	1.5–20	2–13	1.5–10
Hourly wage ($)	5.00	4.50	4.37	5.50	4.98	5.00
Range ($)	2.00–15.00	2.50–8.70	1.50–11.40	3.35–12.00	2.00–8.50	2.50–11.00
Monthly family earnings[a] ($)	1,031	1,072	1,000	1,186	900	1,013
% female interviewees	39.6	39.1	26.4	52.6	25.6	35.0

[a] Includes earnings of both spouses, if applicable.

guans, and 1 Costa Rican. In the tables that follow, Salvadorans are examined separately from the other Central Americans, who are lumped together because of their small numbers.

As Table 1 indicates, Mexicans in San Diego and Dallas were similar in age and education. Mexicans in Dallas, however, had been in the United States for a much longer period of time, and earned about fifty cents more an hour. Salvadorans and other Central Americans had similar socioeconomic characteristics, with little difference between those in San Diego and Dallas. Salvadorans in San Diego had a median of 8 years of schooling, compared to 6 for Salvadorans in Dallas, whereas other Central Americans had a median of 7 years in both places. Salvadorans and other Central Americans in Dallas had a median of 4 years in the United States, compared to 3 years and 2 years for Salvadorans and other Central Americans, respectively, in San Diego. The median age of Salvadorans in both San Diego and Dallas was 30 years, and that of other Central Americans in both places was similar. Central Americans in Dallas earned slightly more than those in San Diego, but they had been in the country longer. Monthly family income includes the earnings of both spouses.

The growing interest in differences between politically motivated migrants and economically motivated migrants raises questions about the relationship between such motivations and residence intentions (Pedraza-Bailey 1985). Undocumented immigrants from El Salvador, Nicaragua, Guatemala, and Honduras living in San Diego migrated for many reasons, some of which sound similar to those of Mexican immigrants I have interviewed (Chavez 1988, 1991). Few Central Americans, however, had the long family histories of migration common to many Mexican immigrants (Chavez 1992).

Table 2

Central American interviewees citing political reasons for migrating.

| | San Diego | | Dallas | |
Country Of Origin	N	%	N	%
El Salvador	92	65.2	86	60.5
Honduras	24	20.8	6	0
Nicaragua	15	60.0	6	83.3
Guatemala	11	54.5	47	6.4
Costa Rica	3	33.3	1	100.0
Total	145	55.9	146	41.8

Table 2 shows the proportion of Central Americans who mentioned political reasons for migrating to the United States. The question was open-ended, so they could respond in any way they desired. A person could cite more than one reason, but if at least one of the reasons for leaving was related to political conflict and turmoil then the person is listed here as having a political motive for migrating. Most of the Salvadorans, Guatemalans, and Nicaraguans cited reasons for coming to the United States that included references to political turmoil their countries were experiencing.

Political motives among the undocumented Central Americans included a general fear that their lives were in danger. They were concerned about being caught in a political, and very real, cross fire. According to one Salvadoran woman, "There is much danger because of the rebels and the army." A Salvadoran man added, "Because of the conflict in El Salvador, there's no respect for the life of others." Others linked the disruption of the economy with the political turmoil their countries were experiencing. The dangers inherent in the political conflicts caused some of the people I interviewed to feel a great deal of anxiety for their children's safety. And then, association with a political faction or the government placed some people in politically sensitive situations.

A note on indigenous groups in the sample: Oaxacan Indians often worked as temporary agricultural laborers in Northern San Diego County. However, network sampling is biased against such transient migrants, and they were not interviewed in this study. In earlier work, I have specifically targeted fieldworkers and interviewed Oaxacan Indians (Chavez 1992). Ethnic Guatemalan Indians have settled in Houston, but were not a significant part of the Latino population of Dallas (Rodriguez 1987). As a result, none of the interviewees in the sample discussed here indicated that they spoke an indigenous language at home in the United States. The interviewees were predominantly Mestizo members of their national cultures.

IMMIGRANTS VIEWS OF BELONGING TO THE LOCAL COMMUNITY

Obviously, it is difficult to ask people if they imagine themselves to be part of a community. Anderson was trying to get at perceptions about community membership that are taken for granted, and yet reflect the notion of belonging to some social grouping "out there" that is intuitively known as the "community" and extending that sense of belonging to others who also belong. To try to elicit interviewees' perceptions in this area, we asked a number

Table 3

Frequencies on variables used in logistic regression

Variable	VALUE	MEXICANS (%)	CENTRAL AMERICANS (%)
Intention To Stay Permanently in the United States			
Yes	0 —	34.5	53.6
No	1 —	65.5	46.4
Monthly family Income			
less than $800 a month	0 —	27.1	31.8
$801–$1,289 a month	1 —	35.0	36.1
$1,290 or more a month	2 —	37.9	32.1
Education			
0 to 5 years of school	0 —	34.1	26.6
6 to 8 years of school	1 —	33.3	33.5
9 or more years of school	2 —	32.6	39.9
Years in the United States			
3 years or less	0 —	29.2	54.8
more than 3 years	1 —	70.8	45.2
Spouse and/or children in the United States			
No	0 —	45.0	54.3
Yes	1 —	55.0	45.7
Relatives Live Nearby			
No	0 —	33.2	42.2
Yes	1 —	66.8	57.8
Location			
Dallas	0 —	51.3	50.2
San Diego	1 —	48.7	49.8
Politically Motivated Migration			
No	0 —	NA	51.2
Yes	1 —	NA	61.2
Place of Origin Other Central			
American country	0 —	NA	38.8
El Salvador	1 —	NA	61.2
Sex			
Male	0 —	53.7	68.0
Female	1 —	46.3	32.0
Feels Part Of The Community			
No	0 —	39.7	52.1
Yes	1 —	60.3	47.9

Table 4

Logistic regression, undocumented Mexicans' intention to stay permanently in the United States as dependent variable

	MODEL 1[b]			MODEL 2[c]		
	β	SE	OR	β	SE	OR
Monthly family salary						
Less than $800						
$801–$1,289	.1712	(.4438)	1.1868	.0955	(.4709)	1.1002
$1,290 or more	-.4534	(.5033)	.6354	-.6723	(.5274)	.5105
Education						
0–5 years						
6–8 years	-.6450	(.4185)	.5245	-.4347	(.4414)	.6455
9 years or more	-.1862	(.4285)	.8301	-.5082	(.4526)	.6016
Years in U.S.						
3 years or less						
more than 3 years	.7680*	(.3386)	2.1554	.7077*	(.3587)	2.1613
Spouse and/or children in u.s.						
no						
yes	.9928*	(.4008)	2.6987	.8795*	(.4158)	2.4098
Relatives live nearby						
no						
yes	.2963	(.3515)	1.3449	.3280	(.3765)	1.3882
Location						
Dallas						
San Diego	-1.2337***	(.3494)	.2912	-1.1696**	(.3715)	.3105
Politically motivated migration						
No	NA					
Yes						
Place of origin						
Other Central Amer. country	NA					
El Salvador	NA					
Sex						
Male						
Female	.7114*	(.3412)	2.0368	.4924	(.3583)	1.6362
Feels part of the community						
Yes					1.3471***	(.3694)	3.8464

[a] β = Beta: SE = standard error: OR = odds ratio. [b] Summary statistics for Model 1: Model chi-square = 65.510 (p < .001), degrees of freedom = 9, classification table = 76.17%, N = 235.

[c] For Model 2: Model chi-square = 76.518 (p < .001), degrees of freedom = 10, classification table = 78.48%, N = 223.   * p < .05   ** p < .01   *** p < .001

Table 5

Logistic regression, undocumented Central Americans' intention to stay permanently in the United States as dependent variable. [a]

	MODEL 1 [b]			MODEL 2 [c]		
	β	SE	OR	β	SE	OR
Monthly family salary						
less than $800						
$801-$1,289	.7265	(.3742)	2.0678	.5717	(.3393)	1.7713
$1,290 or more	1.2760**	(.4481)	3.5822	.9495*	(.4631)	2.5845
Education						
0-5 years						
6-8 years	-.0543	(.3712)	.9472	-.2727	(.3982)	.7613
9 years or more	-.0461	(.3702)	.9550	-.3523	(.3983)	.7031
Years in u.s.						
3 years or less						
More than 3 years	.9953*	(.3123)	2.7056	.8734**	(.3232)	2.3950
Spouse and/or children in u.s.						
No						
Yes	.1613	(.3450)	1.1751	.4904	(.3692)	1.6330
Relatives live nearby						
No						
Yes	-.2969	(.3125)	.7431	-.1846	(.3325)	.8314
Location						
Dallas						
San Diego	.9717**	(.3295)	2.6423	.7262*	(.3523)	2.0672
Politically motivated migration						
No						
Yes	-.1517	(.3274)	.8592	-.0557	(.3466)	.9459
Place of origin						
Other Central Amer. country						
El Salvador	1.1064***	(.3324)	3.0235	1.0169**	(.3530)	2.7645
Sex						
Male						
Female	.5838	(.3250)	1.7928	.5117	(.3451)	1.6681
Feels part of the community						
No						
Yes				1.5660***	(.3268)	4.7875

[a] β = Beta: SE = standard error; OR = odds ratio.

[b] Summary statistics for Model 1: Model chi-square = 54.404 ($p < .001$), degrees of freedom = 11, classification table = 69.29%, N = 241. [c] Summary Statistics for Model 2: Model chi-square = 76.887 ($p < .001$), degrees of freedom = 12, classification table =

of questions about their relationships to their places of origin and to the United States, and whether they desire to return or stay. One question is particularly apt: Do you now feel like you are a part of the American (*Norteamericano*) community? We then asked them to explain their answers by asking them, Why do you think that? We left the definition of community intentionally vague, in order to allow interviewees to interpret its meaning.

Responses to this question (Table 3) indicated that, overall, more Mexican than Central American interviewees had begun to consider themselves part of their communities. Qualitative data reveal that undocumented immigrants had many reasons why they personally felt or did not feel themselves to be part of the community.

As for those who did not feel as though they were part of an American community, some mentioned that their families were back in Mexico or Central America. Others found cultural differences hard to transcend: their beliefs, behaviors, and languages kept them apart. Still others lived isolated and secluded from the larger society, and so believed they were not part of that society. Overall, however, the single most important reason why undocumented immigrants felt themselves to be outside their local communities was immigration status. As one Mexican immigrant, Hector Gomez (all names are pseudonyms), commented,

> There's lots of discrimination against the illegal. That's one of the major things, because no matter where you are they call you "illegal" or "wetback." Wherever you go, at times you are humiliated because you are not legal. In all things you come last. Even our own race humiliates us.

On the other hand, many undocumented settlers felt that they were part of local communities. They spoke of adapting to local life and becoming interested in local events, as did this Mexican immigrant: "I have adapted to the society. I'm concerned about the community. I'm interested in things that happen in this city, this country." For a Nicaraguan woman, it was only a matter of time: "With time, I have become accustomed to the way of life and to the people." Feeling like you are part of the community appears to be related to overcoming feelings of isolation, developing a network of family and friends in the local community, acquiring local cultural knowledge, and reconciling yourself to the possible threat of deportation.

Once again, Hector Gomez serves as a good example of someone who became involved in community activities despite his undocumented status. He and his wife Felicia and their children attend church regularly and participate in many church-related social groups. Hector has also taken many self-improvement classes,
for example, training to be an electrician. Not only have such activities provided him and his family an escape from the isolation of
the avocado farm where they live and he works, but in his own es-
timation, he has grown from a rather timid rural person into
someone who is not afraid to express himself, even with English-
only speakers. Moreover, these activities have given them a sense
of community, as Hector notes:

> There's a lot of work to be done in the community. That's
> how the community grows. I like to participate a lot. We
> hardly ever miss a [church-related] meeting. We go every
> month, as sick or tired as we are we must go. So, I think I
> have a lot of help because I am conscientious and I'm con-
> stantly at our meetings, and that's what helps us. The doors
> are never closed to us. We have help when we need it and
> that's the advantage. Participate in whatever is in your com-
> munity, work hard, and that's the point, so that we can have
> everything, friends, acquaintances, and there's the salvation.

The friends Hector and his family made through their community involvement proved instrumental in their long battle to stay
in the United States. After being apprehended by the Immigration
and Naturalization Service for a second time in 1980, Hector and
his family faced a series of deportation deadlines. Each time a
deadline arrived, the family received a reprieve as a result of the
letters and petitions friends and church officials sent to the immigration authorities. After years of stalling deportation, the Gomez
family's status finally became legal under the 1986 immigration
law.

Some undocumented immigrants felt they had earned the right
to feel part of the community; they had "paid their dues" in one
form or another. As a fellow from Mexico said, "Since I have been
here I have contributed to the community by paying taxes and so I
am part of the community." A Salvadoran echoed this sentiment,
"I pay taxes, I shop in the stores, I eat in restaurants. I am part of
the community." A Salvadoran woman went even further when
she said, "Because of all the abuse I have suffered since I arrived, I
feel I am of this community." Jorge Diaz Adds yet another per-

spective that helps us to understand why undocumented immigrants might feel part of the community:

> I feel like part of the community. Of course, why shouldn't I? As Latinos we form a community within the United States. . . . Because of our roots, because there are Latinos who are legal, we communicate whether we are legal or illegal. Even among the Americans, we communicate with them at work and in the environment that we all live in.

The long history of Mexicans in the American Southwest and the presence of legal immigrants provide Jorge with a sense of community. And for Jorge, interacting with those around him helps him feel like he belongs.

Beatriz Valenzuela feels part of the community because she receives notices about community events. This makes her feel accounted for and considered by the community:

> I do feel part of the community because when there are meetings here in the neighbourhood, they send me a notice or an invitation, so that I will be able to attend those meetings. They always send me information on whatever programs there are. That's why I feel like part of the community.

Enrique, Beatriz' husband, also likes what he perceives as the government's general respect for the law. At the same time, both Beatriz and Enrique realize that their feeling that they are part of the community is somewhat illusory, and their situation could change dramatically if they were deported.

> You may have something, but you have a lot of fear, too, because the whole time you think that they might take it away from us because we are not here legally in this country. So for us the [immigration] papers are the most important thing.

The Vanezuelas also were legalized several years after the 1986 immigration law went into effect.

Federico Romero emphasized the importance of friends in giving him a sense of community:

I've always felt like part of the community since I arrived in 1979, because I've had friends and relationships with a lot of people. I've always felt part of the community despite the fact that I have that fear that doesn't allow me to go out and develop in the way that I would like, that doesn't even permit me to take my children to Disneyland.

Although Federico feels part of the community, he, like many others, also includes the reality of his undocumented status that ultimately serves to undermine those personal feelings of belonging to the community. Undocumented immigrants are drawn into or increasingly incorporated into American society and culture through work, raising children who attend local schools and acquire local culture, and developing friendship networks. These experiences can lead to increasing feelings of being a part of the local community. But even if they do imagine themselves to be community members, their full incorporation into the larger society does not depend on their own beliefs or actions; it depends ultimately on the larger society's perceptions of undocumented immigrants. Federico Romero perceptively made this point:

To be treading on land that is not ours [is a problem], and we say that because at one time it was [ours], but that's past history. Now, legally, we are treading on territory that is not ours. Many people may believe we [Mexicans] are people without education and that we don't have an ability to develop better things, [but] we want, and hope, for an opportunity to show them that we can make it and that we don't need to depend on government aid in order to subsist and achieve what we want.

In sum, these qualitative data indicate that, over time, undocumented immigrants develop the kinds of ties to the local economy and society that result in their staying and settling in American communities. Experiences such as finding relatively steady employment, acquiring on-the-job responsibility, forming a family, giving birth to children in the United States, raising children who attend U.S. schools and acquire local culture, learning to navigate in the larger society, and ultimately, perhaps achieving legal immigration status begin to incorporate an undocumented immigrant into the new society. Moreover, establishing a network of friends and relatives, some of whom may be from the same community of origin, increases sentiments of solidarity with the new society.

These factors begin to counterbalance the forces encouraging return to the country of origin, and are, I believe, the reason why many undocumented immigrants defiantly assert their intentions to stay and be a part of their local communities despite their immigration statuses.

Let me add here that for these immigrants, feeling like part of their American communities does not translate as severing ties to their home communities; sentiments, social contacts, and economic relationships continue. For example, over half (56.2 percent) of the Mexicans who felt like part of their American communities continued to send money to their families in Mexico, as did most (84 percent) Central Americans who shared this view.

COMMUNITY AND SETTLEMENT: A TESTING OF HYPOTHESES

How important are the factors that influence undocumented Central Americans to settle in the United States? Forming a family, working and earning money, having friends and relatives in the area, time, and political motivations are all factors that appear to influence settlement. Moreover, I hypothesize that once immigrants perceive themselves to be part of an American community, for whatever reason, they will be more likely to desire to stay in the United States. This means that despite the negative experiences, status, and harsh economic conditions, if immigrants perceive or imagine themselves to be part of an American community, their orientation will be not that of a sojourner but that of a settler.

A logistic regression was used to test the relative importance of some of the influences on settlement. Logistic regression is a particularly useful statistical technique for anthropologists since it allows dichotomous variables to be used as the dependent variable. Anthropologists often ask questions for which a scale does not exist and there is no quantity to measure, as there would be with, for example, earnings. We often have responses that can be categorized as yes or no answers, although they can also be elaborated on with the use of extensive qualitative data. With logistic regression we can take these basically qualitative variables and measure the influence of another variable or variables on them. When more than one variable is placed in the model as an independent variable, logistic regression measures the effect of one variable while holding the other variables constant, which helps to disentangle the relative affect of each of the variables in question.

A particularly appealing statistic that can be computed with this analysis is the odds ratio. The odds ratio suggests the odds of something happening to the dependent variable as a result of the independent variable. For example, say we had a variable that was defined as having two values, o = low income and 1 = high income, and we had another variable with the values o = males and 1 = females. With logistic regression we can derive a hypothetical odds ratio of 3.1, which means the females were a little over three times more likely than males to be in the high-income category. If the odds ratio were -3.1, then the females would be three times more likely than males to be in the low-income category.

The variables used in the logistic regressions of interest here and the summary statistics are presented in Table 3. The dependent variable is the intention to stay permanently in the United States.

The results of the logistic regression are presented in Tables 4 and 5. Model 1 includes all the variables except "feels part of the community." Model 2 includes "feels part of the community."

In Model 1, for undocumented Mexicans, income, education, and having relatives living nearby are not significant influences on intentions to stay permanently in the United States, at least when the other variables are held constant. Significantly, however, those with more than three years in the United States were over twice as likely as those with less time to intend to stay in the United States. Having a spouse and/or child in the United States was also significant: the odds ratio indicated that those with a spouse or child were almost three times as likely to intend to stay as those without such family members with them. Mexican interviewees in Dallas were more likely than those in San Diego to intend to stay in the United States. This makes sense, given that Mexicans in San Diego were generally in the United States less time than those in Dallas, and San Diego is on the United States-Mexico border, allowing for easy return.

Also significant, females were twice as likely as males to desire to stay. These findings generally support evidence from the previous studies that suggest female Latin American and Caribbean immigrants resist leaving, and often find ways to undermine plans for return migration (Pessar 1986).

For Central Americans, Model 1 indicates that having a family income in the top third of all incomes is significant, when controlling for all the other variables. The odds ratio suggests that Central Americans with higher family incomes were 3.5 times more likely to desire to reside permanently in the United States than those with lower incomes. Having an income in the middle third of all incomes is just above the significance level ($p = 0.0522$), and those in this category are about twice as likely to intend to stay permanently as the others.

Residing in the United States for more than three years is also significant. The odds ratio indicates that Central Americans with more than three years in the United States are almost three times as likely as those with fewer years to desire to stay permanently in the United States.

Interestingly, living in San Diego was significant, everything else being equal. Central Americans living in San Diego were about 2.5 times as likely as their counterparts in Dallas to desire to stay permanently. In contrast to Mexicans, geographical proximity to the United States-Mexico border was not a negative influence on desires to stay. In addition, among the Central Americans, Salvadorans were three times as likely as other Central Americans to desire to stay.

What is not significant among Central Americans is also interesting. When time in the United States and the other variables are controlled for, having a spouse and/or children in the United States and having relatives who live nearby were not statistically significant influences on residence intentions. Migrating for political reasons was also not significant, nor was being female significant. This does not mean, however, that these variables did not influence settlement. For example, a spouse in the United States who works increases family income, which is significant, and other relatives and friends might assist you in finding a job, which would produce income. Moreover, the odds ratio suggests that women were 79 percent most likely than men to intend to stay permanently in the United States.

Adding "feels part of the community" to the model (Model 2) improves the statistical significance of the model for both Mexicans and Central Americans. For Mexicans, three or more years in the United States, having a spouse and/or child in the United States, and living in Dallas continue to have significant influences on intentions to stay in the United States. Being female was no longer significant, although females were still 64 percent more likely than males to intend to stay.

The results clearly underscore the importance of feeling part of the community. Not only is the influence on the dependent variable statistically significant, but the odds ratio indicates that those who feel part of the community are almost four times as likely to intend to stay in the United States as those who do not feel part of the community.

For Central Americans, having a higher family income and more than three years in the United States continue to be significant in Model 2, as do living in San Diego and being Salvadoran.

Importantly, for the general hypothesis put forward earlier, perceiving oneself to be a part of the community was also significant among Central Americans. Indeed, those who perceived themselves as part of the community were almost five times more likely to intend to stay permanently in the United States than those who did not feel like part of the community. Although having a spouse and children in the United States and relatives living nearby were insignificant statistically, I believe they contribute, if indirectly, to a Central American immigrant's perception of community membership.

A brief note on the influence of speaking English is in order. In addition to the variables examined here, the models were run with the variable "English" added. The variable compared interviewees who indicated that they spoke English well to those who responded they spoke English "a little" or none at all. With the other variables held constant, English did not have a significant influence on the desire to settle. The other influences were considerably more important. English was, however, significant in a regression on the natural log of wages. Perceiving oneself as confident with the English language was related to earning more money; thus, English competency may indirectly affect the desire to settle.

CONCLUSIONS

Undocumented Mexicans and Central Americans migrate to the United States because of economic hardships and political turmoil in their home countries. Some come intending to stay permanently in the United States; others are sojourners who intend to return home after a period of time. Although they may have arrived alone, knowing few people, over time undocumented immigrants acquire social and economic ties to the United States, a finding that does not contradict Massey et al.'s (1987:255) assertion that undocumented immigrants are less likely than legals to acquire such ties. It does suggest, however, that the formation of linkages to the larger society does occur among undocumented immigrants and that these linkages are important for understanding why they settle in the United States.

Although some segments of the larger society may like to imagine undocumented immigrants to be rootless, unattached, and temporary residents in U.S. society, the evidence here suggests that this is not the case. In contrast to, perhaps even in defiance of, such images of them as temporary residents and as outsiders, many undocumented immigrants perceive themselves as part of the community and intend to become long-term or even permanent settlers. This is a process that appears to occur independently of public policies that restrict their presence, although legalization may speed up the process, as Massey et al. (1987) suggest. But in contrast to much accepted wisdom in the field of migration studies, I find that legal immigration status is but one of many possible factors contributing to a migrant's sense of belonging to a community.

Settlement by some undocumented immigrants occurs because an international migrant, even one who migrates outside of legal authority, can, and often does, develop a sense of belonging to multiple communities and of having multiple identities, some connecting him or her to a community "back home" and some created by his or her presence in a "host" community. Over time, an undocumented immigrant develops ties to the local economy and society. Experiences such as finding relatively steady employment, forming a family, giving birth to children in the United States, raising children who attend U.S. schools and acquire local culture, learning to navigate in the larger society, and even hoping to someday regularize one's immigration status are the types of linkages that influence the formation of a sense of community. Therefore, in contrast to most other work on international migrants, especially that on Mexicans in the United States, I find that immigrants can have multiple identities; they can imagine themselves to be part of their communities "back home," and they can also imagine places for themselves in their "new," or host, communities. An immigrant is not necessarily restricted to an either/or classification when imagining his or her community or, more accurately, communities.

Feeling oneself to be part of the local community is a powerful influence on settlement. For whatever reason particular undocumented immigrants may have come to this perception, once they do so, they are likely to intend to stay permanently in the United States. Less likely to desire to stay permanently in the United States are those who do not perceive themselves as part of a community, be it because of inadequate time, attachment to family and community back home, or perception of isolation, experience of discrimination, an internalization of the larger society's image of the temporary "illegal alien" who does not really belong in the United States, or some combination of these and other factors.

These conclusions attest to the power of the imagined community. Imagining oneself to be part of a community influences other perceptions, desires, and behaviors. On the other hand, imagining oneself to be part of a community is often not enough. Others in that community may have a counterimage, which, given the structure of power relationships, influences to a great degree the "truth" that is created about undocumented immigrants. The real-life implication of this truth making is the creation of public policies based on that truth. For example, undocumented students attending the University of California are classified as nonresidents of California, where they are charged foreign-student tuition, even though they may have lived for years in the state and their parents may be taxpayers. In 1991, Representative Elton Gallegly (R-Simi Valley) introduced legislation to Congress that would amend the U.S. Constitution to disallow the right of citizenship for children born in the United States with undocumented parents.

Many other such examples could be put forth, but the point has been made that imagining oneself to be part of a community may be less important, in some ways, than how the larger community defines community membership. Yet what I find remarkable among the undocumented immigrants I have interviewed is that the process of community formation occurs regardless of these constraints. It attests, perhaps, to the ability of humans to form social relationships and develop a sense of community under adverse conditions. This, too, is a form of power that will increasingly inform anthropological theories concerning community, identity, and nationalism as anthropologists continue to work among the many displaced and mobile populations of the world.

NOTES

Acknowledgements. The fieldwork on which this article is based was supported by a grant from the Inter-University Program for Public Policy Research on Hispanic Issues. Earlier drafts benefitted greatly from the advice and comments of Juliet McMullin, Ramom Torrechilha, Frank Cancian, and the anonymous reviewers for *AA*. I am, of course, solely responsible for the arguments made here as well as for any errors or omissions.

1. Of course, the settlement of legal immigrants and refugees is also of considerable interest (see Lamphere 1992).
2. More than 80 percent of undocumented immigrants live in five states: California, New York, Texas, Illinois, and Florida (Passel and Woodrow 1984). California attracts the largest proportion of undocumented immigrants of all nationalities. For example, Cornelius (1988) found that in 1987, California had approximately half (1.74 million) of the nation's undocumented immigrants. Not surprisingly, most undocumented immigrants from Mexico also choose California as their state of residence. California alone absorbs at least half of the total flow of undocumented Mexican immigrants (Cornelius 1988:4). Of the approximately three million people legalized under the 1986 Immigration Law, most (55 percent) lived in California (CASAS 1989).
3. See Chavez (1991) for an extended analysis of the explanations interviewees gave for why they did or did not feel part of the community in the United States.
4. See also Malkki's (1990) work on the differences in historical consciousness among Hutu refugees in Tanzania for an example of how notions of a moral community are constructed under different conditions of exile.
5. Estevan T. Flores, with the assistance of Marta Lopez-Garza, coordinated data collection in Dallas.
6. Dallas County had, in 1980, approximately 1.5 million inhabitants, of which about 10 percent were Latino, of whom 92 percent were of Mexican origin. In 1990, Latinos were 16.6 percent of the 1,852,810 inhabitants, with those of Mexican origin accounting for 14.5 percent. As for Central Americans, 14,729 were counted in 1990 (U.S. Bureau of the Census 1984:6-1206, 1990). In 1980, the Dallas-Ft. Worth metro area had about 44,000 undocumented persons, of whom 32,000 were born in Mexico (Passel and Woodrow 1984).
7. For analyses that make extensive use of the qualitative data, see Chavez 1991 and 1992.
8. Because the English proved insignificant, the models were left out to meet space constraints.
9. A model was also tested using "feels part of the community" as the dependent variable and with the same independent variables as in the models above. The betas, significance levels, and odds ratio for the variables that proved significant were for Mexicans: 6-8 years of schooling (= -; p = ; OR = .46), more than 3 years in the United States (= .7368; p = .039; OR = 2.1), English (= .9961; p = .005; OR = 2.7). For Central Americans: High income (= 1.4117; p = .002; OR = 4.1), San Diego (= 1.0135; p = .002; OR = 2.8), 9 or more years of schooling (= .7239; p = .053; OR = 2.1).

REFERENCES CITED

Anderson, Benedict
1983   Imagined Communities. London: Verso.

Appadurai, Arjun
1991   Global Ethnoscapes: Notes and Queries for a Transnational An-
            thropology. *In* Recapturing Anthropology. Richard G. Fox, ed.
            Pp. 191-210. Santa Fe: School of American Research Press.
Arensberg, Conrad M., and Solon T. Kimball
1965   Culture and Community. New York: Harcourt, Brace and World.
Baca, Reynaldo, and Dexter Bryan
1980   Citizenship Aspirations and Residency Rights Preference: The
            Mexican Undocumented Work in the Binational Community.
            Compton, CA: SEPA-OPTION.
Biernacki, R., and D. Waldorf
1981   Snowball Sampling. Sociological Methods and Research 10:141-
            163.
Brimelow, Peter
1992   Time to Rethink Immigration? National Review 22 (June):30-
            46.
Brow, James
1990   Notes on Community, Hegemony, and the Uses of the Past. An-
            thropological Quarterly 63:1-5.
Browning, Harley L., and Nestor Rodriguez
1982   The Migration of Mexican Indocumentados as a Settlement
            Process: Implications for Work. *In* Hispanics in the U.S. Economy.
            George J. Borjas and Marta Tienda, eds. Pp. 277-297. New York:
            Academic Press.
CASAS (Comprehensive Adult Student Assessment System)
1989   A Survey of Newly Legalized Persons in California. Prepared for
            the California Health and Welfare Agency. San Diego: Compre-
            hensive Adult Student Assessment System.
Chavez, Leo R.
1985   Households, Migration, and Labor Market Participation: The Ad-
            aptation of Mexicans to Life in the United States. Urban Anthro-
            pology 14:301-346.
1986   Immigration and Health Care: A Political Economy Perspective.
            Human Organization 45:344-352.
1988   Settlers and Sojourners: The Case of Mexicans in the United
            States. Human Organization 47:95-108.
1991   Outside the Imagined Community: Undocumented Settlers and
            Experiences of Incorporation. American Ethnologist 18:257-278.
1992   Shadowed Lives: Undocumented Immigrants in American Soci-
            ety. Ft. Worth: Harcourt, Brace and Jovanovich College Publish-
            ers.
Chavez, Leo R., Estevan T. Flores, and Marta Lopez-Garza
1990   Here Today, Gone Tomorrow? Undocumented Settlers and Im-
            migration Reform. Human Organization 49:193-205.
Clifford, James
1988   The Predicament of Culture. Cambridge, MA: Harvard Univer-
            sity Press.
Cornelius, Wayne A.
1980   America in the Era of Limits. Working Paper No. 3. La Jolla: Cen-
            ter for U.S.-Mexican Studies, University of California, San Di-
            ego.

1982   Interviewing Undocumented Immigrants: Methodological Reflections Based on Fieldwork in Mexico and the United States. International Migration Review 16:378-411.

1988   The Persistence of Immigrant-Dominated Firms and Industries in the United States: The Case of California. Paper presented at the Conference on Comparative Migration Studies, June 20-23, Paris, France.

Diaz-Briquets, Sergio

1989   The Central America Demographic Situation: Trends and Implications. *In* Mexican and Central American Population and U.S. Immigration Policy. Frank D. Bean, Jurgen Schmandt, and Sidney Weintraub, eds. Pp. 33-54. Austin: The Center for Mexican American Studies, The University of Texas at Austin.

Durkheim, Emile

1984[1893]   The Division of Labor in Society. New York: The Free Press.

El Financiero

1992   Gross Domestic Product. El Financiero, Mexico Business News (Weekly International Edition) 1(49[June 8]):1.

Evans-Pritchard, E.E.

1972[1940]   The Nuer. Oxford: Oxford University Press.

Graham, Otis L., Jr., and Roy Beck

1992   To Help City, Cut Flow of Immigrants. Los Angeles Times, May 19, B11.

Gupta, Akhil, and James Ferguson

1992   Beyond "Culture": Space, Identity, and the Politics of Difference. Cultural Anthropology 7:6-23.

Hannerz, Ulf

1980   Exploring the City: Inquiries toward an Urban Anthropology. New York: Columbia University Press.

Jehl, Douglas

1992   Buchanan Raises Specter of Intolerance, Critics Say. Los Angeles Times, March 17, A-1.

Lamm, Richard D., and Gary Imhoff

1985   The Immigration Time Bomb. New York: Truman Talley Books.

Lamphere, Louise

1987   From Working Daughters to Working Mothers. Ithaca: Cornell University Press.

Lamphere, Louise (ed.)

1992   Structuring Diversity: Ethnographic Perspectives on the New Immigration. Chicago: University of Chicago Press.

Malinowski, Bronislaw

1961[1922]   Argonauts of the Western Pacific. New York: E.P. Dutton and Co., Inc.

Malkki, Liisa

1990   Context and Consciousness: Local Conditions for the Production of Historical and National Thought among Hutu Refugees in Tanzania. *In* Nationalist Ideologies and the Production of National Cultures. American Ethnological Society Monograph Series, Number 2. Richard G. Fox, ed. Pp. 32-62. Washington, DC: American Anthropological Association.

Marmora, Lelio
1988   Social Integration and Employment of Central American Refu-
            gees. *In* When Borders Don't Divide. Patricia Pessar, ed. Pp. 142-
            155. New York: Center for Migration Studies.
Marx, Karl
1967[1867] Capital. New York: International Publishers
Massey, Douglas S.
1987   Understanding Mexican Migration to the United States. Ameri-
            can Journal of Sociology 92:1372-1403.
Massey, Douglas S., Rafael Alarcon, Jorge Curand, and Humberto Gonzalez
1987   Return to Aztlan. Berkeley: UC Press.
Melville, Margarita B.
1978   Mexican Women Adapt to Migration. International Migration
            Review 12:225-235.
Montes Mozo, S., and J.J. Garcia Vasquez
1988   Salvadoran Migration to the United States: An Exploratory
            Study. Washington, DC: Center for Immigration Policy and
            Refugee Assistance, Georgetown University.
Newsweek
1992   What They [Primary Candidates] Think. Editorial, March 16, p.
            33.
Palmer, David S.
1992   Central America: Starting Over. Hemisfile: Perspectives on Politi-
            cal and Economic Trends in the Americas 3 (3[May]):1-2.
Papademetriou, Demetrios B., and Nicholas DiMarzio
1986   Undocumented Aliens in the New York Metropolitan Area: An
            Exploration into Their Social and Labour Market Incorporation.
            New York: Center for Migration Studies of New York.
Park, Robert
1969[1928] Human Migration and the Marginal Man. *In* Classic Essays on
            the Culture of Cities. Richard Sennet, ed. Pp. 131-142. New York:
            Appleton-Century-Crofts.
Passel, Jeffrey S.
1985   Estimates of Undocumented Aliens in the 1980 Census for
            SMSAs. Memorandum to Roger Herriot, Chief, Population Di-
            vision, Bureau of the Census, August 16, 1985.
Passel, Jeffrey S., and Karen A. Woodrow
1984   Geographic Distribution of Undocumented Aliens Counted in
            the 1980 Census by State. International Migration Review
            18:642-671.
Pedraza-Bailey, Silvia
1985   Political and Economic Migrants in America: Cubans and Mexi-
            can Americans. Austin: University of Texas Press.
Pessar, Patricia
1982   The Role of Households in International Migration and the
            Case of U.S.-Bound Migration from the Dominican Republic.
            International Migration Review 16:342-364.
1986   The Role of Gender in Dominican Settlement in the U.S. *In*
            Women and Change in Latin America. June Nash and Helen
            Safa, eds. Pp. 273-294. Westport: Bergin and Garvey.

Piore, Michael J.
1986   The Shifting Grounds for Immigration. Annals of the American
            Academy of Political and Social Science 485:23-33.
Portes, Alejandro, and Robert L. Bach
1985   Latin Journey: Cuban and Mexican Immigrants in the United
            States. Berkeley: University of California Press.
Redfield, Robert
1956   The Little Community and Peasant Society and Culture. Chi-
            cago: University of Chicago Press.
Reinhold, Robert
1991   In California, New Discussion on Whether to Bar the Door.
            New York Times, December 3, A1.
Rodriguez, Nestor P.
1987   Undocumented Central Americans in Houston: Diverse Popula-
            tions. International Migration Review 21:4-26.
Rouse, Roger
1991   Mexican Migration and the Social Space of Postmodernism. Di-
            aspora 1:8-23.
Simon, Rita J.
1985   Public Opinion and the Immigrant. Lexington, MA: Lexington
            Books.
Sin, Paul
1987[1953] The Chinese Laundryman: A Study in Social Isolation. New
            York: New York University Press.
U.S. Bureau of the Census
1984   Money, Income and Poverty Status of Families in the United
            States: 1983. Series P-60, No. 145, August. Washington, DC: Gov-
            ernment Printing Office.
1990   U.S. Census Summary Tape file 3A. Washington, DC: Govern-
            ment Printing Office.
1991   Census Bureau Releases 1990 Census Counts on Specific Racial
            Groups. United States Department of Commerce News, June 12
            (CB91-215). Washington, DC: Economics and Statistics Admini-
            stration, Bureau of the Census.
U.S. House of Representatives
1986   Immigration Reform and Control Act of 1986. Conference Re-
            port. 99th Congress, 2d Session. Report 99-1000. Washington,
            DC: U.S. Government Printing Office.
Weber, Max
1978[1947] Economy and Society, Volume 1. Berkeley: University of Cali-
            fornia Press.
Whiteford, Linda
1979   The Borderland as an Extended Community. In Migration across
            Frontiers: Mexico and the United States. Fernando Camara and
            Robert Van Kemper, eds. Albany: Institute for Mexican American
            Studies. State University of New York at Albany.
Woodrow, Karen A., and Jeffrey S. Passel
1990   Post-IRCA Undocumented Immigration to the United States:
            An Assessment Based on the June 1988 CPS. In Undocumented
            Migration to the United States: IRCA and the Experiences of
            the 1980s. Frank D. Bean, Barry Edmonston, and Jeffrey S. Passel,
            ed. Pp. 33-75. Washington, DC: The Urban Institute Press.

I3

Introduction

In a way characteristic of scholarship in many disciplines, Penelope Eckert's "Cooperative Competition in Adolescent 'Girl Talk'" spans realms seemingly remote from one another, these realms embodied in the language of the article itself. On the one hand, readers encounter wordings derived from highly theoretical, formal accounts of the social order:

> women's influence depends primarily on the accumulation of symbolic capital (Bourdieu, 1977): on the painstaking creation and elaboration of an image of the whole self as worthy of authority. This is not to say that men are not dependent on the accumulation of symbolic capital but to say that symbolic capital is the *only* kind that women can accumulate with impunity. (388-89)

And, on the other hand, readers also encounter wordings derived from practical, informal accounts of the social order — the conversation of schoolmates:

> I mean I know them by face and —
> 　　　but you know, Al Jones —
> = their FACES I've heard so much aBOUT them
> 　　　　　　everybody looks up to him.
> 　　　　　　　　I mean you know, as we were=(419)

Although the two realms are each substantially represented in the language of the article, the relationship between them is not exactly symmetrical: the theoretical, scholarly voice typically has the last word, transforming the speech of everyday life into terms useful to research purposes. So, even though vernacular speech opens the article —

> I think girls just talk too much, you know, they — they — talk constantly between themselves and — about every little thing.... I think girls talk about, you know, every little relationship, every little thing that's ever happened, you know. (386)

— that speech is immediately converted to more scholarly wordings, wordings the speaker himself would (probably) never have used: "it is commonly believed that girls and women regularly engage in long and detailed personal discussions about people, norms, and beliefs and that boys and men do not" (386-87). (With this conversion, "norm," for example, is now available for complex reasoning about community, interaction and status, as on 389-90). Even when the wordings of the everyday domain are preserved in the research discourse, they are defined in abstract terms which, in turn, can contribute to elaborate conceptualization. So high-school "popularity" — something familiar to most people who have grown up in North America — is defined as

> the community's joint recognition of an individual's good personhood, in other words, a measure of his or her symbolic capital.... because popularity is accorded by the community as a whole, it requires not only likability but also sufficient, well-managed visibility to draw the community's attention to that likability. (391)

This conversion of the materials of everyday life to the materials of research links the two domains. But the link is a one-way street.

Everyday life and research life are connected at another level, too, in this article. The first paragraph refers to what is "commonly believed" about women's and girls' ways of talking, and how these ways differ from those of men and boys. It is not entirely clear who believes these things, but the quotation from the "adolescent boy" suggests that these are non-specialist beliefs — common wisdoms or folk beliefs. The second paragraph shows, however, that these matters also concern researchers, and that researchers' ideas are somewhat parallel to folk ideas about gender and talk (e.g., "Writers frequently refer to women's conversational style as 'cooperative' ..." [387]). And we might note generally that both folk knowledge and scholarly knowledge are concerned with gender differences.

But these two paragraphs also suggest that both folk and scholarly knowledge of gender differences are inadequate. Eckert poses a research question — what is accomplished by these observed patterns in male and female styles of interaction? — and immediately follows this question with a principal claim: "The difference between male and female group dynamics is, I argue, based on difference in gender roles in society as a whole" (388). To keep Eckert's aim in focus, and especially to keep in focus the theoretical section on "Women and Symbolic Capital," you might try to answer these questions:

- What does Eckert's claim — what she "argues" — have to do with the research question (388)?

- How does her research address the inadequacy or incompleteness of both folk and scholarly knowledge of gender differences in styles of speech?

The title of Eckert's article contains what appears to be a contradiction – "cooperative competition." Her theoretical account of "symbolic capital" explains the circumstances which bring about this seemingly contradictory behaviour, and her interpretive analyses of the girls' conversation demonstrates it in practice. But still it is a complicated idea: how can competitive and cooperative behaviours co-occur? (Current debates on education, for example, seem to separate rather than connect these behaviours: while some people argue for "cooperative" learning – members of groups helping each other – others reject this model and call for a return to competitive models, where students strive for individual success and recognized rankings.) You might look at the idea of "gossip" (396-97) (another term shared by both folk and scholarly discourse) to bring this seeming contradiction into focus.

- How does the speech genre *gossip* enact both community (cooperative) and individual (competitive) values?

In Western culture, many generations have typified women's speech as "gossip," and this typification seems to have persisted to the present day.

- How far does Eckert's research go in confirming or denying traditional, folk beliefs about women's speech?

- How does she account for social change and its effect on women's and girls' ways of speaking?

Cooperative Competition in Adolescent "Girl Talk"

PENELOPE ECKERT
University of Illinois at Chicago and Institute for Research on Learning

DIFFERENCES BETWEEN MALE AND FEMALE participation in speech events are based in differences in gender roles in society as a whole. Fruitful discussion of such differences, therefore, must account for the function of male and female interaction within a social theoretical framework. Such an approach is taken here to girl talk, a typically female speech event involving long and detailed personal discussion about people, norms, and beliefs. It is argued that the function of girl talk derives from the place of females in society, particularly as a function of the domestication of female labor. Deprived of direct power, females are constrained to focus on the development of personal influence. Thus constrained to define themselves, not in terms of individual accomplishments, but in terms of their overall characters, females need to explore and negotiate norms that govern their behaviour and define this character. Girl talk is a speech event that provides females with the means to negotiate these norms and to measure their symbolic capital in relation to them. An examination of 2 hours of girl talk among six adolescent girls show the verbal means by which this negotiation is accomplished. The girl talk interaction constitutes a temporary community within which norms are cooperatively defined through a painstaking process of negotiation and consensus.

I think girls just talk too much, you know, they- they- talk constantly between themselves and- about every little thing. Guys, I don't think we talk about that much. (*What kinds of things do you talk about?*) Not much. Girls . . . cars, or parties,

you know. I think girls talk about, you know, every little relationship, every little thing that's ever happened, you know.

As reflected in the foregoing quotation from an adolescent boy, it
is commonly believed that girls and women regularly engage in
long and detailed discussions about people, norms, and beliefs and
that boys and men do not. Such speech events are frequently but
inaccurately referred to as gossip session. Although they often
contain instances of gossip, they also contain a great deal of other
kinds of discussion. For want of a better name, I will call these
events by their alternative popular name, "girl talk." This paper
examines part of a girl talk events involving six adolescent girls,
with a view to uncovering its purpose as a gender-specific speech
event and the verbal means by which it accomplishes its purpose.

The real gender specificity of girl talk or its components is not
altogether clear because we lack a systematic ethnographic account of the verbal repertoires of men and women. As Goodwin
(1980) shows, for instance, gender differences in norms of interaction in one kind of speech event (in this case norms concerning direct confrontation among black elementary school girls) might not
apply in another. And inasmuch as the significance of gender is not
uniform throughout society, one cannot assume that what holds in
one set of observations is true of society as a whole. Indeed, gender differences in interaction much be studied within the context
of the situations in which they are observed, with an understanding of the significance of those situations to men and women
in that cultural group. There is some evidence that middle-class
women in our society are more prone than men to pursue personal topics in discussion (Aries, 1976). My own observations
among adolescents and Wodak's (1981) data on therapeutic interactions show this to be less true for working-class, as compared
with middle-class speakers. Aries (1976) shows that in same-sex
groups of college undergraduates, women talk about themselves,
their personal feelings, and their relationships, and men engage in
competitive conversation comparing knowledge and experience
and recounting competitive exploits. There is also some evidence
that women are more prone to share the floor than men, at least in
same-sex interactions. Aries found a tendency in men's groups for
a individual or individuals to gain control and dominate the group
in the current and subsequent interactions, whereas the women
tended to draw each other out, spreading the talk around. Writers
frequently refer to women's conversational style as "cooperative"
— women have been found, not only to encourage each other to

participate, but also to build on each other's utterances and stories (Jones, 1972; Kalcik, 1975). However, because this is based primarily on the examination of women's behavior and not systematically compared with men's, the status of these differences remains highly speculative.

One obviously cannot conclude from the available evidence of sex differences in conversation that men do not engage in cooperative personal revelation, or women in impersonal competition. One might, rather, ask, what competitive discussion of impersonal topics accomplishes in all-male groups and what personal and cooperative conversation accomplishes in all-female groups. The difference between male and female group dynamics is, I argue, based on differences in gender roles in society as a whole.

WOMEN AND SYMBOLIC CAPITAL

The origins of gender differences in styles of interaction can be traced to the traditional roles that relegate women to the domestic realm and men to the economic marketplace, and although these roles have changed to some extent in our society, the social norms and the norms of interaction they have created remain to complicate and thwart social change. The domestication of female labor involves a strict division of roles, with men engaged in the public marketplace and women's activities restricted to the private, domestic sphere (Sacks, 1974). The man competes for goods and power in the marketplace in the name of the family and controls these within the family. Thus, although the woman is solely responsible for maintaining the domestic unit, she has no direct control over that unit's capital. Whereas a man's personal worth is based on accumulation of goods, status, and power in the marketplace, a woman's worth is based on her ability to maintain order in, and control over, her domestic realm. Deprived of power, women can only gain compliance through the indirect use of a man's power or through the development of personal influence.

Women can use men's power indirectly by winning men's cooperation through social manipulation or by borrowing men's status through the display and exploitation of connections with men. It is not, therefore, surprising that women are more concerned with the shape of their social networks, with their connections to people in those networks, and with their ability to understand and influence people. Although it is frequently said that women are more status conscious than men, it would be more accurate to say that they are more status *bound*.

Actual personal influence without power requires moral authority. In other words, women's influence depends primarily on the accumulation of symbolic capital (Bourdieu, 1977): on the painstaking creation and elaboration of an image of the whole self as worthy of authority. This is not to say that men are not dependent on the accumulation of symbolic capital but to say that symbolic capital is the *only* kind that women can accumulate without impunity. And indeed, women's symbolic capital becomes part of their men's symbolic capital and, hence, part of the household's economic capital. Men can justify and define their status on the basis of their accomplishments, possessions, or institutional status, but women must justify and define theirs on the basis of their overall character and the kinds of relations they can maintain with others. Women, therefore, unlike men, are frequently obsessed with being the perfect spouse, the perfect parent, the perfect friend.

Whereas men compete for status in the marketplace, women must compete for their domestic status. The "better" woman gets the "better" domestic situation, the better deal in that situation, and ultimately greater access to the goods that men control. However, although the situation is inherently competitive, one cannot overtly compete in the accumulation of symbolic capital, for it is in the nature of symbolic capital that it should not appear to have been consciously accumulated. Because good personhood is supposed to be an inherent property, its possession specifically excludes competitiveness or the need for competition. Norms against women's competitiveness stem from two sources, therefore: Competition in the marketplace violates men's cultural prerogative, and competition in the personal realm contradicts the underlying definition of personal worth.

The marketplace establishes the value of men's capital, but women's symbolic capital must be evaluated in relation to community norms for women's behavior. The establishment and maintenance of these norms requires regular monitoring, and, because it is women who must compete in relation to these norms, it is they who have the greatest interest in this monitoring. To the extent that they can control norms, women can increase their competitive edge. Girl talk, I will argue, is the major means by which they do this. Although it is certainly reasonable to assume, as is generally done, that this activity of women's is a conservative force, particularly the gossip that can enter into girl talk, I argue that gossip and girl talk not only keep track of individuals' behavior in relation to the norms but also keep track of the norms in relation to individuals' behavior. In this light, girl talk can be seen as an agent of social change, as well as of social control. By engaging in the negotiation of norms, women can also increase their stake in the norms, simultaneously tying together the community and tying themselves to it. One might say that women's negotiation of norms is an important part of what makes communities. Harding (1975) characterizes much of women's talk as "climbing . . . the figurative fences between households" (p.302), providing a flow of information that, in effect, maintains communication within communities.

The fact that women today are entering the marketplace does not change, but complicates, these dynamics. The strong norms associated with the domestication of women function to limit women's participation in the marketplace, and the verbal behavior that serves these norms takes on new significance, serving simultaneously as an adaptive strategy and as a barrier to access to the marketplace. For, as norms become more problematic, the need to negotiate them increases. It is reasonable, then, that girl talk should intensify with the double bind that marketplace participation imposes on women. However, at the same time, women's engagement in girl talk is taken as evidence of their unsuitability for the marketplace.

FEMALE SYMBOLIC CAPITAL IN THE HIGH SCHOOL SETTING

Girls in high school spend a great deal of time engaging in girl talk. They are at a life stage in which they are just learning women's roles and acquiring new and unfamiliar norms. In addition, the high school poses a double bind for many girls, for the emphasis on competitive status in the school institution conflicts with norms for women's behavior. Although there are any number of ways to function in high school, and certainly more than one context in which to achieve success and status (academics, music, ROTC, office assistance, etc.), there is a clear mainstream acknowledged, not only by the students, but by the school itself (Eckert, 1989). Individuals of both sexes are expected to compete for personal mainstream success, which involves the accumulation of power through the domination of a small range of social, political, and athletic activities and membership in the social networks that dominate those activities. Although the importance of particular activities differs somewhat from school to school, the existence of a mainstream status group is common to public high school across the country. Most high school students feel that the status system that defines mainstream success in the high school is unfair, even some of those who have benefited from it. But they are locked in an institution that supports this system and, as a result, must come to terms with it in some way.

Because the roles are arranged hierarchically and because there are few of them in relation to the size of the student population, school activities constitute a competitive marketplace. This competition creates a double bind for the girls who, therefore, transform it to suit their own symbolic needs. The terms of boys' and girls' competition in school are, therefore, very different. Central to this difference is the notion of popularity. Popularity is the community's joint recognition of an individual's good personhood, in other words, a measure of her or his symbolic capital. In view of females' greater dependence on the accumulation of symbolic capital, it is reasonable that girls should be more concerned with popularity than boys and that they should compete for it. But, because popularity is accorded by the community as a whole, it requires not only likability but also sufficient, well-managed visibility to draw the community's attention to that likability. The visibility gained through elected office and other formal roles in the school activity marketplace thus increases one's access to popularity. This involves not only competition but also a certain measure of exclusivity (being associated with only prestigious people), to maximize visibility. The result is a double bind created by the conflict between competition and exclusivity on the one hand and likability on the other.

This conflict is played out in the instance of teenage girl talk to be presented here. This tape-recorded session took place in the course of 2 years of participant observation in a Detroit suburban high school. During this time I followed one graduating class through their last 2 1/2 years of high school. The six girls involved in this interaction are all members of that graduating class. The analysis is based on the broader ethnographic context and on my relatively long-term and regular familiarity with the participants in this interaction and with many of their approximately 600 classmates. This interaction did not occur spontaneously: I had asked one of the participants, Karen, to get together a bunch of friends after school to talk about "stuff." At the time of this interaction, the six participants, Karen, Betty, Miriam, Carol, June, and Pamela, were at the end of their junior year in high school.[1]

All of them except June had been friends in Rover Junior High School, where they had been members of the same social cluster.

---

[1]   All names are fictitious.

June, who had gone to a different junior high school, was casual friends with all of the girls in this interaction and had been invited to come along to this session at the last moment as the girls were at their lockers getting ready. As a result, she said relatively little during the interaction, but she served as a kind of observer.[2]

The Rover girls had been part of the "active" group in junior high school, a fairly large network of boys and girls who dominated school activities and who pursued informal, large-group, social activities outside of school. These girls, like many of their peers in that group, agreed that ninth grade had been their "best year ever." When their class merged in high school with classes from two other junior high schools, the competition for status and opportunities in the new setting was fierce, and success required learning who was who from the other schools and establishing contacts with them. There was, therefore, a race to get to know as many people from the other schools as possible and, in particular, to get to know the powerful people from the other schools. Ultimately, one had to run this race as an individual, and slower friends were typically left behind. Betty's account (on another occasion) of the history of her friendship with Karen, Miriam, and Pamela during this period of transition is a particularly poignant account of the process that yielded their current relations.

> We're pretty much alike. But as soon as we got into high school, which was kind of strange, we all just kind of drifted away, you know, and we were just like, you know, new friends here, new friends there, but then it just all came back together again, you know because you can't really — you're never that much different . . . as soon as you get into high school, it's like popularity, popularity — everybody's like, you know, you have to be popular, that's what-that's what's in you know, so you have to try to get the popular friends, the people who are really popular. Well if, you know, you

---

2   One could say that this interaction had five members, one inside observer (June), one outside observer (me), and six mechanical observers (tape recorders). Each girl wore a lavalier microphone attached to a separate tape recorder. The girls controlled their own tape recorders, turning them on and off and changing the tapes. Although it is common in sociolinguistics to try to make taping as unobtrusive as possible, to reduce the speakers' self-consciousness, I have found that, in group sessions where individuals were implicated in their own recording, there was less awareness of the machines than otherwise.

feel that you really- the popular friends aren't too terrific, then, you know, you always fall back on just your friends that have been friends for so long.

The session under analysis is the first time these girls have gotten together as a group since junior high school, and this interaction, like any reunion, prompts them to measure their own progress in relation to each other's. Thus, it is inherently competitive: Each girl has a stake in showing herself and the others that she has "done well." The terms of this competition, however, are complex for two reasons. *First*, there is the conflict between their need to show that they have succeeded in the competitive marketplace and their need to show that they are likable. Thus, they must compete without appearing to. *Second*, to the extent that the girls in the interaction have been following different paths in high school, they need to negotiate what "doing well" is. In addition, they are competing, not only over status in the marketplace, but also over the very likability that makes it impossible for them to compete openly. Therefore, their noncompetitive performance in this interaction, which allows each girl to display her understanding of human nature and her ability to resolve conflict and create community, can be seen as part of the competition. The result is that the main activity of the interaction is the negotiation of a set of norms that allows equally for the accomplishments, behavior, and beliefs of all the girls involved.

The girls in this interaction are all good students with different measures of mainstream involvement and success in high school. None of them are full-time members of the most popular and powerful group. Inasmuch as every one of these girls admits to having aimed for mainstream success in 10th grade, they have to account for themselves and to each other both for the things they did in seeking it (the likability issue) and their perceived success or failure to attain it (the status issue). Each girl has to either establish her own mainstream status or account for her lack of it. Establishing mainstream status involves the display of formal roles and/or social contacts, and almost all of the girls in this interaction make such displays in the course of this interaction.

One can account for lack of mainstream status by denying the values of mainstream success, by establishing the preferability of an alternative status system, and by affirming one's success in it. This is one main theme in the discussion, and it is linked to the issue of personal autonomy, another problematic issue for adolescents, particularly adolescent girls. Betty, Miriam, and June have taken the mainstream route, confining their interactions primarily to the network surrounding the mainstream popular crowd in their own graduating class and pursuing the school activities that bring mainstream status. Karen, Carol, and Pamela are involved in alternative networks in the junior and senior classes and pursue some less mainstream activities. Carol and Pamela, for instance, are involved in the band. They present themselves in the interaction as more autonomous or independent by virtue of their exploration of social alternatives and their transcendence of their own graduating class. In much of the discussion, Karen and Carol, on the one hand, and Betty and Miriam, on the other, form two sides in the discussion. Associated with the juxtaposition between mainstream and alternative networks is Karen and Carol's pride in their sophistication and their liberal outlook, whereas Betty and Miriam willingly cast themselves as "innocents." (Their innocence stems from personal traits not necessarily associated with their mainstream identities.)

THE GIRL TALK

The main body of the discussion lasts one hour and 55 minutes and flows through a variety of topics. After everyone gets settled around the table, discussion begins with my asking a question about how they find things out in school. The discussion turns quickly to information management: preventing unfavorable information from getting out and promoting the dissemination of favorable information. This leads to a discussion of how girls can let boys know they "like" them, which introduces the section on boys. This section centres around relations with boys and ends in a discussion of who the popular boys are and what they are like. This leads to a discussion of popular people in general, popularity itself, and people who will do anything to gain popularity. A discussion of one girl who has been particularly responsive to peer pressure leads to the conclusion that she suffers from lack of family support. This leads into the discussion of family relations, in particular the need for mutual respect between parents and children. Further discussion of people who have bad relations with their parents leads Carol to tell about one such person who has been supported in her family difficulties by her religious faith. This leads to the discussion of religion, which ends with a discussion of the number of people in school that unexpectedly belong to church groups. This leads to a brief discussion of unguessable things about people, particularly people with family problems. Carol, Miriam, and Karen then tell a story each about past resolved conflicts with parents. After Karen's story, Carol points out how well Karen turned out in spite of this conflict because she has basically a strong relationship with her parents. This leads the conversation to how they have all changed since junior high school. This is an extremely important topic, because it deals explicitly with the covert agenda of the discussion. At this point, the discussion begins to move back and forth among topics already covered and ultimately leads to a discussion of their upcoming senior year, including the impending loss of their senior friends, the necessity of getting their own class together in senior year, and the responsibility of being the school leaders (as a class). From here on, the conversation jumps quickly from topic to topic and, in a variety of ways, wraps up the entire conversation with implicit and explicit reference to earlier parts.

Shared norms imply community, and the negotiation of norms both reaffirms and requires community. The building of consensus is the building of community through the development of a shared account of themselves as a group. Communities build through repeated interactions among the individuals that constitute them, and each of these interactive events constitutes, in some sense, a temporary community of its own.[3] Each interaction builds an internal history as it progresses. Stories can be built on, points can be elaborated, and even a history of linguistic usage can develop, all of which can be invoked through the interaction. If the temporary community is sufficiently memorable, its participants may refer later either to the interaction as a whole or to community devices within it. The girl talk under consideration here is a prime example of the creation of community in an interaction. These girls are together for the first time after 2 years, and their separation has involved events and developments that continue to divide them. To be able to interact as friends, they need to become a community, but a temporary one, for they intend to resume their separation when they leave this interaction. They are not trying to recreate a community that existed earlier but a community that bridges the gap between their earlier relations and the present and that allows them to anticipate separating again without ill feeling or awkwardness. The particular value of this temporary community to each of them is to allow her to show herself and the others how far

3   I owe a great deal in this section to discussions with Charlotte Linde.

she has come and to demonstrate that her actions and choices have been worthy.

Disagreement is an important way of getting norms onto the table. Because these girls have followed somewhat different paths, and because each girl's claim to status depends on the group's recognition of her path, the paths themselves have to be worked into the consensus. To a great extent, therefore, the discussion is a long sequence of claims, counterclaims, and negotiated consensus. In these cases, a pattern is followed in which one girl makes a statement of opinion or belief, which someone else contradicts. Others might or might not take explicit sides at this initial stage, but then one or the other side presents support in the form of either an argument or an illustration. This might be countered by another argument or illustration, or consensus negotiation could begin immediately. Consensus is negotiated by finding a position that includes both positions presented or by refining one or both of the positions to eliminate the disagreement. Consensus is built not only through the accumulation of items, but also through a hierarchical development, with fairly trivial items of agreement combining to yield a broader item of agreement. As the girls discuss a given topic, each subtopic leads to a related subtopic. Discussion of each subtopic leads to some kind of consensus, and the progress through subtopics leads to the development of agreement on a higher level or a more general topic. It is clear at times that one or more of the participants finds herself stuck in a consensus that she probably does not really share, by virtue of having agreed to the earlier items of consensus and not being able to argue against the other participants' logic in building the higher level item.

Illustrations of behavior in relation to norms (what is normally referred to as gossip) are an important component of the history of a girl talk event. Gossip has been seen both as a means for building community and emphasizing community membership (Gluckman 1963) and as a means for personal advancement within communities (Paine 1967). It is perhaps in girl talk that the lack of contradiction between these two is the clearest. Within this interaction, gossip builds community in several ways. It provides stories that can be built on and referred to throughout the interaction, creating an interactional history. It also provides an opportunity for the group to align itself in relation to the people being discussed (or at least to their foibles, problems, or behavior), setting them off from the rest of the population as a temporary community. It allows the participants, singly and as a group, to display their compassion for the transgressors and maturity in analyzing the causes of the transgression. And it defines the community by virtue of the issues it raises. As Gluckman (1963) points out, one must be a member of a group to know how to gossip in it and to be allowed to. On the other hand, the same device provides opportunities for the teller to enhance her position in the interaction. Unlike a regular conversational turn, telling a story allows the individual a relatively long time slot. It thus allows the individual to expand on her point of view or to insert more information about herself than she could otherwise, without competing for the floor. Gossip also emphasizes the teller's individual network and information sources, and a personal story about a popular or powerful individual, for example, enhances the teller's claim to mainstream status. It is generally believed in our society that women are more likely than men to repeat confidences. I believe this to be true in certain circumstances, for where one's status depends on affiliation, repeating confidences is a way of displaying these affiliations. In most circumstances, women are more bound to prove affiliation than men. It has been my observation that, in situations where the same is true of men, they do the same.

Illustration can also be powerful in manipulating the point-by-point building of consensus discussed earlier, because illustrations are always specific and the use of items of consensus built on them is at times quite free. In the process of building consensus on a more general topic, therefore, illustrations allow the group to build consensus little by little, first by agreeing on the relatively non-threatening interpretation of an individual example, then by gradually weaving the examples into a higher level and more general agreement that might in face, not be equally satisfactory at all.

Talk About Boys

The remainder of this paper focuses on the first section of the girl talk event, the discussion of boys, because it contains illustrations of all of the devices and strategies just discussed and sets the tone for the entire interaction. It establishes the "sides" in the discussion, it establishes the norm of consensus negotiation, and it introduces what emerge as the two main themes of the entire interaction: popularity and independence. The underlying issues in the discussion of boys are (1) the issue of maturity and independence, as measured by the nature of one's relations with boys; and (2) the sticky issue of mainstream status, as measured by involvement with popular boys.

The discussion can be divided into 4 episodes. It begins with issue (1), focusing on two issues concerning how to behave with boys; using go-betweens (Episode A) and asking boys out (Episode B). There is initial disagreement on both subjects, and each is resolved in turn. The process of resolution of each of these specific issues sets up Karen, Carol, and Pamela as more familiar with boys and as more mature and independent in their relations with them. Karen and Carol then close the discussion of handling boys by introducing what becomes a superordinate item of consensus: that one should not idolize boys. It becomes apparent in the course of the conversation that people are less likely to idolize boys if they know boys as *just people*. There is an implicit understanding that the girls who orient themselves toward popular boys have been denied this familiarity. By emphasizing the importance of not idolizing boys, therefore, Karen, Carol, and Pamela are leading the group into an endorsement of their involvement with nonmainstream boys. This sets the stage for Episodes C and D, in which the discussion turns to popular boys and the relative merits of different kinds of boys. The final resolution (in Episode D) is that nonmainstream boys and popular boys are desirable for different reasons. This is a major step toward resolving the differences between the girls' notions of "doing well."

Episode A: Third Parties. As already mentioned, this section of the discussion begins with the question of how girls can go about letting boys know that they "like" them. Carol and Pamela let the group know that they have one juicy story on this topic, but when they do not tell it right away, June tells a story about an unnamed person who made a fool of herself by having a friend act as a go-between. The first disagreement comes as June finishes the story, saying that the strategy didn't work out. Karen denounces the use of go-betweens, or "third parties," and Miriam agrees (1).[4] Carol

4   To represent as clearly as possible the relations between different participants' utterances, I have organized the transcript as a musical score, with each speaker represented at all times. Overlaps are indicated as precisely as standard orthography allows. Successive uninterrupted lines of speech (i.e., lines representing the speech of all six participants) are numbered sequentially, and it is these numbers that are referred to in parentheses in the text. There are several departures from transcription conventions normally observed in conventional analysis: (1) Laughter is represented by exclamation points(!), (2) *hs* are used to represent inhaled laughter, (3) all speech is represented in standard orthography, (4) blank spaces are rough indications of pause length.

and Pamela then disagree and refer again to their own as yet un-
told story, which the others then beg them to tell (3-7).

1

```
June:    ... it just didn't work out.
Miriam:                                             No they don't.
Betty:
Karen:                        Oh third parties NEVER work.
Carol:
Pamela:
Eckert:
```

2

```
June:
Miriam:                         I don't think so.
Betty:
Karen:    DON'T EVER use a third party.
Carol:                                They do SOMEtimes.
Pamela:                                           They do sometimes !!
Eckert:
```

3

```
June:
Miriam:
Betty:    hhh
Karen:    It's never worked for me. !!!
Carol:                          This is the voice of experience
Pamela:
Eckert:                          Apparently it just worked over here.
```

4

```
June:
Miriam:                                             Yeah I know !!
Betty:
Karen:                          God now I'm dying to know !!!
Carol:                     yeah
Pamela:   ((cough))       ! yeah !!
Eckert:   really?
```

5

June:	
Miriam:	Let's see here's gossip. We all=
Betty:	! ! ! ! ! ! ! ! ! ! ! ! ! ! ! ! ! !
Karen:	
Carol:	
Pamela:	! ! !
Eckert:	Are are you dying to tell it or not? ! !

6

June:	
Miriam:	=want to hear it. Come on, tell us.
Betty:	! ! ! ! ! ! ! ! Come on Pam !
Karen:	! ! ! Come on, Pamela.
Carol:	Everybody just lean =
Pamela:	
Eckert:	

7

June:	
Miriam:	Yeah I know.
Betty:	! ! ! ! hhh
Karen:	! !
Carol:	=forward. What was it? um Okay we might as well get it out.
Pamela:	((cough)) ! ! yeah right.
Eckert:	

Carol and Pamela agree to tell the story together, and the telling begins jointly with Pamela helping Carol locate the incident in time (8-9). However, after their initial collaboration in establishing the approximate date of the incident in question, Pamela assumes a role as antagonist by virtue of her role as victim in the story by denying responsibility for the motives of Carol's action (13). Throughout the telling, the other girls, including Pamela, provide commentary on the story, jokingly challenging Carol's contention that she had acted spontaneously (16-17) and invoking external evaluations by filling in the boy's reactions (19-20). One might say that the group participation in the story in the form of laughter and comments implicates them all, already mitigating the disagreement that Carol's and Pamela's stance raised in the earlier discussion.

8

June:
Miriam:
Betty: !!!!!   snicker snicker hh
Karen: m hm
Carol: It was at a party earlier this year like   November   like was it
Pamela: m hm
Eckert:

9

June:
Miriam:
Betty:
Karen:
Carol: late about   late October early November and um =
Pamela: November
Eckert:

10

June:
Miriam:
Betty:
Karen:
Carol: =everybody's in REAL good mood from the party OK? and two=
Pamela:
Eckert:

11

June:
Miriam:
Betty: hhh
Karen: !!
Carol: =people are sitting there and I knew this one girl   who wanted to go to S-
Pamela:
Eckert: ! !   who=

12

June:
Miriam:
Betty: hh
Karen:
Carol: right   wanted to go to Sadie Hawkins OK which=
Pamela:
Eckert: =will remain unnamed

13

June:
Miriam:
Betty:
Karen:
Carol: =is the girls ask
Pamela: not ALWAYS not really I was talked into it !! to go
Eckert: right

14

June:
Miriam:
Betty: hhh
Karen:
Carol: she   she wasn't sure she wanted to go but I was confident ! she did !!
Pamela:
Eckert:

15

June:
Miriam: !
Betty: ((cough)) !
Karen:
Carol: and things just kept talking and so I asked the guy you know we were=
Pamela: !!
Eckert:

16

June:
Miriam:
Betty:
Karen: just HAPPENED
Carol: =just it just happened to come up in the conversation
Pamela: just HAPPENED?
Eckert:

17

June:
Miriam: ! ! !   sort of directed
Betty: hh !!
Karen: !
Carol: yes. So we=
Pamela: she just happened to bring it up
Eckert:

18

June:
Miriam:
Betty:
Karen:
Carol:
Pamela: =were talking about it I said "so eh   John are you going to uh Sadie's?"
Eckert:

19

June:
Miriam:
Betty:
Karen: John ! !
Carol: said "no" said "would you like to go?"   he looks at me=
Pamela: he looks at her !
Eckert:

20

June:

Miriam: he goes "phew" no I'm only kidding !

Betty:

Karen:

Carol: =and I said "not with ME" goes "oh SURE I'd love to go"

Pamela:

Eckert:

21

June:

Miriam: =I'm only joking ! ! !

Betty:

Karen:

Carol: and I go "Pamela wants to go with you"   !

Pamela: hhhh   ((sniff))

Eckert:

22

June:

Miriam:

Betty: hh !!!   !!!

Karen:

Carol: =he goes "OH GREAT we'll go." They've been going out ever since.

Pamela: hh   hh

Eckert:

At the end of the story, Miriam resolves the disagreement about third parties by refining Karen's original statement that third parties never work (1), making it compatible with Karen's story. According to Miriam's revised version, it would be all right for a third party to operate on her own, so long as it was not instigated by the first party (27). Now that the terms of consensus have been established, Carol continues with a further story about another girl who misused a third party (32-33). This extreme example gives everyone the opportunity to reaffirm the consensus by engaging in ridicule, aping, and laughter over this particularly ridiculous transgressor, uniting them as a group in opposition to the kind of people who do such silly things (34-36). The hilarity in this segment marks the end of the issue of third parties, which has now been resolved to everyone's satisfaction.

```
23
June:    So what did YOU do Pamela did you know she was going to say that=
Miriam:
Betty:   ! ! !
Karen:
Carol:
Pamela:
Eckert:
```

```
24
June:    =to him?
Miriam:
Betty:                                                         hhh
Karen:
Carol:                                      she was sitting=
Pamela:      No I didn't              YES I was sitting right next to him
Eckert:      You were sitting right there?
```

```
25
June:
Miriam:                              !
Betty:
Karen:
Carol:   right next she was talking to somebody else though ! !
Pamela:                                        yeah
Eckert:                                              so you=
```

```
26
June:
Miriam:
Betty:                 ! ! !                    ! !
Karen:                                      m hm
Carol:                          She ignored it
Pamela:      Oh I HEARD it  ! !          I heard it but it's just=
Eckert:  =didn't hear it
```

27

June:	
Miriam:	Well those kind of third parties I think work when like=
Betty:	hhhh
Karen:	m hm I know !!
Carol:	
Pamela:	=OH GOD!
Eckert:	

28

June:	
Miriam:	=someone would go up to someone and you didn't know they were=
Betty:	
Karen:	Oh that's that's silly. It's too silly
Carol:	
Pamela:	
Eckert:	

29

June:	
Miriam:	=saying it but um the one where like I would say to Karen, "would you=
Betty:	
Karen:	
Carol:	
Pamela:	m hm ((sniff))
Eckert:	

30

June:	
Miriam:	=please tell this guy that I like him" or something Those never-
Betty:	
Karen:	Oh that's=
Carol:	Yeah.
Pamela:	m hm
Eckert:	

31
June:
Miriam: because yeah it just never get-
Betty:
Karen: =that's silly   it's too SILLY
Carol: Yeah yeah a friend of mine =
Pamela: right
Eckert:

32
June:
Miriam:
Betty:
Karen: juvenile and turns you off.
Carol: = did that and she's been doing it since uh last year and I think this=
Pamela:
Eckert:

33
June:
Miriam:
Betty:
Karen:
Carol: =guy is really getting sick of it because she keeps telling him or she
       keeps telling all these other people "well I really like him" and "kinda
       drop the hint that I like him" I I think I'd get really turned off by that.=
Pamela:
Eckert:

34
June:
Miriam:
Betty:
Karen: =Oh yeah.   That's=
Carol: ((cough))   SAME GUY. yes.
Pamela:
Eckert: She's been dropping a hint about this one guy for a year?

```
35
June:
Miriam:        And you eh you know he probably has gotten the hint.  ! !
Betty:                      ! ! !          ! !                                ! ! ! !
Karen:     =disgusting.  ! !                                          I'm=
Carol:
Pamela:                  ! !
Eckert:
```

```
36
June:
Miriam:                                                              yeah
Betty:                                          it's true  ! !
Karen:     =sure he's gotten it, yeah.                             Ohh
Carol:                     And it hasn't been too subtle either.
Pamela:    ! ! !                                                        ! !
Eckert:            Yeah right. !!
```

The use of third parties is a key issue in relations with boys because of its association with what the girls now see as the childish practices of junior high school. In this consensus, the participants have all affirmed that they are not silly about boys (as they might have been in ninth grade) and that they know how to deal with them in a mature way. Carol's final story, cementing the group's disapproval of immature dealings with boys, becomes a group story, which turns up later in this section.

Episode B: Asking Boys Out. Episode B continues directly from Episode A. Now that an end has been put to the issue of third parties, I ask whether they would ever ask a boy out (37). This question raises a new issue that results in a disagreement and conflict resolution sequence analogous to those in Episode A, continuing with the general issue of know-how in relations with boys. In answer to my question, Miriam quickly says "never" and is contradicted by Carol's "yes" (37). (Of course, inasmuch as each is answering for herself, this is not so much a contradiction as a difference that must be resolved.) Negotiation is consensus on the issue of asking boys out is accomplished early on by Miriam's admission that she'd like to and Karen's mitigation of her statement that she has (38-39). Karen then expands on this subject, giving a rough description of the time she asked her current boyfriend out (39-45) and emphasizing the fact that she had been friends with her boyfriend before they started going out. This both introduces the fact that Karen has a boyfriend (which Carol and Pamela did not know) and shows her to have graduated from sex-segregated behavior with boys to more open, mature relationships.

```
37
June:
Miriam:                                    Never.    I WISH I could but I never would
Betty:                                                                              !
Karen:                                                        yeah
Carol:                                     Yes.
Pamela:                                                        oh yeah NOW I do
Eckert:    Would you ever ask a guy out?
```

```
38
June:                      Betty!
Miriam:                          ! ! Oh Betty !
Betty:     =NEVER AGAIN ! ! !          ! !
Karen:                         hh       I have.          but I mean it=
Carol:                                     I have.
Pamela:                      ! !
Eckert:        !!
```

```
39
June:
Miriam:
Betty:                    !
Karen:     =was like after we knew each other   pretty well.   Not that=
Carol:                                          very well.
Pamela:                                   after          yeah! after=
Eckert:
```

```
40
June:
Miriam:
Betty:         hhh          hhh
Karen:     =well but I mean it was like         we both    we both were like=
Carol:
Pamela:    =you'd been going out with him uh !
Eckert:
```

41
June:
Miriam:
Betty:
Karen: =said we were friends and stuff and it was a PLATONIC THING but=
Carol:
Pamela:
Eckert:

42
June:
Miriam: N:O it=
Betty: !!!!!!!
Karen: =I asked HIM out. so   no.!   !
Carol:
Pamela:
Eckert: and it stayed platonic.   oh.

43
June:
Miriam: =didn't !
Betty:
Karen: but it was for a while but it it's I did ask him out it=
Carol: no. !
Pamela:
Eckert:

44
June:
Miriam:
Betty:
Karen: =was nothing and it was very relaxed. I was surprised. I thought I'd=
Carol:
Pamela:
Eckert:

45
June:
Miriam:
Betty:
Karen: =be so nervous.   but it was it was good.
Carol: It's easier=
Pamela:
Eckert: yeah. m hm

At the end of Karen's turn, Carol joins her by supporting the importance of friendship (45-48) and denouncing "love at first sight" (48-49). By referring back to Carol's story in Episode A, of the girl who kept sending hints, Karen then binds together the general subject of boy handling and allows them all to agree that one should not idolize boys (49-53). Carol's expansion of that story (53-54) allows the group to cement their agreement with vociferous contempt for those who have not transcended junior high school behavior with boys (54-57).

46
June:
Miriam: Mm hm
Betty: ((sniff))
Karen:
Carol: =it's easier when they build from like small friendships.
Pamela: friendship
Eckert:

47
June:
Miriam:
Betty:
Karen: Oh yeah and it's probably, you know, it'll STICK longer if it's a=
Carol:
Pamela:
Eckert:

48
June:
Miriam:
Betty:
Karen: =FRIENDSHIP instead of you know-
Carol: Yeah. Love at first sight=
Pamela:
Eckert: does that happen a lot?

49
June:
Miriam:
Betty: hh
Karen: No. It's not good either if one=
Carol: =Voom you know that's not good.
Pamela: hhh
Eckert:

50
June:
Miriam:
Betty:
Karen: =person IDOLIZES the other person. It's like the one girl said she's been=
Carol:
Pamela:
Eckert:

51
June:
Miriam:
Betty:
Karen: =dropping hints and "oh God I just WANT to get to know him" well, you=
Carol: m hm
Pamela: ((cough))
Eckert:

52
June:
Miriam:
Betty:
Karen: = know, it's like "I worship you" and lalala and all of that sort of thing.
Carol:
Pamela:
Eckert:

53
June:
Miriam: I know
Betty:
Karen: HE can't relate to that.   uncomfortable
Carol: and the things that that make her so excited=
Pamela:
Eckert:

54
June:
Miriam: m hm
Betty: ! ! ! !   ! !
Karen: ! !
Carol: =are like "He SMILED at me today."   Whoopee
Pamela: Those things just OHH GOD
Eckert:

55
June:
Miriam: ! !   ! ! ! ! ! ! !
Betty: He gave me a GLANCE over ACROSS the room. ! ! !
Karen: yeah !
Carol:
Pamela:
Eckert: by mistake

```
56
June:
Miriam:
Betty:                                    ! ! ! ! !
Karen:              big mistake
Carol:        yes ! ! !           the big one that I hate is "he bumped into me in=
Pamela:
Eckert:                   ! ! ! ! !
```
_____

```
57
June:
Miriam:
Betty:              uh huh
Karen:              W:OOPS
Carol:   =the hall."              "hello."        Oh you got a long way to . . .
Pamela:                 ((cough))          hello .mm
Eckert:
```

Episode C: Popular Boys. The girls have now agreed on appropriate behavior with boys, and Karen and Carol are assuming roles as authorities on boys. An important measure of mainstream success is familiarity with the popular boys. Karen, Carol, and Pamela are on friendly terms with boys who are not part of the popular crowd, whereas June, Miriam, and Betty are more oriented toward the popular boys who, by virtue of their status, are generally available on only the most casual basis. There arises a tension, therefore, between the value of popular contacts, on the one hand, and close experience with boys such as Karen and Carol have displayed, on the other. The issue of desirability of popular boys takes longer and is more complex than the issue of how to behave with boys.

Following the discussion of girls who idolize boys, I ask which boys girls tend to idolize. This sparks a somewhat confused disagreement about whether people look up to older boys, leading to the following segment that starts with June's pronouncement on which boys people in general look up to (1). This elicits the expected lineup of opinion: agreement from Miriam and Betty and disagreement from Karen, Carol, and Pamela (1-2). Karen and Carol then begin to expand on their view of popular boys, while Pamela says that she doesn't know them (2-4). My question, along with Miriam's answer (5), can be seen as a challenge to Carol's assertion that popular boys have big heads and no personality, and she quickly backs down (5). Karen, however, saves her position for her (6) by saying that "it CAN be true." Carol then disavows contact with these popular boys, with humorous support from Miriam and Pamela, and with June providing the reason (7-11). More discussion ensues of what makes boys popular (such as sport, student government, looks, well-roundedness).

1

June:	mostly your BIG POPULAR people.
Miriam:	Yeah, I think so too, just like you=
Betty:	Yeah. hh
Karen:	I don't think so at=
Carol:	
Pamela:	! !
Eckert:	

2

June:	
Miriam:	=know I- Looking up?
Betty:	hh
Karen:	ALL It's different for me. pular
Carol:	I find that that turns me off. the big No. The big popular
Pamela:	those I don't know them. yeah big popular
Eckert:	

3

June:	
Miriam:	
Betty:	
Karen:	whoo h turnoff. h
Carol:	macho guy. That's one thing that I just do NOT like.
Pamela:	ooh no I can't=
Eckert:	

4

June:	
Miriam:	
Betty:	hh
Karen:	
Carol:	Yes. It's the big heads and no personality.
Pamela:	=stand it.
Eckert:	Why not?

5
```
June:
Miriam:                                              Not all the time
Betty:           no comment  hh
Karen:     Yeah                          I-
Carol:                                   no it's not. I think that's just a=
Pamela:    mm hmm
Eckert:          Is that really true?
```

6
```
June:
Miriam:
Betty:          I think it's a front. yeah
Karen:     stereotype                                It CAN be true=
Carol:              stereotype       I don't have a lot of oh
Pamela:
Eckert:
```

7
```
June:
Miriam:
Betty:
Karen:     =though
Carol:         a lot of watchacallit        No uh well that's the word but=
Pamela:                        interaction
Eckert:
```

8
```
June:
Miriam:               relationships  friendships       hh
Betty:
Karen:                            ! !              m ! ! !
Carol:     =it's not the one I                   Action. ! ! ! I don't=
Pamela:                   I know                        ! !
Eckert:                                                ! ! !
```

9
June:
Miriam:
Betty:
Karen: yeah   oh see I
Carol: =have a lot of exposure to a lot of those guys.   I just don't see them.
Pamela:
Eckert:

10
June: You're not a cheerleader you're not you're not=
Miriam:
Betty:
Karen:
Carol: I don't talk to a lot of those guys.
Pamela:
Eckert:

11
June: =involved with them.
Miriam:
Betty:
Karen: No.
Carol:
Pamela:
Eckert:

Episode D: Flaws. Episode D begins when I ask who exactly these popular boys are that they are talking about. Two boys are mentioned (1), who serve as the focus of the ensuing conversation. Karen cuts off the naming of popular boys (1) with a disavowal of contact with such boys (1-4) and an introduction of her alternative network. There ensues a short competition between Karen and Pamela over which of them has less to do with popular boys, at the same time displaying her familiarity with them (6-10). Carol supports her, first by providing the key word for her utterance (*change*) (9), then by repeating Miriam's evaluation (10). She then displays her own familiarity with Al Jones (10-12).

1

June:

Miriam: John Smith

Betty: Al Jones !

Karen: See now I'm I'm around=

Carol: Al Jones.

Pamela: Al Jones

Eckert

2

June:

Miriam:

Betty:

Karen: =the guys who are more inTELLIgent when- they're seniors and=

Carol:

Pamela:

Eckert:

3

June:

Miriam: yeah

Betty: hh   that's true.

Karen: =BOY they're a LOT NICER ! !   Yeah I don't really=

Carol: m hm Yea   huh huh

Pamela:

Eckert:

4

June:

Miriam:

Betty:

Karen: =even MESS with these guys I mean

Carol: Oh I don't either. I-

Pamela: I don't know them.

Eckert:

5

June:
Miriam:
Betty: yeah
Karen: I don't even know=
Carol:
Pamela: I mean I know them by face and-
Eckert:

6

June:
Miriam: but you know, Al Jones-
Betty: =their FACES I've just heard so much aBOUT them
Karen:
Carol:
Pamela:
Eckert:

7

June:
Miriam: everybody looks up to him. I mean you know, as we were=
Betty:
Karen:
Carol:
Pamela: mm m
Eckert:

8

June:
Miriam: =saying, falling all over him and he- at first his appearance to me that he
           was really you know big head and that, but when I met him it was it=
Betty:
Karen:
Carol:
Pamela:
Eckert:

9
June:
Miriam: =was so such a refreshing-   change that he was not like that=
Betty: uh exactly
Karen: hh
Carol: change
Pamela:
Eckert:

10
June:
Miriam: =at all. He was really nice.
Betty: he IS nice
Karen:
Carol: He IS. He's a very nice guy. I've worked=
Pamela: I don't=
Eckert:

11
June:
Miriam: yeah.
Betty:
Karen:
Carol: =with him on makeup for one of the plays   and he was=
Pamela: =know him.   m hm
Eckert:

12
June:
Miriam: looks
Betty:
Karen:
Carol: =really nice.
Pamela: looks
Eckert: How do people GET into that position? how-

When I ask how boys get popular (12), Miriam, Pamela, and
Karen agree that "looks" are important, but then Miriam brings
up John Smith's broader qualities (13-14) and find support from
the others (13-15).

13

June:	
Miriam:	I think hmmmm
Betty:	HIS case is looks but there there's like John Smith's case where=
Karen:	lot is looks
Carol:	
Pamela:	looks he's smart
Eckert:	

14

June:	
Miriam:	
Betty:	=it's just like sports and smartness and good personality yeah
Karen:	
Carol:	
Pamela:	sports and smart he's a
Eckert:	

15

June:	
Miriam:	
Betty:	! ! ! ! !
Karen:	an apple pie face.
Carol:	
Pamela:	he's a basic all around American guy.
Eckert:	

If consensus is to cover each girl's behavior, it must allow for the desirability of both the popular boys and the boys that Karen, Carol, and Pamela are involved with. It is Karen who offers the terms of consensus. Her description of John Smith as having an "apple pie face" (15) provides a transition to her evaluation of popular boys as too perfect (16). Her humorous expression of affection for flaws (17-18) brings the others into participation in her preference for non-mainstream boys. Miriam, who until now has been the greatest defender of popular boys, expands on Karen's statement, explicitly raising the theme of individuality for the first time (20-21), and Carol's observation that there is a lot of individuality in the band (22) brings this topic home. The girls have now agreed that nonmainstream activities and networks have a special quality. The orchestration of the discussion of faults allows all the girls to agree on the perfection of popular boys, the importance of individuality, and the frequent disjunction between the two.

16
June:
Miriam:
Betty: right. apple pie face ! !
Karen: I don't know - but they're so perfect.
Carol:
Pamela: mm
Eckert:

17
June:
Miriam: and it's it's-
Betty: They ARE.   It IS pathetic
Karen: you just wouldn't-   Yeah, the people that are=
Carol: It's pathetic.
Pamela:
Eckert:

18
June:
Miriam: Yeah.   m
Betty: m hmm
Karen: =more appealing are the people with the flaws.
Carol:
Pamela:
Eckert:

19
June:
Miriam:
Betty: ! !
Karen: I- I really go for like a big nose. ! ! ! I DO. Things that are WRONG=
Carol:
Pamela: ! !
Eckert:

20
June:
Miriam: It's just- they so- you know what it is, they're individual
Betty: ! !
Karen: =are GOOD.   It's so-   Oh yeah
Carol: yes
Pamela: ((cough))
Eckert:

21
June:
Miriam: individualized by that and it's so much more-
Betty: so much-
Karen: Individuality is a=
Carol:
Pamela:
Eckert:

22
June:
Miriam:
Betty:
Karen: ts ahh
Carol: =good thing you can find in uh band. Now see I don't when when I I=
Pamela: yeah yes
Eckert:

23
June:
Miriam: m hm
Betty:
Karen: m hm
Carol: =came to Belton I was not appealed by any of the big jocks and I found=
                        Pamela:
Eckert:

June:	
Miriam:	
Betty:	
Karen:	
Carol:	=myself not in any group . . .
Pamela:	
Eckert:	

It is at this point that one could consider the issue of boys to be re-solved, and indeed the discussion turns immediately to popular girls. The smaller issues resolved in the discussions of third parties and asking boys out combine to give the higher level agreement that boys are just people and not to be worshipped. This discussion also establishes Karen and Carol as ahead of at least some of the others in "normal" relationships with boys. The affirmation of the merits of popular and alternative boys allows for all six girls to jus-tify their preferences because they have acknowledged the validity of a choice of independence over the "popularity route."

CONCLUSION

The themes of independence and popularity continue throughout the interaction, as do the verbal strategies for their negotiation and the personal alignments. Consensus on the issue of independence becomes increasingly broad, and, during the discussion on parents, the general consensus develops that, ultimately, one must make her own decisions about values and behavior. This consensus, now built on a solid and expanding consensus about the importance of independence, takes an interesting twist in the discussion of relig-ion. Early in the discussion, Miriam comes out against mixed mar-riages, on the grounds that the family must have a single religion if the children are to develop strong values. At the end of the discus-sion, however, because of the differences in religious backgrounds and opinion in the group, Carol offers the resolution, once again, that each person must ultimately make his or her own decision, this time about religious choice. Miriam is forced into an uneasy participation in this consensus by her participation in all the pre-vious steps that led to it. The flimsiness of this consensus empha-sizes the strikingly constant negotiation of consensus in the inter-action. The development of common norms for the group is suffi-ciently crucial to the maintenance of the group and its interaction that not one topic is allowed to conclude without an expression of consensus.

The norms that govern this interaction are clearly derived from the play that women and girls find themselves in society. Their need to define themselves in terms of their overall character and the constraints placed on their participation in the world at large create a need to explore and negotiate the norms that govern their behavior. In fact, their ability to create freedom to function in the world depends on their understanding of, and control over, these norms, and girl talk events like the one described here are a major source of that understanding and control.

REFERENCES

Aries, Elizabeth. (1976). Interaction with patterns and themes of male, female and mixed groups, *Small Group Behavior*, 7 7-18.

Bourdieu, Pierre. (1977). *Outline of a theory of practice.* Cambridge: Cambridge University Press.

Eckert, Penelope. (1989). *Jocks and burnout.* New York: Teachers College Press.

Gluckman, Max. (1963). Gossip and scandal. *Current anthropology*, 4, 307-315.

Goodwin, Marjorie Harness. (1980). Directive/response speech sequences in girls' and boys' task activities. In Sally McConnell-Ginet, Ruth Borker, & Nelly Furman (Eds.), *Women and language in literature and society* (pp. 157-173). New York: Praeger.

Harding, Susan. (1975). Women and words in a Spanish village. In Rayna Reiter (Ed.), *Toward an anthropology of women* (pp. 283- 308). New York: Monthly Review Press.

Jones, Deborah. (1980). Gossip: Notes on women's oral culture. In Cheris Kramarae (Ed.), *The voices and words of women and men* (pp. 193-198). Oxford: Pergamon Press.

Kalcik, Susan. (1975) ... like Ann's gynecologist or the time I was almost raped. — Personal narratives in women's rap groups. *Journal of American Folklore*, 88, 3-11.

Paine, Robert. (1967). What is gossip about? An alterative hypothesis. *Man*, 2, 278-285.

Sacks, Karen. (1974). Engels revisited: Women, the organization of production and private Property. In Michelle Zimbalist Rosaldo & Louise Lamphere (Eds.), *Women, culture, and society* (pp. 207- 222). Stanford, CA: Stanford University Press.

Wodak, Ruth. (1981). Women relate, men report: Sex differences in language behaviour in a therapeutic group. *Journal of Pragmatics*, 5, 261-285.

14

Introduction

Mary Englund's account of her years in a residential school at Mission, British Columbia, is the only selection in this volume that is not scholarly prose. In a sense, it is not "prose" at all, but a transcription of an oral narrative, tape-recorded by a researcher in 1980. And, although her story is now in print, you will find in it features characteristic of speech. For example, as she concludes her story, she says, "Well I came up *here* and never went back" (442, emphasis added). Where is "here"? Referring to the editor's introduction to the transcription (429), and to evidence in the narrative itself, we might interpret "here" as Lillooet, a place in British Columbia's southwestern interior. We could also say that "here" is the location at which the utterance was produced — a reference to the speaker's physical surroundings, a context shared, at the moment of utterance, by the speaker and her primary audience, the researcher and her tape recorder. Nowhere else in this volume will you find a direct reference to the physical moment of speech, embodying the physical proximity of speaker and listener. Like many other forms of literate expression, scholarly writing systematically erases the signs of the particular localities of utterance. (Some genres are at the boundary of writing and speech: a note on an office door, for example, might report that the writer/occupant will be "*here* to receive assignments at 2:00.") Speech encodes immediate context in a way that writing does not.

Englund's narrative distinguishes itself from other selections in other ways, too. As narrative, it does have some elements in common with other passages in this book: McDougall's story of maternity-leave legislation in France; Scott's report of the Civil War and aftermath in some Louisiana parishes, for example. Like these passages, Englund's account is ordered chronologically, beginning with her departure for school and ending with her return home. Like the other chroniclers of the past, she not only tells what things were generally like but also focuses on specific instances as representative. But unlike McDougall and Scott, Englund refers to no other sources to substantiate her account — only to her own memories. And, unlike others who write about the past, she neither begins nor ends with high-level interpretive abstractions (like McDougall's "social and fiscal conservatism," or Scott's "labour relations" and "boundaries of freedom") to control her audience's understanding of detail. Accordingly, even at paragraph level, readers are left to construct for themselves the gist of her narrative. So a "paragraph" (constructed by the editor, since speech doesn't exactly have paragraphs) which begins with mention of "one girl" from her own village who was "very good to" Englund (431) might lead us to think of earlier remarks about how people on the reserve "looked after one another more or less" (429) and get an idea of mutual help and community (remember Counts and Counts' discussion of "reciprocity" among RVers). But the paragraph doesn't continue along this line. Instead, it develops mention of dormitory routines and monitoring: the procedures for washing and grooming and the Sister's vantage point. We might connect this material with other mentions elsewhere of procedural regularity in daily life (eating, dressing, hair-dos) and relentless surveillance (even extending to a system which recruits the girls to report on one another when they are out of sight of the school staff). In constructing gist this way — finding abstractions like "community" and "surveillance" — we are making meaning out of materials available, going beyond the paragraph and its organization to build higher-level connections.

But perhaps we should be careful about building these high-level platforms from which to view a landscape of faraway figures and episodes and lifetimes. Englund did not say "community" or "surveillance." Maybe this is not what she intended. Like Kabeer, who asked Bangladeshi women in the London garment industry why they chose to work at home and then "[goes] beyond" their answers, we are "[going] beyond" what Englund said. As readers and writers in the research genres, we seem obliged to extrapolate from the loose ends (what happened to Englund's brother? to her mother?), contradictions (a paragraph beginning with the claim that "[m]ost of [the nuns] were pretty nice" and ending with an expression of "bitterness"), and discontinuities (why, after all this, did Englund want to become a nun?), and construct larger interpretations which serve the present interests of academic inquiry. What are our responsibilities in this regard? Our generalizations and interpretations are conditioned by academic culture; the Sisters' generalizations about and interpretations of the schoolgirls in their care were conditioned by Christian European culture. How do we know that our typifications are more innocent, less damaging and self-serving or self-interested than theirs? This is a hard question, and perhaps the best we can do is to keep asking it.

As you will have seen from the selections in this volume, many members of the academic community make a practice of collecting the words of people in typifiable social groups (Bangladeshi garment workers, RVers, undocumented immigrants, residents of ethnically mixed, inner-city neighbourhoods, high-school girls) and *rewording* their speech into the abstractions which inform and organize the discourse of the research genres. For the time being, it seems that this practice can shed light on aspects of the social order. So, we too might go after such illumination and find in the words of Mary Englund evidence of patterns larger than those which she herself identifies. You might notice, for example, that she describes two long trips: she was conducted, by priests, first from the reserve to Mission, then from Mission to Ladner, which, she says, was "worlds away" from the convent school.

- What higher-level term can you find to interpret these journeys?

- Or you might analyze Englund's frequent and complex mentions of *home* — the place the Sisters call "camp." (Dorothy Counts and David Counts (77) refer to theories of *home*: are these applicable to Mary Englund's experience?)

- You might also bring into focus Englund's mentions of language, reading (including the reading aloud of "big [speeches]" (437), writing, and school-leaving (441).

- What role did language and literacy play in Englund's experience? Along these lines, Mary Englund's narrative could also be read in the larger contexts of literacy instruction and its historical connection with missionary enterprises and European imperialism. Don F. McKenzie (1987) has documented one instance of the links between literacy, religious mission, and colonization —- Christian efforts in the 1830s to teach the Maori to read and write (and to confine pupils' reading to religious materials). Whereas Englund offers an aboriginal point of view, MacKenzie cites (with some scepticism) contemporary Europeans' descriptions of the Maori response to this literacy campaign. For example, one observer reported that

about 200, old and young, were soon employed teaching and learning the letters with greatest possible interest. ... They easily learn to read and write without the necessity of constant teaching. (cited in McKenzie 167-68)

Another European observer, a printer of educational materials, reported that, at the arrival of a printing press in 1835, "the Natives ... danced, shouted, and capered about in the water, giving vent to the wildest effusions of joy" (cited in McKenzie 173). "[J]oy," "greatest possible interest" — these accounts suggest that the Maori received their schooling with more enthusiasm than Mary Englund expresses about hers.

- What might account for the difference between nineteenth-century Europeans' interpretations of Maori education and Mary Englund's description of her schooling in early twentieth-century British Columbia?

- Keeping in mind Lu's analysis of various ideologies of education, you might also speculate on the relation between literacy and power, schooling and domination, language and racialism.

WORK CITED

McKenzie, Don F. 1987 The sociology of a text: Oral culture, literacy and print in early New Zealand. In *The Social History of Language*, ed. Peter Burke and Roy Porter. Cambrige UP.

An Indian Remembers

MARY ENGLUND

MARY ENGLUND WAS BORN IN LILLOOET, the home of her mother's people, in 1904. Her father, a French-Canadian, named her Marie Anne. Until she was about six years old, the family lived at what is now Bralorne, approximately 35 miles west of Lillooet, but when her father died in 1910 the family returned to the Indian reserve. An older brother and two sisters had attended and left the Indian residential school at Mission before Mary and a younger brother were taken there in 1912. The school was run by the Oblates who had charge of the boys, while the Sisters of St. Ann had charge of the girls. Mary has strong memories of her school days; some things she remembers with pleasure, some she recalls with bitterness. Still a faithful Catholic and lay spiritual leader, she is nevertheless quite candid about her school experiences.

MARY ENGLUND: By this time [1912] we were old enough — my brother and myself — to go to the boarding school. There was no school around so the priests used to come and collect the children to go to school like from Fountain and Lillooet and Bridge River and all around. That was Father Rohr and Father Chirouse and all those. They'd come around once or twice a year and they'd count the children and take stock I guess you might as well say. And then they would say when you were ready to go to school. Your parents had to supply you with clothes such as shoes, underwears and before that, when my older sisters and brother went to the school, they had to have blankets and sheets and everything. So mother figured since she already supplied all that, that would be there so we didn't have to take any. But even at that our clothes were pretty skimpy.

Life was tough. It wasn't very nice, you see, because my mother was alone. My grandmother really kind of kept an eye on us, looked after us and kept us together. Because mother had to go out and work. However, we managed to get along. There was my uncle, then there was my grandmother, you see we all lived in the village. We each had our own house but everybody took care of one another. If grandmother wasn't around my uncle who was the chief then he took care of us. Everybody looked after one another more or less. Of course mother was home a good part of the time but there was times she had to leave us otherwise we never got anything to eat.

Father Chirouse picked us up when the train came to Lillooet. I was really excited, because we'd never been anywhere outside of going here and there to one reserve and another either in a canoe or boat and on horseback. It was something really exciting to go on the train. We were left alone so many times we never had the tendency to say, "Well, I'm sorry I'm going to go away and leave my mother" because we were alone most of the time. And I couldn't understand why they were cryin'. My brother and I, we enjoyed it you know. We enjoyed the train ride as far as that went. It was fun. It was something new. It was the old steam engines. Father Chirouse was the one that took us. He was awfully nice. I remember he talked to us and then he'd go further and get in the other seats and we'd look over to see what he's doing. We were able to open the windows and look out to see what we were passing. It was really fascinating until we got to Squamish and then we had to go on a boat and by this time it was dark. After we got to Vancouver I remember walking along the street with *big buildings* — fascinating — we couldn't understand all these big buildings. Finally we got on another train and we finally got to Mission. And then we had to walk. I thought we'd *never* get there.

Then I had to leave my brother. I couldn't understand why I had to leave him in this other building while I went to the other building. You see there was a big building where the boys lived, and then you went along and there was a big church, and then you went along and that's where the girls lived. These were three-storey buildings. There was the main floor and the second floor and on the third floor we slept, all the girls slept. And I remember when I got there I couldn't figure out why I had to leave my brother . . . and I kept asking but they said that he had to stay with the rest of the boys. I wanted to know why.

I had never seen a nun in my life. So these people with their covered up heads and white around and then their black robes and black veil — how the Sisters of St. Ann dressed — I couldn't figure out why they had to wear such clothes. And I used to ask the girls, "Why's she dressed like that?" "Because she's a Sister." "Well, what's a Sister?" They told us we had to stay there for a whole year, well I didn't know what a year was. That was the other problem, "When's the year going to end?"

So anyway this one big girl — she'd been there quite a while — she took me over to this other building. Way at the back of the convent was another big building where they did all the washing and you did your bath and there were square wooden tubs. You heat the water and you filled it and that's where you had to have your bath. You didn't go to bed — when you first got there — without your bath. Every girl that came in they had to be taken to the laundry and put through the wash. And then you had to take all your clothes off and leave them there and then they gave you other clothes to put on. Sort of a uniform. They were white blouses, they buttoned at the back and there was a sort of a jumper with frills around the sleeves and buttoned at the back — 'course I couldn't button them so I had to have somebody help me — and underwears and long black stockings and underwears down to the ankle and then the black stockings over it. Oh my! It didn't please me. I very seldom had these big longjohns on — I would call them now, long underwear — and then these big black stockings on, because at home we never wore any of those things. We had little panties on down to the knees with little frills around and I couldn't figure out these long things and then these stockings over. And then we had to have garters to hold them up. Then black shoes with little high-top laces . . . the only shoes I had were boys' lecky boots in those days and I thought, "Oh boy I was dressed up." Because we at home hardly ever wore any shoes. We wore moccasins and we ran all summer bare-footed. I really was uncomfortable. But they were handy when it came cold.

But oh my was I *ever* homesick. You know home wasn't much, in fact the nuns didn't call it home, they called it our *camp*. And that used to hurt me. It still does when I think about it. When we'd talk about going home, they'd say, "You're not going home you're going back to your camp." That was their impression of the reserve. Well in a way they were right because the homes we had in those days were made out of great big log houses. And the house we got into didn't even have a floor in it. It was just dirt floor. Then we used to have to every so often go out and chop boughs and put them on the floor to keep the dust down, until mother was able to get some lumber and put the floor down. You know we were raised in a hard way, so going to school and going in the convent it was very unusual.

This one girl she was very good to me. Apparently she had come from the same reserve I did but I don't ever remember her. So anyway she was awfully good with me. She helped me in the mornings to dress. We were given a basin and a towel, tooth-powder and toothbrush and comb. That was ours. We had little squares in the washroom and the washroom was quite a length and all window in front so the Sister could look in from the dormitory.

And this great big galvanized trough with the cold water, cold taps, and in there were the basins. You filled up your basin then you went over to the counter — no hot water, all cold water — then you had to scrub your teeth in the sink, then you had to wash your basin and put it underneath the counter. You had to fold up your towel and take it with you and put it at the head of your bed. And there was squares for your comb and your toothbrush and tooth-powder. So that was our gadgets.

An older girl saw to it that you were dressed. Then of course it took us time to put on these long stockings and high boots, and laces. And your hair had to be braided at the back and put up in a nob. You couldn't have one little hair hanging on your face. It had to be smoothed back. So she used to help me comb my hair. She'd wet my hair and comb it and braid it here and braid it there, then she'd braid it at the back and roll it up and pin it up. That was the way we were supposed to have our hair. At home we got up, washed our face and we didn't think of combing our hair; we just took it and tied it up and that was it.

We lived a simple life you know and then to go into these places where we didn't know that we didn't have to talk. That was another big thing. Everything was *silent*. You lived by the bell. The bell rang you shut up. Not another word. And here we'd keep on talking, us that were new, and we had to be shushed and shaken and what-not. Then we had to go in lines you see, one behind the other, go upstairs. No matter where you went you were in line. You never moved until the bell rang. There was a little bell always, no matter where you went. Or one of those desk push-bells.

I never forget that night when we first went there. We were outside in the yard and this bell rang inside. I said, "What's that for?" "Oh come on, come on. We've got to go for supper." So away we went and had supper. We got in there. "Don't talk, don't talk. No, don't talk just get in line. No, not one word." And then we went into the dining room and they put us in certain places and then the grace was said. The bell rang, then you sat down. Great big long tables — there must be 20 on each table — and the benches and galvanized plates — or tin plates as we called them — the same with saucers. And we had a fork and a spoon. There was never much of knives because you didn't get no butter and you didn't get no meat to cut up; everything was grounded up. And green tea. We never got no milk except skim milk to put in your tea. Of course me — I was not knowing the rules — I was talking to this girl who was with me. She told me what to do, "You don't talk before the bell rings and you don't talk after the bell rings either." So we kept on talking, the bell was ringing and we were still talking and she'd come over and shush me up.

'Course the Sisters were pretty good in a way too you know. If they knew you were new and didn't know the rules they'd say, "Here! You remember now you're not supposed to talk after the bell rings?" I remember this one Sister, her name was Sister "V," she'd great big eyes you know. She was a French nun. My she was *miserable*. She'd roll her eyes around. Gosh we had to watch for her. This Sister "V" was a real needle in the side and you know the Indians they have a name for everything and the owl always has a big eye you know and so this nun we all called her chkilulek, the owl.

You got up around five-thirty in the morning. The bell rings and you had to get up. You had to go and wash and dress and get your hair combed and make your little — we had little cots and the mattresses were full of straw — and you had to make your bed, make it really neat. You can't just slip-slop, everything had to be tight. If you didn't make your bed right the nun would come along and pull all the sheets and blankets off and you had to make it over. You had to fold up your nightgown and put it under your pillow. You had a little closet to hang your clothes in. If those weren't neat in there you either had to kneel down somewhere in some corner or kept silent at the dining room meal time.

After breakfast each one had their offices to go to. They called them offices, that was jobs. A certain amount of girls went to the dormitory, they had to put white spreads on the beds. A certain amount of girls went to the kitchen, a certain amount of girls stayed in the dining room and washed the dishes. See there were 51 girls and there was certain ones that swept the halls and cleaned the halls. My first job was in the classroom. I went with these two big girls to go to the classrooms; they were to clear the classroom out. There was one classroom and we had shifts. The middle ones went to school in the morning, the big girls went to the sewing room. We had to clean the boards, clear the brushes and dust everything, dust the desks and swept the floors. So this was where I had my first experience that you were not to touch a nun.

This one girl, she was an older girl — 'course most of the time I didn't know what to do so I just stood around and helped move the desks once in a while — she took this brush and she laid them alongside the windowsill and you could see down to the street from where our classroom was. I didn't put them there. She must have. When the teacher — she was a nun — came in and saw these brushes on the window ledge she wanted to know who put them there. And of course the other girl didn't want to get into trouble so she said I did. I said, "I didn't!" Oh, I was determined I wasn't going to be told that I did it. So the nun came up to me and she kind of tapped me on the face. She said, "Did you put the brushes on the windowsill?" "No, I didn't." I pushed her. She pretty near went over the desk. She could have hurt herself very badly. But how was I to know that I wasn't to touch her? She was supposed to be something precious that you can't lay your hand on. So anyhow she left me alone and I cried all morning, didn't do my work. And that was another thing. I couldn't talk at dinnertime. That was my punishment. So this girl she told me we were not to touch the Sisters. "Well," I said, "she slapped me!" Oh I wasn't going to be slapped. That smoothed over after that I remember, and I told the Sister that I did not put those brushes on the window ledge. But you see when you're new they take advantage of you.

Everybody went to catechism eight thirty in the morning until nine and then there was school. The older girls went to the sewing room and they mended socks and underwear and whatever there had to be mended and that's where I made my first encounter with a nun too. She would give us those long black stockings — sometimes they wore off on the heel or the toe — and you'd stick your hand in there and they'd give you a darning needle and you'd mend them, darn them in other words. I didn't want to darn in one place because it was thin, so I just mended the hole and that was it. We had to go and show them to the Sister when we had finished and she'd stick her hands in the sock and work her finger out. If her finger went through it was just too bad. You had to do it over again. She put her finger through my sock and I don't know what I said to her but she got really annoyed at me. She says, "Now stick your hand out." She had great big scissors and she hit me. I was really annoyed. I didn't cry at first and she looked at me and I don't know what she saw in my face but I know she looked terrible to me. I went and sat down and I banged down. You know how you do when you get mad. She says, "Come back here. You kneel right there and finish your sock." On my knees! I didn't have no thread in my needle so I just sat there and sucked my needle.

But later on when I got a little higher and a little older I used to go to the sewing room in the morning and she started teaching us how to run the machines and sew. First it was aprons — we all had to wear aprons — so she gave me this material she cut it out — she never let us cut it out — and then she showed us where to sew and your stitching had to be straight. So I started this zig zag. She'd make me rip it over and I'd sit there and cry and rip, and the names I didn't call her. 'Course to myself. It never came out because I didn't dare. I didn't trust nobody; you couldn't in a convent you know. You'd say one thing and this girl might go and tell Sister and you got punished for it so you had to say things to yourself that you didn't like.

We weren't allowed to speak our language in school. We had to speak English right from day one. I was pretty well bilingual you might as well say. When we first moved to the reserve we couldn't talk Indian either. We had to learn from the kids we played with and during this time while we were on the reserve we kept pretty well, at least I did, to our language and we talked in Indian too. So it didn't bother me too much although it was kind of different and you got mixed up. It was a difficult situation. See they had different Indian dialects. Along the Fraser Valley they had the Stalo and the Thompson and us here was the Chehalis. We talked very differently than they did. So if we talked to them it was all English. Even if we could talk with one another, the nuns wouldn't allow it. Of course there was a lot of us that could talk the same language; you take from Fountain to Pavillion down to Mount Currie we all talked the same language. When we were alone in some corner we did talk our own language and if the Sister caught us it was, "You talk English!" That's where a lot of girls kind of forgot their language. If you're there, stayed there a certain length of time, you forget certain words in Indian. You couldn't explain yourself too much in Indian as you would in English. They said it was better for us to speak English because we could learn English and read and write better if we kept our English, if we spoke English instead of talking Indian.

When the principal came over — Father Rohr; he was French — they'd sit and talk French and we knew very well they were talking about us, all of us, they could talk French. We used to tell them that, "How come you can talk in French in front of us, and you wouldn't allow us to talk Indian in front of you?" And of course they got after us for that. You weren't allowed to question. Oh yes, they weren't very nice in that respect.

Of course all the parents thought that was great you see, that we should talk English and be able to write so that we'd be able to write letters when we got home, to do things for the Indian people. You were something great when you come home, "Oh she can write now." They were kind of proud of us in a way once you were able to write your name, your mother's name, your father's name and whoever was in the family. We were doing all right. They were proud of you then. I remember my grandmother — I don't know how old she was but she was partly blind and she was all crippled with arthritis — she'd pat us on the head because we can write.

We were not to tell our parents what went on in the school. That was another rule. We were not allowed to discuss what goes on in school when we go home. We never got sugar at school, no sugar in our porridge or in our tea so when we went home I guess this one girl was telling her parents how she never got sugar at school. When she got back to school she was really reprimanded by the principal Father Rohr. And he didn't go about it in a nice way. He went about it in a way very insulting, telling you what you did in your *camp* and what you told your father and mother and the tattletales. And your parents never had anything to say of what you were doing in the school because they didn't know. I was told I was not to tell my mother of what went on. Whatever we did outside the school when we went home, if it wasn't just what it should be, we heard about it when we got back to the school. We were punished for it. If the girls that went to school with you saw you in the village with so and so, if they had anything against you or felt jealous of you in anyway, they'd tell the Sister and you'd get reprimanded for it. But I was lucky, there was nobody else from my village, just me.

But you didn't dare rebel, whatever they said was gospel. There was two girls that got dismissed while I was there. That was a terrible thing. I don't know, sometime in September or October I think it was they ran away from school. We were staying up quite late that evening until 9 o'clock. We were having games and so on and all at once these girls disappeared. And come line-up time to get ready to go to bed they weren't there. Boy that was terrible for us. We were concerned you know. So anyway we went to bed. We thought maybe they're just hiding downstairs somewhere. And once you go to bed, once you get up in the dormitory there's a trapdoor that goes over the stairs and that's got a great big bolt that Sister puts in there. Nobody can get through there. So you were locked up there. I often think afterwards, when I got older, what would we do if the bottom part of the building got burnt? How would we get out of there? But anyway they were brought back about a month or so later on. They were found and brought back and their parents were notified. And they really got reprimanded. They not only got reprimanded I remember they went to bed one evening and there was one big husky Sister, she came up and she had a great big — you know they used to use the razor straps for shaving? Well she had one of those with a wooden handle on it. They laid on their stomach on the bed and they really went to work on them. I don't know how many straps they got but we were all crying, everybody was sniffling and crying. That strap was used on very serious occasions.

They gave you notes. Like in school you have certain notes, if it's "A" you're perfect, "B" you're not too good, "C" you're gettin' worse and "D" you're very poor and you need reprimanding and you need the strap or something. I lost my note, this was really funny, I was working in the kitchen. I used to work in the pantry helping the Sister. She was grinding up this meat to make meatballs for *their* table — they had a dining room by themselves — so I cleaned up the meat grinder. 'Course I had scraps of meat left and I came down into the kitchen. Sister was French, she could hardly talk English. There was a pot of hash on the stove for the girls, ground up meat and potatoes and everything was in that big pot of hash, so I went and I asked her what was I to do with this handful of scraps of meat. Instead of saying "hash" she said, "Put it in your ass." And I started to laugh, and oh she was annoyed at me. She went right away and told Sister Superior and of course I lost my note for that. We were reprimanded because we're not to condemn the nuns because they couldn't speak very good English and they reminded us that we weren't perfect in English either because we spoke Indian.

Every occasion that comes up like a principal's birthday, like Father Rohr's birthday, or he'd go away and he'd come back and we'd have a welcoming party, and the Sister would write out a speech and you had to read that to the priest. And there was always somebody to read that big speech, you had to read this in long sheets you know and you had to read *every word perfect*. I read it several times but my cousin she was always getting chosen to read this, and you had to practise that. You had to practically memorize it in order to make a perfect recitation. Sister "V" would say, "Now if you weren't an Indian girl you could do that perfectly well, better; a white girl she would go over that very well, nicely."

They were always degrading us because we were Indian. We didn't come from homes we came from *camps* and we didn't know how to live. We ate rotten fish so they didn't seem to be particular in what they gave us to eat. They never let us forget that we were *Indian*, and that we weren't very civilized, that we were more or less savages. The other nuns weren't too forward with their mentioning of Indians, but this particular nun, Sister "V," she looked after us in the recreation room and she looked after us in the dining room — once in a while the other nun would come and take her place — and she looked after us in the dormitory. She was constantly with us, which I think was too much of a strain for her. If they had changed places I think it would have eased her tension a little more and she wouldn't have been so hateful towards us.

There was a couple of Sisters that really showed their affection. One was Sister Mary André. Whenever I met her in the hall she'd put her arms around me and she really showed that she was a happy-go-lucky person. And then there was our teacher, Sister Mary Hildegard. You were privileged if you could go down town with the Sisters, if they had something to do down town, to go and mail letters or go and pay bills and you were privileged if you were chosen to go with the Sister. We'd go down town and you see you were not to touch them but the minute we got outside the door and out the yard she'd hold my hand. Oh it was really a privilege.

Most of them were pretty nice. Like our teacher, she was pretty nice but we were told that we were expected to stand up and if we didn't she used to report us to Sister Superior. We were called rude if we didn't stand up whenever any of them entered. Same way if you passed them in the hall or anywhere, you're to stop and bow your head. They were really up on the pedestal. I guess it was good training in a way. I don't know. They sure put themselves somewhere where you couldn't touch them. You couldn't reach them and you had to bow to them, that's something I could never . . . it made me to a certain extent very bitter by the time I left school.

Another thing that made me very rebellious was the punishment. They used prayer to punish you. If you were late or you disobeyed in one way or another you knelt down and you said 10 Hail Marys or 10 Our Fathers or something like that. Well saying these things was against your nature. You know it wasn't a praying thing and therefore I rebelled against it. I couldn't see the sense of using prayer as a punishment.

And going in the chapel you couldn't look at the next person. We wore veils and we went in there with our hands folded and even if we nudged there's a nun watching way at the back and she saw everything that went on. You got your ears pulled or you got a slap in the face. On special occasions we wore great big veils that came down. You wore that and you had uniforms to go with that, and we thought that was great to wear a great big long veil. You were an angel or something. They were pinned in our hair and they had to stay there. But I guess it was a way of teaching you respect. You were not to look around but there were little instances as you came in the church, because the boys sat on one side and we sat on the other. It got so the older girls, the minute you'd come in a certain boy would cough and of course some girl would answer. Finally the nuns would catch on, "Who was that that did that?" and of course nobody didn't dare tell. No, you were a tattletale if you told. You were not to talk to a boy unless it was your brother. And you were not to have any way of showing any kind of signs or anything to a boy.

I tell you one instance. The boys were cleaning the eaves. They'd get full of moss and they were cleaning and there was great big long ladders put up and this one ladder was left at the end of the building and that was going into the lavatories. And the windows were able to be opened, screens could be taken off and opened. Apparently a bunch of the boys had decided that they were going to go over to the convent and raid the girl's dormitory. I think there was four or five of them, quite big boys, and they got into the dormitory about midnight by using the ladder. The dormitory, sleeping 50 girls, is quite a large place and away in one corner the nun slept. She had her little caboose, we called it, a walled-off room. And they got down the middle of the dormitory and they were waking some of the girls up. In those day, when you're young, you're scared of anything in the dark. 'Course there was dim lights all over the dormitory but you couldn't see very well. One of the girls, she was so scared she crawled on the floor and went and knocked on the nun's door. This one boy he was trying to crawl into bed with one of the girls and she was trying to push him off the bed, and then the nun came out and they all took off — down through the ladder again. One boy he was still in the middle of the dormitory and they had blackened their faces so they wouldn't be seen. We were all talking because the Sister had gone downstairs to tell Sister Superior and all at once, as we looked up, this black thing came up at the foot of my bed. I hollered and I pulled my blanket and my feet were stickin' out! He went downstairs. I don't know how he got out but he went downstairs. We had a new Father Superior by this time and they got a strapping and the girls of course they got blamed for enticing the boys to come over. Some of the girls apparently were getting familiar with the boys, so they decided they were going to go and visit the girls. You could call them gutsy.

When you went home you missed the companionship of the others. You felt alone. Although the family was there, my brothers were there, my older brother, my uncle, my grandmother — we always had an uncle live with us because he was blind — but you were lonely. At least I was, and children on the reserve were not of your . . . oh they were *people* you know, but they weren't like the ones you had in the convent. So it was different. You talked to them, they were nice to you, they wanted to know what the school was all about. And we'd go swimming. Things were different but mother always tried to make life easier for us. She always had a garden. We'd weed the garden and then when we got through the horses were saddled and we packed up a lunch and we went up in the hills picking berries. We spent our holiday that way. We'd come down and then we'd get ready before we went back to school. There was washing and ironing and getting ready and bathing and hair-washing. Then we'd hit the train. We never felt that we were leaving somebody that we loved. We were glad to get away. Wasn't that something? We were anxious to get on that train; we were anxious to be on our way. We never thought that well maybe we should say good-bye to mother she'll feel bad.

She died while I was in school. But then we weren't allowed . . . once you had no parents, there was no home to go to, you weren't allowed out of the school. I wasn't allowed out anyway. My younger brother and myself, we stayed in the school. We did have family at home, but after my mother died we weren't allowed to go home. We weren't even allowed to go to the funeral which hurt me very much because I was old enough to understand. So there I was kind of left with my two brothers to look out for. My one brother was two years younger than me and the little one he was just about eight or nine years old.

I wanted to be a nun and I spoke to them about it, but you see your father and mother had to be married and you had to produce their marriage certificate and you had to have a certain amount of money, otherwise it was useless. You might as well go talk to the wall. I wanted very much to be a nun. Sister Bernadette, she was our Mother Superior there for a while. I told her. So she says, "You know you can't get married, you can't have children?" I said I didn't want any, I wanted to be a nun. I was about 15 then. She says, "Did you know your father and mother have to be married in the Church?" which they weren't. She says, "You'll need money you know." I didn't have no money. I never even got money from home at times. I didn't, that was another thing that I rebelled very much against. For money and because my mother and father weren't married I couldn't join but I still had that desire to become a nun.

I was there for just two years after, I was about 16 then, when the principal came over one day. He thought I had gone as far as I could go. In those days the grades weren't as high as the public schools were. If you were in grades five and six you were equal to grades eight and 10 in public schools and I was in grade six. I could have gone to high school or finished school anywhere but I wasn't allowed to because that's as high as I was going to go, that's high as *Indian* girls went. You worked around the convent if you stayed there. You did the cooking, you did the washing, you did the supervising if you wanted to stay at the convent. You didn't get paid for it though.

We'd got a new principal by this time, his name was Father Duplanil and him and Father Hartmann came over one day and said, "You're no good to this school anymore and you can't go any higher so you may as well go out. There's a lady in Ladner that would like a girl to keep house for her. She'll teach you how to cook. She'll look after you." She was 83 years old and she was a well-to-do woman. So they took me down there. I didn't know what I was getting into. The money was more fascinating to me because I knew I'd have money to be able to do something with my brothers, to be able to buy them nice clothes and I would be able to buy nice clothes. I was told I'd get $35 a month, oh it was big money in those days, but I never did. I never got no more than $20 a month. It was just to get me there you see. And I used to cry. Because Ladner was worlds away from where I'd been. And being with a bunch of girls all these years, well pretty near 10 years, and then to go and live with this cranky old woman was just ridiculous. And she was more strict than the nuns were.

She was Scotch. She had high blood pressure and she had arthritis. She couldn't walk properly, and you had to wait on her hand and foot. I was there for a year and she took sick. She had pneumonia and pleurisy and the doctor used to come from Vancouver and she had trained nurses to come look after her and she was so miserable they didn't last. One lasted three days and another lasted three or four days and she took off. So I had to do all the work, looking after her. I'd sit up all night. She had a kettle by her bed with Friar's Balsam in it and I had to keep that filled and I'd sit by her bed all night long. Very little sleep. It got towards spring I took sick so when the doctor came over he ordered me out of there — Ladner's very damp — so he told me to go to a drier climate for two or three weeks. Well I came up here and I never went back. She sent the two priests after me but I told them I'd go back next week but I never did go back because that $20 a month didn't seem important to me, my health was more important.

Acknowledgements

Alan Apter, Mohammed Abu Shah, Iulian Iancy, Henry Abroamovitch, Abraham Weizman, Samuel Tyano 1994 "Cultural effects on eating attitudes in Israeli Subpopulations and Hospitalized Anorectics."

Harriet Baber 1994 "The Market for Feminist Epistemology," *The Monist* 77 (4). Copyright 1994, *The Monist*, La Salle, Illinois 61301. Reprinted by permission.

Cheshire Calhoun 1994 "Separating Lesbian Theory from Feminist Theory." *Ethics* (April 1994 104. Reprinted with permission.

Leo R. Chavez 1994 "'The Power of the Imagined Community': The Settlement of Undocumented Mexicans and Cultural Americans in the United States." *American Anthropologist* 96 (1). Reproduced by permission of the American Anthropological Association from *American Anthropologist* 96:1, March 1994. Not for sale or further reproduction."

Dorothy Ayers Counts and David R. Counts 1992 "They're my Family Now: The Creation of Community among RVers," *Anthropologica* 34. Copyright 1992 *Anthropologica*, Department of Sociology and Anthropology, Laurentian University, Sudbury, Ontario P3E 2C6. Reprinted by permission.

Reed Way Dasenbrock 1987 "Intelligibility and Meaningfulness in Multicultural Literature in English," *PMLA* 102. Copyright 1987. Reprinted by permission of the Modern language Association of America.

Genetic, Social and General Psychology Monographs 120 (1). Reprinted with permission of the Helen Dwight Reid Educational Foundation. Published by Heldref Publications, 1319 Eighteenth St., N.W., Washington, D.C. 20036-1802. Copyright 1994.

Penelope Eckert 1990 "Co-operative Competition in Adolescent 'Girl Talk,'" *Discourse Processes* 13. Reprinted by permission of Ablex Publishing Corporation, 355 Chestnut Street, Norwood, New Jersey 07648."

Naila Kabeer 1994 "The Structure of 'Revealed Preference': Race, Community and Female Labour Supply in the London Clothing Industry," *Development and Change* 25. Reprinted by permission of Sage Publication Ltd. 6 Bonhill Street, London EC2A 4PU, England.

Min-Zhan Lu 1992 "Conflict and Struggle: The Enemies or Preconditions of Basic Writing," *College English* (December 1992). Copyright 1992 by the National Council of Teachers of English. Reprinted with permission.

Mary Lynn McDougall, "Protecting Infants: The French Campaign for Maternity Leaves, 1890-1913." *French Historical Studies*, 13:1 (1983), pp 79-105.

Rebecca J. Scott 1994 "Defining the Boundaries of Freedom in the World of Cane: Cuba, Brazil, and Louisiana after Emancipation," *American Historical Review* (February 1994). Reprinted by permission of author.

Nick Tiratsoo and Jim Tomlinson 1994 "Restrictive Practices on the Shopfloor in Britain, 1945-1960: Myth and Reality," *Business History* 36 (2). Reprinted by permission from the 36th issue number 2 of *Business History* published by Frank Cass & Company, 890/900 Eastern Avenue, Ilford, Essex, England. Copyright Frank Cass & Co. Ltd.

Maykel Verkuyten, Wiebe de Jong, and Knees Masson 1994 "Similarities in Anti-racist and Racist Discourse: Dutch Local Residents Talking About Ethnic Minorities," *New Community* 20 (2). Reprinted by permission of Carfax Publishing Company, 871-81 Massachusetts Avenue, Cambridge, MA 02139.

Concert of Voices

An Anthology of World Writing in English

edited by Victor J. Ramraj

"a wide-ranging, eclectic, and stimulating anthology;
the selection is very impressive."

Rowland Smith, Wilfrid Laurier University

"a rich range of authors, representing a wide range of
issues; this is an important and worthwhile project."

Shalini Puri, University of Pittsburgh

Combines poetry with fiction and essay in a
wide-ranging anthology of some of the best
writers in English. Included are a number of
established writers, who despite their great
reputations, are all too often left out of the
mainstream canon (such as Wole Soyinka, Nadine
Gordimerand Derek Walcott). Most selections,
however, are by a wide range of much less
established authors, from Olive Senior and Keri
Hulme to Rohinton Mistry and M.G.Vassanji.
A sparkling collection and a great read!

1995 6x9 paper 400pp
1-55111-025-3
U.S. $19.95   CDN $24.95

Her Kind:

Stories of Women from Greek Mythology
Jane Cahill

Everyone knows that Medea betrayed her father and left her homeland for love of Jason. Then when he abandoned her, she murdered her children. But did she? And what of Clytemnestra, the conniving adulteress? For ten years she plotted the murder of her husband Agamemnon, King of Mycenae and Conqueror of Troy. How would she have told her story?

The Greek myths as we know them were told for men by men. Yet they were the culmination of a long oral tradition in which both men and women shared. Using extant ancient literary sources as her guide, including the works of Homer, Aeschylus, Euripides and Apollodorus, Jane Cahill reconstructs the stories as they might have been told to women by women. These are stories of wronged women, inspired women,determined women, tender women. Medusa tells how it is to know that one look at her face will turn a man to stone, to be hated and feared for all time. Jocasta, Queen of Thebes, confesses her love for the young man who came to save her city from the Spinx—her son, Oedipus.

Each story is accompanied by extensive notes which discuss the ancient sources, explain relevant Greek concepts and customs, and serve as a guide to further study.

Jane Cahill is both a professional storyteller and a professor of Classics at the University of Winnipeg.

November 1995 6x9 192pp
1-55111-042-3
U.S. $ 16.95 CDN $18.95

Wisdom of the Mythtellers

Sean Kane

Mythtelling: the ideas and emotions of the Earth expressed through stories—stories distilled from millennia of treading warily in nature, rather than undertaking to rearrange her furniture. *Wisdom of the Mythtellers* explores four kinds of dream-mapping of the natural world: Native Australian, Native American, Celtic, and Greek.

◆◆◆◆◆◆

"a rare and wonderful introduction to mythic thought, it marks an advance in relating this profound human activity to our entire relationship with the earth and the world we live in."
Robert Lawlor, author of *Voices of the First Day: Awakening in the Aboriginal Dreamtime*

"Loren Eiseley once speculated that there must be a small, simple, child-sized hole in the metaphysical hedge we all walk along in life—an entrance into the awesome mind-scape of the Spirit of the Earth. He was convinced a child would spot it easily—and spent the rest of his life in search of it. Sean Kane, I believe, has found it."
Calvin Luther Martin, Professor of History, Rutgers University. Author of *In the Spirit of the Earth: Rethinking History and Time*

1994 5 1/2 x 8 1/2 paper 288pp
1-55111-041-5
U.S. $14.95   CDN $19.95